Emerging Trends in Database and Knowledge-Base Machines

The Application of Parallel Architectures to Smart Information Systems

Edited by

Mahdi Abdelguerfi
Simon Lavington

IEEE Computer Society Press
Los Alamitos, California

Washington • Brussels • Tokyo

Library of Congress Cataloging-in-Publication Data

Emerging trends in database and knowledge-base machines: the application of parallel architectures to smart information systems / edited by Mahdi Abdelguerfi and Simon Lavington.
    p.   cm.
   Includes bibliographical references.
   ISBN 0-8186-6552-1
   1. Parallel computers.   2. Database management.   3. Expert systems
(Computer science)   I. Abdelguerfi, Mahdi.   II. Lavington, S.H. (Simon Hugh), 1939– .
QA76.58.E45 1995
005.74 ' 0285 ' 435—dc20

            94-34327
            CIP

Published by the
IEEE Computer Society Press
10662 Los Vaqueros Circle
P.O. Box 3014
Los Alamitos, CA 90720-1264

IEEE Computer Society Press Order Number BP06552
IEEE Catalog Number EH0407-7
Library of Congress Number 94-34327
ISBN 0-8186-6552-1

Additional copies can be ordered from

IEEE Computer Society Press
Customer Service Center
10662 Los Vaqueros Circle
P.O. Box 3014
Los Alamitos, CA 90720-1264
Tel: (714) 821-8380
Fax: (714) 821-4641
Email: cs.books@computer.org

IEEE Service Center
445 Hoes Lane
P.O. Box 1331
Piscataway, NJ 08855-1331
Tel: (908) 981-1393
Fax: (908) 981-9667

IEEE Computer Society
13, avenue de l'Aquilon
B-1200 Brussels
BELGIUM
Tel: +32-2-770-2198
Fax: +32-2-770-8505

IEEE Computer Society
Ooshima Building
2-19-1 Minami-Aoyama
Minato-ku, Tokyo 107
JAPAN
Tel: +81-3-3408-3118
Fax: +81-3-3408-3553

Technical Editor: Ali Hurson
Production Editor: Lisa O'Conner
Cover Photo: Courtesy of Digital Semiconductor, a business unit of Digital Equipment Corporation.
Cover Layout: Joe Daigle

Printed in the United States of America by Braun-Brumfield, Inc.
99 98 97 96   5 4 3 2

 The Institute of Electrical and Electronics Engineers, Inc.

Contents

USING MASSIVELY-PARALLEL GENERAL COMPUTING PLATFORMS FOR DBMS

KNOWLEDGE-BASE MACHINES

ARTIFICIAL INTELLIGENCE MACHINES

1

Introduction
Parallel Database and Knowledge-Base Systems

Mahdi Abdelguerfi[†] and Simon Lavington[††]

†Computer Science Department, University of New Orleans, USA
††Computer Science Department, University of Essex, UK

1.1 INTRODUCTION AND SCOPE

Database technology has been extended into many new applications areas such as computer-aided design and manufacture, geographical information systems, and real-time intelligent decision making. Such applications bring with them demands for richer information models and the capability to handle larger quantities of heterogeneous data. Furthermore, increasing numbers of online users are expecting some form of smartness from their information systems. We use the term *smart* information systems, or knowledge-base systems, to describe computer applications that incorporate nontrivial features such as the ability to adapt and evolve, or to carry out inferencing. All these factors combine to produce a need for improved performance and additional functionality.

This book consists of 13 invited papers, chosen to illustrate ways in which novel parallel hardware is being used to provide improved performance and additional functionality for a variety of information systems. Two of the machines described have each sold to well over one hundred customers (see Chapters 8 and 9). Two more are in the final stages of product launch (see Chapters 8 and 11). The rest of the machines described in this book are research prototypes. Overall, they provide a survey of the latest trends in performance-enhancing architectures for smart information systems. The book will thus appeal to all engaged in the design or use of high-performance (parallel) architectures for nonnumeric applications.

The machines featured in this book have been designed to support various information systems, ranging from relational databases to semantic networks and other artificial-intelligence paradigms. Knowledge-representation formalisms, as such, are not described in any detail. Although expertise in knowledge representations is not required for an understanding of the hardware architectures in this book, readers wishing for background information on this subject may refer to Frost.[1]

The topic of database and knowledge-base machines is a large one, and no single volume can hope to cover the field in a truly comprehensive manner. Particularly, this book does not touch on distributed or federated databases,[2] heterogeneous databases,[3] or related issues. However, many of the projects we have chosen to emphasize contain generic architectural ideas that may be used to support several sets of higher-level requirements. In other words, some of the machines are based on hardware designs that strive to be semantics-free. For completeness, we list the major review books, conference proceedings, and survey papers that have appeared within the last ten years on the hardware and software of database and knowledge-base machines.[4-14] Papers describing ongoing research appear from time to time in several journals, particularly in the *IEEE Transactions on Knowledge and Data Engineering*, in the *Proceedings of the ACM SIGMOD*, and in the *Proceedings of the International Conferences on Very Large Databases*.

1.2 THE TECHNICAL CONTEXT

Many mainframe database management systems already have difficulty meeting the I/O and CPU performance requirements of information systems that support large numbers of concurrent users, and/or handle massive amounts of data.[15] To achieve the required performance levels, several mainframe designers have incorporated add-on special-purpose accelerators. ICL's Content-Addressable File Store is an early example of an add-on hardware accelerator, the latest version of which is now incorporated into every Series 3 ICL mainframe.[16] CAFS is designed to alleviate the disk I/O bottleneck and reduce CPU loading. Rinda was developed at NTT to accelerate the execution of relational database queries, and is now connected to NTT's general-purpose DIPS series mainframes.[17] Hitachi's largest mainframes can now be purchased with an optional hardware accelerator (the integrated database processor) that performs sorting and merging.[18] Greo is a very-large-scale-integration sorter and merger used as a performance accelerator for Mitsubishi machines.[19] On a more specialized topic, there are add-on performance accelerators that undertake particular tasks such as free-text searching. An example is the High Speed Text System designed to be connected to a PDP/11.[20]

The hardware parallelism, where it exists in the above add-on accelerators, is quite localized. For example, it does not usually extend to whole-structure operations such as those implied by dyadic relational algebraic operators—a theme we return to later. An emerging trend in database technology is to employ parallelism more explicitly.[15] For conventional database management systems that use industry-standard database models, such as the relational, the approach to parallelism can take one of two forms.

Firstly, massively parallel general-purpose computers such as Intel's iPSC, nCube, and the Distributed Array Processor marketed by Cambridge Parallel Processing, have all become platforms for DBMS and related commercial software.[21-23] DBMS vendors such as Oracle have been active in promoting these developments. Some of the newer players in the high-performance parallel computer market, like Kendall Square Research Corp., are taking business and commercial applications seriously. Thus, high-performance platforms, which have hitherto been targeted at numeric applications, are also being used in the nonnumeric, that is, symbolic, area. On a somewhat related theme, parallel processing has been shown to give spectacular commercial advantages in the field of financial modeling and securities trading.[24] These developments are bound to make end-users of conventional data processing equipment restless, and in the long run encourage fresh architectural initiatives on the part of computer manufacturers.

In the second approach to parallelism in DBMS, some of these initiatives are already apparent. This approach is based on the use of arrays of off-the-shelf components, such as microprocessors and (cheap) disks, to form parallel add-on database machines and performance accelerators. For the most part, these hardware systems are based on multiple instruction, multiple data, shared-nothing, parallel architectures.[25] Besides providing high performance, such systems are often modular and therefore easily scalable. The current market leader is Teradata's Database Computer DBC/1012,[26] which makes use of Intel microprocessors and a special interconnecting network known as the Ynet. Teradata has recently become part of NCR, which has announced the NCR 3700 as a successor to the DBC/1012.[27] This system uses a high-performance multistage interconnection network, known as BYNet, and redundant arrays of inexpensive disks (RAIDs).[28] A new United Kingdom company, White Cross Systems, has just announced a database machine using arrays of transputers.

Unlike conventional mainframes, the above parallel systems can usually be scaled up to meet the future performance needs of conventional database software. Furthermore, parallel computing platforms such as nCube are reported to be more cost-effective than mainframe solutions, by factors of 20 or so.[21] Of course, a company that adopts a massively parallel solution may have considerable difficulty running its existing programs and ready-made software packages. Nevertheless, the performance and cost benefits of parallel solutions are compelling. In addition, the availability of high-performance platforms will encourage designers of information systems to experiment with advanced features, for example, deductive, object-oriented, temporal reasoning, and fuzzy logic, which may have previously introduced unacceptable overheads on conventional uniprocessor platforms. However, adding such advanced features does itself bring additional challenges for the systems architect—as is discussed shortly.

Apart from the machines mentioned previously, many more parallel database hardware systems exist in the development stages or as research prototypes. Examples are Multibackend Database Supercomputer MDBS,[29] GAMMA,[30] IDIOMS,[31] the Datacycle project,[32] and the parallel multi-wavefront work of Su.[33] MDBS is a multibackend database system having the interesting property that, despite an increase in the size of the database, a transaction's response time can be kept constant by increasing the degree of backend parallelism. GAMMA is a multiprocessor system in which a set of identical computers, each with its local main memory and secondary storage, is interconnected by a ring bus. The latest version of GAMMA is based on a 32-node Intel iPSC/2 hypercube with a disk attached to each node. The IDIOMS machine, Professor Su's prototype, and Datacycle all employ transputers. IDIOMS is of interest because it is designed to support both online transaction processing and the decision-support queries that result from management information systems that use the same OLTP data. Su's multi-wavefront parallel database system uses the object-oriented paradigm as its underlying data model. The Datacycle parallel system supports SQL plus some extra functionality such as fuzzy queries. These last three systems are examples of projects that go beyond classical (relational) DBMS, in response to user's needs for smarter information systems.

The functional requirements of smart information systems involve the efficient implementation of tasks such as rapid pattern-directed searching and whole-structure operations such as join and transitive closure—tasks that are believed to be generic to knowledge-base systems. There is much natural parallelism to be exploited in these tasks. It is felt by several researchers that such tasks highlight the mismatch between the functional requirements of knowledge-base systems and the operational characteristics of both conventional von Neumann uniprocessors and many existing parallel architectures. Particular examples are the mismatch (1) between logical data-objects of varying size and granularity and blocks of linearly addressed memory and (2) between the rich variety of data types used by knowledge-base software and the limited scalar primitives supported by conventional arithmetic logic units. These mismatches result in overcomplex software and unacceptably long runtimes. How to overcome these mismatches is a topic of current research; the IFS/2 project (see below) represents one possible approach.

Adding more functionality to produce "smart" systems covers a range of software paradigms. Many of these draw on the insights of artificial intelligence. It is convenient to divide the resulting hardware architectures into two categories: those that take a broad approach to knowledge representation, and those that focus on one representation or problem-solving paradigm. The first category, which may be called knowledge-base machines, often remains compatible with the *n*-ary relational model but extends this model toward deductive databases and the support of object-based and rule-based systems. Support may also be given to some AI-like knowledge representations such as semantic networks, while still retaining an ability to deal with commercially realistic quantities of data. An example of this first category of machines is the European Declarative System, a collaboration among ICL, Siemens, and Bull.[34] Some of the EDS insights originated in a research project to design a parallel graph reduction machine for functional languages. However, the production EDS takes relational databases as its starting point. EDS supports Extended SQL,[35] as well as LISP and PROLOG. Research into knowledge-base machine architectures includes the recent work of Stolfo[36] and the IFS/2.[37] Professor Stolfo has examined rule-based systems such as Datalog and OPS5, with a view to extracting the common inherent parallelism. The IFS/2 uses a modularly extensible array of single instruction, multiple data search engines under transputer control, to achieve associative processing of structures such as relations, sets, and graphs. At the AI end of the smart information system spectrum come machines whose architecture is focused on one particular knowledge representation or one (declarative) language. There exists a long tradition of machines dedicated to production-rule systems such as DADO.[38]

More recent examples of machines designed to support semantic networks are SNAP[39] and IXM/2.[40] Computers designed to speed up execution of declarative languages (that is, logic and functional) are well reviewed in Kogge.[9] An interesting example of a PROLOG engine is the Knowledge Crunching Machine, which comes from the European Computer Manufacturers' Research Centre in Munich.[41] Unfortunately, not many of these architectures perform well when handling commercially realistic volumes of data. (By "commercially realistic" we mean at least several tens of megabytes for the knowledge-base systems and perhaps several tens of gigabytes for the more conventional smart DBMS applications). On the very-large-scale-integration front, there have been several associative (that is, content-addressable) memory chips that contain added facilities for declarative languages.[42] There are also several examples of VLSI accelerators for the more general forms of pattern-directed search, as found in Stormon.[43]

1.3 GUIDE TO THE REST OF THE BOOK

The main text is divided into four sections, which broadly follow the developments described above.

(1) *Database machines:* In this category come add-on machines and performance-enhancing units that employ parallel hardware mainly in support of conventional database models such as the relational. Object-oriented systems are also beginning

to emerge. However, SQL typically forms the programmer's interface to the majority of machines featured in this section.

(2) *Using massively parallel general computing platforms for DBMS:* Two examples are given to illustrate how high-performance computers can be used to support database and related software, even though some of these platforms (in this case a single-instruction, multiple-data array processor) may originally have been designed with scientific/numeric applications in mind. Once again, the emphasis is on information systems that follow conventional models or service well-known applications.

(3) *Knowledge-base machines:* This section features projects that go beyond the relational model toward what has been called "smart" information systems. The ability to handle realistic quantities of data is retained, but this data may have a complex structure that includes rules. These machines thus attempt to combine some of the management features of DBMS with techniques drawn from artificial intelligence. The programmer's interface may be extended SQL (that is, with deductive features) or a declarative language.

(4) *Artificial-intelligence machines:* Two examples are given of machines that are deliberately designed to speed up a particular knowledge-representation formalism or a particular problem-solving paradigm. The projects in this section can be regarded more as research prototypes than products; nevertheless, experience gained with such machines will no doubt influence the development of future architectural features relevant to smart information systems.

Mahdi Abdelguerfi, University of New Orleans, USA
Simon Lavington, University of Essex, UK
November 1994

REFERENCES

1. R.A. Frost, *Introduction to Knowledge-Based Systems*, Collins, London, England, 1986.
2. S. Ceri and G. Pelagatti, *Distributed Databases: Principles and Systems*, McGraw-Hill, New York, N.Y., 1985.
3. D.K. Hsiao and M.N. Kamel, "Heterogeneous Databases: Proliferation, Issues, and Solutions," *IEEE Trans. Data and Knowledge Eng.*, Vol. 4, No. 3, June 1992, pp. 45–62.
4. D.K. Hsiao, *Advanced Database Machine Architectures*, Prentice-Hall, Englewood Cliffs, N.J., 1983.
5. S.Y.W. Su, *Database Computers: Principles, Architectures, and Techniques*, McGraw-Hill, New York, N.Y., 1988.
6. J.S. Kowalik, *Parallel Computation and Computers for Artificial Intelligence*, Kluwer Academic, Norwell, Mass., 1988.
7. M. Kitsuregawa and H. Tanaka, eds., "Database Machines and Knowledge-Base Machines," *Proc. 5th Int'l Workshop Database Machines*, Kluwer Academic, Norwell, Mass., 1988.
8. H. Boral and P. Faudemay, eds., *Proc. 6th Int'l Workshop Database Machines*, Springer-Verlag, New York, N.Y., 1989.
9. P.M. Kogge, *The Architecture of Symbolic Computers*, McGraw-Hill, New York, N.Y. 1991.
10. P. America, *Parallel Database Systems*, Springer-Verlag, New York, N.Y., 1991.
11. P. Valduriez, *Parallel Processing and Data Management*, Chapman and Hall, London, England, 1992.
12. A.R. Hurson, et al., *IEEE Tutorial: Parallel Architectures for Database Systems*, IEEE CS Press, Los Alamitos, Calif., 1989.
13. Hurson, A.R., et al., "Parallel Architectures for Database Systems," *Advances in Computers*, Vol. 30, 1989, pp. 107–151.

14. "Database Prototype Systems," *IEEE Trans. Knowledge and Data Eng.*, Special Issue, Vol. 2, No. 1, Mar. 1990.

15. D. DeWitt and J. Gray, "Parallel Database Systems: The Future of High-Performance Database Systems" *Comm. ACM*, Vol. 35, No. 6, 1992, pp. 85-98.

16. V.A.J. Maller, "Information Retrieval Using the Content Addressable File Store," *Proc. IFIP-80 Congress*, North Holland, Amsterdam, The Netherlands, 1980, pp. 187-190.

17. T. Satoh and U. Inoue, "Rinda: A Relational Database Processor for Large Databases," Chapter 4 in this book.

18. S. Kojima, et al., "IDP—A Main Storage Based Vector Database Processor," *Proc. 5th Int'l Workshop Database Machines*, Kluwer Academic, Norwell, Mass., 1988, pp. 47-60.

19. M. Kitsuregawa and W. Yang, "Evaluation of 18-Stage Pipeline Hardware Sorter," *Proc. 6th Int'l Workshop Database Machines*, Springer-Verlag, New York, N.Y., 1989, pp. 142-145.

20. *HSTS: High Speed Text Search System Product Literature*, Operating Systems Inc., 1982.

21. M. Stroud, "Massively Parallel Computer Makers Begin to Target Database Applications," *Investors Daily*, June 1992.

22. J. Spiers, "Mapping a Fourth Generation DBMS to a Range of Parallel Machines," in *Parallel Processing and Data Management*, P. Valduriez, ed., Chapman and Hall, London, England, 1992, pp. 53-67.

23. N. Bond and S. Reddaway, "A Massively Parallel Indexing Engine Using DAP," Chapter 9 in this book.

24. S. Zenios, "Parallel and Supercomputing in the Practice of Management Science," *Proc. UNICOM Seminar on Commercial Parallel Processing*, Uxbridge, Middlesex, England, 1992, pp. 67-95.

25. M. Stonebraker, "The Case for Shared-Nothing," *Database Engineering*, Vol. 9, No.1, 1986, pp. 4-9.

26. J. Page, "High-Performance Database for Client/Server Systems," in *Parallel Processing and Data Management*, P. Valduriez, ed., Chapman and Hall, London, England, 1992, pp. 33-51.

27. F. Cariño, et al., "Industrial Database Supercomputer Exegis—the DBC/1012, the NCR 3700, the YNet and BYNet," Chapter 8 in this book.

28. D.A. Patterson, et al., "The Case for Redundant Arrays of Inexpensive Disks (RAID)," Proc. *ACM SIGMOD*, ACM Press New York, N. Y., 1988, pp. 109-116.

29. D.K. Hsiao, "From DBC to MDBS—A Progression in Database Machine Research," Chapter 3 in this book.

30. D. DeWitt, et al., "The GAMMA Database Machine Project," *IEEE Trans. Knowledge and Data Engineering*, Vol. 2, No.1, Mar. 1990, pp. 44-62.

31. J. Kerridge, "IDIOMS: A Multitransputer Database Machine," Chapter 2 in this book.

32. T.F. Bowen, et al., "The Datacycle Architecture: Applying VLSI Filters to Large Databases," Chapter 7 in this book.

33. S.Y.W. Su, et al., "Parallel Multi-Wavefront Algorithms for Pattern-Based Processing of Object-Oriented Databases," Chapter 6 in this book.

34. L. Bormann, et al., "EDS: An Advanced Parallel Database Server," Chapter 11 in this book.

35. G. Gardarin, et al., "ESQL: An Extended SQL with Object and Deductive Capabilities," *Proc. Int'l Conf. Database and Expert System Applications*, Springer-Verlag, New York, N.Y., 1990, pp. 299-307.

36. J.S. Stolfo, et al., "A Parallel and Distributed Environment for Database Rule Processing: Open Problems and Future Directions," Chapter 12 in this book.

37. S.H. Lavington, "The IFS/2: Add-On Support for Knowledge-Base Systems," Chapter 10 in this book.

38. J.S. Stolfo and D.E. Shaw, "DADO: A Tree-Structured Machine Architecture for Production Systems," *Proc. Nat'l Conf. Artificial Intelligence*, Morgan Kaufman, Pittsburgh, Penn., 1982, pp. 242-246.

39. D. Moldovan, et al., "SNAP: A Marker-Propagation Architecture for Knowledge Processing," *IEEE Trans. Parallel and Distributed Systems*, Vol. 3, No. 4, July 1992, pp. 397-410.

40. T.S. Higuchi, "IXM/2: A Parallel Associative Processor for Knowledge Processing," Chapter 13 in this book.

41. J. Noye, "An Overview of the Knowledge Crunching Machine," Chapter 14 in this book.

42. I. Robinson, "A Prolog Processor Based on a Pattern Matching Memory Device," *Proc. 3rd Int'l Conf. Logic Programming*, Springer-Verlag, New York, N.Y., 1986, pp. 172–179.

43. C.D. Stormon, et al., "An Architecture Based on Content-Addressable Memory for the Rapid Execution of Prolog," *Proc. 5th Conf. Logic Programming*, MIT Press, Cambridge, Mass., 1988, pp. 1448–1474.

2

IDIOMS: A Multitransputer Database Machine

Jon Kerridge

National Transputer Support Centre, Sheffield Science Park, Sheffield, England, UK

ABSTRACT

The aim of the IDIOMS project is to build a shared-nothing database machine that can support both online transaction processing and decision support queries that result from a management information system. It was essential that both processing styles were integrated into a single architecture to support a perceived need of commercial organizations. This need arises from organizations that have acquired over a long period a large amount of low-level data critical to their viability. Unfortunately, current technology does not permit the organization to extract management information or provide decision support in a low-cost scalable manner. The IDIOMS project has demonstrated the feasibility of building a scalable multitransputer shared-nothing database machine that can undertake both styles of processing at low cost.

2.1 INTRODUCTION

The timely availability of management information and facilities to support decision making is vital to the well-being of an organization. Unfortunately, for most organizations such systems are not feasible if they manipulate a large volume of online data subject to some form of online transaction processing. Typically, the system used for OLTP is incapable of supporting the extra processing required for management information systems and decision support, even if the data were stored in a form that enabled both types of processing. This bulk data is generally well structured so as to support efficiently the mission-critical capability of the organization. That is, the data has to be structured in order to provide the transaction processing capability. This very structure inhibits the manipulation of the data by traditional programming techniques, normally used to obtain management and decision support information.

9

The advent of relational database technology appeared to offer a solution to the dilemma of answering ad hoc queries. Highly structured data could be held in a flat-file or tabular form and could be queried using the values of columns to access data. It was not necessary to know how the data was stored. It was thus relatively easy to formulate an ad hoc query. The only problem was that the processing time, for all but the simplest query, was prohibitively long for everyday use.

In the mid-1980s the bench mark wars commenced,[1] in which the comparative performance of a number of relational systems was determined. This competition led to performance improvement. However, these improvements were focussed on the transaction-processing capabilities of the relational database systems, because there were such benchmarks already available for specially constructed application-specific transaction processing systems. There was no universally accepted benchmark for query processing. The setting up of the Transaction Processing Performance Council and the consequent benchmarks, such as the TPC-A and B, and Wisconsin benchmarks, ensured that appropriate metrics were used. It could be argued that this development led to relational database technology being developed in a direction (transaction processing) for which it was not intended. Transaction-processing performance was obtained at the expense of having poor query-processing performance. The required optimizations for one style of processing are inappropriate for the other.

To overcome these performance limitations, a number of different solutions were attempted, based upon dedicated hardware. Typical were those of Britton-Lee and Teradata.[2] Other companies, such as Oracle, Ingres, and Sybase, were adopting a different approach based upon the use of shared-memory multiprocessors, because they were using different platforms, which required a common software architecture framework, including single processor systems.

The Britton-Lee and Teradata[3] approach used dedicated hardware that improved the data access and relational-processing part of database manipulation. The user interface was retained on the host mainframe originally used to support the database in its entirety. The advantage of off-loading data access is that the customer retains the user interface, which occupies most of the application development time. Database users do not have to be retrained, and existing communication structures can be retained. Thus, rather than having to upgrade the central resource, a database accelerator is bought, providing a very real advantage if the mainframe manufacturer has not yet produced the required more powerful machine. However, this hardware is expensive and not easy to scale after installation.

The approach adopted by third-party vendors has been to develop their database architecture to execute on shared-memory multiprocessor systems. The original architectures were developed for single processor systems and thus a major architectural redesign was not required. Thus, in the short term, a performance advantage was easily obtained by moving to such share-everything multiprocessor systems. However, it has become apparent that the load placed upon a shared-memory multiprocessor by database software is such that it is not usually possible to fully utilize all the processors that could be connected, typically a maximum of eight to 16 processors, when up to 32 could be used. That is, the performance limit of the shared memory had been reached, and the addition of further processors yielded no improvement in performance.

It was within this framework that the IDIOMS project[4] was proposed to investigate the feasibility of constructing a distributed-memory share-nothing multiprocessor system that could support both OLTP and MIS functionality on the same data set. It was also vital that the scalability of the system should be demonstrated, and that it should be designed for large data volumes, at least 10 Gbytes. The system had to be scalable both on first installation and, subsequently, when the system was upgraded.

2.2 THE IDIOMS COLLABORATORS

IDIOMS (intelligent decision making in on-line management systems) is a collaboration between the National Transputer Support Centre (NTSC) in Sheffield , the Bristol Transputer Centre (BTC), Strand Software Technologies, Ltd. (SSTL), and TSB Bank. The NTSC's role is to develop the database engine that supports both OLTP and MIS processing. The BTC is developing parallel algorithms that allow large volumes of on-line data to be processed using neural networks, constraint-satisfaction networks, and genetic algorithms for decision support. SSTL is providing a parallel environment, called STRAND,[5] which will enable the easy construction of an interface between the MIS and the SQL queries required for the database engine. TSB is providing data from both banking and credit-card systems, to enable the construction of two demonstrations of the IDIOMS approach. These demonstrations will be using real data from each of the applications to ensure that any comparisons drawn with their existing systems are realistic.

The aim of the IDIOMS project is to build a demonstration of transputer-based[6] hardware to construct a shared-nothing distributed-memory parallel database machine. Of particular interest to TSB are the aspects of performance in both OLTP and MIS modes separately and combined, and the ease of system scalability.

Currently TSB has one system that provides a repository for the banking data and is accessed solely in OLTP mode, with batch runs overnight. These batch runs generate some statistics, but it is not possible to query the data in an MIS mode. A separate system, based upon a Teradata machine, is used to provide a customer information database. There is some duplication of data between the banking and customer information systems. The credit-card system is kept on a totally separate system even though many of the customers are common. TSB is atypical of most UK banks in that it actually updates the banking information on-line, rather than the more usual check-clearing run overnight. This practice results from the fact that account holders have passbooks as well as checkbooks, and there is a need to be able to update the customer's passbook while the customer is being served. If the online data could be accessed in an MIS decision-support mode then the TSB would be able to improve both its services and its profitability.

2.3 OVERVIEW OF THE IDIOMS DESIGN

The block architecture of the IDIOMS machine is shown in Figure 1. It shows that the OLTP and MIS functions of the machine are completely separate but that they both have access to the shared-data storage. The shared-data storage is fundamental to the IDIOMS design and arises from an appreciation of the differing processing characteristics of OLTP and MIS.

An OLTP transaction is generally of short duration and manipulates one or more related records, using both read and write operations. An OLTP record is usually accessed via a unique generated key, such as account number. It is therefore normal in an on-line environment to build an index based upon the key, to optimize access to the data. Normally the data is organized into one large record so that, with one disk access, all the possibly relevant information can be fetched regardless of the particular transaction to be undertaken. This procedure is a nonrelational way of storing the data, because it is generally not normalized. For example, a bank account record contains sufficient space for as many

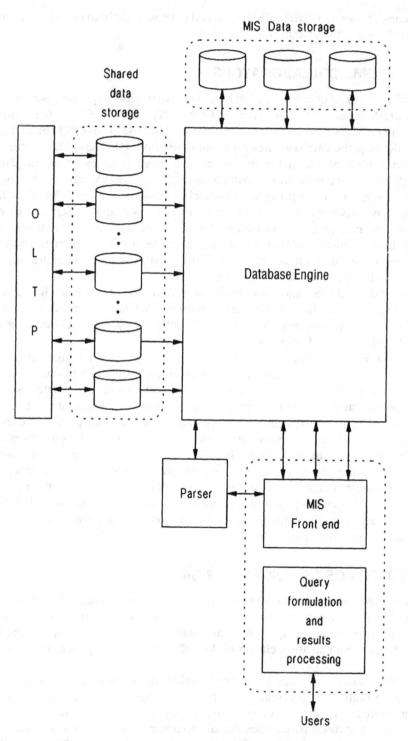

Figure 1. Block diagram of the IDIOMS system.

account movements (transactions) as appear on a statement. Thus the record contains a repeating group. In the IDIOMS machine we have separated the slowly changing information concerning an account, such as name and address, from the account movements, into two tables so that all the movements (up to the length of a statement) occur as a single group in the table. Thus, the OLTP system can access the whole group of movements, whereas the MIS can access each row independently. Effectively we have used the grouping column of the movements table to control the physical placement of the data on disk.

The data is range-partitioned across the shared disks. The account number is used as the key for range partitioning; transactions for a particular account are directed to the disk upon which the account data is stored. The shared data storage is organized so that access requests from OLTP are given priority over MIS requests.

The MIS makes requests for data from the shared-data storage as though the data were stored in relational tables. The MIS only makes SELECT requests upon the shared-data storage. The MIS can access the MIS data storage for any type of SQL query and the data is stored as pure relational tables, as opposed to the combined form used in the shared-data storage. Queries are passed from the MIS front end to the parser, which determines what parts of the database engine are required to satisfy the query. The resultant data is returned in a number of parallel data streams to the MIS, where the data is further processed to provide management and decision-support information.

2.4 DETAILS OF THE IDIOMS DATABASE ENGINE

Figure 2 shows the detail of the database engine. Each of the squares represents a transputer. In the actual demonstrator there are nine OLTP disks (D_o) and three MIS disks (D_m), all 100 Mbytes in size. There are three relational engines R with associated buffer processors B. The rings, made up of C processors, comprise a scalable communications network.[7] The design of the internal processes that make up each of the processors is given by Kerridge.[4] Each of the disks is interfaced to the system by a transputer with associated small computer systems bus interface (SCSI). It is this processor that gives priority to the OLTP system, using firmware provided on the processor.[8] The processors T receive the transactions to be carried out via a routing network.[9] Each of the T processors is capable of carrying out all the transactions. As stated earlier, the data on disks D_o is range partitioned and this ability to carry out all transactions is a necessity. The ring of T and I processors is required to implement transactions that need access to more than one account, where the account information is stored on different disks. This event would occur in transactions involving the transfer of funds from one account to another.

For the purposes of this demonstration we have assumed that a customer does not have accounts on different disks. Thus the customer information pertaining to several accounts held by the same customer is always on the same disk, as is the account information. This assumption is not unreasonable for the purposes of the demonstration, as the number of real-life situations is small where this condition is not the case. The transaction code is written in C encapsulated in an Occam2 harness.[10] The transaction code has been written as a pair of parallel processes, one which requests data from the disk, processes the data, and writes any results back to the disk. The other process accesses the disk, using the key value provided, and accesses the disk for the correct record. The layout of data on the disk is held in the data dictionary and is communicated to each of the T processors using the I process at system boot time. The role of the data dictionary will be described later.

The database engine comprises the disks D_o and D_m and the processors S, C, B, and R. P/DD is the parser/data dictionary processor. Each of the S engines comprises a number of

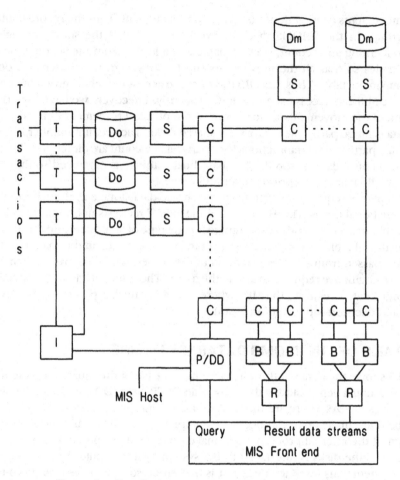

**Figure 2.   Detailed structure of the IDIOMS parallel
database machine.**

table handler processes running in parallel, one for each table stored on the disks. Each table handler is initialized with details of the table structure and physical disk placement from the dictionary at boot time.

The table handler then contains processes, yet again running in parallel, which undertake the basic manipulations of SQL (*select, update, insert,* and *delete*). These processes are allocated to a particular query on an as-needed basis, by the parser. The basic premise of the database engine is that data filtering (equivalent to the relational select and project operations) is carried out in the table handler associated with the disk. The selected rows are then transferred round the network of C processors to the relational engines (B, R) where two table operations are carried out. In the case of S processors connected as part of the shared data (disks D_o) then they are restricted to *select* operations only. Thus a query being processed by such an S engine can be stopped while the disk is accessed by a T processor during an OLTP operation. This feature does mean that an MIS query will probably see the data in an inconsistent state, but for such processing this problem is not critical. We are developing scalable concurrency management algorithms that will overcome this problem.

In the demonstrator we chose not to implement any indexes, either primary or secondary, on the MIS data. This selection arises because most of the queries will be based on ranges of values, and the natural keys of the data, account, and customer numbers will not normally form part of an MIS query. In due course we hope to be able to add indexes in order to measure performance improvement, if any, with indexes. We have implemented a mechanism of scanning the data set and, for the selected tuples, doing a memory-based sort, so that subsequent join-processing can use a sort-merge join. The sorting process can also be used for *distinct* and *group by* operations. We have thus traded runtime performance of a query for the ease of table modification and not having to maintain indexes. Current performance measurements indicate that this practice is proving not to be desperately expensive, because we have subdivided the data into such small units. The sort of selected tuples is carried out in the table handler process within the S processor. A further advantage of this approach is that we can sort any column of a table on an as-needed basis. We are not restricted to carrying out selections and joins on tables for which there is an index.

Data from the S processors is then directed to one or more of the relational engines. These engines comprise two B processors and an R processor that does the actual operation. The resultant data stream can either be sent directly to the MIS front end, or, in the case of nested operations, redirected to another relational engine, using the B processors and the communications network.

From the foregoing description it is apparent that there is a need for control within the database engine. In the next section we look at how the control of the database machine is achieved and the software infrastructure that has been developed.

2.5 THE DATA DICTIONARY AND SYSTEM CONTROL

One of the early decisions taken in the design of the IDIOMS database machine was to base the dictionary structure upon that contained in the Working Draft Database Language SQL2.[11] This decision proposes an information schema that describes the structure of the database being managed. It is equivalent to the catalogue of IBM's DB2. In the parallel IDIOMS machine it was decided that the dictionary should hold physical placement data and resource availability information, so that it can be used by the query optimizer contained in the data dictionary. The operational model of the IDIOMS database engine is one of query decomposition into dataflow graphs, with nodes of the graph undertaking *project*, *select*, *join*, and other operations. In a parallel environment this operation can be further extended by undertaking parts of the query concurrently on different processors.[12]

Earlier it was stated that the data is range-partitioned. This partitioning means that queries that use the partitioning column(s) in their predicate can be optimized to access only those partitions where it is known that data appropriate to the query is stored. As part of the IDIOMS project, a data-storage description language (DSDL) has been developed,[13] allowing the partitioning of data to be specified. The partitioning information is then stored in the dictionary, so that it can be used by the query optimizer.[14]

This decision is further reinforced by the use of the transputer as the processing element. As well as providing memory, processor, and communications capability, the transputer also contains a process scheduler.[15] In fact, the transputer contains a high-and low-priority scheduler. The former is a non-preemptive scheduler that allows a process to execute until it needs to communicate, enabling implementation of lightweight processes that are the basis of OLTP systems; the low priority scheduler is a preemptive scheduler, which is ideal for MIS query processing. Thus, the traditional process-scheduling aspects of an operating system are actually provided by the transputer hardware.

The transputer was designed to support dedicated embedded systems, normally manifesting themselves as real-time control systems. However, a database machine is an embedded system. It accepts commands in the form of OLTP transaction requests or MIS queries, and then carries out the transaction or supplies a stream of data corresponding to the query.

The processes that actually access the disk data storage have been encoded to deal with the table structures that occur in relational database systems. Thus, the file management system normally provided as part of an operating system is not required. The IDIOMS database machine does not use a traditional operating system. It merely accepts queries or transactions and returns the corresponding results.

This change has one major benefit, in that portable database management systems usually build a direct interface to data storage by using the system level calls provided by the operating system. Thus, a layer of software has to be traversed, which is totally redundant. Secondly, because operating systems provide a general-purpose process-scheduling strategy, assuming a number of concurrent independent users, most database systems implement their own process-scheduling strategy running as a single process within the host operating system. Yet again, this software layer can be avoided by the use of the transputer.

2.6 TEST CONFIGURATION

In order to evaluate the performance of the IDIOMS machine, a test hardware configuration was constructed. The test configuration comprised nine disks in the shared-data storage, three relational engines, and no disks in the MIS data storage. Each of the disks was a 100-Mbyte SCSI drive connected to an SCSI controller contained on a transputer module (TRAM). The data was passed from the SCSI TRAM along a link operating at 10 Mbits/sec to either the storage processor S or the transaction processor T. The S and T processors were 20-MHz T800 TRAMs with 2 Mbytes of memory. Each relational processor R comprises two buffer processors acting as the input to the join processor. The three R processors were then connected to a PC containing a transputer board that consumed the output stream. The buffer processors were T800, 20-MHz, 1-Mbyte TRAMs, and the join processor was a T800, 20-MHz, 2-Mbyte TRAM. The relational processors output an ASCII-printable string corresponding to the output data needed to satisfy the query. The PC software then outputs this data to screen and/or file or neither. This latter option is required to ensure that performance measurement is not limited by the PC to transputer communications software.

2.7 OLTP PERFORMANCE

The performance was measured using both a TPC data set[1] and data provided by TSB. The following figures for TPC-B performance have NOT been audited.

2.7.1 TPC-B Performance

The TPC-B data set was loaded and configured for the size of data required for the given performance. The data set increases with increasing claimed performance. The data was evenly distributed over the nine disks. A sustained performance of 15 transactions per second (tps) was achieved against the nine disks. A peak performance of 20 tps was achieved during some processing periods, giving an estimated cost/tps ratio of $0.85k. Perhaps, more usefully, we can express this cost as 1.66 tps per disk, because the aim of the IDIOMS machine was to demonstrate a low-cost scalable system. In other experiments we have demonstrated that the OLTP performance is linear in the number of attached disks.

2.7.2 TSB Data Set Performance

The TSB data was also loaded evenly onto the nine disks, using a range-partitioning technique based upon account number. The total data set was about 5,000 accounts. This data comprises the test data set used by TSB, and as such contains realistic data as opposed to the TPC data set, in which the records are unrealistically small. A performance of 6 tps was obtained from the nine disks, or 0.66 tps per disk. The difference in performance between the TPC dataset and the TSB dataset can be accounted for in the size of records that were manipulated and the complexity of the real transactions that were undertaken for the TSB data set.

We can also compare this performance with that of existing TSB systems. For the same number of accounts the current system has an average performance of 0.13 tps. Thus, the IDIOMS machine has a performance improvement of about 45 times. However, in order to store the number of accounts currently maintained by TSB, a large number of disks would be required, giving a performance in excess of that which is required. A balance would therefore have to be achieved between size of disk, desired OLTP performance, disk reliability, and amount of MIS processing required. The performance improvement was seen by TSB to be a contribution to the way in which they would design OLTP systems in the future.

It also has to be stated that the IDIOMS mechanisms contained no means of transaction recovery or rollback, which is included in the current TSB system. However, a completely separate parallel architecture with minimal overhead, developed for recovery and rollback, is currently being implemented.[16-18]

2.8 MIS PERFORMANCE

The data for the OLTP system, which is shared with the MIS, comprises five tables. For the performance measurement exercise we only used three of these tables. The salient details of these tables are presented in Figure 3, in which only the columns used in the queries

```
CREATE TABLE ACCOUNT
     (     AC_NUMBER        CHAR(12) NOT NULL,
           BALANCE          DOUBLE PRECISION NOT NULL,
           OVERDRAFT_LIMIT  DOUBLE PRECISION DEFAULT 0,
           FILLER           CHAR(44),
     PRIMARY KEY (AC_NUMBER)
     )
CREATE TABLE CUSTOMER
     (     CUSTOMER_NUMBER  CHAR(12) NOT NULL,
           TITLE            CHAR(8),
           INITIALS         CHAR(3),
           SURNAME          CHAR(25),
           FILLER           CHAR(208),
     PRIMARY KEY (CUSTOMER_NUMBER)
     )
CREATE TABLE CUST_ACCNT
     (     AC_NO            CHAR(12) NOT NULL,
           CUST_NO          CHAR(12) NOT NULL,
     PRIMARY KEY (AC_NO, CUST_NO),
     FOREIGN KEY (AC_NO) REFERENCES ACCOUNT,
     FOREIGN KEY (CUST_NO) REFERENCES CUSTOMER
```

Figure 3.   Schema table structure.

are detailed. The ACCOUNT table holds the fixed details of an account. The queries have been organized so that predicates are evaluated on the ACCOUNT table, which are then selected directly, or used subsequently in conjunction with the CUSTOMER table, using a join operation. The CUSTOMER table holds fixed details concerning customers. The table CUST_ACCNT is a linker table that implements the many-to-many relationship that exists between CUSTOMER and ACCOUNT. (A customer may have many accounts. An account may be used by many customers.) Thus, to find out details about a customer who uses an account, it is necessary to form a join between ACCOUNT and CUST_ACCNT and between CUST_ACCNT and CUSTOMER.

The database contains two further tables, which hold details of the current statement and the previous statement. It should be noted that currently TSB cannot hold the previous statement on-line, due to the data volumes involved.

The performance was evaluated using two different database sizes. The first was a small test database of 90 accounts and customers, in which there were no many-to-many relationships. The second was the complete test data set provided by the TSB, in which there were a representative number of many-to-many relationships between customers and accounts. In addition to the 3000 account records there were 4000 customer records and 5000 rows in the linker table CUST_ACCNT.

2.8.1 Selecting Data from a Single Table

A series of predicates were evaluated on the ACCOUNT table, which reduced or filtered the amount of data that was output. These predicates are shown in Figure 4. A query of the form:

```
SELECT AC_NUMBER, BALANCE, OVERDRAFT_LIMIT
    FROM ACCOUNT
    WHERE P
```

was evaluated for each of the predicates P.

The performance achieved is shown in Table 1. Table 1a shows the timings using the 90-row database. The time column just gives the time to access the disk and select the rows for the given predicate, which are then output to the PC connected to the relational engine. The final sorted time column gives the processing time when the selected rows are sorted before being output. Sorting is valuable when the output rows are then used as an input to a join process, rather than being directly output. It can be seen that for this small database

P	Predicate
0	no predicate (all rows selected)
1	BALANCE < 2000
2	AC_NUMBER > 300000000000
3	OVERDRAFT_LIMIT = 0
4	P1 AND P2
5	P2 AND P3
6	P1 AND P2 AND P3

Figure 4.   Predicate values.

Table 1a. Timings for the 90-row database.

Predicate	Rows output (secs)	Time (secs)	Sorted Time (secs)
0	90	0.34	0.36
1	11	0.30	0.29
2	40	0.29	0.35
3	89	0.34	0.35
4	8	0.29	0.28
5	39	0.29	0.35
6	8	0.31	0.35

Table 1b. Timings for the test data set.

Predicate	Rows output (secs)	Time (secs)	Sorted Time (secs)
0	3317	5.1	18.5
1	482	3.5	8.5
2	1367	2.8	11.0
3	3268	5.3	18.3
4	457	2.5	4.9
5	1332	3.1	10.9
6	448	2.9	5.3

the time is dominated by the time to access the disk. Table 1b gives the same timings for the complete data set of 3317 rows.

2.8.2 Join Performance

In order to evaluate the join performance, a query of the form shown below was evaluated.

```
SELECT CUSTOMER_NUMBER, TITLE, INITIALS, SURNAME
   FROM CUSTOMER, CUST_ACCNT, ACCOUNT
   WHERE P
   AND AC_NUMBER = AC_NO          (JP1)
   AND CUST_NO = CUSTOMER_NUMBER (JP2)
```

To examine the effect of this query, take the case of P4 on the 90-row database. We know that P4 generates eight rows of output and that each account happens to be used by a unique customer (which is not the case in the test data set.). Thus the AC_NUMBER column in each of the eight rows that are output has to be compared (JP1) with AC_NO in all 90 rows of CUST_ACCNT. The resulting CUST_NO in each row in which AC_NO = AC_NUMBER is then used to access (JP2) the desired row of CUSTOMER to extract the columns that are to be output. Assuming we use some form of testing rows in a loop to implement the join, then P4 is evaluated 90 times, resulting in eight rows, JP1 is evaluated 720 times, resulting in eight rows, and JP2 is also evaluated 720 times.

Table 2a. Join performance on the 90-row table.

	NOT OPTIMIZED			OPTIMIZED		
P	JP1	JP2	Secs	JP1	JP2	Secs
1, 11	8100	990	0.77	90	495	0.63
2, 40	8100	3600	2.1	90	1800	1.4
3, 89	8100	8010	3.1	90	4005	1.8
4, 8	8100	720	0.73	90	360	0.63
5, 39	8100	3510	2.0	90	1755	1.4
6, 8	8100	720	0.74	90	360	0.64

This sequence can be optimized if we sort the outputs of the intermediate stages and/or use indexes, as suggested by Valduriez.[19-21]. However, the use of such techniques in themselves consumes time. In the basic IDIOMS design very little use has been made of such optimizations. The major optimization is that, when data is selected from a table by evaluating a predicate (even if the predicate selects all rows), we can sort the rows into any order, based on the value of any column or group of columns. The relational engine is then able to carry out optimizations based upon the input data streams. No optimization is possible if both data streams are unsorted, and the full cartesian product has to be evaluated, using the nested-loops technique, as described above.

Different optimizations are possible if the sorted order is based upon a column that either does or does not have the UNIQUE (or PRIMARY KEY) attribute. Thus, the join between ACCOUNT and CUST_ACCNT (JP1) results in a unique sorted data stream from ACCOUNT and a sorted data stream from CUST_ACCNT. The join between CUSTOMER and the output from JP1, referred to as JP2, results in an unsorted data stream from JP1 being joined to a sorted unique data stream from CUSTOMER. In effect, this means that the average search in the join JP2 can be reduced to one half of that without the optimization. Table 2 shows the performance of the join operations for the two cases where, first, the sort optimization is not used and, second, when the optimization is used. All times are in seconds. The columns labelled JP1 and JP2 give an estimate of the number of comparisons that were undertaken to satisfy the particular join predicate identified. The P column gives the predicate number, together with the number of rows that were output. The column labelled Secs gives the time for the query.

Table 2a demonstrates that the processing time is dominated by the fact that the output from the first join JP1, which is unsorted, directly influences the number of operations that have to be undertaken in the second join JP2. Thus, the nonoptimized version shows substantial processing times when the number of rows output from JP1 is high. In the optimized version we see that the processing time is drastically reduced for those predicates that generate a larger number of rows from JP1. The implication is that a sort would be beneficial after the first join has been evaluated.

Table 2b reinforces this aspect even more. In general, there is at least a 50 percent improvement in the optimized version over the nonoptimized version. In some cases it approaches 60 percent. The actual population of the tables was as follows: ACCOUNT: 3317 rows, CUST_ACCNT: 5234 rows, and CUSTOMER: 4175 rows. It can be seen that the optimized version reduces JP1 to the size of the linker table CUST_ACCNT. The next stage is governed by the number of rows that result from JP1. If we had a sort engine available such as that described by Kerridge,[22] then the size of JP2 would be reduced from the figures given to the size of the CUSTOMER table (4175), because we could use a merge sort.

Table 2b. Join performance on the complete database (m = million).

	NOT OPTIMIZED			OPTIMIZED		
P	**JP1**	**JP2**	**Secs**	**JP1**	**JP2**	**Secs**
1, 1494	17.36m	6.24m	1963	5234	3.12m	1007
2, 2071	17.36m	8.65m	3791	5234	4.32m	2210
3, 5154	17.36m	21.52m	6737	5234	10.76m	3385
4, 641	17.36m	2.68m	1204	5234	1.34m	701
5, 2018	17.36m	8.43m	3697	5234	4.21m	2149
6, 625	17.36m	2.61m	1176	5234	1.30m	683

A further access optimization is available, which is to use an index. This procedure would reduce JP2 to the number of rows output from JP1. However, the index has to be maintained and this is only feasible for columns that are used as a primary key, or are a foreign key to another table.

2.9 FURTHER WORK

From the foregoing discussion it is apparent that further work is needed to investigate the efficacy of using a sort after each stage of join processing. It is not a foregone conclusion that such sorting will have the dramatic improvement that would be expected, because the sort itself will take time to set up and process. Sorting large streams of data does take a long time.[22]

We also intend to investigate the use of indexes to reduce processing times in joins. The advantage of using an index may be outweighed by the time taken to maintain the index in the overall system processing time. Our current system has a degree of flexibility that an index-based system does not. We can sort after predicate evaluation into any order of any columns. Generally it is not feasible to maintain indexes on all columns. Gray[1] suggests that no general MIS query would be attempted on a column for which an index is not provided. We do not believe this to be a reasonable restriction for any database system; hence our emphasis on building a system that does not use any indexes.

We wish to investigate the situation where more than one relational processor R was allocated to each part of the join. In the current configuration we used two of the R processors from the three that were available, one for JP1 and the other for JP2. If more were available, then these extra resources could be allocated to the parts of the join operations individually. For example, if there were sufficient resources, each S processor could be allocated its own relational processor R. This would have the effect of reducing the overall processing time. This reduction may be to the extent of nullifying any benefits that might be obtained by using sorting and indexes. We undertook some evaluation of the system and determined that the performance was not influenced by the communication structure.[7] In operation it does appear that the machine is I/O-bound during simple select operations but during complex join processing this is not the case; this area of inquiry needs further investigation.

Finally, we are investigating index structures to support foreign key joins that commonly occur when a linker table is used. We are also investigating the implementation of parallel hash techniques to support *group by* and *join* processing. A parallel pipelined join processor is also being constructed.

Eventually, we would wish to undertake the comparison of the IDIOMS style machine with other database machines and systems. Before this comparison can be done there needs to be further development of the IDIOMS machine so that it provides all the functionality normally associated with a database system. It is also important to appreciate that the IDIOMS machine was designed to undertake concurrent OLTP and MIS operation. Thus, it will also be necessary to obtain a benchmark that accurately reflects that style of operation. Furthermore, such a benchmark has to be based upon a realistic mimic of an actual system.

2.10 CONCLUSIONS

This chapter has discussed the design strategy of a share-nothing parallel database machine. It has shown how the use of transputer-based processor technology has enabled a radically different approach to integrated OLTP/MIS operation. This is the environment in which the use of parallel technology will have its most dramatic effect, enabling data being used to provide decision support during transaction processing. This development could open up many uses for data, currently infeasible due to the lack of processing power provided by current database systems.

We have also shown that the performance obtained with this design, especially in OLTP, is a worthwhile improvement over current mainframe-based technology. We have identified places where the performance could be improved and discussed ways in which that improvement could be achieved.

ACKNOWLEDGMENTS

Most of the work described in this chapter has been carried out by a number of people. Those at the Transputer Centre include R. England, R. Guiton, S. Hanson, G. Jones, J. Kerridge, J. Krug, G. Miller, P. Thompson, and D. Walter. In addition, there has been a major contribution to the work by people in the Dept. of Computer Science at the University of Sheffield, including S. North, M. Unwalla, R. Oates, and S. Addy.

REFERENCES

1. J. Gray, *The Benchmark Handbook*, Morgan Kaufmann Pub., San Mateo, Calif., 1991.
2. S. Su, *Database Computers—Principles, Architectures, and Techniques*, McGraw-Hill, New York, N.Y., 1988.
3. J. Page, "A Study of a Parallel Database Machine and its Performance, the NCR/Teradata DBC/1012," in *Advanced Database Systems* (BNCOD10), P.M.D. Gray and R.J. Lucas, eds., Lecture Notes in Computer Science 618, Springer-Verlag, New York, N.Y., 1992, pp. 115-138.
4. J. Kerridge, "The Design of the IDIOMS Parallel Database Machine," in *Aspects of Databases*, M.S. Jackson and A.E. Robinson, eds., Butterworth & Heinemann, Oxford, England, 1991, pp. 128-149.
5. I. Foster and S. Taylor, *STRAND: New Concepts in Parallel Programming*, Prentice-Hall, Englewood Cliffs, N.J., 1989.
6. Inmos, Ltd., *Transputer Data Book*, Prentice-Hall, Englewood Cliffs, N.J., 1987.
7. D. Walter and J. Kerridge, "A Scalable Communications Network for a Parallel Database Machine," in *Occam and the Transputer—Current Developments*, J. Edwards, ed,. IOS Press, Amsterdam, The Netherlands, 1991, pp. 201-216.
8. *SCSI TRAM Databook*, TTM-11, Transtech Devices, Ltd., High Wycombe, England, 1991.
9. P.J. Thompson and S.W. Waithe, "The Design and Implementation of the IDIOMS On-Line Transaction Processing Simulator," in *Transputer Applications '91*, T. Duranni et al., eds., IOS Press, Amsterdam, The Netherlands, 1991, pp. 329-334 .
10. Inmos, Ltd., *Occam2 Reference Manual*, Prentice-Hall, Englewood Cliffs, N.J., 1988.

11. *Database Language SQL2*, ISO/IEC JTC 1/SC 21/ N 5215, Committee Draft, Dec. 1990.

12. J. Kerridge, "Transputer Topologies for Data Management," in *Commercial Parallel Processing*, P. Valduriez, ed., Chapman and Hall, London, England, 1992, pp. 107–120.

13. "A Data Storage Description Language for Database Language SQL," Internal Report CS-91-05, Dept. of Computer Sci., University of Sheffield, Sheffield, England, 1991.

14. M. Unwalla and J. Kerridge, "Control of a Large Massively Parallel Database Machine Using SQL Catalogue Extensions and a Data Storage Description Language in Preference to an Operating System," in *Advanced Database Systems* (BNCOD10), P.M.D. Gray and R.J. Lucas, eds., Lecture Notes in Computer Sci. 618, Springer-Verlag, New York, N.Y., 1992, pp. 138–155.

15. Inmos, Ltd., "The Transputer Implementation of Occam," in *Communicating Process Architecture*, Prentice Hall, Englewood Cliffs, N.J., 1988.

16. R. Oates and J. Kerridge, "Adding Fault Tolerance to a Transputer-Based Parallel Database Machine," in *Transputing '91*, P. Welch et al., eds., IOS Press, Amsterdam, The Netherlands, 1991, pp. 449–461.

17. R. Oates and J. Kerridge, "Improving the Fault Tolerance of the Recovery Ring," in *Transputer Applications '91*, T. Duranni et al., eds., IOS Press, Amsterdam, The Netherlands, 1991, pp. 608–613 .

18. R. Oates, *Transaction Recovery Architectures for Parallel Database Machines*, PhD thesis, Univ. of Sheffield, Sheffield, England, 1991.

19. P. Valduriez and G. Guardarin, "Join and Semi-Join Algorithms for a Multiprocessor Database Machine," *ACM Trans. Database Systems*, Vol. 9, No. 1, 1984, pp. 133–161.

20. P. Valduriez, "Join Indices," *ACM Trans. Database Systems*, Vol. 12, No. 2, 1987, pp. 218–246.

21. P. Valduriez and S. Khoshafian, "Parallel Evaluation of the Transitive Closure of a Database Relation," *Int'l J. Parallel Processing*, Vol. 12, No. 1, 1988, pp. 19–42.

22. J. Kerridge and G. Miller, "A Transputer-Based Parallel Sort Engine," in *Transputer Applications '91*, T. Durrani et al. eds., IOS Press, Amsterdam, The Netherlands, 1991, pp. 452–457.

3

From DBC to MDBS—A Progression in Database Machine Research

David K. Hsiao[†], IEEE Fellow, and Wilson T. S. Wang,[††] Distinguished International Professor

[†]Computer Science Department
[††]Chinese University of Hong Kong,
Shatin, NT, Hong Kong

ABSTRACT

This chapter is about the multibackend database supercomputer (MDBS). In fact, it is a summary of the long paper on MDBS published in IEEE MICRO.[1] *In order to highlight the architecture of MDBS and its design rationale, we contrast MDBS with its predecessor, the database computer (DBC). With these contrasts, one can perhaps conclude that MDBS attempts to distinguish itself in software-and-architecture innovations, rather than in hardware-and-component innovations, as in the case of DBC.[2] The conclusion may also suggest more than one way to provide innovations in database machine research, that is, by way of software-and-architecture elements as well as by way of hardware-and-component modifications.*

3.1 A TALE OF TWO DATABASE MACHINES

The multibackend database supercomputer (MDBS) is a research database machine of the mid- and late 1980s and early 1990s, which distinguishes itself in the innovations in data structures, database algorithms, software elements, and architectural configurations.[1] It is devoid of special-purpose hardware and uniquely designed chips. All the hardware elements of MDBS are off-the-shelf supermicrocomputers, storage devices, and communication lines. Nevertheless, the complexity of the data structures, database algorithms, software organizations, and architectural configurations is great. In Section 3.2 we describe only briefly the various hardware elements. We concentrate instead on the sophistication and innovation of their software counterpart.

The database computer (DBC) is a research database machine of the late 1970s and early 1980s, which focuses its innovation in hardware elements.[2] Neither conventional microcomputers nor traditional disk drives are used without hardware modification. Many of the

software-and-architecture innovations of MDBS are not employed in DBC, which attempts
to ride out of the performance issue with the sheer improvement of its hardware elements.
In Section 3.3 we describe the major and most innovative hardware elements of DBC.

In Section 3.4 we contrast these two research database machines. In Section 3.5 we conclude our experience with these two database machines by anticipating the kinds of database machines of the coming decades.

3.2 THE MULTIBACKEND DATABASE SUPERCOMPUTER (MDBS)

The use of off-the-shelf hardware elements is a major characteristic of MDBS, as depicted
in Figure 1. Each database processor is a supermicrocomputer with a Motorola 68020
processor, an address-translation capability, and a 6-megabyte main memory. Each supermicrocomputer also supports three disk drives: a medium disk of 96 Mbytes for paging, another medium disk for meta data, and a third 500-Mbyte disk for base data. For

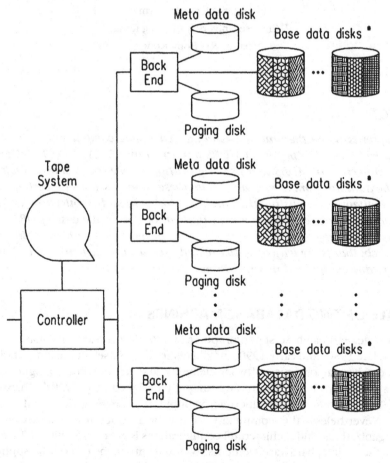

* Tracks with the same shading consist
of records belonging to the same cluster.

Figure 1.   The architecture of MDBS.

intercomputer communications, each supermicrocomputer has a communication backplane with two Intel microprocessors, 80186 and 82586, and a small amount of main memory. All the backplanes of all the corresponding supermicrocomputers interface with each other by way of an Ethernet cable. At the present there are eight such supermicrocomputers connected on the Ethernet via their respective transceivers. They are called database backends. Their meta-data disks and base-data disks are termed the database stores of their respective database backends.

In order to coordinate the parallel execution of database transactions by the database backends, a ninth supermicrocomputer is connected to the Ethernet. This supermicrocomputer is different from the other eight in that it has neither the meta-data disk nor the base-data disk. Instead, it has a tape drive for backup and recovery of the backend software and data. As the sole interface with the user, it is called the database controller of the backends. The controller receives the user transactions, broadcasts each transaction to all the backends simultaneously, postprocesses the results given by the backends, and routes the final result to the user.

From the above description we learn that all the hardware elements are off-the-shelf, requiring no special design and modification. On the other hand, there are considerable innovations in the data structures, database operations, software designs, and architectural considerations. They are delineated and discussed in the following paragraphs.

3.2.1 Broadcasting and Multicasting Capabilities

Consider the communication software provided by Ethernet and its backplanes. Ethernet is intended to provide the reliable point-to-point (that is, single-backend-to-single-backend) communication, and does not provide reliable broadcasting. When every backend is broadcasting to the others, there is multicasting communication. Since broadcasting is not reliable on Ethernet, multicasting is not reliable either. We must provide them in the new communication software. Essentially, we provide the reliability by requiring each backend to acknowledge the receipt of the broadcast message in a fixed period. If certain backends have not acknowledged in the prescribed period, a copy of the message will be sent to these backends, one backend at a time, using the point-to-point protocol. The reliability in broadcasting and multicasting is therefore built into the software at the expense of the parallel communications among the backends.

3.2.2 SQMD and MQMD Operations

The single-query-or-transaction-and-multiple-database-streams (SQMD) and multiple-queries-or-transactions-and-multiple-database-streams (MQMD) operations are the best for any parallel machine. For SQMD operations, the relevant data for the same query or transaction must come from multiple database stores in parallel. Thus, the relevant data must first be grouped together and placed in equal portions on the separate disks of the database stores. The use of multiple keys in the query, and for the clustering of data in the database, is aimed at supporting the even distribution of the clustered data on the database stores. Consequently, the effective access time for relevant data is typically the time to access all the disk tracks of the relevant data on a single backend. For MQMD operations, every backend must maintain a query or transaction queue so that, if there is no relevant data on the backend's database store for the query or transaction, the next query or transaction in the queue will be executed by the backend. Parallel database operations are therefore supported in the software of backends.

3.2.3 Nonreplicated Base Data, Replicated Meta Data, and Replicated System Software

From the above discussion of database operations, we observe that base data, although clustered and distributed, is not replicated. On the other hand, every backend must consult its meta data for the identification of those keys of the query appearing in the meta data. Thus, meta data is replicated. Lastly, the software in every backend must carry out the same operations required by the same query or transaction that has been broadcast to this and other backends. Thus, all the software processes in a backend are identical to those in the other backend. In other words, all the backends have the identical system software.

3.3 THE DATABASE COMPUTER (DBC)

The use of specially designed hardware is a major characteristic of DBC, as depicted in Figure 2. When there are several competing technologies for a hardware component, there have been different designs for the same component, each of which utilizes the outstanding characteristics of a given technology. We discuss some of the major components of DBC in light of the discussion made on MDBS in the above section.

3.3.1 Pipelining in Lieu of Broadcasting and Multicasting

In DBC there are separate hardware components for processing meta data and base data. Thus, a query or transaction must first be piped through a series of components for processing the query or transaction against the meta data, and then be piped through a number of components for getting the results from the base data to the user. The former is termed the structure loop of hardware components consisting of keyword transformation unit (KXU), the structure memory (SM), the structure memory information processor (SMIP), and index translation unit (IXU). The latter is termed the data loop of hardware components, consisting of the mass memory (MM) and security filter and postprocessor (SFP). In other words, the query or transaction is not broadcast to all the aforementioned components of DBC for simultaneous processing and accesses. Instead, in DBC the pipelining of the query or transaction is used.

3.3.2 The SQMD or MQMD Operation at the Component Level

SM is used to store the meta data, whereas MM is used to store base data. However, the memory of SM is organized as banks of blocks. A bucket of indices corresponding to a key is stored in blocks, each of which is in a separate bank. Thus, the effective access time for a bucketful of indices is typically the time to access a single block, since there are many parallel blanks in SM. These blocked-oriented memory blanks may be realized in the charge-coupled-devices technology. Thus, we have achieved the multiple-data-streams operation for the meta data by accessing multiple blocks of meta data in parallel.

On the other hand, MM is still based on moving-head disk technology. There are three modifications of the technology: (1) the I/O bus between the disk drive and the disk controller is replicated for each read/write head of the disk drive, (2) there is a base-data processing unit in the disk controller for each I/O bus, and (3) the read/write heads of all the tracks of a given cylinder may be activated simultaneously for reading or writing. As far as the base data is concerned, we have achieved the multiple-data-streams operation by accessing, in parallel, all the tracks in a given cylinder. This modification is also known in moving-head disk technology as the logic-per-head approach.

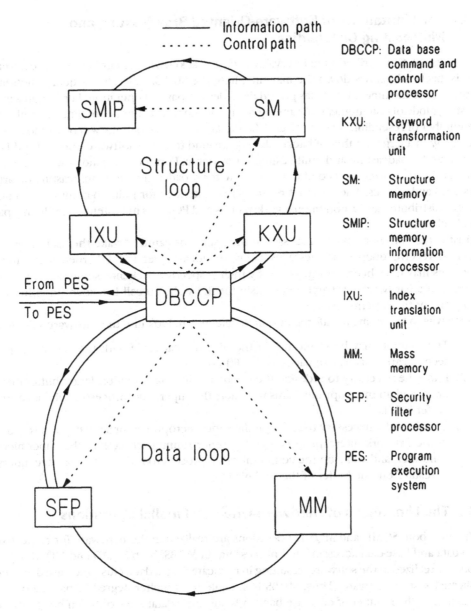

Figure 2.   The architecture of DBC.

3.3.3 No Replicated Data and Software

With the use of exclusive components in the structure and data loops for storing and processing meta data and base data respectively, the need for common software and replicated
data disappears. Thus, there is no replication of meta data or system software in DBC.

3.4 A CONTRAST OF MDBS AND DBC

There are pros and cons to software innovations in lieu of hardware innovations. They
are discussed in separate sections below.

3.4.1 The Limitations of Software-Oriented Broadcasting and Multicasting Capabilities

The use of a prescribed time interval for sensing acknowledgments from the receivers, that is, backends, slows down the machine, here the MDBS. Resending a query, message, or result after the time interval has passed degrades the parallel operation. Further, in a multicasting mode of communications among many backends, the number of time intervals and the number of resendings may be large. Their delays and degradations will be pronounced. Clearly, with a large number of backends (say, beyond ten), the software-oriented and Ethernet-based broadcasting and multicasting is not viable. Further, the bandwidth of the Ethernet at the 10-Mbyte-per-second rate is narrow for broadcasting and multicasting of large messages and queries. The Ethernet protocols are intended for point-to-point communications of distributed and autonomous workstations and PCs. It is not intended for highly parallel backends.

Lastly, the communication processes in the backends cannot "wake themselves up" in order to receive queries or messages being broadcast over the Ethernet, since these processes may have been "put to sleep" by their respective backends some time ago. The absence of a hardware interrupt mechanism for the wake-up call is evident in either the backplane or the supermicroprocessor.

One way to overcome the aforementioned defects is to look into the hardware solutions:

(1) The solution may be in the use of the fiber-optical cable with the 100-Mbyte-per-second capability as a replacement of Ethernet;

(2) It may be necessary to redesign the backplane with faster chips, larger buffer memories, and an interrupt mechanism to alert the supermicroprocessor whenever the buffer is full;

(3) It may also be necessary to redesign the supermicroprocessor so that it will respond to the network interrupt, preempt any other running process in the supermicrocomputer, and wake up the communication process to receive the message, query, or result from the buffer of the backplane.

3.4.2 The Limitations of Hardware-Oriented Parallel Operations

In DBC, both SQMD and MQMD operations are realized in the hardware for respective meta-data and base-data accessing and processing. In MDBS, both SQMD and MQMD operations are realized in the software, resulting in replicated meta data, clustered base data, and replicated system software. Thus, MDBS is scalable for a higher degree of parallel operations; that is, the number of database backends and their database stores can be increased for the purpose of performance gains or capacity growth or both. For an upscaled MDBS, we merely need to replicate the meta data on the meta-data disks of the new backends, replicate the system software on the new backends, and redistribute the clustered base data on all the base-data disks, whether they are existing or new.

On the other hand, to upscale DBC for a higher degree of parallelism, it is necessary to replace the existing DBC hardware with the next DBC model with greater performance and larger capacity. This kind of upgrade of machine performance and database capacity is traditionally more disruptive. Literally, we must shut down the existing DBC and replace it with a set of newer and more powerful DBC components.

We know that to upscale a computer system with identical computers and storage devices is cheaper than to upscale the computer system with newer and more powerful replacements. Further, off-the-shelf hardware does not lock the user into a specific maker of computers and devices, whereas the replacement by specially designed computers and logic-per-head devices tends to be monopolized by their maker.

3.5 CONCLUDING REMARKS

From DBC to MDBS, we have made a dramatic change from the use of purely-hardware innovations for the database machine to purely-software innovations for the database computer. Such change is very natural in a research environment, because we want to explore the strong and weak points of either approach to innovations.

The purely hardware innovations tend to produce database machines that are difficult and expensive to upgrade, that is, to scale up for performance gains and capacity growths. However, they tend to yield highest absolute performance in database management. The purely-software innovations tend to produce database computers that are easy and inexpensive to upgrade, that is, to scale up readily and cheaply for performance gains and capacity growths. However, on a machine-vis-a-vis-computer basis, the individual hardware-oriented database machine has a higher absolute performance than does the software-oriented database computer. The use of a software-oriented database computer is therefore not for its absolute performance but for its relative performance, that is, relative to the cost.

In the paper on MDBS, we have shown the multiplicity of backends as a function of performance gains and as a function of capacity growths. These benchmark results have shown that there is a direct correlation of the backend multiplicity and the relative performance of MDBS. In other words, the more parallel backends used in an MDBS configuration, the higher performance the MDBS may sustain. This result is indicative of the relative performance of MDBS.

In the real world, we may employ some hardware innovations to improve the absolute performance of the communication net, the individual backends, and the meta-and base-data disks, and rely on some of the software innovations to improve the relative performance of the database computer as a function of the number of database backends and their database stores. In this way, we can achieve greater scalabilty and higher parallelism with lower expenses and easier upgrades.

ACKNOWLEDGMENTS

The author wishes to thank NPMTC, NPS, and ONR, for their support for the work reported in this chapter.

REFERENCES

A number of referenced articles on MDBS can be found in:

1. D.K. Hsiao, "A Parallel, Scalable, Microprocessor-Based Database Computer for Performance Gains and Capaicty Growth," *IEEE MICRO,* Vol. 11, No. 6, Dec. 1991, pp.44-60.

A number of referenced articles on DBC can be found in:

2. J. Banerjee, D.K. Hsiao, and K. Kannan, "DBC—A Database Computer for Very Large Databases," *IEEE Trans. Computers*, Vol. C-28, No. 6, June 1979, pp. 414-429.

4

Rinda: A Relational Database Processor for Large Databases

Tetsuji Satoh and Ushio Inoue

NTT Network Information Systems Laboratories, Japan

4.1 INTRODUCTION

In recent relational database systems, high-speed query execution is required for retrieving over 1-gigabyte databases. Relational database accesses are classified into queries and updates; queries are also classified into nonindexed and indexed ones. Conventional database management systems, which run on general-purpose computers, execute indexed queries and updates efficiently, using indexes created before the execution. A typical indexed query is the selection of a single row in a table by using a previously associated unique index. The response time of such queries and updates is fairly good on current database management systems even if the size of the database is very large. However, these systems cannot take advantage of indexes for nonindexed queries. Examples of nonindexed queries are selections of multiple rows by partial matching of a character string, joins of two tables with nonunique join keys, and aggregations of a whole table with groups of rows in it. A general purpose computer consumes a lot of processing time executing such nonindexed queries, because searching and sorting are computationally intensive operations.[1,2]

Various database machine architectures have been studied and developed to solve the performance problems that occur in processing nonindexed queries. These problems are caused by two primary bottlenecks: the I/O bottleneck and the CPU bottleneck. CAFS[3] was designed to solve the I/O bottleneck problem between the main memory and disks, and uses special purpose processors attached to the disk controllers. Each processor executes row selections and restrictions within the row readout time from the disks. Greo,[4] with a special hardware sorter, and IDP,[5] with an expanded vector processor, were designed to solve the CPU bottleneck problem caused by sorts and joins. The Teradata DBC/1012[6] and Tandem NonStop series[7] are parallel database machines for solving both the I/O and CPU bottlenecks. They consist of several processors and disks each of which can run independently.

At NTT, we developed a database machine called Rinda (*relational da*tabase processor) to accelerate the execution of nonindexed queries.[8] Rinda is composed of content search processors and relational operation accelerating processors. The content search processor, or CSP, searches rows in a disk storage and transfers the selected and restricted rows to the main memory of the host computer. A relational operation-accelerating processor, or ROP, filters and sorts the rows to enhance the performance of joins, sorts, and some other aggregate functions.[9] Rinda was designed to solve both the I/O and CPU bottlenecks in processing nonindexed queries by using CSPs and ROPs. The CSP has specialized hardware for searching, while the ROP has specialized hardware for filtering and sorting. Three-phase join algorithms[10] and multiway merge algorithms[11] are used in the ROP to enhance the hardware utilization.

This chapter presents an outline of Rinda from a specialized hardware viewpoint. Section 2 is an overview of Rinda's architecture and query processing. Sections 3 and 4 discuss the search and join-and-sort algorithms used in the CSP and ROP, and also describe the design and implementation of them, respectively. Finally, Section 5 discusses Rinda's performance, as well as the effect of CSPs and ROPs in a benchmark system.

4.2 SYSTEM DESIGN

4.2.1 Design Considerations

The performance of relational database systems has been improved by using indexes effectively. However, some types of queries, that is, selection by nonindexed columns, sorts, joins and aggregations, cannot take advantage of indexes. For these nonindexed queries, searching and sorting are fundamental operations. Searching is selecting rows and columns from a table according to predicates in a query. Disk reads are needed when a table is stored on a disk. Therefore, searching takes a long response time, because it must transfer all rows from the disk to the main memory. It also takes a great amount of CPU time because all rows in a table must be qualified. Queries with sort and join operations require additional CPU time. Sorting is ordering rows in a table using a key, which may be composed of several columns. The major problem in sorting is its complexity. With ordinary algorithms, comparisons of the order $N*log(N)$ must be done, where N is the number of rows. Another problem is its memory requirements. Additional disk accesses are required if the main memory size is insufficient.

The amount of CPU and disk-read time to perform nonindexed queries increases according to the number of rows in a table. The goal of Rinda is to relieve host computers from heavy loads caused by nonindexed queries. The solution for searching is an intelligent disk controller that performs searches at the disk storage. Transferring only selected rows saves both CPU and table read time. The solution for sorting is a hardware sorter with a large memory, which sorts rows in time of order N. Therefore, Rinda had to satisfy the following requirements:

- Application programs and/or programmers should not be aware of the underlying Rinda architecture. Users improve performance by using Rinda without changing application programs.
- Rinda should be based on a scalable architecture in order to maintain constant response time. When a database is small, small hardware is sufficient, but when the database is large, powerful hardware is required.

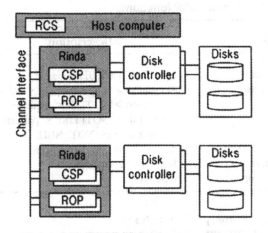

RCS: Rinda control subsystem
CSP: Content search processor
ROP: Relational operation accelerating processor

Figure 1. Rinda system organization.

To meet the first requirement, the Rinda system realizes an SQL[12] interface in order to avoid any modification in user programs. The functions of Rinda's hardware were designed based on a subset of the SQL functions. The software in the host computer fills the gaps between a full-set SQL and Rinda. It also supports dedicated algorithms for Rinda, and optimizes the execution with Rinda hardware. To meet the second requirement, Rinda is composed of two independent special purpose processors: CSPs and ROPs. Any number of CSPs and ROPs can be used in a system to achieve the appropriate performance required by users.

4.2.2 Hardware Architecture

A typical Rinda system organization is shown in Figure 1. Rinda is a collection of CSPs and ROPs, each of which is connected to a host computer by a channel. The major components of the system are a DIPS series general-purpose computer developed by NTT, standard disk controllers, disk units, and CSPs and ROPs. The numbers of CSPs and ROPs in the system are determined independently by its database size and performance requirements. For example, if the database is very large, several CSPs can be used in parallel to reduce the response time. The CSPs and ROPs are controlled by channel commands and order tables created by the Rinda control subsystem, RCS, which runs in the host computer.

A CSP directly searches a database table stored on disks, selects rows and columns specified by a query, and then transfers only the results to the host. Therefore, heavy CPU loads for searching can be reduced by the CSP as well as the loads for disk read operations. Table 1 shows its primary functions, which cover most single-table queries of relational databases. The CSP performs these functions at the data transfer rate of the disk.

An ROP sorts the rows in a table transferred from the host, and transfers the results back to the host. Its primary functions, listed in Table 2, include removal of unnecessary rows to accelerate joins and nested queries. The ROP performs these functions at the data transfer rate of the channel in a pipeline manner. The CSP and ROP will be discussed later from the viewpoint of algorithms and hardware organization.

Table 1.   Primary CSP functions.

Function	Description
Predicates	Specified in a WHERE clause
Comparison	< column > < comp-op. > < value >
In	< column >[NOT] IN < value list >
Like	< column >[NOT] LIKE < pattern >
Null	< column > IS [NOT] NULL
Boolian expression	Any combination of predicates
Column selection	SELECT < column list >
Set function	COUNT(*)

Table 2.   Primary ROP functions.

Function	Description
Sorting	ORDER BY < column [ASC|DESC] list > (also used for joins, subqueries, and GROUP BY clause)
Filtering	Removal of unnecessary rows (used for joins and nested queries)
Duplicate removal	DISTINCT < column list >
Set function	COUNT(*) with a GROUP BY clause

4.2.3 Software Architecture

The software structure on the host computer is shown in Figure 2. The Rinda control subsystem, RCS, was attached to an existing relational database management system forming a new integrated DBMS. A query including both indexed and nonindexed is described in a form of SQL statements. An application program written in Cobol language includes queries with embedded-SQL statements. Some users issue an adhoc-query with SQL statements. These queries, described by either an embedded or adhoc SQL in the first step, are parsed by the language processing subsystem of DBMS and translated into intermediate language. Then, a global optimizer decides the access path: the Rinda route using the specialized hardware, or the software route using indexes. If the query is nonindexed—we use the term "nonindexed query" as the query executed using Rinda—RCS functions are called. The RCS provides functions to optimize and execute queries using Rinda, that is, CSPs and ROPs. Thus, the Rinda system provides a two-phase optimization: global optimizer for access path decision, and either Rinda optimizer on Rinda route or local optimizer on the software route. The principles of the access path decision are as follows:

- A transaction, in general, is composed of several SQL statements, each of which can be executed either with Rinda or without Rinda. Thus, the access path is determined one by one by an SQL statement. Query execution by the RCS is controlled by the concurrency controller in order to keep the database consistency when nonindexed queries and indexed updates are executed concurrently in multiuser environments.
- The access path is decided by the estimated times of the disk I/O operations because CPU consumption is expected to be proportional to the I/O times. It is a rough estimation indeed; however, we believe that quicker decisions of the access path are more

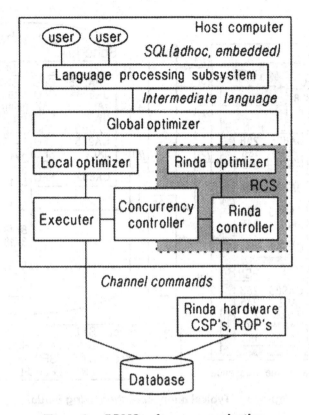

Figure 2.   DBMS software organization.

important than strict ones. To avoid a penalty for taking a long response time, we select the Rinda route when we are not sure of the access path decision. The reason is that Rinda achieves a constant and predictable response time, while the response time of the software operations is not so; sometimes it takes several hours.

A typical procedure to execute a nonindexed query is shown in Figure 3. This query gets the number of passengers, PSN, boarding planes for San Francisco, "SFO" on 1 August. To execute it, "Schedule" and "Flight" tables are selected by the condition of DST='SFO' and DATE='8/1' respectively; selected rows are then joined by the flight number, "FL" column. The global optimizer decides the Rinda route in executing selections and a join, because both tables do not have indexes.

The RCS sends a command to the CSPs to select the "Schedule" table, and to transfer the selected rows to the RCS buffers in the main memory—sequences (1) to (3) in Figure 3. Then, it sends another command to an ROP with the selected rows in "Schedule," which prepares the join, that is, the set-and-sort operation of the single-table filtering method described in Section 4.2.2—sequence (4). Selection of table "Flight" is executed by the condition of DATE='8/1'—sequences (5) to (7). Next, the RCS sends the refer-and-sort command, which also appears in Section 4.2.2, to the ROP to filter unjoinable rows—sequences (8) and (9). In sequence (9), the RCS receives the results at least satisfying the condition of the query. Finally, the RCS returns the results to the application program according to the SQL form.

The RCS can store a table distributed over multiple disks and conduct parallel CSP searching on the disks shortening the search time in sequences (2) and (6). In the case of Fig-

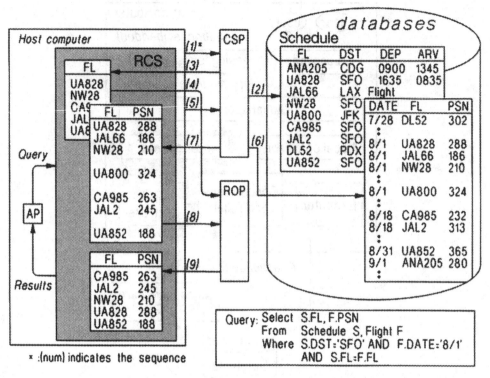

Figure 3.   Typical query execution using Rinda.

ure 3, sequences (4) and (5) to (7) may be done in parallel because the CSP and ROP are separated. If two or more CSPs exist, the execution sequences (1) to (3) and (5) to (7) may be done simultaneously. That is the reason why we designed the Rinda consisting of independent CSP and ROP modules. In the current status, only parallel CSP searching has been implemented in the RCS.

4.3 CONTENT SEARCH PROCESSOR

4.3.1 Search Algorithms

4.3.1.1 Design Considerations

Search conditions in an SQL statement are translated into a Boolean equation of predicates by using Boolean operators such as AND, OR, and NOT. A CSP is designed to evaluate the Boolean equation directly and its predicates to relieve host computer loads. However, to support all kinds of predicates against all kinds of attribute types, integers of single and double precision, packed and unpacked decimals, and so forth, requires a huge amount of hardware. Therefore, selected predicates, which are used many times in general applications, are implemented in the CSPs. In Table 1, <value> and <value list> include the attribute type of integers and decimals, and <pattern> includes wild-card characters of one byte and two bytes (for handling Japanese kanji characters).

A hybrid architecture between the CSP hardware and the RCS software is designed to fill the gap of full-set SQL and CSP specifications. Cooperative evaluation of Boolean equations is achieved between the CSPs and the RCS using the following sequences.

1. The language subsystem translates a nonindexed query into a conjunctive canonical form of the Boolean equation. In the following equation, the CSP executable predicates, $p_1, p_2, \ldots$, and CSP not-executable predicates, $p_x, p_y, \ldots$, are separated in the former and latter part of it.

$$\underline{(p_1 \ OR \ p_2 \ OR \ \ldots \,) \ AND \ (\ldots)} \quad \underline{AND \ (p_x \ OR \ p_y \ OR \ \ldots \,) \ AND \ (\ldots)}$$

$$\textit{CSP executes} \qquad\qquad\qquad \textit{RCS executes}$$

2. The RCS sends the commands to the CSPs to execute the former part of the equation, which consists of only CSP executable predicates. A CSP returns the rows that satisfy the former part of the equation.
3. The RCS examines the latter part of the equation with the rows returned by the CSPs. The RCS can easily take over the evaluation of the equation from the CSPs because the equation is described using the conjunctive canonical form.

4.3.1.2 Predicate Evaluation

A search condition is expressed by predicates and Boolean operators, AND, OR, and NOT. In SQL, each column may have a null value instead of zero or space, when the value is undefined. As a result, the truth value of a predicate in the condition may be true, false or unknown. Therefore, Boolean operators are defined by the three-valued (true, false, and unknown) logic shown in Table 3. To treat three-valued logic, ASLM[13] decomposes a maybe query to several subqueries, any of which includes unknown values or not. The query is performed by iterative evaluation of subqueries with two-valued logic. In the ASLM, each subquery is executed quickly by using specialized hardware called associative module.

Rinda takes another approach in handling three-valued logic. If unknown is substituted for false in the evaluating predicates, the three-valued logic is localized into two-valued logic, and the CSP is implemented simply. A where-clause in an SQL statement, WHERE <search condition>, selects rows whose final truth value of the <search condition> is true. Therefore, unknown can be substituted for false in the last stage of the evaluation. In the truth table shown in Table 3, the NOT(unknown) column is important. If unknown is simply substituted for false, the result may be unreasonable, because NOT(false) is true while NOT(unknown) is false. Therefore, if and only if there is no NOT operator in the search condition, unknown can be substituted for false, and the three-valued logic can be localized into two-valued logic.

Table 3.   Truth table of three-valued logic.

AND	True	False	Unknown
True	True	False	Unknown
False	False	False	False
Unknown	Unknown	False	Unknown
OR	**True**	**False**	**Unknown**
True	True	True	True
False	True	False	Unknown
Unknown	True	Unknown	Unknown
NOT	**True**	**False**	**Unknown**
	False	True	Unknown

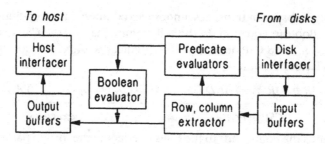

Figure 4. CSP hardware configuration.

The following procedure transforms any search condition into another search condition having the same effect without NOT operators:

1. Transform a search condition into a conjunctive canonical form, mentioned in the previous section.
2. (a) If there is no predicate with NOT, then the translation procedure ends.
   (b) If there is a predicate with NOT, then remove NOT in the predicate and reverse the comparison operator in the predicate. For example, NOT(column1 > x) is replaced by (column1 ≤ x).

In Rinda systems, the RCS transforms a search condition into a conjunctive canonical form without NOT operators, and creates an order table for the CSP. The CSP substitutes unknown for false in the evaluation of predicates and applies two-valued logic.

4.3.2 CSP Organization

4.3.2.1 Database Storage

A database stored in disks consists of several database spaces, each of which is a collection of pages stored in one or more continuous disk areas. A database space may be distributed over several disks. When a table is created in a database space, adjacent pages are assigned to the table. As the table grows, a constant number of adjacent pages are added to the table. Thus, a table is stored in multiple disk extents. Each page holds rows of a single table, and no row is stored across page boundaries. Each table has control records indicating its disk extents on separate pages, and this information is used to perform CSP searching under control of the RCS.

4.3.2.2 Hardware Organization

A block diagram of the CSP is shown in Figure 4. The search process in a CSP is performed in two ways: synchronous and asynchronous. In the synchronous mode, a data stream from a disk is processed on the fly, while in the asynchronous mode, reading and searching are decoupled by buffers. In the CSP, an asynchronous mode is employed for the following reasons:

- A disk controller has error-detecting and -correcting facilities for data pages recorded. This procedure is completed after the last byte of the page is transferred from the disk to the buffer storage.
- The page format has been designed without considering hardware-searching mechanisms. Changing the page format in order to attach Rinda hardware was impossible because the pages are shared and accessed concurrently by both Rinda and the software DBMS.

The CSP transfers pages successively from a disk to its buffers by the multitrack-read method, and scans the page in the buffer before the next page comes. Therefore, the CSP can perform searching within the page transfer time, similar to on-the-fly of the synchronous mode.

4.3.2.3 Search Operation Flow

In Rinda systems, searching with CSP is performed using the following procedure.

1. The RCS running on the host acquires the RCS buffers and prepares a set of channel commands and an order table for appropriate CSPs. An order table has disk access information that includes the disk unit number, extent addresses to be searched, the RCS buffer size, and the search condition.
2. The order tables are sent from the host to the CSPs by channel commands.
3. According to the order table, each CSP generates new channel commands to the disk to read pages successively, using the multitrack-read method. When the first page comes, the CSP begins to select rows from the page. To keep up the data transfer rate, the CSP uses multiple input buffers that hold pages transferred from the disk, and multiple output buffers that hold new pages containing selected rows.
4. When one of the output buffers is filled, the CSP transfers the page to the host asynchronously.

This procedure continues without any interruption to the host DBMS until all of the extents have been read by the CSP or all of the RCS buffers are occupied. In the latter case, the RCS saves the selected rows on a work disk and repeats the above procedure.

4.4 RELATIONAL OPERATION ACCELERATING PROCESSOR

4.4.1 Sort

Sorting is one of the fundamental relational database operations, and is performed on the selection results with respect to the database. Thus, it is impossible to know in advance how many rows or records are to be sorted. It may also be necessary to sort a huge number of records, depending on the application. It is thus difficult to optimize the number of merge circuit stages in the case of conventional sorters,[14] where the maximum number of sorting records is dependent on the number of merge circuit stages.

By separating the record comparator from the record storage circuit, however, the authors have developed a multiway merge algorithm that satisfies two independent requirements at the same time: the maximum number of sorting records, and sort speed.

4.4.1.1 Hardware Configuration

The basic structure of the sorter is shown in Figure 5. It consists of a linear sorting array that performs the parallel comparisons on the records as strings, a working storage to hold the records, and a merge controller. The sorting array is configured as a one-dimensional array structure consisting of sorting cells in which two records are compared. A major departure from conventional pipeline merge sorters[15] is that the centralized working storage is implemented in a small area circuit board using large-capacity dynamic-RAM chips. The k-way merge operations are controlled by the merge controller. Many k strings, each of which has many records, are merged at one time using the sorting array. The merged string output from the sorting array is re-stored in the working storage as a new string. Many records can be sorted in a few stages of k-way merging because the number of sorted records is k^n where n is the number of stages.

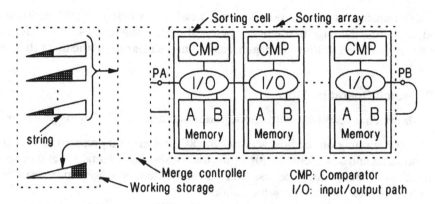

Figure 5.   Block diagram of multiway merge sorter.

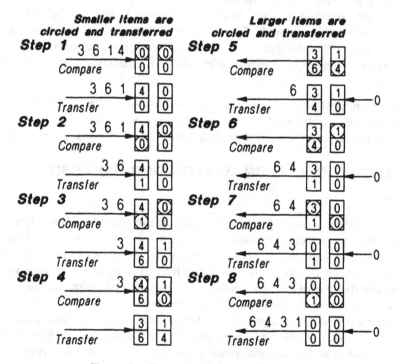

Figure 6.   Example of descending sort.

A parallel comparison of the sorting array is illustrated in Figure 6. Records represented by integers are sorted in descending order. A comparison operation and a transfer operation based on the comparison result are synchronously performed in each sorting cell. During an input operation, records are input from the left edge of the sorting array. The smaller record in either memory-A or memory-B is selected and transferred to the neighboring rightward cell. Conversely, during an output operation, the larger record is selected and transferred to the neighboring left cell. The largest record in the array is thus always kept in the left-most sorting cell at any input/output step. For a sorting array consisting of $[k/2]$ cells, k records are sorted and k strings merged within the time it takes to input and output the records, where $[k/2]$ denotes a ceiling number of $k/2$.

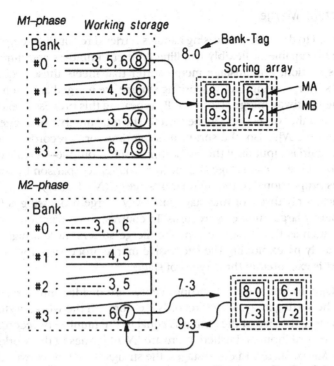

Figure 7. Continuous multiway merge diagram using bank tags.

4.4.1.2 Multiway Merge Algorithm

A large volume of records can be sorted with few merge stages by implementing a large number of merge ways. Here we describe a data-driven string-selection technique using bank-tags that permits a high throughput to be maintained without complicating the control mechanism, even expanding the number of merge ways. A k-way merge control using bank-tags is depicted in Figure 7. The figure shows an example of four-way merging in descending order. Four strings indicated by the bank numbers #0 to #3 have been stored in the working storage.

M1-phase: The sorting array is filled with the largest records in all the strings to be merged, that is, the records located at the tops of the strings. Bank-tags are attached to the records to indicate which strings the records belong to.

M2-phase: Merge operations—a record output and subsequent input to the sorting array—are performed successively until all merging strings are empty. The largest record in the sorting array is immediately output with the bank-tag. This is the largest record included in all the merging strings. The second-largest candidate records are limited to any of the remaining ones in the sorting array, or the top one in the string indicated by the largest record's bank-tag. This top one is input to the array and is compared with the remaining k-1 records. Successive multiway merging is achieved by this alternate record output-input operation.

The bank-tag controlling the k-way merge processing is attached to the least significant part of the record so as not to affect the record comparison. The minimum number of required bits for the bank-tags is $[\log_2 k]$; thus, a large number of k-way merges can be easily achieved employing a sorting array with $[k/2]$ sorting cells, with very little control overhead.

4.4.1.3 Multistage Merge

A sorter applied to database processing handles retrieval results in a temporary table, and must therefore be capable of flexibly handling different numbers and different lengths of records. In this section, a multistage merge sorter that meets these requirements is described. In this sorter, k strings in the working storage are merged and then re-stored there according to the multiway merge algorithm. By repeating this process in each k-way merge stage, a massive number of records can be sorted. The total number of merge stages for sorting N records is [$\log_k N$]. Also, the sort-processing time for N records—the interval from when the first record is input until the last sorting result is output—is realized in $O(N)$ time because the processing in each stage is done as a parallel comparison by the sorting array. The time is thus proportional to the number of stages $O(N * \log_k N)$.

To be practical, only three- or four-stage multiway merge processing is fully capable of sorting a sufficiently large number of records. In contrast to conventional multistage hardware schemes, such as those used in pipeline merge sorters, here a high-speed sorter is achieved compactly by exploiting the successive merge-processing approach. The multistage merge sort is executed in three types of stages:

Pre-merge Stage: In this stage, all sorting records are divided into k-record strings and sorted in the sorting array. Sorted records are stored in the working storage as strings of size k where the size of the strings is equal to the number of records they contain. When the record input is finished, there are [N/k] strings in the working storage.

Intermediate Merge Stages: In these stages, the strings stored in the working storage are successively merged in iterative k-way merge processes. At each stage of the intermediate merge processing, the k strings stored in the working storage are merged one at a time and then re-stored as a single string. The size of the generated strings is increased k times and their number is decreased in $1/k$. The intermediate merge stage processing continues until the number of strings is below k.

Output Merge Stage: In this stage, the strings in the working storage, which have been reduced to less than k in the intermediate merge stage processing, are merged and output.

The processing of the pre-merge and output merge stages is carried out concurrently while records are being transferred between the host computer and the sorter. Thus, the latency time in the sorter (from the end of record input to the beginning of output) is $N*([\log_k N]-2)$, where $N \geq k^2$. Typically this is equal to the time required for one stage—at worst the two stages—of the intermediate merge processing. Furthermore, since the sort processing is carried out through successive merges, the maximum number of records that can be sorted is disassociated from the hardware configuration. Here we summarize some of the unique properties of the sort algorithm.

1. A multiway (several tens of ways) merge circuit is easily achieved by combining the parallel comparison on the sorting array and data-driven string-selection technique using bank-tags. Merge processing can be executed in $O(N)$ for a large number of merging ways, and thus a large number of records can be sorted very quickly with few stages. In actual applications employing the multiway merge algorithm, processing times of $O(3N)$ or $O(4N)$ have been achieved.

2. The maximum number of sorting records depends on the capacity of the working storage, and is not dependent on how the sorting array or controller is configured. Moreover, by increasing the scale of the sorting array and expanding the number of merge ways, the duration of sorts can be shortened with fewer merge stages. This

means the sorter can be configured flexibly to optimize either the sorting speed or the maximum number of sorting records.

3. Since the sorting array where the records are compared and the working storage are implemented separately, great flexibility is available in terms of scale and extent of hardware implementation. For example, by adding a sorting array to a general purpose computer, merge operations with conventional software can be greatly accelerated. Or, by constructing an all-hardware sorter including merge controller, a very fast and compact sorter can be achieved. In the Rinda system, we applied the latter approach.

4.4.2 Join

4.4.2.1 Three-Phase Join Algorithms

Conventional join algorithms mainly comprise three groups: nested-loop join, sort-merge join, and hash-join algorithms.[16, 17] In nested-loop join algorithms, each row in the first table is repeatedly compared with all rows in the second table. Thus, this algorithm can be used only if both tables are small because, although it requires no work space, it requires a very large number of comparisons. In hash-join algorithms, both joining tables are split into many packets by a hashing mechanism. Actual join operations are executed between split packets in which every row has the same hashing value. Therefore, a hash-join algorithm is suitable for parallel execution. In sort-merge algorithms, the amount of merge-join computations decreases to a linear order by separating sort operations for both tables. We selected a sort-merge algorithm in the Rinda system because sort operations are rapidly executed by using specialized hardware.

As mentioned above, the three-phase join method based on the sort-merge algorithm is implemented in Rinda. It consists of filtering, sorting, and merge-join phases. Unjoinable rows are removed in the filtering phase. The remaining rows, each of which is a candidate row of the join in both tables, are sorted in the sorting phase. After that, the sorted rows are merged and the matched rows are connected together in the merge-join phase.

The concepts behind how the filtering and sorting phases are achieved by hardware are described below. In the first filtering phase, unjoinable rows are removed by a filtering method with hashed-bit-arrays.[18] The remaining rows, after the filtering phase, are sorted and then merged. Thus, if all unjoinable rows are removed in the filtering phase, useless sorting and merging operations for unjoinable rows are eliminated. However, a few unjoinable rows inevitably remain, due to collisions of hashed results. Therefore, a refined hashing function is required because the number, data type, and distribution of the keys are unknown before the hashing operation. Moreover, operations in this filtering phase are done on the largest amount of rows in the three phases. Therefore, we decided the filtering operations should be executed by specialized hardware.

It is well known that sorting operations consume a lot of power. We also decided sorting operations should be executed by specialized hardware. The number of keys and its data type are generally changed dynamically. Thus, we implemented the multiway merge sorter mentioned in Section 4.1 that can easily handle any number and types of keys. The multiway merge sorter is a compact large-capacity hardware sorter.

In the merge-join phase, the number of input rows is decreased by filtering operations, and the rows are already sorted. Therefore, merge-join operations are executed with little computation. The configuration of result rows generated by merge-join operations is assigned many variations by users. That is the reason why merge-join operations are executed by software on the host computer.

4.4.2.2 Implementation of Join Algorithms

Three-phase join can be attained through single-table filtering and dual-table filtering methods. These methods, shown in Figure 8, are described below.

(a) Single-table filtering method: Temporary tables for join operations, R' and S', are made by the CSP from the base tables, R and S, respectively. Rows in the first table R' are input into the ROP to set a hashed-bit-array and to be sorted as a set-and-sort operation. Sorted rows are output from the ROP as sorted table R". After that, rows in the second table S' are input to the ROP to refer the hashed-bit-array and to be sorted as a refer-and-sort operation. Unjoinable rows in table S' are removed by this set and refer operations. Sorted rows are also output as a sorted table S". Finally, each row of both sorted tables, R" and S", is merged and concatenated in the host computer. Thus, unjoinable rows in the second table S' are removed in the single-table filtering method.

(b) Dual-table filtering method: Rows in the first table R' are input to the ROP only for setting a hashed-bit-array as a set operation. Rows in the second table S' are then input for filtering unjoinable rows. The remaining rows in table S' set another hashed-bit-array and are sorted as a sorted table S" as a refer-sort-and-set operation. Rows in table R' are then input again for filtering, using the second hashed-bit-array set by the remaining rows in table S'. The remaining rows in table R' are sorted as a sorted table R". That is the same refer-and-sort operation in the single-table filtering method. Finally, each row of both sorted tables, R" and S", is merged and concatenated in the host computer. Thus, unjoinable rows in both tables are removed in the dual-table filtering method.

Join operations based on either method can be done when the number of remaining rows after filtering is below the capacity of the sorter. Therefore, tables whose rows exceed the capacity of the sorter can be handled if the number of rows in the filtered table is below the capacity. Moreover, both row transferring time and join operations in the host are decreased by filtering unjoinable rows.

Dynamic optimization of join methods is implemented in the Rinda optimizer illustrated in Figure 2. The optimal join method, in single-table filtering, dual-table filtering, or nested-loop join methods, is selected by the number of rows counted by the CSP. The nested-loop join method is performed when both temporary tables read out by the CSP are small and can be joined without extra I/O operations. The single-table filtering method is performed when the temporary table, R' or S', is small enough compared with the other, S' or R'. In other cases, the dual-table filtering method is performed.

4.4.3 ROP Organization

4.4.3.1 Key Extractor

A block diagram of the ROP, which performs filtering and sorting operations, is shown in Figure 9. Rows are generally composed of several columns, each of which has a different data type, such as an integer or a decimal number with or without sign or character string. A null (unknown) value, which means the value of that column is undefined, may appear.

The ROP has key-extract hardware that composes internal keys from rows. This hardware translates from a row having several kinds of data to a comparable key, and makes it a fixed-length from a variable-length or a null value. Therefore, filtering and sorting operations for fixed-length keys are rapidly executed by simple hardware.

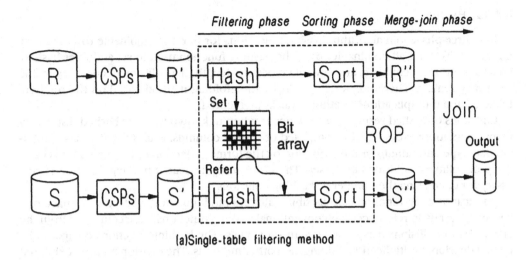

(a)Single-table filtering method

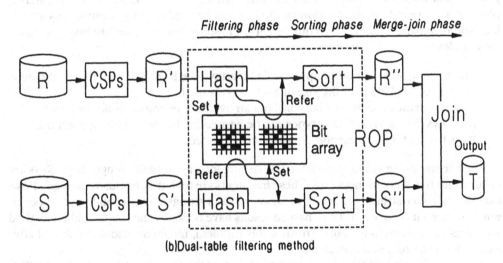

(b)Dual-table filtering method

Figure 8.   Three-phase join algorithms using Rinda.

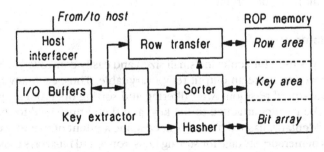

Figure 9.   ROP hardware configuration.

4.4.3.2 Hasher

In a three-phase join algorithm, hashing functions for filtering unjoinable rows are very important. To filter all unjoinable rows, the hashing function used to set and refer hashed-bit-arrays must not collide in any key data types and length. If a collision occurs, unjoinable rows may remain. Therefore, a new multiplication-folding method based on the rotation-folding[19] and multiplication[20] methods was implemented.

Collisions of hashed results generally occur when unknown keys are hashed. Especially in join operations, keys may be composed of several columns, each of which has a different data type and nonuniform distribution by the former selection operations. In this case, the probability of collisions increases. Therefore, a sophisticated hashing function is necessary for decreasing the number of hashing collisions.

An ideal hashing function can distribute all keys randomly in the addressing space of a hashed-bit-array. In references[19, 20] conventional hashing functions were compared from the viewpoint of collisions using fixed-length short keys. The hashing functions compared included division, multiplication, folding, and other methods. The division method exhibited good results with fewer collisions for an unknown set of keys. However, in the filtering phase of join operations, the division method cannot be used directly because keys may be long and of variable length. The requirements of hashing functions for filtering operations are as follows:

- The hashing table can be composed of a bit-array. The loading factor, that is, the number of hashing keys over the size of a bit-array, is small.
- It is important to decrease collisions, but an overflow operation is not necessary.
- Any keys having various data types can be hashed by the same hashing function.
- Keys having long and variable-lengths can be hashed.

The exclusive-or method is available for hashing long and variable-length keys. Keys are divided into fixed-length fragments. These fragments are folded by exclusive-or logic. However, in character strings, especially in Japanese kanji strings, the probability of '1' occurrence in each bit is not even. Thus, hashed results have biases by the simple folding method with one- or two-byte fragments. To solve this problem, fragments should be folded after shift or bit-order reversed operations.

A new multiplication-folding method for key hashing was developed for Rinda. This method is composed of a folding method with a bit shift operation and a multiplication method for fixed-length fragments. The multiplication method is applied to randomize the character code, and the folding method is applied to handle variable-length keys. The multiplication-folding method is achieved by compact specialized hardware such as exclusive-or and simple multiplication circuits.

4.4.3.3 ROP Memory

An internal key is used for achieving small sized and easily controlled hardware. Original rows must be stored to make an output temporary table. Thus, each key has a pointer assigned to the row stored position. After filtering and sorting operations, appropriate rows are read out by the pointer attached to the key, and then transferred to the host as a temporary table. Incidentally, hashed-bit-arrays need some amount of memory capacity. Therefore, three types of memory storage for storing keys, rows, and bit-arrays must be in the ROP.

Single working memory storage is implemented in the ROP for storing keys, rows, and bit-arrays. This storage unit is compact because it is composed of large-capacity RAM chips.

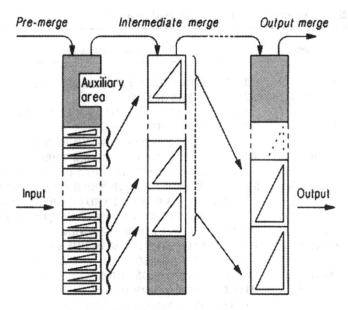

Figure 10. Multistage merge sequence.

The size of the bit-array is assigned by the constant ratio of the working storage capacity to keep the loading factor low. If the storage capacity is increased, so is the size of the bit-arrays. Keys and rows are stored in the remaining area of the working storage. The boundary between the keys and rows moves dynamically because the length of each row is variable.

Here, we discuss the utilization of the key area. In the intermediate merge stages of the successive k-way merge processes, k strings are read out from the working storage, merged, then re-stored there. Thus, an efficient memory management method is essential to effectively exploit the memory space that is available. We now evaluate a number of memory management schemes in terms of the effective memory utilization factor, LN / (storage capacity), assuming N records of L length are to be sorted.

Conventional memory management algorithms include the dual-memory, the pointer, and the block-division methods.[21] In the dual-memory approach the working storage is divided into two areas for alternate use. Control is quite simple but the utilization factor is $1/2$. The pointer method manages the available space by adding a pointer to each record that indicates the next record to be accessed. The method offers very simple control, but its memory utilization factor is L / (L + pointer length), and efficiency declines for shorter records. In the block-division method, fixed-sized blocks are allocated to store some or part of the strings and are reused by implementing pointer chains for control within the blocks. This represents a finer level of subdivision than just partitioning the memory in two, as in the dual-memory approach, and thus provides a better utilization factor. With the block-division method, auxiliary k blocks equaling the k-way merge number are required. This method is effective in areas where the way number is small.

Considering the drawbacks of conventional methods, we investigated an area-store method for memory management in the multistage merge sorter that yields a memory utilization factor of $k/(k + 1)$. With this method, the utilization factor is enhanced as the number of merge ways is increased. The merge process using the area-store method is shown in Figure 10. In the pre-merge stage, input records are sequentially stored as strings of size k in the working storage starting from the bottom address. A single string is stored

Table 4. SQL statements for performance evaluation.

Query	Type	SQL statement
Selection	1 row	SELECT* FROM THUK WHERE UNIQUE2 = 999
	1 percent	SELECT * FROM THUK WHERE UNIQUE2 >=500000 AND UNIQUE2 < 510000
	10 percent	SELECT * FROM THUK WHERE UNIQUE2 >= 500000 AND UNIQUE2 < 600000
Join	AselB	SELECT * FROM HUNKA A,HUNKB B WHERE A.UNIQUE1 = B.UNIQUE1 AND A.UNIQUE1 < 10000

	CselAselB	SELECT * FROM HUNKA A,HUNKB B TENKA C WHERE
		   C.UNIQUE1 = A.UNIQUE1 AND C.UNIQUE1 = A.UNIQUE1
		   AND A.UNIQUE1 < 10000 AND B.UNIQUE1 < 10000

Minimum	Scalar	SELECT MIN(UNIQUE1) FROM HUNKA
	Group-by	SELECT MIN(TWOTHOUS) FROM HUNKA GROUP BY HUNDRED
Count	Scalar	SELECT COUNT(*) FROM HUNKA
	Group-by	SELECT COUNT(*) FROM HUNKA GROUP BY HUNDRED

in a continuous area, a practice which permits uncomplicated memory management. At the end of this stage, the auxiliary area is located above the area containing the strings. The intermediate merge stages are performed so as to maintain a continuous auxiliary area, and merged strings are continuously stored from the top and bottom of the working storage in alternating odd-even stages.

An auxiliary area, distinct from the area where the k input strings are kept, is prepared to store the output merged strings. Its capacity is equal to the maximum size of the strings stored in the working storage. In other words, it is equal to the size of the largest string output in the last intermediate merge stage.

In order to minimize the size of the auxiliary area, the size of the output string generated in the last intermediate stage must consist of uniform-sized k strings. This can be accomplished by generating a string equivalent to k^2 strings in the preceding last intermediate merge stage. In effect, this means that a string equivalent to an exponential power of k strings is produced in the working storage at the first stage of the intermediate merge processing. At the first stage of intermediate merge stages, power-of-k strings can be generated with a size differential of no more than k even in the worse case, because the number of input records is definitely known at the end of the pre-merge stage.

4.5 PERFORMANCE EVALUATION

4.5.1 Models

The performance of Rinda was evaluated by using the extended Wisconsin Benchmark.[22,23] The database table consisted of 100k rows in HUNK and 1000k rows in THUK, and each row was 208 bytes long. The Rinda system was composed of the NTT DIPS-V30E super minicomputer[24] as the host, and two CSPs and an ROP. The database was stored in two 1.3-Gbyte disks whose data transfer rate is 3 Mbytes per second.

The elapsed time was measured in the host computer from the start of query execution to the return of the last result row to the user program. To measure the performance under a real application environment, all of the result rows were transferred to the user program one by one, by using fetch commands of SQL. The queries executed were classified into four categories: simple selections, joins, Minimum functions, and Count functions, as shown in Table 4. The Count functions are additional queries to evaluate the pure hardware performance of Rinda. Their response times were almost equal to Rinda's hardware response times because they returned only one or a few values to the applications.

4.5.2 Results

The performance improvement using Rinda is show in Figure 11. The speedup is the elapsed time without Rinda divided by one with Rinda. The queries for one row, 1 percent, and 10 percent selections and scalar Minimum and Count are executed with only the CSPs, while the others are performed by a combination of the CSPs and the ROP.

Table 5 shows the query execution time in seconds with Rinda as well as some other database machines measured by DeWitt et al.[23] The query execution times do not include fetch operations but include storing the result rows on the work disk. The DBC/1012 and the Gamma consisted of 24 and 17 processors, respectively.

4.5.3 Considerations

Figure 11 shows that the speedup of queries by CSPs depends on the number of result rows. In general, the speedup is larger as the results are smaller. For example, the speedup was 72.1 in the 1 row selection using 2 CSPs, while it was only 3.7 in the 10 percent selection. The reason is that a lot of CPU time is consumed transferring rows from the result table to the user program using the RCS. In other words, the fetch operations take a long time when the number of result rows is large, because they must be performed in the host computer in serial.

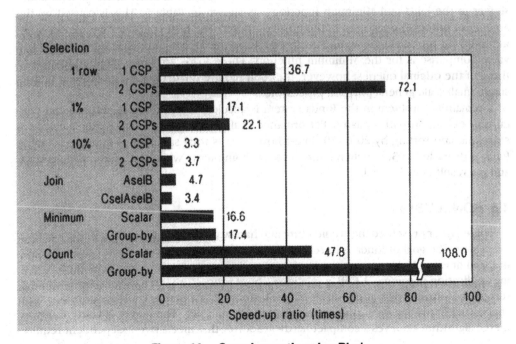

Figure 11. Speed-up ratio using Rinda.

Table 5.   Query execution time in seconds.

Query	Type	Rinda	DBC/1012	Gamma
Selection	1 %	52.5	213.1	134.9
	10 %	92.0	1106.9	181.7
Join	AselB	136.8	235.6	35.8
	CselAselB	128.5	95.7	37.9
Minimum	Scalar	31.7	18.3	15.5
	Group-by	47.3	27.1	1934

The speedup of the scalar Minimum was smaller than that of the scalar Count, because the Count is directly supported by CSPs while the Minimum is not. As for the Minimum, specified column values of all rows are transferred from the CSPs to the RCS, which determines the minimum value.

The speedup by the ROP becomes apparent by comparing the scalar and GROUP-BY in the Minimum or Count functions in Figure 11. In spite of the additional load caused by sorting, the speedup did not decrease, because the ROP sorts dozens of times faster than the host computer. The AselB join query also demonstrated the effect of the ROP in contrast with the 10 percent selection. The speedup of the join query was similar to that of the 10 percent selection because the join query returns the same number of rows. The join operation of this query is performed by the single-table filtering method after 10 percent selection by the CSPs. In the benchmark, the number of rows after filtering was 10,000 by a collision-free filtering operation, because the join column is a unique attribute. Thus, the row transferring time from the ROP to the host and storing as a sorted temporary table is decreased substantially. Moreover, row comparing time in the host is dramatically decreased because most unjoinable rows have already been removed by the ROP.

By comparing Rinda with DBC/1012 and Gamma,[23] Rinda was faster in the selections and slower in the joins and Minimum functions, as shown in Table 5. This is caused by the amount of processing required in the host computer. The host computer has almost nothing to do for the selections, while it must perform the merge-join phase for the joins and value comparisons for the Minimum function. These loads are fairly small compared to those of the original queries; however, they still require relatively long processing time in single small-scale general-purpose processors.

A remaining problem in the Rinda system is acceleration of fetch operations and concurrent execution with updates. Performance evaluations showed that Rinda accelerates searching and sorting by 20 to 50 times; however, its total speedup of queries including fetch is degraded to 3. In general, Rinda shows high merits when the source table is large and the result table is small.

4.6 CONCLUSION

This chapter presented the architecture and hardware organization of the Rinda database processor. The goal of Rinda is to relieve its host computer of heavy loads caused by non-indexed queries. Users can get the improved performance by using Rinda without rewriting application programs. A CSP, a special purpose processor with hardware for searching, selects rows from a disk at the disk's data transfer rate. An ROP is another processor with specialized hardware for sorting rows selected by the CSPs. The newly devised multiway merge algorithm achieves a compact hardware sorter that meets two independent requirements: the maximum number of sorting records and sorting speed, at the same time. For join queries, the single-table and dual-table filtering methods based on the three-phase join algorithm are employed with the hardware filter and sorter in the ROP. Rinda composed of CSPs and ROPs substantially reduces the CPU and I/O time of the host computer. The performance study showed Rinda accelerates nonindexed queries from three to a hundred times compared with conventional DBMS software.

Currently Rinda is in operation in several business database systems. Rinda is mainly used to retrieve rows by adhoc queries or to get statistical reports from very large tables. The role of Rinda is increasing as database applications become more advanced.

ACKNOWLEDGMENTS

The authors would like to thank Masato Haihara and Kenji Suzuki for their useful suggestions and discussion. The authors are also grateful to Toshio Nakamura and Jyunichi Kuroiwa for their helpful assistance with the measurements.

REFERENCES

1. H. Boral and S. Redfield, "Database Machine Morphology," *Proc. 11th Int'l Conf. Very Large Databases*, Morgan Kaufmann Pub., San Mateo, Calif., 1985, pp. 59-71.
2. U. Inoue and S. Kawazu, "A Relational Database Machine for Very Large Information Retrieval Systems," in *Database Machines*, A.K. Sood and A.H. Qureshi, eds., NATO ASI Series, Vol. F 24, Springer-Verlag, New York, N.Y., 1986, pp. 183-201.
3. E. Babb, "Implementing a Relational Database by Means of Specialized Hardware," *ACM Trans. Database Systems*, Vol. 4, No. 1, 1979, pp.1-29.
4. M. Kitsuregawa and W. Yang, "Evaluation of 18-Stage Pipeline Hardware Sorter," *Proc. Int'l Workshop Database Machine*, Springer-Verlag, Berlin, Germany, June 1989, pp. 142-145.
5. Kojima K., S. Torii., and S. Yoshizumi, "IDP—A Main Storage Based Vector Database Processor," in *Database Machines and Knowledge Base Machines*, M. Kitsuregawa and H. Tanaka, eds., Kluwer Academic, Norwell, Mass., 1988, pp. 47-60.
6. Teradata Corp., "DBC/1012: Data Base Computer System—Introduction," 1986.
7. S. Englert, et al., "A Benchmark of NonStop SQL Release 2 Demonstrating Near-Linear Speedup and Scaleup on Large Databases," Technical Report 89.4, Tandem Part No. 27469, May 1989.
8. U. Inoue, et al., "RINDA—A Relational Data-Base Processor for Non-Indexed Queries," *Proc. Int'l Symp. Database Systems for Advanced Applications*, 1989, pp. 382-386.
9. H. Takeda and T. Satoh, "An Accelerating Processor for Relational Operations," *Proc. Int'l Conf. PARABASE*, IEEE CS Press, Los Alamitos, Calif., 1990, p. 559.
10. T. Satoh, et al., "Acceleration of Join Operations by a Relational Database Processor, RINDA," *Proc. 2nd Int'l Symp. DASFAA*, World Scientific Pub., Singapore, 1991, pp. 243-248.
11. T. Satoh, H. Takeda, and N. Tsuda, "A Compact Multiway Merge Sorter using VLSI Linear-Array Comparators," *Proc. Int'l Conf. Foundation of Data Organization and Algorithms*, Springer-Verlag, Berlin, Germany, 1989, pp. 223-227.
12. ISO, "Information Processing Systems—Database Language SQL," *Int' l Standard*, ISO 9075, June 1987.
13. L.L. Miller and A.R. Hurson, "Maybe Algebra Operations in Database Machine Architecture," *Fall Joint Computer Conf.*, IEEE CS Press, Los Alamitos, Calif., 1986, pp. 1210-1218.
14. S. Todd, "Algorithm and Hardware for a Merge Sort Using Multiple Processors," *IBM J. Res. and Dev.*, Vol. 22, No. 5, Sept. 1978, pp. 509-517.
15. M. Kitsuregawa, et al., "Implementation of LSI Sort Chip for Bimodal Sort Memory," *Proc. Int'l Conf. VLSI*, Elsevier Science Pub. B.V., North Holland, 1989, pp. 285-294.
16. M.W. Blasgen and K.P. Eswaran, "Storage and Access in Relational Data Bases," *IBM System J.*, Vol. 16, No. 4, 1977, pp. 363-377.

17. M. Kitsuregawa, M. Tanaka, and T. Moto-oka, "Application of Hash to Data Base Machine and Its Architecture," *New Generation Computing*, Vol. 1, No. 1, 1983, pp. 63–74.

18. D.R. McGregor, R.G. Thomson, and W.N. Dawson, "High Performance Hardware for Database Systems," *Systems for Large Data Bases*, North-Holland, Amsterdam, 1976, pp. 103–116.

19. V.Y. Lum, P.S.T. Yuen, and M. Dodd, "Key-to-Address Transform Techniques: A Fundamental Performance Study on Large Existing Formatted Files," *Comm. ACM*, Vol. 14, No. 4, 1971, pp. 228–239.

20. G.D. Knott, "Hashing Functions," *Computer J.*, Vol. 18, No. 3, 1975, pp. 265–287.

21. M. Kitsuregawa, et al., "Memory Management Algorithms in Pipeline Merge Sorter," *Proc. Int'l Workshop Database Machine*, Springer-Verlag, Berlin, Germany, 1985, pp. 208–232.

22. D. Bitton, D.J. DeWitt, and C. Turbyfill, "Benchmarking Database Systems—A Systematic Approach," *Computer Sciences Technical Report #526*, Univ. of Wisconsin-Madison, Madison, Wis., 1983.

23. D.J. DeWitt, et al., "A Single User Evaluation of the GAMMA Database Machine," in *Database Machines and Knowledge Base Machines*, M. Kitsuregawa and H. Tanaka, eds., Kluwer Academic, Norwell, Mass., 1988, pp. 370–386.

24. S. Shiokawa, Y. Obashi, and A. Nagoya, "DIPS-11/5E Series Mainframe," *Rev. ECL*, Vol. 35, No. 6, 1987, pp. 633–641.

FURTHER READING

N. Tsuda, T. Satoh, and T. Kawada, "A Pipeline Sorting Chip," *Proc. IEEE Int'l Solid-State Circuits Conf.*, IEEE CS Press, Los Alamitos, Calif., 1987, pp. 270–271.

5

A Paginated Set-Associative Architecture for Databases

Pascal Faudemay

Masi Lab / UPMC

ABSTRACT

Associative caches, containing content-addressable data, can greatly speed up certain database operations. The cache access mechanism can be set-associative, paginated, or a mixture of these architectures. We present a mixed associative cache architecture system called RAPID-2, which offers hardware assistance for several memory-management and arithmetic functions in addition to its data-storage capabilities. RAPID-2 is implemented as an add-on subsystem to a standard workstation. This chapter discusses data management within the associative cache, architectural details, hardware implementation, and performance evaluation.

5.1 INTRODUCTION

Database management systems have largely replaced file systems. DBMSs enable data sharing between applications, enforce consistency, and make possible data querying through a high-level language. However, their substitution for file systems has been somewhat constrained by too-simple data types, and too low a performance for some applications, such as CAD and decision support.

In order to increase their performance, we can improve the algorithms or use greater computational power. The prospect of more and more powerful processors, with instruction throughput about 1,000 million instructions per second in the next-generation workstations, may seem to be a solution to this problem. However, a straightforward increase in the processing power is unlikely to be sufficient for the demands of new applications such as multimedia, real-time applications, and knowledge bases, or for the execution of persistent programs on a large number of objects.[1-6] Associative memories have been found useful for several of these applications.[1,7-10]

One approach to these problems is to use high or massive parallelism. This approach has been tried for relational databases.[11-13] It is usually based on multiple-instruction, multiple-data execution models implemented on distributed-memory architectures. This solution suffers from a lack of appropriate development environments, and from load-balancing problems. Another approach is that of single-instruction, multiple-data execution models, based on general SIMD architectures (array processors, systolic engines, Connection Machine)[13,14] or on dedicated architectures. In this chapter we describe a solution based on a massively parallel, dedicated SIMD architecture. Other work on dedicated SIMD architectures for databases deals with communication processors for those architectures, sorters, filters, and processors dedicated to relational operations[15-25] and associative memories.[1,7-10, 23-35]

In this chapter we present a set-associative cache architecture, which can also be used as a "paginated associative memory,"[36] particularly for text retrieval. The associative memory to be described, known as RAPID-2, implements hardware rehashing and redistribution of data. It also has an arithmetic capability. It is well adapted to the management of migrations between associative memory and RAM ("cachelike" operation mode), and to the execution of sorting and logical address translation (dereferencing).

We successively present a brief state of the art, the RAPID-2 functionality, its system architecture and implementation, its management of data migration, an example of dereferencing, and finally, performance evaluation.

5.2 ASSOCIATIVE MEMORY: A BRIEF STATE OF THE ART

Associative memory is well adapted to the implementation of a massively-parallel SIMD architecture with a very simple execution model.[25] While load balancing in RAM-based multiprocessors may be a complex task, it is straightforward with associative architectures. Recent surveys on associative memories have been presented.[25,26]

In these memories, and in content-addressable memories, which are usually limited to equality comparisons, access and manipulation of data are based on content and not on address. Associative-memory systems have been the subject of much study for some years.[27] Unlike simple CAM, they retrieve data based on a complex assertion, and can sort, modify, and possibly execute arithmetic operations on data. Associative memories are therefore well adapted to the evaluation of queries on a database or part of a database.

The arithmetic capability of some associative-memory systems gives an important flexibility over more-classical approaches to computation. Associative memory with arithmetic capabilities can form a sort of general SIMD machine.[1,28] This possibility is especially interesting for retrieving data, based on a function of its content. Application to vision tasks has also been demonstrated.[1]

5.2.1 Main Limitations

Most current limitations of associative-memory systems relate to poor performance for inequality comparisons ($>$, $\geq$, and so on), cost of adding computational facilities to "fully associative" memory, restriction to fixed-length data, choice of small-length words, difficulties in representing complex data structures, and the small memory capacity compared to RAM. This small memory size makes it impossible to store significant portions of a database, or even large objects. For example, in 1989, Ogura's associative circuit (implemented in a 2-microns technology) was only 20 kilobits large.[7]

Where an associative-memory system has a small capacity, it may still be used as a filter, in which the user stores query predicates. The program then reads the database sequentially and evaluates each object, or possibly each byte.[30] Filters are not, of course, necessarily associative memories.[22] Furthermore, if the filter is fed by a general processor, it cannot have a larger throughput than the host machine bus, which limits its usefulness.

5.2.2 Memory Size Improvement in Fully Associative Circuits

The purpose of some projects is to reach a comparable memory size to that of RAM memories, or at least to that of static RAMs.

Some circuits with associative capabilities implement a larger memory size by the use of dynamic RAM in each binary cell,[1, 28,29] and possibly the execution of computational operations by a one-bit arithmetic logic unit, which enables easy implementation of inequality comparisons, Boolean functions, and some aggregates (minimum, maximum), with the minimum silicon area. This approach is employed by the DBA (Data Base Accelerator), and the CAPP circuit designed by Herrman and Sodini.[1] CAPP also combines associative operations and arithmetic operations in a 2-D cell network, which is adapted to low-level vision tasks.

However, the use of 32-bit or more ALUs appears to be more effective than 1-bit ALUs for arithmetic and inequality comparisons. Use of dynamic RAM also implies reliability problems in the case of transient failures.

5.2.3 The Set-Associative Approach

Another research approach, which borrows terminology from conventional cache organization, is that of set-associative memory. In this case, an associative cell is made up of one comparator and several data registers. Data are distributed among registers by hashing. A set consists of all data items that are stored at the same register address in the various cells. The number of sets is usually fixed in hardware.

In order to compare a data item with those stored in the associative memory, the circuit selects the same register address in all cells, according to the comparand hashing value. The ratio between the logic and memory chip-areas can therefore be modified by changing the number of registers per cell. It is then possible to reach a ratio of the area dedicated to memory of about 0.4, compared with 0.5 in RAM.[36]

An advantage of the set-associative approach is that it does not introduce any constraint on the ALU word size. Therefore, set-associative circuits can execute inequality comparisons in a bit-parallel mode, which is not usually the case. Although many set-associative circuits are indeed limited to equality comparisons, they can also evaluate inequality comparisons using interval-based hashing.[31] Fast arithmetic calculations are also possible.

Large set-associative memories can be implemented by using separate existing RAMs, and comparators. This approach is used by the IFS-1 and IFS-2 database machine projects from Lavington and others.[8,32,33] However, it may lead to some limitations, such as increase of circuit I/O with memory size, restricted data format in the associative memory, and/or difficulties in implementing hardware text retrieval.

Another approach is to integrate memory and comparators in the same chip, as in the dictionary search processor by Motomura and others.[31] This chip also includes a dedicated module for interval-based data hashing. The chip is implemented in a 0.8-microns technology, and has a 160-Kbit capacity.

5.2.4 The Paginated Approach

A comparable approach is that of paginated associative memory. These memories contain a fixed number of data "pages." In each cell, one register corresponds to each page. The search is done in parallel in all registers of the same page, then of the next one, and so forth. An example of a paginated associative memory is the pattern associative memory presented by Robinson.[36] In the case of large data elements, PAM first stores them in the registers of a same page, then in the registers of the next page, and so on. Data can also be stored successively in the successive pages of one cell, then of the next cell, and so forth.

The set-associative architecture may be viewed as a special case of the paginated architecture, with the inclusion of a hardware-hashing mechanism for selecting single pages.

Paginated architectures are well suited to the retrieval of a sequence of text stored in the system. This application is proposed for the PAM, which also includes the capability to retrieve text patterns into structured texts with variables. Set-associative architectures are less suitable for text retrieval, except for retrieving short sequences stored in the circuit as, for example, in the DISP dictionary management chip.

Another advantage of paginated memories is that they guarantee a very good memory utilization ratio, which is not always the case with a set-associative memory. In set-associative memories, the memory occupation ratio depends on the distribution of hashing values. For example, if one set is twice as large as the other ones, then the memory occupation ratio is about 0.5. (However, a better utilization ratio can be achieved by adapting the number of sets to the data distribution characteristics).

However, an advantage of set-associative memory is that it executes a retrieval on a single page, while paginated associative memory usually retrieves data from several or all pages. A combination of paginated and set-associative architectures may therefore display the best efficiency for all types of retrieval, while guaranteeing a good memory utilization ratio. The Rapid-2 system implements such a mixed architecture.

5.2.5 Set Associativity and Redistribution

When using a set-associative memory, it is important to choose the right hashing function. This function usually favors some sets of queries, and must be modified when the query type changes. In existing set-associative memories, this modification can only be done by reloading the associative memory. If this condition occurs for each operation, the operation duration becomes at least equal to that of reloading, and associative memory is not faster than a filter that would browse the data sequentially. Data rehashing and redistribution using associative memory are not implemented in existing set-associative memory systems.

5.2.6 Dedicated Associative Memory

Associative-memory systems are often dedicated to specific applications; some examples are memory management (such as "translation look-ahead buffers" in memory management units,[34]) vision applications,[28,35] text retrieval,[30,31] other database applications,[8,29,32,33] and symbolic processing.[36] The RAPID-2 architecture, which we now describe, is dedicated to database operations.

5.3 SYSTEM FUNCTIONALITY

The RAPID-2 system is an add-on associative cache, designed to support the functional requirements of object-oriented databases and extended relational databases. Physically, the RAPID-2 system consists of one or more printed-circuit boards attached to a host workstation's bus. Each RAPID-2 board typically contains 16 application-specific integrated circuit chips. Each chip consists of a number of cells (presently 16). Each cell includes an area of memory (currently 64 words of 32 data bits plus tags), an ALU, and some control logic. The memory in each cell is accessed associatively, using a mixture of the paginated and set-associative modes of access. The whole RAPID-2 system acts as an add-on associative cache, with a typical capacity of 64 kilobytes per board.

The host computer contains some driver software that communicates with the RAPID-2 cache. The interface between host and cache consists of a number of complex instruction-set computinglike instructions, so that the RAPID-2 system may in some respects be regarded as a coprocessor as well as a data cache. Complex database queries may be executed in a simple way, using high-level instructions that are directly executed by hardware. Furthermore, RAPID-2 implements all the main functionalities of a set-associative memory.

The functions needed by a set-associative memory to support databases are *write* and *update*, *select*, *read*, redistribution (that is, memory management), aggregation (in the sense of relational languages), and arithmetic and logical processing. The RAPID-2 chip implements these functions. It is intended to be suitable for efficient use in various database or persistent language applications, such as graph traversal, relational or set-oriented operations of an object system, retrieval of text fields in complex data, or data retrieval in text or image bases. In the rest of this section we describe the layout of data within the RAPID-2 cache, methods of accessing this data associatively, and the RAPID-2 instruction set. The following section describes the hardware implementation.

5.3.1 Data Segments and Data Migration

Data are stored in pages or contiguous groups of pages, which we call containers. Containers hold data segments. Each segment is composed of a collection of data that satisfies a common logical assertion, or that belongs to the same data type. One container may hold one or more segments. The container to which a piece of data belongs is known by the driver program, and the container's address is included in the storage or retrieval instruction.

In Figure 1 we present the RAPID-2 cache contents for multiprogrammed querying of three data types: a byte string, stored in container 1, a PERSON (NAME, CITY, PHONE_NUMBER, IDENTIFIER) relation divided into two segments, which is stored in container 2, and <object identifier, address> pairs, stored in container 3. Segments in container 2 are hashed into four pairs of pages (see below), according to a common hashing function. Unused pages (container 4) are shown as "empty" in Figure 1.

One data segment in container 2 is defined by the logical assertion or condition: "all tuples of type PERSON (NAME, CITY, PHONE_NUMBER, IDENTIFIER), who live in Paris." The application program may, for example, use the RAPID-2 cache to find the phone number or identifier of all persons with names beginning with 'AB' and living in Paris. Before querying the segment, it must check if the cache contains a segment with "DATA_TYPE = 'person', CITY = 'Paris' and NAME beginning with 'AB'," or any superset of this segment. If this condition exists, the program may use the cache to execute the query. If not, the query must be executed by host software, or the segment must first be moved into the cache. The decision whether or not to use the cache may use a heuristic, hopefully simple, embedded in the driver.

The driver has the capability to decide whether a segment defined by a given assertion, or a superset of this segment, is present in the associative memory. This task is accelerated by the cache. Each segment is mapped with a descriptor, which is stored in the cache. Descriptor retrieval is executed in a few cycles by a simple selection query.

If the driver decides to load a new segment, and there is a container overflow or cache overflow, some existing segments must first be deleted, and in some cases existing containers have to be grouped together. Overflow detection is performed by hardware. Segment suppression and container grouping are executed by the RAPID-2 system in a few cycles, under program control.

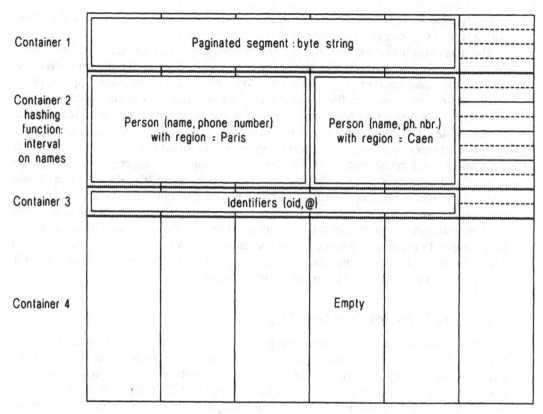

Figure 1.   Segmentation.

We assume that all useful data are moved from or to the host's RAM. This is valid for the "main-memory database" assumption.[36-38] If this is not the case, the operating system or the object manager will first move relevant data into RAM. Data migration (segment checks, loading, and deletions) between RAM and the RAPID-2 associative memory is independent of data migrations between the host's RAM and disks.

Data migration at the segment level between associative cache and associative disk has been studied by the IFS-1 project,[8,33] in the context of purely set-associative memory. With some differences, the method can be adapted to a mixed associative architecture. Data migration with a smaller granularity, such as migration at the chip level, is also possible with RAPID-2. The basic circuit mechanisms enable the management of data ages (that is, usage) and the enforcement of an LRU policy on data. This policy is intended to be used for object reference segments. A complete presentation of RAPID-2 migration mechanisms is outside the scope of this chapter.

5.3.2 Data Types

The associative cache processes structured data composed of one or more elements. In the rest of this chapter, we shall generally refer to elements as "data items" or "tuples." In the relational data model, tuples correspond to structured data with a fixed number of elements, or attributes. Each attribute belongs to a predefined type, and may have a fixed or variable length. However, we also process data with a variable number of elements (collections), such as sets (where elements have no duplicate) and lists (where it is possible to insert or delete an element at a given place), or nonstructured data such as byte strings. Operations on byte strings include retrieval of a sequence from any point in the string, or starting at previously marked places.

Data-elements are objects that can be identified by the same persistent reference during the whole life of the object. Data may contain one or more identifier words, which can be read as a query result. In the case of large byte strings, bytes are grouped into 4-byte words. Each word may be identified by a word tag.

The element types are byte strings and integers. Byte strings are organized as sequences of 4-byte words, each word being completed by special bits (word tag). Special bits include data *begin-and-end* markers, element *begin*, *null* element, *empty* byte flags, element numbers, segment number, and writeable flags. Data can be masked at byte level. Integers may be 32-bit integers or 8-bit integers. Each 32-bit word holds four 8-bit integers, which can be processed in parallel.

5.3.3 Access Modes

Within a container, two data access modes are possible. The first one is a paginated organization, where any word retrieval is carried out on a page specified in the instruction. The other access mode is a set-associative one, and is a specific case of the paginated access mode. In this mode, the number of the processed page within the container is a hashing value calculated by the RAPID-2 circuit, possibly added to some offset included in the instruction. An example is given later. The paginated access mode is appropriate for large byte strings, while the set-associative one is appropriate for other data types.

5.3.4 Data Organization within the RAPID-2 Chip

Data within a container is structured into blocks. A block may be composed of one or more 32-bit words, and all the words of a block occupy consecutive words in the same cell. A container is composed of an arbitrary number of blocks, within the limits of the circuit capacity (when data may have more than one block, we speak of "variable length" data). In order to simplify the presentation, we shall assume that there is a single block size in the whole chip, which is of course not necessarily the case in practice.

In a given container, the number of sets is equal to the number of pages, divided by block size. Therefore the number of sets depends on the block size and the size of the container. The choice of the block size must be made when creating a new container. Within a block, a specific word can be accessed by specifying an offset in the instruction. Block organization can ease the adaptation of the number of sets to data distribution, and also facilitate parallel processing of structured data.

For example, if tuples of type PERSON (NAME, CITY, PHONE_NUMBER, IDENTIFIER) are stored as byte strings in a paginated associative memory like PAM, the NAME of the first PERSON will be in cell 0, CITY in cell 2, and so on. Therefore, when selecting tuples on NAME, most cells could be idle. While a block organization can be simulated to some extent in a paginated memory, it is not the case in a set-associative or mixed architecture, as block size is a parameter of address calculation. Therefore, blocking data must be considered explicitly in circuit design.

5.3.5 Interest of the Mixed Associative Architecture

A main purpose of the RAPID-2 system is to study the optimal combination of paginated, set-associative, and block-oriented utilizations.

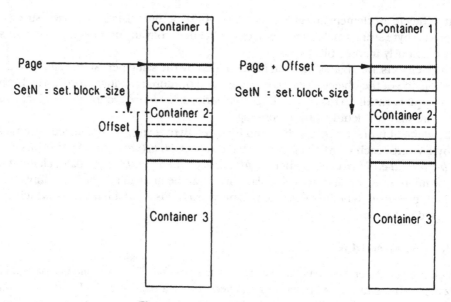

Figure 2.   Mixed data access.

A mixed paginated and set-associative architecture is simple to implement and enables the host program to divide the cache into several containers with different set (and possibly block) organizations. Each container can thus hold a different data type. Several containers may also correspond to the same data type, but with different query and hashing criteria. It is therefore possible to load data into the cache depending mainly on access probability, even if the data are of different types.

It is possible to notice that a paginated access to a group of sets and the use of offsets within a block can be combined easily . If the first page of a container is PAGE, and the offset within a block is OFFSET, and the hashing value is SET, then the address of the relevant word in each cell is :

$$\text{ADDRESS} = \text{PAGE} + \text{SET} * \text{BLOCK\_SIZE} + \text{OFFSET}.$$

A consequence is that the relevant word can also be found by using a PAGE value equal to PAGE + OFFSET, and calculating the word address as:

$$\text{ADDRESS} = \text{PAGE} + \text{SET} * \text{BLOCK\_SIZE}.$$

As BLOCK_SIZE is always a power of two, the address calculation only requires an adder, a hashing device, and some shifting mechanism. Access to the relevant word in a container is presented in Figure 2, for the two cases.

It can be seen that the mixed paginated and set-associative architecture has no significant effect on the complexity of instructions or on the circuit sequencing. In fact, it should make possible a much better use of the cache than a purely paginated or a purely set-associative approach.

5.3.6 Instruction Set

RAPID-2 is sequenced by microprograms, which are stored in RAM within the control section. Therefore, the instruction set can be adapted to each application class. In this chapter we present the "Basic instruction set," which was used for the initial RAPID-2 processor design.

Update instructions

LOAD :	the following data are to be stored into the cache
MODIFY :	marked data are replaced in parallel
SUPPRESS :	marked data are deleted and replaced by a null filler
INSERT :	each data is inserted after its predecessor in some order
CHANGE-LIMITS :	loads limits for hashing by interval

Retrieval instructions

SELECT :	marks all data that satisfies some predicate and/or is already marked
READ :	returns the previously selected data with their tags

Redistribution instructions

REHASH :	calculates a new hashing value for each data
REDISTRIBUTE :	redistributes data between sets after rehashing

Integer arithmetic and binary operations

AGGREGATE :	calculates an aggregate (count, sum, min, max) on virtual classes
OPERATION :	performs an arithmetic or binary operation on a page in parallel (add, sub, mul, div, shift, rotate, and, or, xor, not, comparisons)

Register copying

ALTER-TOKEN :	operation on tokens, such as shift, propagate, set, reset . . .
COPY :	copies an element of a marked data item into a register, or the converse
MOVE-CONT :	moves a container toward empty pages, to free pages.

Figure 3.   RAPID-2 basic instruction set.

The basic instruction set is composed of a small number of high-level instructions, with a CISC-like approach. The system is controlled by data-transfers and most instructions execute as long as data are sent to the circuit, and as long as the host program does not modify the current instruction. The instruction set is presented in Figure 3. The format of a SELECT instruction is presented in Figure 4.

5.4 ARCHITECTURE AND IMPLEMENTATION

5.4.1 Global Architecture

The RAPID-2 chip architecture is based on a cascadable set-associative subsection. Each RAPID-2 associative cache printed-circuit board is composed of a number of set-associative components and a control component. The associative component will include, in present chip technology, about one million transistors. A host machine will use one or more associative boards; however, we shall only consider a single associative board in the following description.

Registers having the same name in all the associative subsections are placed at the same address in the host machine address space. The host CPU (or one of them, in the case of a

CODOP	12 bits	corresponding microprogram address
CTRL field (5 bits)		
BYTE	1 bit	8 / 32-bit mode
HCSEL	2 bits	address type (use hash-code, use former-hashcode, use page value)
TKMSHIN	2 bits	mode of the token mesh (input 0, input 1, or loop)
PARAM field (15 bits)		
PAGE	6 bits	page number
BS	3 bits	block-size
HCS	3 bits	hash-code size
(NOT USED)	3 bits	
TOTAL	32 bits	

Figure 4.   Format of the SELECT instruction.

multiprocessor) communicates with the board by writing to or reading from one of the registers of the control component.

The control subsection is composed of a sequencer, an external interface, a global arbitration tree, and an error-management module. The sequencer is made of a control store and a microsequencer. Conditional branches in microprograms depend on three possible conditions: value of the global OR of all cell states (that is, cells inhibit tokens), global counter overflow, or processor overflow. Only one of these conditions can occur at any given time.

Each associative subsection is composed of an array of associative cells, and a local arbitration tree. The state of a cell is defined by the content of its register file, auxiliary registers, memory registers, and token registers. Each cell has four tokens :

- the RTKN stores the ALU result
- the ITKN stores the cell activation state
- the ETKN enables the cell to write to the data bus when ordered by the appropriate microinstruction
- the FTKN sets the cell to the "faulty" state. In that case it is bypassed in all further operations, except the reset of FTKN.

Figure 5 presents an abstract view of the chip block-diagram. In this figure, local and global arbitration trees are grouped into a single block.

The control section communicates with the host machine through the section's I/O registers. In the same way, communications of associative cells with the control component imply reads or writes in their I/O registers or in their memory. Thus, there is an input and output data pipeline. This pipeline is needed for the effective operation of the circuit, and it is an important factor in the circuit response times. Communication of a cell with the outside is a distinct action of the cell. The architecture of the control component interface module is presented in Figure 6.

Data shifts can also be executed simultaneously from each cell to the next or previous one, thus enabling data insertion. Shift is conditional: data are copied into the next cell if the "token" activation flag is set in this cell. This mechanism supports incremental memory compaction (garbage collection) in a relatively automatic manner.

The address management module calculates the hashing value of the data to be stored into the cache (or of the constant of the evaluated predicate), and adds the page number

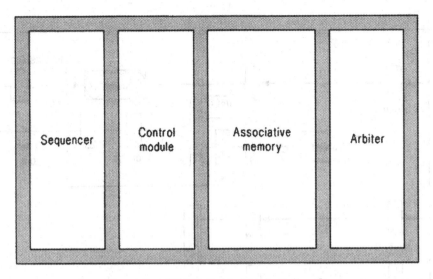

Figure 5.   RAPID-2 chip block diagram.

and/or the offset and mixed-operation mode. The hashing function may be based on folding or intervals. Folding calculates some signature of an element. Hashing by intervals compares the hashed element to a set of limits, and the hashing value is the number of the first larger limit. Hashing by folding uses a specific combinatorial module (see below).

5.4.2   Cell Architecture

Each cell is composed mainly of a register file, a dedicated arithmetic and logic unit, and several auxiliary registers. A cell can therefore be viewed as a dedicated reduced instruction-set computing heart with its register bank. The word size is 38 bits, including 32 data bits and a 6-bit word tag ("special bits"). The memory size is 64 words.

The estimated cell size is about 50,000 transistors, and the complete chip includes the maximum number of cells possible. In the present design the number of cells per circuit is 16 in 0.5 microns complementary metal-oxide semiconductor technology. Therefore, the memory capacity per chip is 32 Kbits of data. The cell architecture is represented in Figure 7.

The choice of a 32-bit word width, without the tag, is a compromise between the processing power available in one cycle, and the desired level of parallelism. The choice of 32 is well suited to integer arithmetic and to present bus widths, making it possible to limit the number of words per cell to 64, while having a good ratio between the chip's memory area and the total circuit area. With a minimum of two words per block, the number of page-sets is limited to 32, which limits the effect of data skew. For example, with a 6 percent data skew (6 percent of hashing values are the same) and 32 sets, the memory occupation ratio is 0.5, which seems to be an acceptable minimum. In case of too much data skew, data can be stored in a purely paginated mode.

However, larger numbers of registers may be acceptable later, since the number of sets is also reduced if there are several containers. Therefore, the optimal memory size may evolve with the technology, and will be the subject of further studies.

The ALU width is 32-bit. For some operations (text retrieval), it is divided into four 8-bit ALUs. The associativity (proportional to the number of comparators in parallel) is then multiplied by 4. The use of 8-bit ALUs also makes an 8-bit arithmetic feasible, which can result in a speedup and capacity improvement of up to 4 for some operations.

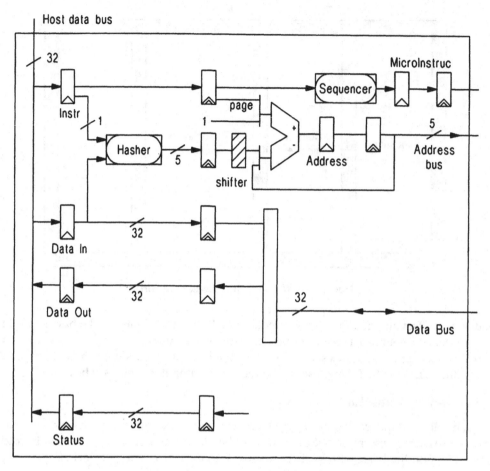

Figure 6.   Interface module of the control component.

5.4.3 Hashing and Redistribution

A similar hashing module is used in the cell and in the address management module, in order to calculate folding functions. Hashing is applied to a single element of each data item (usually to a single word). The address-management hashing module is used to calculate the page number of an item when it is input to the cache. The cell hashing module is used in the cell for data rehashing, before a redistribution operation. The hashing value is then stored in the word tag. Redistribution is a special case of sorting by hardware with a very limited amount of memory. It makes large use of the arbitration mechanism, which is a characteristic of this type of associative memory.

The hashing module is adapted to the calculation of the hashing value in one cycle on a one-word data element. All hashing values in the associative board can therefore be calculated (by folding) in at most 32 cycles (one per set). Folding on n bits is implemented by successive n-bit shifts on one-data word, followed by an XOR operation with the previous folding result. Folding continues as long as the data word is not back to its initial position. If a word folding on 5 bits were to be executed with a nondedicated ALU in each component, it would need a number of cycles $32*N$ times greater, with N being the number of cells in the component.

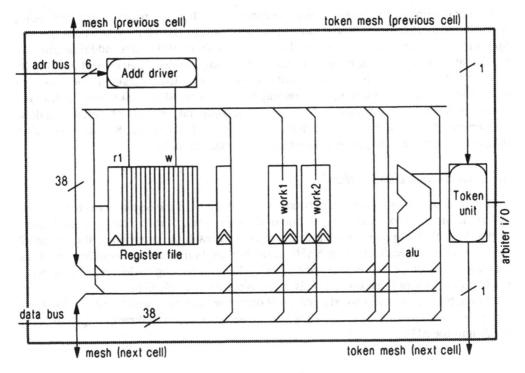

Figure 7.   Cell architecture.

Folding can also be applied to several words in a block, or several words in consecutive blocks. In this case the circuit executes parallel XORs between word-pairs in the same cells, or in two consecutive cells, before applying word-folding on the result.

An important problem during folding is the possibility, with some nonuniform data distributions, that significant bits may not be distributed on all bits of the folding result. This may be the case, for example, if the element is a number $A = aX + Y$, where $a = 255$, $X = 0, 1,..3$ and $Y = 0, 1, ..3$. A has 16 possible values, but the number of variable bits in case of a folding on 4 bits would be limited to 2. Similar results could be obtained with other values of a. In order to avoid an excessive data skew and consequential circuit overflow, folding should then begin by an identical "random" bit permutation in all hashed elements.

Another possible hashing mode is hashing by intervals. The domain of the hashed element is then partitioned into intervals. The hashing value is the number of the interval that includes the element. One way to calculate the hashing value is to compare successively each hashed element, in all cells, with all interval limits. This approach is used for redistribution. Another approach is to compare the hashing element in parallel with all limits, previously stored in one register per cell. This approach is used at storage or evaluation time.

5.4.4 Arithmetic Operations

Arithmetic functions in RAPID-2 have been limited to integer arithmetic. Addition is needed for aggregate calculations. More generally, arithmetic capabilities enable the host program to evaluate assertions on functions, and not only on raw data, without needing to reload data into the cache. Many database numbers are integers or fixed-point numbers that can be represented by integers.

Integer multiplications and divisions are executed with a minimal chip-area cost, using two shifters (limited to a 1-bit shift) and one adder per cell. Therefore, a 32-bit integer multiplication is executed in 34 cycles, and a division in about 100 cycles. Addition and subtraction are executed in one cycle (plus pipeline loading). In case of an error (for example, capacity overflow), a flag is set in the word tag, and it can be used to exclude the data from further operations. Arithmetic operations may also be executed on 8-bit words, with an important performance improvement for image retrieval operations. The 8-bit multiplications are performed every 8 cycles, on 4 numbers in each cell. Therefore, 8-bit multiplication throughput is 16 times larger than 32-bit multiplication throughput.

5.4.5 Updating a Data Word

During an operation, it is often necessary to rewrite part of the 38-bit words read for this operation. Modifications can apply to one of the data bytes, or to the tag field. Updating a field is done by multiplexing each previous bit with a result bit, returned by the cell result module (TOKEN module), or by the ALU, or the hasher. In the case of a modification of the data field, either all 32 bits or none are replaced. The multiplexing device, called MIX, is driven by a control word that corresponds to the various updatable fields.

Although any result data word or external data word can be stored in the WORK auxiliary registers, bypassing this register is also possible in order to directly input memory words into the ALU.

5.5 AN EXAMPLE: DEREFERENCING

Translation of logical addresses into physical addresses (dereferencing), is a frequent operation when programming in a virtual-memory environment or in an object-oriented environment. Use of associative memories for dereferencing is a classical application, to be seen in devices such as memory management units. This operation is presented here to illustrate the RAPID-2 cache utilization, as it implies both selects, updates with incremental garbage collection, overflow management, and data suppression.

In object bases, references are persistent pointers that can be translated into logical or physical addresses. We shall assume that the identifier is a 64-bit word, and that the physical address is a 32-bit word, as is the case with the VROOM object manager.[39] When an object is first accessed during a session, the identifier-address pair cannot be present in the associative cache, and so the address is obtained by software. So long as the object is present in the host's main memory or in the swap volume, the identifier-address pair is stored in a data structure (access graph) in main memory, which makes it possible to map the address with the identifier. If the identifier must be translated again into an address, it is possible to execute this translation by software, by traversing the access graph. However, it is also possible to store the identifier-address pair into a large associative memory, select this pair by its identifier, and return the address.

5.5.1 Reference Retrieval in the Circuit

The sequencing of this operation is described in Figure 8, which presents a Register Transfer Level diagram of retrieval. The instruction is first present on the host data bus at cycle 0, then it is stored in the instruction input register (cycle 1), and decoded. It is then stored in a decoded instruction register, and used for sequencing. The value of the decoded instruction register remains unchanged, as long as no other instruction was written in the

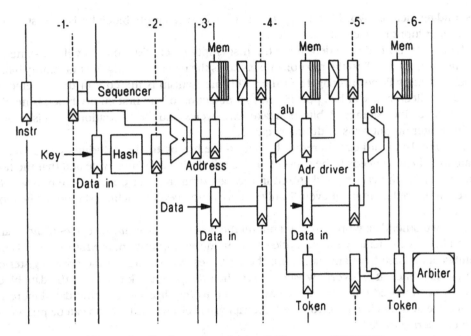

Figure 8.   Register transfer level diagram of SELECT.

input register during the previous cycle. The first data word, called the hash key, is then stored in the data input register (cycle 2). It is hashed using the current hashing function present in the instruction. The resulting value is then added in the second phase to the page number in order to obtain the current address, which is stored in the read-address registers (cycle 3).

The first word of the data itself is then stored in the data input register (cycle 4). In some cases, optimization can be done by using the first data word as the data key, but this is not always possible. Comparison with the corresponding data present in the cache is then executed, and the result is stored in the token register (cycle 5). Next, local arbitration (at circuit level) and global arbitration (at board level) each take one cycle, and the arbitration result is written into the arbiter result register at cycle 7.

The address part of the reference, if it has been found, can then be output on the host data bus using the READ instruction. If there is no answer from a cell, the arbiter outputs a null value on the bus. The null data tag value is a fixed arbitrary value, which is not used in the data tag.

We do not detail age (that is, usage) incrementation and reset, because this is still being optimized. The next instruction can be present on the host data bus at cycle 9. Therefore, the retrieval operation takes 9 cycles (8 if the hash key is the first data word).

5.5.2 Data Replacement

In the case of a null answer, the identifier-address pair must be retrieved by host software through the access graph. If it is present in this graph, it is then stored in the RAPID-2 cache.

The storage instruction is first put on the host data bus (cycle 0), and decoded as before. The hash key is put on the host bus during cycle 1, and stored in the data input register at cycle 2. The page-set address is then stored in the address registers at cycle 3, and the corresponding memory word is read in the same cycle. The empty block bit is then stored in the arbiter input register during cycle 4.

Arbitration is needed to determine the first empty block. Data blocks will be shifted in parallel from each cell to the next one up, as far as the cell containing the first empty block. Block shifting will not propagate further. This mechanism is the core of the incremental garbage collector. It will be appreciated that detection of the first empty block is needed for effective block storage. Arbitration takes two cycles, and the arbitration result is present in the arbiter output register during cycle 6.

The first data word can therefore be put on the bus by the host during cycle 5 (we assume that the data needs to be present on the bus during only one cycle and that the host does not delay the cache), and stored in the data input register during cycle 6. It will be stored in the cell memory at cycle 7 only if there is no overflow, which should be the most frequent case.

The two other data words are then put on the bus by the host during cycles 6 and 7, and stored in the cell memory during cycles 8 and 9. In this application, the fourth word is not significant and can have any value, but the host uses cycle 8 to read the error register on the global arbiter. If an overflow value is set, then the program knows that the data block has not been stored effectively. It must proceed to the deletion of some data before restoring the new block. If no error is set, then another retrieval instruction can be put on the host bus during cycle 8.

Therefore, the storage of a new reference into the circuit takes 9 cycles, including the operation of the incremental garbage collector.

5.5.3 Data Deletion

If an overflow error has been detected, the program must then delete some data in the cache. It can either suppress a data item with a given age (that is, usage) or all data with this age. The first solution is quite costly, so we shall not consider it.

If references are more or less equally distributed between ages 0 to 3, the best solution seems to be to replace data with age 3, and then increment all ages. The delection and incrementing can either be done in the page-set where an overflow has been observed, or in all sets. These choices will be studied in future simulations.

In order to suppress data with a given age, the host selects data based on the age value. Age is stored within the tag in flags 1 and 2. The duration of a SELECT on a tag value is the same as a SELECT on a data value. However, when a SELECT is followed by a SUPPRESS, there is no need for arbitration cycles. Therefore the SELECT duration is 4 cycles per set.

SUPPRESS is done by writing the EMPTY bit into the corresponding tags. Therefore it takes one cycle per page, and two cycles per set.

Age incrementation takes advantage of the token unit functionalities. In each set, it includes the steps presented in Figure 9 (with one cycle per step) :

Thus, data delection and age incrementation in one page take 15 cycles per set. If the RAPID-2 board were to contain 800 cells, and data are equally distributed among ages, this operation should take place every 200 updates. Therefore, its cost is negligible.

5.6 PERFORMANCE EVALUATION

In this section we evaluate the cache performance for dereferencing and image retrieval. Speedup for redistribution, text retrieval, and arithmetic operations have also been studied and will be published in future papers.

—conditional incrementing of bit 1 of age:

(1) RTKN <- flag0   —we assume bit 0 of age is in flag 0, bit 1 in flag 1
(2) ITKN <- RTKN
(3) RTKN <- flag 1   —this action is conditioned by ITKN
(4) RTKN <- 1 OR RTKN
(5) flag1 <- RTKN

—conditional incrementing of bit 0 of age:

(6) RTKN <- flag0
(7) NOT RTKN
(8) ITKN <- RTKN
(9) flag 1 <- RTKN   —flag 1 is set if RTKN = 1, but is not reset in the opposite case

Figure 9.   Age incrementation algorithm.

5.6.1 Dereferencing

The average time for this operation is a function of the number of references to the same object, during the lifetime of its residence in the associative memory. The time varies between the delay for a retrieval (9 cycles) in the case of frequently utilized data, to the delay for software access to the data (about 5 microseconds on a 12-MIPS workstation), plus the delay for a replacement (9 cycles), in the case of a single access reference.

Therefore, the speedup ratio depends on the hit-ratio of the RAPID-2 system, considered as an associative cache. The speedup ratio is:

$$R = \text{soft} / (\text{hit} * \text{retrieval}) + (1\text{-hit}) * (\text{soft} + \text{replace})$$

where "soft" is the duration when the operation is only executed by software, "hit" is the hit ratio, "retrieval" is the delay for a retrieval using the circuit, and "replace" is the delay for a replacement. The improvement ratio as a function of the hit-ratio, for a 12-MIPS and a 60-MIPS workstation, and for a circuit cycle time of 20 nanoseconds can reach 5.5 if the reference locality is very high. Therefore using the cache for dereferencing can be useful, but it is not a major application of the RAPID-2 system.

5.6.2 Retrieval in an Image Database

Retrieval in an image database consists of recognizing database images that are similar to a pattern belonging to the observed image, whether a fixed image or a video. Pixel images are first transformed into collections of vectors or elementary areas by low-level vision tasks. These tasks can also be accelerated by the RAPID-2 circuit. However, there are other associative circuits that can process most of these operations in real time.[1] Patterns must then be compared with many possible sub-images. Recognition is often required to be carried out in real time.

This operation can be executed as a comparison of the image vectors with all vectors of the database images (relational semi-join between vector descriptors). The recognition program must then count the number of matching vectors for each image in the database. When this number is greater than some threshold (pattern dependent), then the database image is similar to the pattern.[40] Counting the number of matching vectors for each image is a relational aggregation operation.

When the join is executed by software, its duration can be estimated to be in $O(n+m)$, where n and m are the cardinalities of the source relations (the number of vectors in the database and the incoming pattern). We base this estimation on the assumption that the join is implemented by hashing, followed by cartesian product on hashing buckets. The duration of the hashing phase is linear vs. relation sizes. Assuming that average bucket size is constant and there are no data skew effects, the duration of the cartesian product phase is also linear vs. relation sizes.

The aggregate duration has the complexity of sorting, that is, $O(n \log n)$ where n is the number of vectors in the database. The duration of the aggregation on n vectors should be at least equal to that of a join on relations with the same size.

When using the RAPID-2 system, it is preferable to assume that the database fits in the associative memory. Therefore, the cache size is an important parameter. Previous image recognition using associative memories has been limited to small image bases, such as for vehicle number plates (a few tens of images). If the cache size is sufficient, the join is executed in time $t = a*m$, where m is the number of vectors in the pattern. The aggregate is executed in time $t = b*(\text{Max}\,(m(i))$, where $m(i)$ is the number of vectors in image i.

The improvement ratio can then be approximated as :

$$R = (3*n + m) \text{ join } / \text{ MIPS } / (a*m + b* (\text{Max } (m(i))).$$

where join is the duration of a 500 000*500 000 tuples join (1 million elementary steps) on a 1-MIPS machine, and MIPS is the average power in MIPS of the host machine. We assume that join = 20 seconds (which assumes quite a fast algorithm), a = 240 nanoseconds, b = 20 nanoseconds, and MIPS = 100 MIPS.[41]

The value of a corresponds to the fact that there are four attributes per vector and each attribute evaluation takes three cycles. There is no arbitration or result return; the cache only marks relevant data. The value of b corresponds to the fact that the aggregate is calculated by shifting a numerical token from one cell to the next in each class (image data are sorted by image number). When recognizing a 30-vector pattern in a database of 3000 vectors, the improvement ratio is greater than 400.

The operation duration can be reduced still further, by a factor of 4, if attributes are 8-bit integers. In this case the number of vectors in the database can be four times larger while using the same RAPID-2 system. A further increase in the database size and in the improvement ratio can result from technology improvements (with a probable increase by a factor of above 100), and from the use of several boards in the same host machine. Therefore, this approach seems very promising for image recognition in future multimedia database systems.

5.6.3 Other Remarks

A common assumption for our evaluations is that the host processor copies a data item from memory to the RAPID-2 cache in no more than two circuit cycles. This assumption may be unrealistic when the host processing power is not large enough. In the above example we have made comparisons with software operations using a 100-MIPS machine. This processing power may be the minimum necessary to sustain the 2-cycle assumption.

However, the existence of an instruction cache can reduce the number of I/Os between associative memory and host. Where an instruction cache is present, RAPID-2 can be used as an add-on board even for a PC; this also simplifies the board design.

Redistribution and arithmetic operations within RAPID-2 can be significantly more efficient than external processing and data reloading, even with the most recent workstations.

Using these operations followed by a SELECT may also be much more efficient than executing the SELECT with software. In this chapter, we have only presented a brief sketch of the RAPID-2 potential.

5.6.4 Redistribution

Redistribution is preceded by a hashing operation, which is done in parallel in all cells. In the frequent case where the hashing attribute is in the first data block (or if data items have fixed lengths), parallel hashing on all data is executed in no more than 33 cycles.

Redistribution is executed by block permutations. Each permutation costs $10 + 2*b$ cycles, where b is the block size in words. Therefore, with sufficient block sizes (at least 8 words), the number of cycles per permuted word is generally four or less.

The idea of the operation is that most permutations are done in parallel in all cells, some are done in parallel in all chips, and the rest are done sequentially. The efficiency of our hardware redistribution depends on the parallelism of nonsequential permutations, and the proportion of sequential ones. It is easy to ascertain which values of these parameters favor a parallel execution of redistribution.

5.7 CONCLUSION

Set-associative and paginated associative cache architectures make possible larger-capacity associative memories, in which the memory size per chip may be comparable with that of RAMs using the same technology, or at least with that of classical data caches. In RAPID-2, 47 percent of the cell area is dedicated to the register file, which has the same density as static RAM. Thus, the system's memory capacity is about half that of a static RAM using the same technology. Use of dynamic RAM as in Herrmann's early work[1] was discarded on speed and complexity grounds. With 64 kilobytes of data per board, RAPID-2 capacity can be compared to that of internal data caches of existing processors.

Associative memories can therefore be used like a data cache, in which data can be retrieved based on its content. Data migration can be executed at the word level, or at the level of data sets defined by predicates, which we call data segments. Associative-memory mechanisms may be used to manage segment migrations. Data segments have also been studied by the IFS-1 project.[8,32,33]

A combination of the paginated and set-associative approach is helpful for managing various data segments, corresponding to different data types or interrogands, in the same circuit. This combination is easy to implement, and promotes a good utilization ratio of the associative memory. For set-associative utilization, it seems important to hash data by hardware (as in Motomura,[31] but with more general hashing functions), and also to have a capability to rehash data and to redistribute it in the associative cache.

The associative cells of the RAPID-2 system can be used for general parallel applications (but without floating point operations), as well as for comparisons or updates. Computational functions are implemented with the minimum circuit area and are not very costly. Addition is imperative anyway for some operations, such as aggregates (for example, the sum of the values of an attribute in several data groups).

The RAPID-2 system is a new project[42] that implements a mixed associative architecture. It executes high-level CISC-like instructions, which are needed for improved performance and ease of programming. These instructions are interpreted by a global sequencer. Minimizing the complexity of this sequencer, while retaining the main functionalities, has been a major challenge of the project. One way to reach this goal is the use of a RAM control store within the control section. Therefore, the instruction set can be adapted to suit each class of applications. Microprograms can also be debugged independently of the implementation of the rest of the chip.

While RAPID-2 instructions are CISC-like, each cell can be seen as a RISC subunit. The associative board implements a massively parallel machine, which uses a very simple SIMD execution model. Access to the machine is done by simple reads and writes on its I/O ports. Pipelining is used at the cell and chip level.

The RAPID-2 architecture is adaptable to many database applications, including virtual address translation in object bases, and real-time image-retrieval operations for multimedia database systems.

A complete VHDL model of the RAPID-2 coprocessor has now been implemented. We have also designed a detailed C++ simulation for microprogramming purposes. The coprocessor should be sent to fabrication in 1-micron CMOS technology at the end of 1994. Another fabrication should occur at mid-1995 in 0.5-micron CMOS technology. We are also designing a high-level compiled language for easy programming of RAPID-2.

ACKNOWLEDGMENTS

I would like to thank Denis Archambaud, Stphane Audrain, Ivan Saraiva Silva, and Professor Alain Greiner for fruitful comments. Thanks are also due to Michael Novak and Professor Simon Lavington for having revised the final version of this chapter, and to both editors and to the anonymous referees for their fruitful comments.

The MASI Laboratory is an associate laboratory of CNRS. The RAPID-2 project is partly funded by the GdR ANM (Novel Machines Architecture) and the GdR "Informatique et Gnme" (Computer Science and Genomics).

REFERENCES

1. F.P. Herrmann and C. Sodini, "A Dynamic Associative Processor for Machine Vision Applications," *IEEE Micro*, Vol. 12, No. 3, June 1992, pp. 31–41.
2. G. Salton, E. Fox, and H. Wu, "Extended Boolean Information Retrieval," *Comm. ACM*, Vol. 26, No. 12, Nov. 1983, pp. 1022–1036.
3. P. Butterworth, A. Otis, and J. Stein, "The Gemstone Object Database Management System," *Comm. ACM*, Vol. 34, No. 10, Oct. 1991.
4. O. Deux, et al., "The O2 System," *Comm. ACM*, Vol. 34, No. 10, Oct. 1991.
5. S. Zdonik and D. Maier, *Readings in Object-Oriented Database Systems*, Morgan Kaufmann Publications, San Mateo, Calif., 1990.
6. C. Lamb, C., et al., "The ObjectStore Database System," *Comm. ACM*, Vol. 34, No. 10, Oct. 1991.
7. T. Ogura, et al., "A 20-kbit Associative Memory LSI for Artificial Intelligence Machines," *IEEE J. Solid-State Circuits*, Vol. 24, No. 4, Aug. 1989, pp. 1014–1020.
8. S.H. Lavington, S.H. and R.A.J. Davies, "Active Memory for Managing Persistent Objects," *Proc. Int'l. Workshop Computer Architectures to Support Security and Persistence*, in *Security and Persistence*, J. Rosenberg and JH.L. Keedy, eds., Springer-Verlag, London, England, 1990, pp. 137–154.
9. A.R. Hurson and P.M. Miller, "A 16-Kbit Q-Search Associative Memory," *IEEE Micro*, Vo. 13, No. 2, Apr. 1993, pp. 59–65.
10. C.R. Petrie and A.R. Hurson, "A VLSI Join Module," *VLSI Systems Design*, Vol. 9, No. 10, 1988, pp. 46–58.
11. H. Boral, et al., "Prototyping Bubba, A Highly Parallel Database System," *IEEE Trans. Knowledge and Data Engineering*, Vol. 2, No. 1, Mar. 1990, pp. 4–24.

12. D.J. DeWitt, et al., "The Gamma Database Machine Project," *IEEE Trans. Knowledge and Data Engineering*, Vol. 2, No. 1, Mar. 1990, pp. 44–62.

13. H. Boral and P. Faudemay, eds., "Database Machines," *Proc. 6th Int'l Workshop on Database Machines*, Lecture Notes in Computer Science #368, Springer Verlag, New York, N.Y., 1989.

14. C. Stanfill and B. Kahle, "Parallel Free-Text Search on the Connection Machine System," *Comm. ACM*, Vol. 29, No. 12, Dec. 1986, pp. 1229–1239.

15. Teradata Corp., "DBC/1012 Data Base Computer Concept and Facilities," Teradata Corp., Document No. C02-000100, 1983.

16. M. Kitsuregawa, et al., "Implementation of LSI Sort Chip for Bimodal Sort Memory," *Proc. Very Large Scale Integration*, IFIP 10.5, 1989, pp. 285–294.

17. M. Kitsuregawa and Y. Ogawa, "Bucket Spreading Parallel Hash: A New, Robust, Parallel Hash Join Method for Data Skew in the Super Database Computer," *Int'l Conf. Very Large Databases*, Morgan Kaufmann, San Mateo, Calif., Aug. 1990, pp. 210–221.

18. M. Abdelguerfi and A.K. Sood, "A Fine-Grain Architecture for Relational Database Aggregation Operations," *IEEE Micro*, Vol. 11, No. 6, Dec. 1991, pp. 35–43.

19. M. Abdelguerfi, "Special Function Unit for Statistical Aggregation Functions," *Proc. 6th Int'l Workshop Database Machines*, Lecture Notes in Computer Science #368, Springer-Verlag, New York, N.Y., 1989.

20. U. Inoue, et al., "Rinda: A Relational Database Processor with Hardware Specialized for Searching and Sorting," *IEEE Micro*, Vol. 11, No. 6, Dec. 1991, pp. 61–70.

21. M. Penazola and E. Ozkarahan, "Integrating Integrity Constraints With Database Filters Implemented in Hardware," *Proc. 6th Int'l Workshop on Database Machines*, Lecture Notes in Computer Science #368, Springer-Verlag, New York, N.Y., 1989, pp. 230–ff.

22. K.C. Lee, et al., "VLSI Accelerators for Large Database Systems," *IEEE Micro*, Vol. 11, No. 6, Dec. 1991, pp. 8–20.

23. P. Faudemay and M. Mhiri, "An Associative Accelerator for Large Database Systems," *IEEE Micro*, Vol. 11, No. 6, Dec. 1991, pp. 22–34.

24. A.R. Hurson and P.M. Miller, "Modular Scheme for Designing Associative Memories," *J. Computer Systems Science and Engineering*, Vol. 8, No. 3, July 1993, pp. 166–181.

25. L. Chisvin and R.J. Duckworth, "Content-Addressable and Associative-memory: Alternatives to the Ubiquitous RAM," *Computer*, Vol. 22, No. 7, July 1989, pp. 51–64.

26. K.E. Grosspietsch, "Associative Processors and Memories: A Survey," *IEEE Micro*, Vol. 12, No. 3, June 1992, pp. 12–19.

27. K.J. Thurber and L.D. Wald, "Associative and Parallel Processors," *Computing Surveys*, Vol. 7, No. 4, Dec. 1975.

28. F.P. Herrmann, et al., "A Dynamic Three-State Memory Cell for High-Density Associative Processors," *IEEE J. Solid-State Circuits*, Vol. 26, No. 4, Apr. 1991, pp. 537–541.

29. J.P. Wade and C.G. Sodini, "A Ternary Content Addressable Search Engine," *IEEE J. Solid-State Circuits*, Vol. 24, No. 4, Aug. 1989, pp. 1003–1013

30. K. Takahashi, H. Yamada, and M. Hirata, "A String Search Processor LSI," *J. Information Processing*, Vol. 13, No. 2, 1990.

31. M. Motomura, et al., "A 1.2 Million Transistor, 33 Mhz, 20-b Dictionary Search Processor (DISP) ULSI with a 160 Kbits CAM," *IEEE J. Solid-State Circuits*, Vol. 25, No. 5, Oct. 1990, pp. 1158–1165.

32. S.H. Lavington, et al., "Exploiting Data Parallelism in Knowledge Based Systems," *Proc. Parallel Architectures and Languages Europe*, Springer-Verlag, New York, N.Y., 1992, pp., 893–908

33. S.H. Lavington, et al., "Hardware Memory Management for Large Knowledge Bases," *Proc. Parallel Architectures and Languages Europe*, Vol. I, Lecture Notes on Computer Science #258, Springer-Verlag, New York, N.Y., 1987, pp. 226–241.

34. A. Goksel, et al., "A Content-Adressable Memory Management Unit with On-Chip Data Cache," *IEEE J. Solid-State Circuits*, Vol. 24, No. 3, June 1989, pp. 592–596.

35. R. Storer, et al., "An Associative Processing Module for a Hetegeroneous Architecture," *IEEE Micro*, Vol. 12, No. 3, June 1992, pp. 42–55.

36. I. Robinson, "Pattern-Addressable Memory," *IEEE Micro*, Vol. 12, No. 3, June 1992, pp. 20–30.

37. M. Eich, "Main Memory Database Research Directions," *Proc. 6th Int'l Workshop Database Machines*, Lecture Notes on Computer Science #368, Springer-Verlag, New York, N.Y., 1989.

38. K. Salem and H. Garcia-Molina, "System M: A Transaction Processing Testbed for Memory Resident Data," *IEEE Trans. Knowledge and Data Engineering*, Vol. 2, No. 1, Mar. 1990, pp. 161–172.

39. E. Abécassis, "VROOM / C++ : User Interface," IBP research report, Oct. 1992 (available at ftp.ibp.fr in /ibp/softs/masi/vroom).

40. G. Fouquet, "Une machine bases de données temps réel et ses applications àla gestion de bases d'images," (in French), PhD thesis, Univ. Pierre et Marie Curie, Paris, France, Oct. 1991.

41. D.A. Schneider and D.J. DeWitt, "A Performance Evaluation of Four Parallel Join Algorithms in a Shared-Nothing Multiprocessor Environment," *Proc. ACM-SIGMOD 1989*, ACM Press, New York, N.Y., 1989.

42. D. Archambaud and P. Faudemay, "Rapid-2, A Paginated Set-Associative Architecture that Performs String Processing," *Proc. 1st South American Workshop on String Processing*, Belo Horizonte, R. Baeza-Yates and N. Ziviani, eds., Federal Univ. of Minas Gerais, 1993.

FURTHER READING

Archambaud, D., P. Faudemay, and A. Greiner, "RAPID-2, An Object-Oriented Associative Memory Applicable to Genome Processing," *Proc. 27th Int'l Conf. System Sciences* (HICSS-27), IEEE CS Press, Los Alamitos, Calif., Vol. 5, 1994, pp. 150–159.

Greiner, A., Pécheux, F., "Alliance: A Complete Set of CAD Tools for Teaching VLSI Design," *Proc. 2nd Eurochip Conference*, 1992.

6

Parallel Multi-Wavefront Algorithms for Pattern-Based Processing of Object-Oriented Databases

Stanley Y. W. Su, Yaw-Huei Chen, and Herman Lam

Database Systems Research and Development Center
Department of Computer and Information Sciences
University of Florida, Gainesville, Florida

ABSTRACT

The newly developed object-oriented database management systems provide rich facilities for the modeling and processing of structural as well as behavioral properties of complex application objects. Although some initial benchmark tests have shown that some implemented O-O systems can outperform the existing relational systems, their inherent generality, the new functionalities to be added to these systems as they continue to evolve, and the demand for high performance in many application domains would require that these software systems be implemented on parallel-processing hardware systems. Efficient parallel algorithms and architectures would be needed to meet the performance requirement for processing large O-O databases. In our previous work, we have shown that processing OODBs can be viewed as the manipulation of patterns of object associations. In this chapter, we present several parallel multi-wavefront algorithms based on two approaches, that is, identification and elimination approaches, to verify association patterns specified in queries. The identification approach identifies objects that satisfy an association-pattern specification, whereas the elimination approach eliminates objects that do not satisfy the specification. Both approaches allow more processors to operate concurrently on a query than the traditional tree-structured query processing approach, thus introducing a higher degree of parallelism in query processing. A formal proof of the correctness of the elimination approach is given, and a parallel-elimination algorithm for processing tree queries is presented in this chapter. Some simulation results are provided to compare the performance of the identification approach with the elimination approach. We also describe the implementation of a parallel query processor using the identification approach, running on a four-node Transputer network.

6.1 INTRODUCTION

Traditional database systems are mainly designed for supporting business applications. For supporting many new data-intensive applications, such as CAD/CAM, CASE, office information, military command and control, and so on, the needed modeling capabilities and system functionalities have grown beyond what traditional database systems can handle effectively and efficiently. Object-oriented database management systems, which provide better structural and behavioral abstraction facilities, give a promising alternative to manage data in such applications. Since the early 1980s, the field of OODBs has been growing rapidly and has become a major area of research. Many OODBMSs have been implemented, including ODE,[1] EXODUS,[2] O_2,[3] ObServer,[4] ORION,[5] POSTGRES,[6] OSAM*,[7] and Iris.[8] Other OODBMSs have become commercially available, including GemStone from Servio Logic, Vbase and ONTOS from Ontologic, ObjectStore from Object Design, VERSANT from Versant Object Technologies, and Objectivity/DB from Objectivity. An OODBMS provides rich structural and behavioral abstraction facilities for the user to model complex data-intensive applications. Some initial benchmark tests (for example, SUN Microsystem benchmark) have shown that some implemented OODBMSs can outperform the existing relational systems. However, the inherent generality of OODBMSs, the added functionalities to those systems as they continue to evolve, and the continuous demand for high performance would require that they be implemented on parallel systems to meet present and future application requirements. In order to achieve high performance, efficient parallel algorithms and architectures are needed to support large and complex OODB processing.

As pointed out by Jenq,[9] most existing techniques developed for relational query processing can be applied directly to object-oriented queries against a single target class. For example, the tree-based query processing techniques for relational databases are also used in OODBs.[9-12] The traditional tree-based query processing has two potential problems: (1) it may generate large intermediate results and (2) the tree representation implies an inherent sequential bottom-up evaluation of operators even if some pipelining query processing strategy is employed. In distributed query processing, the semijoin operator[13] is used to reduce the sizes of relations and/or intermediate results. Most research efforts have focused on the problem of finding the optimal execution order of semijoins to reduce the data transmission cost.[14-19] However, this tree-based execution of semijoins may lose the opportunity for exploiting some types of parallelism, such as interoperator parallelism and interquery parallelism. New semijoin execution strategies have been proposed to improve the performance, by executing all applicable semijoins on the relations at a time,[20] and by adding a backward reduction phase to the semijoin and pipelining the execution.[21] Since all reduced relations and/or intermediate results are sent to a final site to perform a multiway join, a large amount of data is transmitted in the network, and the final site may eventually be overwhelmed by the incoming data and become a bottleneck in the distributed query processing. Recently, researchers have begun to understand the alternative query-tree organizations in various database environments.[22-24] In addition to the problems associated with the tree-based query processing, queries in OODBs are usually complex, and are required to retain multiple target classes. Therefore, novel parallel algorithms based on general graph representations are needed for large OODBs.

In this work, all things of interest to an application (for example, physical objects, abstract things, events, and so forth) are uniformly defined as objects. Objects that have the same structural and behavioral properties are grouped together to form an object class that defines the abstract data type for these objects. Furthermore, classes can be associated with one another through different types of associations (for example, aggregation, generalization, and so forth) and the objects of these classes are thus interrelated through these associations. Therefore, an OODB can be viewed as a network of objects interconnected through associations and can be accessed and manipulated by pattern specifications and verifications.[25, 26] We call the operations of finding connected objects from one class to another *association operations*. One of the operators is *Associate*, which constructs a new pattern by concatenating two operand patterns. In the literature, several similar operators have been proposed to find related objects or tuples, such as *class traversal*,[5, 9, 12] *functional join*,[27, 28] *pointer-based join*,[29, 30, 31] and *assembly*.[32] Since a chain query (or a long path of associated object classes) and tree- or network-structured queries are commonly specified in OODB applications, it is important to have a query processor that can exploit interoperator parallelism for queries composed of many Associate operators.

A two-phase query processing strategy, which consists of a context-generating phase and a result-processing phase, has been proposed to avoid accessing and processing a large amount of (sometimes unnecessary) data.[33, 34] In the first phase, objects of interest in the database are identified in the form of object identifiers (OIDs). Then, system- and/or user-defined functions are executed on the objects selected during the first phase to produce the final result. Since only OIDs are processed and propagated in the first phase and the retrieval of sizable descriptive data is postponed until the second phase when the relevant objects have been identified, this technique can reduce or eliminate the I/O bottleneck found in large OODB systems.

This chapter presents two basic pattern-based query processing approaches for verifying object association patterns—an identification approach and an elimination approach. The identification approach, which identifies objects that satisfy the given pattern, has been researched and reported by Thakore.[34, 35] We shall describe a modified identification algorithm to serve as a contrast to the elimination approach. Instead of identifying objects that satisfy the specification, the elimination approach eliminates objects that do not satisfy an association pattern specification given in a query.[36] Queries with tree-structured query graphs can be solved by either the identification approach or the elimination approach. Parallel architecture and data structure are used to represent the OODBs, and multiple wavefront algorithms based on the two approaches are provided.

In Section 2, we illustrate the concepts of data modeling and pattern-based query processing in OODBs by describing the schema graph, the object graph, and the query graph. Then, the query processing problem is formally defined as a special subgraph mapping problem. In Section 3, the identification approach and a multiple wavefront parallel algorithm based on this approach are presented. In Section 4, we describe the elimination approach for evaluating tree-structured queries and give a proof of the correctness of this approach. In Section 5, we present a parallel elimination algorithm for an asynchronous parallel system. The data structure used for storing objects and their associations is also described. In Section 6, we present some simulation results and quantitatively compare the two multiple wavefront query processing algorithms. In Section 7, we present the implementation of a parallel query processor, which is based on the identification approach, on a four-node Transputer network. A summary is given in Section 8.

6.2 QUERY PROCESSING IN OODBS

6.2.1 The Object-Oriented View of Databases

An OODB can be depicted as two graphs—a schema graph and an object graph. In the schema graph (that is, the intensional database), the database is viewed as a collection of

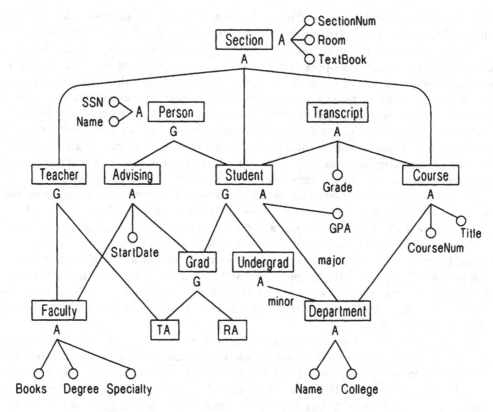

Figure 1. Schema graph of a university database.

object classes interrelated through various types of associations. The schema graph of an example university database is shown in Figure 1.

Rectangle vertices represent entity classes and circle vertices represent domain classes. Objects in entity classes are entities of interest in an application domain. They are assigned with a system-wide unique object identifier (OID). Objects in a domain class are self-naming (for example, integer 2, age 5, and so on) and serve as values for defining or describing other entity or domain class objects. Associations among object classes are represented by edges in the schema graph, and all edges are bi-directional. The edges labeled by G (for Generalization associations) denote superclass-subclass relationships between classes. The edges labeled by A (for Aggregation associations) denote descriptive attributes or object references.

In the object graph (that is, the extensional database), the database is viewed as a collection of objects, grouped together in object classes, and interrelated through type-less associations. The associations are type-less at the extensional level because once a schema has been defined, the user does not have to be concerned about the association types in the formulation of queries since their semantics are constraints of object manipulations enforced by the OODBMS. Vertices in the object graph represent object instances in the database and each edge represents the association between two interrelated object instances. An object instance is a representation of an object (uniquely identified by an OID) in a class. An object instance is composed of an instance identification (IID), the descriptive data of the object instance, and references to other object instances. An IID can be represented by the concatenation of OID and class ID. For example, an object graph of a part of the university database is shown in Figure 2.

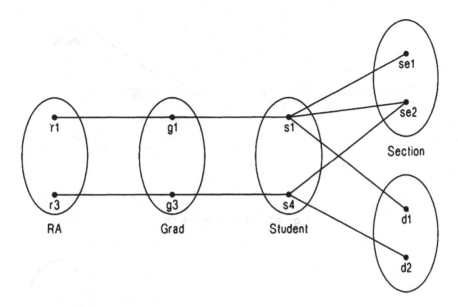

Figure 2. Object graph *OG*.

The *Student* class contains four object instances: *s1*, *s2*, *s3*, and *s4*. Student object instance *s1* is associated with *Grad* object instance *g1*, which in turn is associated with *RA* object instance *r1*; representing that student *s1* is a graduate student and holds an RA position. Student object instance *s1* is also associated with *Section* object instances *se1*, *se2*, and *Department* object instance *d1*. This represents that student *s1* majors in department *d1* and currently takes courses offered as sections *se1* and *se2*. Note that Student object instance *s2* is not associated with any instance of class Grad, which means that student *s2* is not a graduate student.

6.2.2 Pattern-Based Query Processing

In our work on an object-oriented query language[37, 38] and its underlying algebra,[26, 39, 40] we have shown that an OODB can be accessed and manipulated by pattern specifications and verifications. The user can use the query language to specify a complex pattern of object-class associations (linear structure, tree structure with *AND/OR* branches, loops, and so on) as search conditions for identifying those object instances of the corresponding classes that satisfy the pattern. The specified pattern is a subgraph of the schema graph and we call such a graph a *query graph*. For example, the query graph containing classes RA, Grad, Student, Section, and Department as shown in Figure 3 can represent the query "*For all sections, find the majors of those research assistants who are taking these sections.*"

In the query graph, a circle represents a class and an edge represents that the instances of two adjacent classes must be associated with each other. Assuming that the object graph shown in Figure 2 is the extensional representation of the portion of the university database referenced by the query and all branches in the query graph are *AND* branches, instances that satisfy the query pattern are retained in the resulting subdatabase as shown in Figure 4.

This operation completes the first phase of a two-phase query processing strategy.[33, 34] The second phase involves invoking system-defined (for example, retrieve, update, and so

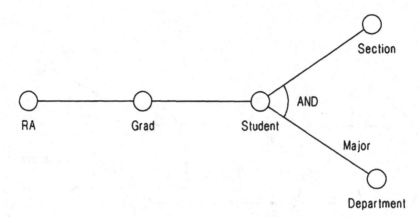

Figure 3.   Query graph *QG*.

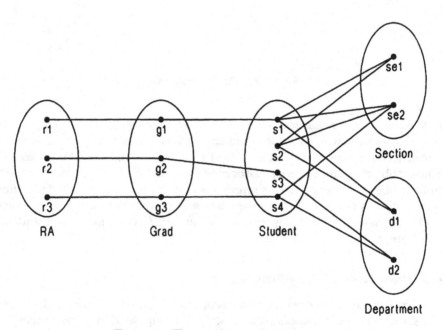

Figure 4.   The resulting subdatabase.

on) and/or user-defined (for example, purchase a part, hire an employee, and so on) operations to these object instances via message passing.

Since query patterns specified by the user can be very complex and pattern searches have to be carried out in a potentially very large extensional database, the first phase of query processing is most time-consuming. In a sequential algorithm to perform a pattern search, a traversal of each object instance through its association links would be necessary to verify that it satisfies a search condition. Often, after a long traversal of a path in an extensional database, it is found that the partially matched pattern does not satisfy the entire search pattern. In that case, the partially matched pattern needs to be taken out of the final result by deleting those object instances and association links that form the pattern. For example, as shown in Figures 2 and 3, if we evaluate the example query starting from class RA, we will mark object instances *r1, r2, r3* in RA, *g1, g2, g3* in Grad, and *s1, s3, s4* in Student when we reach the class Student. After checking the connection information in Student, we find out that $s3$ is not connected to any object in Section and therefore the partially matched pattern $r2—g2—s3$ needs to be deleted through a backward traversal. This deletion of partially matched patterns is called the *ripple-back effect*. Due to this effect, a sequential process cannot identify the correct answer with a single path traversal of the object graph. It is inefficient to trace and delete partially matched patterns that have been previously selected. Moreover, in order to navigate an object graph efficiently, it is necessary to find the optimal traversal plan. Thus, efficient algorithms for pattern verification are needed to support query processing in OODBs.

6.2.3 Definition

The schema graph of an object-oriented database D is defined as $SG_D(C_D, A_D)$, where C_D = $\{Ci\}$ is a set of vertices representing object classes; $A_D = \{(Ci, Cj)\}$ is a set of edges and each edge (Ci, Cj) represents an association between classes Ci and Cj. The object graph of D is defined as $OG_D(O_D, E_D)$, where $O_D = \{Oi_p\}$ is a set of vertices, each of which, Oi_p, represents the pth object instance in class Ci; $E_D = \{(Oi_p, Oj_q)\}$ is a set of edges representing associations among object instances and each edge (Oi_p, Oj_q) specifies that the pth instance in class Ci is related to the qth instance in class Cj through an association between classes Ci and Cj.

We assume that we are given a query Q issued against the database D. The part of D referenced in the query contains k object classes, m association links among classes, and n object instances. The query graph of Q is defined as an undirected graph $QG(C, A)$, where C = $\{Ci\}$ is a set of vertices representing the k object classes and $A = \{(Ci, Cj)\}$ is a set of edges representing the m associations among those object classes, and we assume that all branches in QG are AND branches in the example we shall use in this chapter. The portion of D referenced by Q can be represented by an undirected object graph $OG(O, E)$. In this graph, $O = \{Oi_p\}$, where $Oi_p \in Ci$ and $Ci \in C$, is a set of vertices representing the n objects in the k referenced classes, and $E = \{(Oi_p, Oj_q)\}$, where $Oi_p \in Ci$, $Oj_q \in Cj$, and $(Ci, Cj) \in A$, is a set of edges representing the links between the n objects. Note that the object graph OG is a subgraph of OG_D and the query graph QG is a subgraph of SG_D. We want to identify efficiently all objects that satisfy the given query pattern.

The query processing problem is equivalent to a graph problem of finding the union of all subgraphs of $OG(O, E)$ such that each subgraph can be mapped to the query graph $QG(C, A)$. For each such subgraph $OG'(O', E')$, the vertex set O' is a subset of O and contains k vertices from k different classes in C and the edge set E' with m edges is a subset of E. In addition, for any two vertices in O', Oi_p and Oj_q, $(Oi_p, Oj_q) \in E'$ if and only if $(Ci, Cj) \in A$. Thus, the result of query Q is a union of some subgraphs of the object graph OG and we can transform the query processing problem into a graph problem. It should be noted that we consider only query graphs with *AND* branches in this chapter, but the problem of processing query graphs with *AND/OR* branches can be defined in a similar fashion.

6.3 IDENTIFICATION APPROACH

Identification and elimination are two general processing approaches that can be applied to solving the pattern-based query processing problem. The former approach was introduced in our earlier work.[34, 35] We shall describe a modification of it in this section and use it as a contrast to the new elimination approach to be presented in Sections 4 and 5. Both parallel algorithms to be introduced for processing pattern-based queries are multiple wavefront algorithms. They take advantage of the structural properties of query graphs and eliminate the complexity of the ripple-back effect.

6.3.1 Architecture and Data Organization

The multiple wavefront algorithms are supported by an asynchronous parallel-processing system that consists of a set of processing nodes interconnected by an interconnection network. Each processing node contains a processing unit, main memory, and secondary storage devices. Processing nodes do not share memory or a global clock; they can only communicate by sending and receiving messages. The communication channels are bi-directional. We assume that no messages are lost and that messages are always received in the order in which they are sent. Different interconnection networks can be used to implement the proposed parallel algorithms. Multiple-processor systems with a high degree of connectivity per node (for example, nCube and Hypercube) would be ideal, since the schema graph can be mapped to the processing nodes in a fashion so that connectivity among classes will match as closely as possible to the physical connections of the processing nodes, and communication and data transfer time among processing nodes can be reduced.

In Thakore's work,[35] in order to localize retrieval, manipulation, and user-defined operations and to reduce the overall communication among processors, all the data associated with an object class are initially grouped together to form a cluster. Data associated with their objects are first vertically partitioned[10, 41-43] into binary columns (IID, attribute) so that the values of a specific attribute can be accessed during query processing without having to move unnecessary data from the disk. These vertical partitions are then partitioned horizontally so that the data cluster of an object class having a large number of instances is divided into multiple clusters. The horizontally partitioned clusters are then grouped together to form cluster sets, which may contain clusters belonging to the same or different object classes. The number of cluster sets is equal to the number of physical processors to which these cluster sets are to be mapped. Computation time and communication time of these clusters are estimated based on the data sizes and semantic associations among classes, and are taken into consideration in forming the cluster sets so that the processing time for these cluster sets can be balanced. Heuristics for near-optimal mapping of these cluster sets to the available physical processors have been studied and reported by Thakore.[35]

In this work, since the data clustering, partitioning, and mapping strategies can be applied to both wavefront algorithms to be considered and compared in this chapter, we shall use a simpler data organization and mapping (that is, vertical partition, but without horizontal partition and load balancing and processor-per-class mapping). The associations of instances between two associated object classes can be represented by an adjacency matrix. The rows and columns of the adjacency matrix are represented by two sets of adjacency lists of IIDs in the two classes, one list for each instance. The adjacency list of IIDs for an instance is a list of objects that are associated with it. In the parallel algorithm based on the identification approach, the set of adjacency lists are stored with the instances that they represent. The data structure shown in Figure 5 represents the object graph of the part of the university database referenced in the example query.

The data and methods defined in the five object classes—RA, Grad, Student, Section, and Department—are stored in processors $P1$, $P2$, $P3$, $P4$, and $P5$, respectively. For example, two sets of adjacency lists for Grad instances,

$$g1 \rightarrow r1 \; ; g2 \rightarrow r2; g3 \rightarrow r3$$

and

$$g1 \rightarrow s1 \; ; g2 \rightarrow s3; g3 \rightarrow s3$$

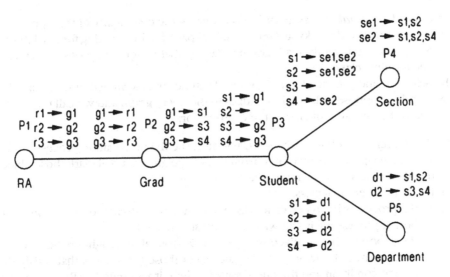

Figure 5. Data structures for the identification algorithm.

are stored in Processor *P2* to specify explicitly their associations with RA and Student instances, respectively. Note that the explicitly stored adjacency lists for each object instance can be viewed as precomputed joins in relational databases. [43, 44]

The above data organization and processor-per-class mapping strategy, although they do not achieve load balancing among physical processors, have a number of advantages. First, methods and constraint rules associated with each class, and applicable to the object instances of that class, do not have to be replicated in multiple processors. Second, multiple queries that may access and operate on different object classes can be executed in parallel by the network of highly connected processors. Third, if object instances of all classes are horizontally partitioned and stored in overlapping sets of processors of different sizes, communications among classes, which are fundamental operations in association-pattern verification, will have to be directed to these different-sized sets of processors. This requirement will make very complicated the communication and control of the network system with a regular interconnection.

6.3.2 The Parallel-Identification Algorithm

The approach of identifying tuples that satisfy some search condition has been commonly applied in relational databases. To reduce the number of tuples involved in the evaluation of a query, semijoin operations can be used to identify tuples that have attribute values satisfying the join predicates. It has been shown that relational queries with tree-structured query graphs can be processed using semijoins.[13] The semijoin program evaluates a tree query in two passes to find the tuples in all the relations that satisfy the query. It first performs semijoins in a breadth-first, leaf-to-root order in every edge of the query graph and then applies semijoins from the root down the tree toward the leaves.

The same identification approach can be used in OODBs. A parallel multiple wavefront algorithm replaces the sequential, two-pass algorithm. The algorithm to be described below is applicable to linear and tree-structured queries. Wavefront algorithms for query structures with loops (that is, a general network structure) are also available.[35] The object classes referenced by a query (that is, those in a query graph) are classified into two types. Classes with more than one edge in the query graph are called *nonterminal classes*. Otherwise, they are called *terminal classes*. In order to eliminate the complexity of the ripple-back effect, this algorithm avoids backward sequential propagation by initiating forward IID propagation processes concurrently at all terminal classes (that is, at the processors that hold the data of the terminal classes).

The selection and propagation of IIDs are dynamically determined in each class by the following rules. Suppose a class C has i edges in the query graph and we call the processor that contains the instances of class C the C processor:

(1) If C is a terminal class, processor C will start the IID propagation process. If processor C receives the stream of IIDs from its only neighbor, it will mark those objects as qualified objects and then terminate.
(2) If C is a nonterminal class,
    a) if C processor has received less than $(i\text{-}1)$ incoming streams of IIDs from its neighboring processors, it will wait for more streams of IIDs to come;
    b) if C processor has received streams of IIDs from all its neighbors but one, it will process the $(i\text{-}1)$ streams of IIDs and select those C instances that satisfy the selection condition and the query pattern; then, it will send the IIDs of the associated instances of the only remaining neighboring class to the corresponding processor;
    c) if C processor receives the ith (that is, the last) incoming streams of IIDs, it will form the final result of the query for class C and then pass the IIDs of those associated instances of all other neighbors to these neighbors except the sender of the ith stream.

Each propagation of IIDs forms a wavefront. Multiple wavefronts will start simultaneously at the terminal nodes and propagate IIDs according to the above rules. Because all branches in the query graph are *AND* branches, a processor cannot propagate IIDs until it has received and treated the $(i\text{-}1)$ incoming streams of IIDs. This waiting condition is added to the algorithm presented by Thakore[34] to avoid misidentifying some unqualified instances under some data conditions. Different from the semijoin approach reported by Bernstein[13] and the active graph model reported by Bic,[44] this parallel algorithm is not restricted to a single root node. Rather, the identification process starts from multiple nodes, thus rendering more flexibility and efficiency.

Using the example query and database shown in Figures 3 and 5, the execution of the parallel-identification algorithm is given in Figure 6. We assume that the propagation of IIDs in each step will take one time unit. The selected instances in all the classes and the IIDs in transit are shown in Figure 6 for each elapsed time unit. It should be obvious to the reader that this parallel algorithm avoids the problem of sequential ripple-back effect and produces the correct resulting subdatabase shown in Figure 4.

6.4 SOLVING PATTERN-BASED QUERIES BY ELIMINATION

An alternative to the identification approach is the elimination approach. Instead of selecting qualified object instances and propagating associated IIDs to its neighbors, algorithms based on the elimination approach delete from the object graph any instances that do not satisfy the search pattern. When an object instance is deleted from the object graph, all its edges are also deleted. This process may create new unqualified instances, causing the elimination process to be repeated until all instances that should be deleted have been deleted. It is shown in this section that tree-structured queries can be solved using the elim-

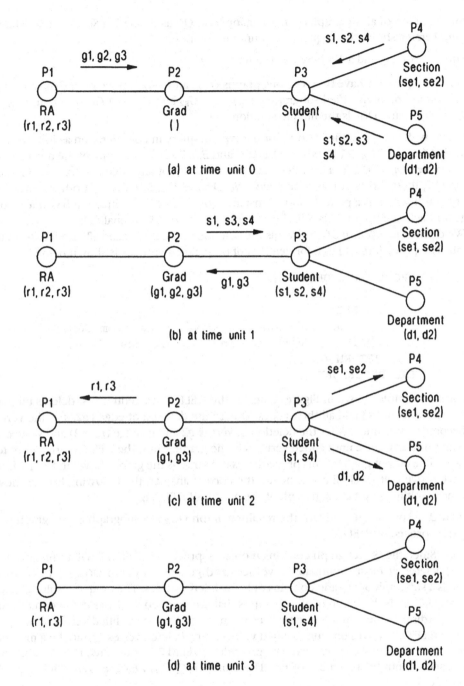

Figure 6. Execution of the identification algorithm.

ination approach. We present this approach more formally below and show that this approach will produce the correct result.

Let $OG = (O, E)$ be the undirected object graph of the part of database D that is referenced by query Q; and let $QG = (C, A)$, in which $C = \{C1, C2, \ldots, Ck\}$, be the query graph of Q. Also, let $OG_R = (O_R, E_R)$, where $O_R \subseteq O$ and $E_R \subseteq E$, be the resulting graph of query

Q (or the union of all subgraphs that are mapped to QG as defined in Section 2.3). The following Lemma shows that a query has a unique solution.

Lemma: For a Q and a D, there exists a unique OG_R.

Proof: Suppose we have two resulting graphs OG_{R1} and OG_{R2}. Since both OG_{R1} and OG_{R2} are the union of all qualified subgraphs, $OG_{R1} \subseteq OG_{R2}$ and $OG_{R1} \supseteq OG_{R2}$. Then, $OG_{R1} = OG_{R2} = OG_R$, and OG_R is the unique solution. $\square$

We now define a qualified vertex for the type of query in consideration as follows. Suppose that $OG_{sub} = (O_{sub}, E_{sub})$, where $O_{sub} \subseteq O$ and $E_{sub} \subseteq E$, is a subgraph of the object graph OG. A vertex $Oi_p \in O_{sub}$ is a qualified vertex in OG_{sub} if, for any edge $(Ci, Cx) \in A$ in query graph QG, there exists at least one edge $(Oi_p, Ox_y) \in E_{sub}$ in OG_{sub}. In other words, the query graph serves as a pattern, and an instance (or vertex) is qualified if it has at least one edge for each neighboring class in the pattern; otherwise it is unqualified.

We define the *deletion of a vertex* as the deletion of the vertex and all its edges from the graph. The procedure DELETE for deletion of unqualified vertices is shown below.

```
PROCEDURE: DELETE(OG)
    OG_out = OG;
    REPEAT
        delete unqualified vertices from OG_out;
    UNTIL all vertices in OG_out are qualified;
    RETURN OG_out;
END PROCEDURE;
```

For the example shown in Figures 2 and 3, the DELETE procedure first deletes unqualified vertices $s2$ and $s3$ and all their edges. Due to the deletion of edge $(g2, s3)$, the vertex $g2$ becomes unqualified. After the deletion of vertex $g2$ and its edge $(r2, g2)$ and vertex $r2$, it cannot find any more unqualified vertices in the graph. Thus, the DELETE procedure terminates. The output graph of this procedure is the same as the graph shown in Figure 4. Before we prove that DELETE can generate the correct answer, the following lemma shows that the resulting graph is a subgraph of the output of DELETE.

Lemma 2:   For any QG and OG, the resulting graph OG_R is a subgraph of the graph generated by procedure DELETE.

Proof: Since the object graph contains n objects, procedure DELETE will terminate after having deleted at most n unqualified vertices and generate a graph $OG_{out} = (O_{out}, E_{out})$, which is a subgraph of OG and contains only qualified vertices. The unique resulting graph $OG_R = (O_R, E_R)$ is the union of all subgraphs that are mapped to QG as defined in Section 2.3. According to the definition, every vertex in O_R must be a qualified vertex. Since procedure DELETE removes only unqualified vertices, any deleted vertex cannot be a member of O_R. In addition, any edge removed by procedure DELETE is connected to an unqualified vertex and cannot be a member of E_R. Therefore, $O_R \subseteq O_{out}$, $E_R \subseteq E_{out}$ and OG_R is a subgraph of OG_{out}. $\square$

Lemma 2 says that OG_R is a subgraph of OG_{out} for any query graph QG. The following theorem shows that if we restrict QG to acyclic graphs, then $OG_{out} = OG_R$.

Theorem 1:   For any Q and D, if QG is acyclic, then Q can be evaluated by deleting all unqualified instances.

Proof: Procedure DELETE generates a graph OG_{out} by deleting all unqualified vertices in OG. As shown in Lemma 1 and Lemma 2, $OG_R = (O_R, E_R)$ is a unique solution to Q and is a

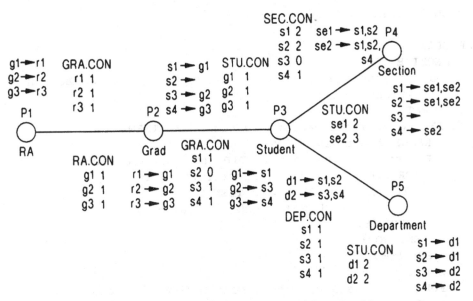

Figure 7.   Data structures for the elimination algorithm.

subgraph of $OG_{out} = (O_{out}, E_{out})$. Assume that vertex Oi_p is a member of O_{out} but is not a member of O_R. Since every vertex in O_{out} is qualified, we can start to traverse the query tree from Oi_p and pick one vertex from each class in the query to form a tree. The tree just created is a subgraph of OG and can be mapped to the query graph as defined in Section 2.3. This contradicts the assumption. Therefore, every vertex is a member of both O_{out} and O_R, and $O_{out} = O_R$. Moreover, since $O_{out} = O_R$, we cannot find an edge that is a member of E_{out} but is not a member of E_R. Thus, $E_{out} = E_R$ and we can conclude that $OG_{out} = OG_R$. $\square$

6.5 THE PARALLEL ELIMINATION ALGORITHM

The elimination-based parallel algorithm uses a different data structure. First, the opposite set of adjacency lists are stored in a class. For example, Figure 7 depicts the data structures used in five processors that represent our example query in Section 2. The adjacency lists for Grad instances that are adjacent to RA instances

$$g1 \rightarrow r1 \; ; g2 \rightarrow r2; g3 \rightarrow r3$$

are stored in processor $P1$, which holds all the data and methods of class RA, and the adjacency lists for RA instances and Student instances are stored in processor $P2$, which holds the data and methods of class Grad. Note that the adjacency lists are stored from the other side of the links in each processor just opposite to the identification approach described before. This reversed storage structure reserves the same connection information as in the original adjacency lists and is used only for processing convenience.

Using an integer array to register the number of connections of each instance is another difference in the data organization for the elimination algorithm. For each class association, one integer array CON is associated with each object class as shown in Figure 7. These arrays are used for storing temporary data and the output of the algorithm. Each element of the array is corresponding to one instance of the class stored in the processor, and the integer value is the number of remaining connections between that instance and the instances of the associated class. For example, as shown in Figure 7, initially the elements of array

```
PROCEDURE ELIM()
    . . .
PAR BEGIN
P1: RECEIVE (QUERY);
      mark object instances that satisfy the local selection
      conditions as qual_for_sel;
    REPEAT
      IF the previous message is not QUERY THEN
        RECEIVE (sender, IIDs);
        FOR every instance p in IIDs DO //delete links
          FOR every q in list sender.LIST[p] DO
            IF sender.CON[q] > 0 THEN
              sender.CON[q] ← sender.CON[q] - 1;
            END IF;
          END FOR;
        END FOR;
      END IF;
      FOR every instance r not deleted from this class DO
        IF (r is unqualified) OR (r is not qual_for_sel) THEN
          FOR every associated class i DO
            IF i.CON[r] > 0 THEN
              i.CON[r] ← 0;
              append r to i.delete_list;
            END IF;
          END FOR;
          mark r as deleted;
        END IF;
      END FOR;
      FOR every associated class i except the sender DO
        SEND (i, i.delete_list);
      END FOR;
    UNTIL FALSE; //detecting termination is described in the text
P2: the same as in P1
    . . .
Pk: the same as in P1
PAR END;
    . . .
END PROCEDURE;
```

Figure 8.   The parallel elimination algorithm.

SEC.CON in class Student, which represent the connections to class Section, have values 2, 2, 0, and 1 for instances $s1$, $s2$, $s3$, and $s4$, respectively. Note that this CON array can be created locally by reading the reversely stored adjacency lists.

Based on the asynchronous architecture and the data structure described above, we can easily convert the DELETE procedure into a parallel algorithm. The checking and deleting tasks can be done locally in every processor and the iteration process can be accomplished in the network by a propagation process. Whenever one processor deletes an object that has connections with other objects in its neighboring processors, the processor propagates the connection information to the neighboring processors and then the processors that receive the messages will start their own checking and deleting procedures. This propagation process will continue until no more elimination can be found.

The parallel algorithm is given as procedure ELIM in Figure 8. All k processors that participate in processing the given query Q run the same segment of codes in parallel. Initially, all processors are idle and waiting for messages. There are two kinds of messages: QUERY and IIDs. The QUERY message sent by a controller contains the query pattern of the receiving processor and the local selection conditions. The controller, which handles the user interface and the control of the parallel algorithm, can be either a host computer connected to the system or any processor with I/O devices within the system. The controller procedure is not shown in Figure 8. The query pattern sent to every processor is a list of adjacent classes of that object class. After receiving the QUERY message, each processor saves the query information received and becomes active.

An active processor checks its CON arrays for deleting instances and then propagates the elimination information, if any exists, to its neighboring classes. According to the definition of a qualified object described in Section 4, an object instance needs to be deleted if it has corresponding elements with zero values in some CON arrays and with nonzero values in other CON arrays. When the CON array element of a deleted instance has a nonzero value, we assign 0 to the CON array element and send the deleted instance's IID to the associated class (that is, its processor). After a processor finishes all the elimination and propagation tasks, it becomes idle again. For example, as shown in Figures 7 and 9(a), both instances $s2$ and $s3$ need to be deleted in class Student because GRA.CON$[s2]$ = 0 and SEC.CON$[s3]$ = 0. After assigning 0 to SEC.CON$[s2]$, DEP.CON$[s2]$, GRA.CON$[s3]$, and DEP.CON$[s3]$, processor $P3$ sends elimination message $s2$ to processors $P4$ and $P5$, $s3$ to processors $P2$ and $P5$, and then becomes idle and waits for new messages.

When a processor receives a list of IIDs from a neighboring processor, it obtains the adjacency list for each received IID from the set of adjacency lists that corresponds to the sending processor. For each local IID in the adjacency list, the processor decreases the value of the corresponding CON element by 1. After processing all the received IIDs, the processor starts the checking process described above. For example, as shown in Figure 9(b), after receiving IID $s3$ from processor $P3$, $P2$ finds that $s3$ connects to $g2$ and then it decreases STU.CON$[g2]$ from 1 to 0. At this time, $P2$ finds out that $g2$ is an unqualified object. It assigns a 0 to RA.CON$[g2]$ and sends an elimination message $g2$ to $P1$. Thus, the deletion wavefront will continue to propagate until it cannot find any more unqualified instances. Note that the processors can process the received IIDs in a pipeline fashion and increase the degree of parallelism.

An asynchronous parallel algorithm terminates if and only if all processors are idle and no message is in transit. The problem of detecting termination is common to all asynchronous parallel algorithms. Many proposed methods can be applied to detect the termination condition in the algorithm; Dijkstra and Huang offer some examples.[45, 46] However, because only tree-structured queries are considered in this research, each processor can determine the completion of the algorithm by simply counting the number of incoming markers, which are issued by processors that start the wavefronts. In the parallel elimination algorithm, all processors start the deletion wavefronts and propagate markers to all its neighboring processors. Therefore, each processor executing the elimination algorithm can complete its computation after receiving the same number of markers as the number of processors participating in the query.

Since the algorithm only removes all vertices that do not satisfy the pattern, as proved in Theorem 1, the procedure ELIM in Figure 8 can identify all objects that satisfy a tree-struc-

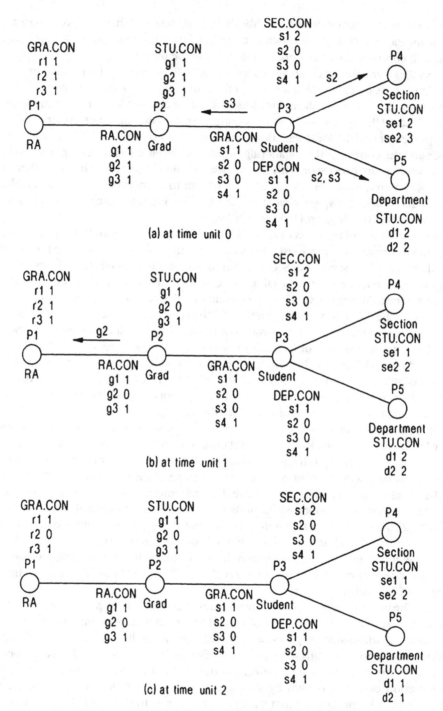

Figure 9.   Execution of the elimination algorithm.

tured query. Each processor in this algorithm becomes active after receiving a message, and it can start processing local data without waiting for any other message. Therefore, one of the deadlock-necessary conditions,[47] that is, *hold and wait*, cannot be true and the algorithm will never get into a deadlock situation. Also, this algorithm will always terminate because there are at most n vertices that can be deleted and the detection method mentioned above will detect the termination condition.

The number of messages and time complexity are frequently used for measuring the cost of an algorithm. The dominant portion of this algorithm is the propagation process. In the worst case, we may need to delete all n object instances. One processor may have to send out as many as $(k-1)$ messages for deleting one instance. Therefore, in the worst case this algorithm issues $O(k * n)$ messages. If a time unit in this analysis includes local delays, processing times, message queue delays, and message transmission times, the algorithm running in a fully connected k-processor system can evaluate a tree-structured query in $O(k)$ time units.

6.6 SIMULATION RESULTS

We have implemented both the parallel identification and parallel elimination algorithms for tree queries using discrete-event simulation techniques on a SUN workstation. The database is represented by IIDs and the links among them. The average connectivity of each object instance can be specified and the simulation program will randomly generate the links accordingly. We assume that the schema graph of the database is perfectly mapped into the simulated processor network. Each object class is stored in one processor and there exists a direct channel between two adjacent processors. By adjusting the communication delay times in interprocessor communication, we can account for the case when this assumption does not hold. By varying the data, query, and system parameters, the total execution time for identifying instances that satisfy the query are obtained and the effects of these parameters are studied. In our simulation, the program actually identifies instances and propagates information, so that it can use the timing data to determine the execution time of the algorithms.

Due to the fact that links between instances in a real database are sparse and can be stored in small adjacency lists, we assume that all instances and their connection information are already in the main memory of each processor before the query processing starts. This assumption is made in the analysis for both algorithms, since their I/O time would be about the same due to the similar data structures they use. The total execution time measured in this simulation consists of the processing time and the communication time. A technique used in the implementation of both algorithms for reducing the communication time is to send the complementary set of IIDs if the number of IIDs that needs to be sent is greater than one-half of the total number of instances. The receiver executing these algorithms can then take the complement of the complementary set to obtain the IIDs intended, because the connection information of two associated classes is replicated on both sides.

However, this step generates additional overhead. Due to the use of a CON array in the elimination approach, we can use another technique to reduce the processing time in the elimination algorithm when large number of instances need to be deleted. After receiving the complementary set of IIDs, the receiver executing the elimination algorithm will first set all elements in the corresponding CON array to 0. It will then obtain the adjacency list for each received IID (that is, a qualified instance) and increase the value of the corresponding CON element by 1 for each local IID in the adjacency list. This method can reduce the time for taking the complement and deleting a large number of connections between the two classes.

The default values of some parameters used in this simulation are as follows. The query contains seven classes and each class has 1,000 object instances. The default query diameter (maximal path length in the query graph) is assumed to be 6; that is, the seven classes are

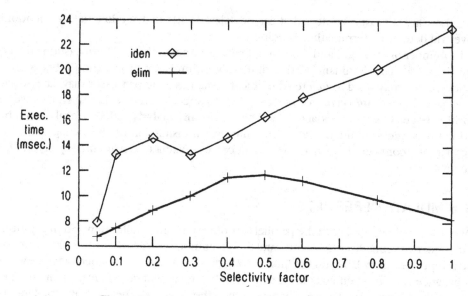

Figure 10.   Execution time versus selectivity factor.

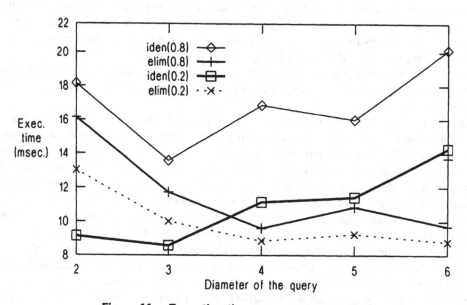

Figure 11.   Execution time versus query diameter.

linearly connected. The default data connectivity is 10, which means that, on an average, an object instance of a class is related to ten instances of an associated class. The communication rate is assumed to be 1 megabyte per second, and each node is an 8-MIPS processor.

The selectivity factor is the ratio of instances in each class that satisfy the local selection condition before the algorithm starts matching the query pattern. Figure 10 shows the total execution time for both algorithms as the selectivity factor is varied.

Due to the technique of sending complementary IIDs when more then one-half of the total IIDs need to be sent, both algorithms will have a peak communication time for sending about half of the IIDs. For the identification algorithm, the communication time increases

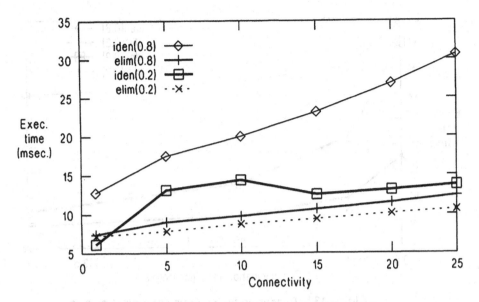

Figure 12. Execution time versus connectivity.

up to the peak around 0.2 selectivity factor and decreases thereafter, while the processing time increases with the selectivity factor. The total execution time of the identification algorithm is the summation of these two time factors and has a local peak around 0.2 selectivity factor as shown in the figure. On the other hand, the elimination algorithm has a peak communication time around 0.5 selectivity factor. Due to the techniques of taking and using the complementary set when many instances need to be deleted, the elimination algorithm has a lower combined execution time even in the lower range of the selectivity factor as shown in the figure. In the rest of the figures we will plot the data for both selectivity factor values 0.2 and 0.8.

Figure 11 shows the execution time of a query with seven classes as the diameter of the query is varied. Generally speaking, when the diameter is long, there will be a longer IID propagation delay. When the diameter is short and the number of classes is kept constant, the query will have more branches and the nodes with branches will have more data to work on. So the performance of a query varies depending on the trade-off between the propagation delay and the possible overloading of those processors with branches. This explains the ups and downs of the curves shown in the figure. Comparing the two approaches, when the diameter is long, the elimination performs better, because it can initiate the elimination wavefronts from every class but the identification algorithm can only initiate the identification wavefronts from a small number of terminal classes.

Figure 12 shows the execution time as the average connectivity of each instance is varied. The processing times of both algorithms increase with increasing connectivities. Due to the peak communication time around selectivity factor value 0.2, the identification algorithm has a local peak execution time in the low range of the connectivity value when the selectivity factor is 0.2. Figure 13 shows the execution time as the communication rate is varied.

The execution times of both algorithms reduce with increasing communication rate. Figure 14 shows the execution time as the processor speed is varied. The result is obvious. A more powerful processor decreases the execution time of both algorithms.

From the above simulation results, it can be observed that the parallel elimination algorithm is better in more cases. However, the identification algorithm is better if a few objects

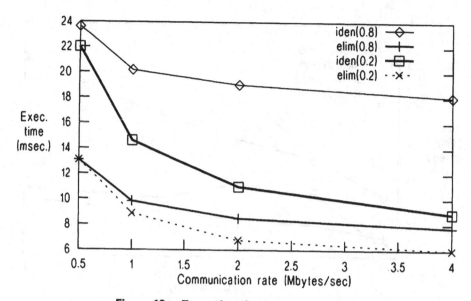

Figure 13.   Execution time versus comunication rate.

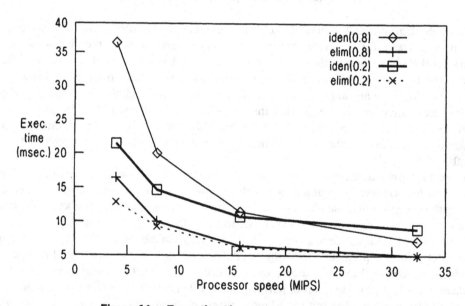

Figure 14.   Execution time versus processor speed.

participate in the identification process and the query has a large number of terminal classes, because the amount of data needing to be processed is dramatically reduced by the low selectivity factor and the low connectivity value, and the algorithm can start the identification wavefronts from all terminal classes simultaneously, thus increasing the degree of parallelism. It is important to note that neither approach is always better; they should be considered as complementary.

6.7 IMPLEMENTATION

In this section, we present the implementation details of a parallel query processor for OODBs, which uses the identification approach for parallel query processing. We first de-

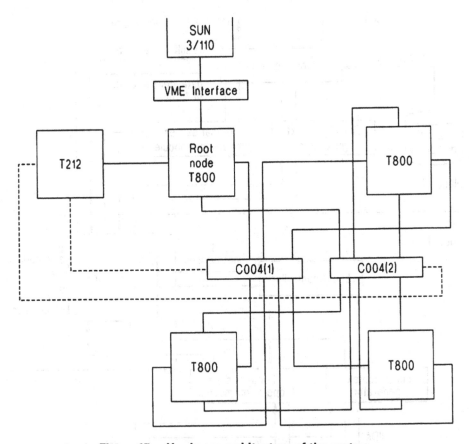

Figure 15.   Hardware architecture of the system.

scribe the hardware and software environment as well as the design choices, and then we present the design and implementation details of the system.

6.7.1 Hardware and Software Environment

The hardware architecture of the system is illustrated in Figure 15. A SUN 3/110 workstation serves as the front-end machine, which provides a friendly user interface and the access to file systems. A Transputer network, consisting of four Transputer modules (TRAMs), is connected to the backplane of the SUN workstation through the VME bus. Each TRAM consists of a T800 Transputer (a 32-bit microprocessor with 11 MIPS) and 1 to 2 Mbytes of RAM. The Transputer network is mounted on a motherboard (B014), which houses two programmable crossbar switches (C004) and a configuration processor (T212). One of the four 20-megabytes-per-second bi-directional serial links of one node, known as the *root node*, is directly connected to the backplane of the front-end machine through the VME interface. Another link of the root node is connected to the configuration processor, which in turn is connected to programmable crossbar switches. This connection facilitates downloading of the configuration code from the front-end machine to the configuration processor. Each of the remaining bi-directional serial links of the four Transputers is connected to a programmable crossbar switch. A connection can be established between any two Transputers by appropriately programming the crossbar switches.

The software platform consists of three major tools: the system-configuration tool, the programming tool, and the program-loading tool. The system-configuration tool, which is a

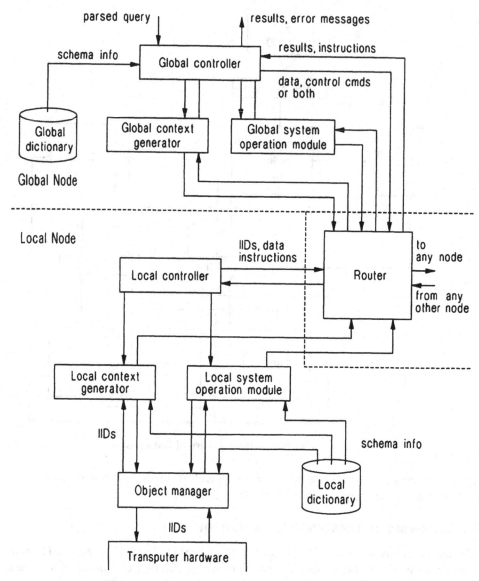

Figure 16.   Software architecture of the system.

part of the Inmos OCCAM toolset, provides a user interface and facility to configure and check the interconnections in the Transputer network. Due to the lack of data abstraction in OCCAM, which is a Transputer-specific language, we choose parallel C as the programming language. The programming tool and the program-loading tool are parts of the Logical Systems C toolset. The former tool consists of C-preprocessor, C-compiler, Assembler, and Linker, and the latter tool provides a facility to download executable machine code onto the root node or onto all nodes present in the system.

6.7.2 Software Architecture

The software architecture of the system is shown in Figure 16. Logically, the software system can be viewed as consisting of two major parts—a global node and a set of local nodes. Each local node is responsible for local processing on one or more object classes and the global node is responsible for the control of execution on all the local nodes. The main components of the global node are Global Controller, Global Context Generator, Global System Operation Module, Global Dictionary, and File Server. The main components of the local node are Local Controller, Object Manager, Local Dictionary, Local Context Generator, and Local System Operation Module. In addition to the logical nodes (global and local nodes), there is also a Router residing at each physical node (T800 TRAM) in the system. Conceptually more than one object class can be mapped into a local node and more than one logical node can be mapped into one physical node. However, in our example we assume that only one class is mapped into one local node and one local node is mapped into one physical node. Hence, the terms of node and object class are interchangeable. Furthermore, the root node contains the global node and a local node. The reason for putting the global node on the root node is that some of the global node I/O operations need a direct access to the link that connects to the server running on the host.

A query is presented to the system in the form of a parsed tree. The Global Controller accepts the query and broadcasts it to those classes that participate in the query. The context generator modules running on the local nodes, upon receiving the query pattern, analyze it to determine the type of the object class. Two types of object classes, terminal and nonterminal, have already been described in Section 6.2. The Local Context Generators asysnchrously initiate and process wavefronts as dictated by the algorithm. The Global Context Generator determines the end of this phase by the messages it received from the local nodes. Following the end of this phase, in which a subdatabase is established, the user- or system-defined operations can be carried out. The system operations are carried out collectively by Local System Operator modules and coordinated by the Global System Operator Module. These operations include Retrieve, Insert Object, Insert Instance, Delete Object, Delete Instance, and Update. The results of the query or error messages, if any, are sent to the Global Controller to be presented to the user. All the operations associated with storage and retrieval of objects into or out of the database are handled by the Object Manager within each local node. All message passing is handled by the Router, which resides on every physical node. All schema and mapping information is supplied by Global and Local Dictionaries. The Global Dictionary contains the mapping and schema information for the database as a whole. Each Local Dictionary contains only the schema information of its local object classes, and their mapping and information pertaining to the association with their neighboring classes.

We describe some key query processor modules necessary to produce the subdatabase as follows. A detailed description of each module can be found in the work of Gorur and Bhethanabotla.[48, 49]

(1) Global Controller: The main function of the Global Controller (GC) is to coordinate the query execution on all nodes. When a query is first presented to the system, the GC identifies the participating object classes and broadcasts the query to the nodes that contain those classes. After this stage, the GC waits in an infinite loop looking for messages that arrive from the local nodes. The messages are processed and then forwarded to appropriate processing blocks depending on the type of the message. Results or error messages are presented to the user, messages indicating end of local processing are forwarded to the Global Context Generator module for further processing, and messages related to system operations, such as Insert Object, Delete Object and so on, are forwarded to the Global System Operator Module.

(2) Local Controller: The Local Controller (LC) is responsible for processing the messages received from the Router on the physical node at which it is present. The mes-

sage packets arriving at the local node are pushed into a FIFO queue. These message packets are then retrieved and processed in the order in which they were received. Every message that arrives at a node needs to be processed depending upon its type. The messages are forwarded to appropriate processing blocks in the same node. The duties of the LC are similar to those of the GC but are restricted to the local node on which it is mapped.

(3) Router: Communication between any two nodes is established by hard and soft channels. Hard channels represent the hard links of the Transputer and facilitate communication between physical nodes. Soft channels facilitate communication between processes running on the same physical node. The Router provides a transparent communication mechanism for processes running anywhere in the system. The Router is implemented as a demon process and has a simple store-and-forward type behavior. There are a number of soft channels and four hard channels (at the maximum) on which messages can arrive at a local node. Both hard and soft input channels are polled in sequence infinitely. When an input is detected on a channel, it is retrieved by reading a fixed-length header followed by a variable-length message. A test on the first field of the header would indicate the destination of the message. If that message was destined for some other physical node, then it is relayed over a hard link. The exact hard link to be used is selected from the routing table, which describes the processor interconnection in the network. However, if the message was destined for the local physical node, then it is pushed onto a FIFO queue for further processing by the LC or GC.

(4) Context Generator: A subdatabase is generated mainly by two modules—Local Context Generator (LCG) module and Global Context Generator (GCG) module. The only function of the GCG module is to process messages that indicate the end of local processing. The GCG keeps a count of these messages and determines the end-of-context generation phase when all the object classes participating in the query have responded. In the local node, the LCG module is mainly responsible for establishing the subdatabase. When a message carrying the query pattern is received at a local node, it is analyzed, and local node behavior is determined to be either terminal or nonterminal. The LCG module does the selection and marking of those selected object instances and then initiates or processes wavefronts of IIDs according to the rules described in Section 3.2.

(5) Dictionary: The Global Dictionary stores the entire schema and class-to-node mapping information. This module is resident on any node that can function as a global node. The Local Dictionary can be viewed as cached subschema information. The purpose of caching schema information at each node is to reduce the number of messages for accessing the global dictionary.

(6) Object Manager: The distributed Object Manager in the system is a collection of identical Object Manager copies running on each node. These copies interact with each other through messages. The distribution of dictionary information across the network facilitates the Object Manager copies at each node to operate independently on their local data. The distributed Object Manager can be classified by its functionality into three groups: operations to support context generation, system-defined operations, and operations for the storage of main memory objects.

6.8 CONCLUSION

OODBMSs and their underlying models possess many desirable features for modeling and processing complex objects in today's data-intensive applications. However, the performance of large OODBs is often limited by the sequential nature of conventional computer systems. Thus, parallel algorithms and architectures are needed to support OODB processing.

In this chapter, we have presented two query processing strategies for OODBs—the identification approach and the elimination approach. The parallel identification algorithm described in this chapter takes advantage of the structural properties of the query and starts the identification process from all terminal classes of the query graph. On the other hand, the elimination algorithm checks every instance in a class according to the query pattern and propagates deletion information to its neighboring classes. Because the parallel elimination algorithm treats all classes the same and can start checking and deleting instances in all classes at the same time, it is intuitively more efficient than the parallel identification algorithm. The simulation results of tree-structured queries also suggest that in most cases the parallel elimination algorithm performs better than the parallel identification algorithm. However, the parallel identification algorithm does perform better in some cases. Thus, the best strategy would be to incorporate these two approaches in a system and to select a suitable strategy according to different data conditions.

A parallel query processor, which is based on the identification algorithm, has been implemented on a four-node Transputer network, using parallel C programming language. The parallel query processor is a component of a parallel processing system for the support of O-O database management, as shown in Figure 16. We have implemented other components of the system, including a distributed object manager, distributed transaction manager, support for system-defined operations, and the integration of a graphical user interface toolset with the system. The system can be used as a testbed for the study of various parallel processing algorithms and techniques for solving very large database problems. Various clustering strategies, mapping algorithms, and so on, are being studied and will be implemented for testing on this system.

ACKNOWLEDGMENTS

A preliminary version of this chapter has appeared in the *Proceedings of the First International Conference on Parallel and Distributed Information Systems*, 1991. This research was first supported by the National Science Foundation grant MIP-8822328 and then by the Fujitsu, Limited, Japan, UPN 93102111. The implementation effort associated with this project is supported by the Florida High Technology and Industry Council grant UPN-90090708. The contributions of Mr. Arun S. Gorur, Mr. Shyam S. Bhethanabotla, and Mr. Gopalan Arun are acknowledged.

REFERENCES

1. R. Agrawal and N.H. Gehani, "ODE (Object Database and Environment): The Language and the Data Model," *Proc. ACM Int'l Conf. Management of Data*, ACM Press, New York, N.Y., 1989, pp. 36-45.

2. M.J. Carey, et al., "The EXODUS Extensible DBMS Project: An Overview," in *Readings in Object-Oriented Database Systems*, S.B. Zdonik and D. Maier, eds., Morgan Kaufmann Pub., San Mateo, Calif., 1990, pp. 474-499.

3. O. Deux, et al., "The Story of O_2," *IEEE Trans. Knowledge Data Eng.*, Vol. 2, No. 1, Mar. 1990, pp. 91-108.

4. M.F. Hornick and S.B. Zdonik, "A Shared, Segmented Memory System for an Object-Oriented Database," *ACM Trans. Office Information Systems*, Vol. 5, No. 1, Jan. 1987, pp. 70-95.

5. W. Kim, et al., "Architecture of the ORION Next-Generation Database System," *IEEE Trans. Knowledge Data Eng.*, Vol. 2, No. 1, Mar. 1990, pp. 109-124.

6. M. Stonebraker, L.A. Rowe, and M. Hirohama, "The Implementation of POSTGRES," *IEEE Trans. Knowledge Data Eng.*, Vol. 2, No. 1, Mar. 1990, pp. 125–142.

7. S.Y.W. Su, V. Krishnamurthy, and H. Lam, "An Object-Oriented Semantic Association Model (OSAM∗)," in *Artificial Intelligence: Manufacturing Theory and Practice*, S. Kumara, A.L. Soyster, and R.L. Kashyap, eds., Institute of Industrial Engineers, Industrial Engineering and Management Press, Norcross, Ga., 1989, pp. 463–494.

8. K. Wilkinson, P. Lyngbaek, and W. Hasan, "The Iris Architecture and Implementation," *IEEE Trans. Knowledge Data Eng.*, Vol. 2, No. 1, Mar. 1990, pp. 63–75.

9. B.P. Jenq, et al., "Query Processing in Distributed ORION," in *Advances in Database Technology EDBT '90*, F. Bancilhon, C. Thanos, and D. Tsichritzis, eds., Springer-Verlag, New York, N.Y., 1990, pp. 169–187.

10. S. Khoshafian, P. Valduriez, and G. Copeland, "Parallel Query Processing for Complex Objects," *Proc. 4th Int'l Conf. Data Eng.*, IEEE CS Press, Los Alamitos, Calif., 1988, pp. 202–209.

11. K.-C. Kim, W. Kim, and A. Dale, "Cyclic Query Processing in Object-Oriented Databases," *Proc. 5th Int'l Conf. Data Eng.*, IEEE CS Press, Los Alamitos, Calif., 1989, pp. 564–571.

12. K.-C. Kim, "Parallelism in Object-Oriented Query Processing," *Proc. 6th Int'l Conf. Data Eng.*, IEEE CS Press, Los Alamitos, Calif., 1990, pp. 209–217.

13. P.A. Bernstein and D.W. Chiu, "Using Semi-Joins to Solve Relational Queries," *J. ACM*, Vol. 28, No. 1, Jan. 1981, pp. 25–40.

14. P.M.G. Apers, A.R. Hevner, and S.B. Yao, "Optimization Algorithms for Distributed Queries," *IEEE Trans. Software Eng.*, Vol. SE-9, No. 1, Jan. 1983, pp. 57–68.

15. P.A. Bernstein, et al., "Query Processing in a System for Distributed Databases (SDD-1)," *ACM Trans. Database Systems*, Vol. 6, No. 4, Dec. 1981, pp. 602–625.

16. A.L.P. Chen, et al., "Distributed Query Processing in a Multiple Database System," *IEEE J. Selected Areas in Communications*, Vol. 7, No. 3, Apr. 1989, pp. 390–398.

17. M.-S. Chen and P.S. Yu, "Determining Beneficial Semijoins for a Join Sequence in Distributed Query Processing," *Proc. 7th Int'l Conf. Data Eng.*, IEEE CS Press, Los Alamitos, Calif., 1991, pp. 50–58.

18. D.M. Chiu, P.A. Bernstein, and Y.C. Ho, "Optimizing Chain Queries in a Distributed Database System," *SIAM J. Computing*, Vol. 13, No. 1, Feb. 1984, pp. 116–134.

19. C. Yu, M. Ozsoyoglu, and K. Lam, "Optimization of Distributed Tree Queries," *J. Computer and Science Systems*, Vol. 29, No. 3, Dec. 1984, pp. 409–445.

20. C. Wang, V.O.K. Li, and A.L.P. Chen, "Distributed Query Optimization by One-Shot Fixed-Precision Semi-Join Execution," *Proc. 7th Int'l Conf. Data Eng.*, IEEE CS Press, Los Alamitos, Calif., 1991, pp. 756–763.

21. N. Roussopoulos and H. Kang, "A Pipeline *N*-way Join Algorithm Based on the 2-Way Semijoin Program," *IEEE Trans. Knowledge Data Eng.*, Vol. 3, No. 4, Dec. 1991, pp. 486–495.

22. Y.E. Ioannidis and Y.C. Kang, "Left-Deep vs. Bush Trees: An Analysis of Strategy Spaces and Its Implications for Query Optimization," *Proc. ACM Int'l Conf. Management of Data*, ACM Press, New York, N.Y., 1991, pp. 168–177.

23. H. Lu, M.-C. Shan, and K.-L. Tan, "Optimization of Multi-Way Join Queries for Parallel Execution," *Proc. 17th Int'l Conf. Very Large Data Bases*, 1991, pp. 549–560.

24. D.A. Schneider and D.J. DeWitt, "Trade-Offs in Processing Complex Join Queries via Hashing in Multiprocessor Database Machines," *Proc. 16th Int'l Conf. Very Large Data Bases*, 1990, pp. 469–480.

25. A.M. Alashqur, S.Y.W. Su, and H. Lam, "OQL: A Query Language for Manipulating Object-Oriented Databases," *Proc. 15th Int'l Conf. Very Large Data Bases*, 1989, pp. 423–442.

26. M. Guo, S.Y.W. Su, and H. Lam, "An Association Algebra for Processing Object-Oriented Databases," *Proc. 7th Int'l Conf. Data Eng.*, IEEE CS Press, Los Alamitos, Calif., 1991, pp. 23–32.

27. M.J. Carey, D.J. DeWitt, and S.L. Vandenberg, "A Data Model and Query Language for EXODUS," *ACM Int'l Conf. Management of Data*, ACM Press, New York, N.Y., 1988, pp. 413–423.

28. C. Zaniolo, "The Database Language GEM," *Proc. ACM Int'l Conf. Management of Data*, ACM Press, New York, N.Y., 1983, pp. 207–218.

29. M. Carey, et al., "An Incremental Join Attachment for Starburst," *Proc. 16th Int'l Conf. Very Large Data Bases*, 1990, pp. 662-673.

30. L.M. Haas, et al., "Starburst Mid-Flight: As the Dust Clears," *IEEE Trans. Knowledge Data Eng.*, Vol. 2, No. 1, Mar. 1990, pp. 143-160.

31. E.J. Shekita and M.J. Carey, "A Performance Evaluation of Pointer-Based Joins," *ACM Int'l Conf. Management of Data*, ACM Press, New York, N.Y., 1990, pp. 300-311.

32. T. Keller, G. Graefe, and D. Maier, "Efficient Assembly of Complex Objects," *Proc. ACM Int'l Conf. Management of Data*, ACM Press, New York, N.Y., May 1991, pp. 148-157.

33. H. Lam, C. Lee, and S.Y.W. Su, "An Object Flow Computer for Database Applications," *Proc. Int'l Workshop Database Machines*, 1989, pp. 1-17.

34. A.K. Thakore, et al., "Asynchronous Parallel Processing of Object Bases Using Multiple Wavefronts," *Proc. Int'l Conf. Parallel Processing*, Penn State Press, University Park Pa., 1990, pp. 127-135.

35. A.K. Thakore, "Data Distribution and Algorithms for Asynchronous Parallel Processing of Object-Oriented Knowledge Bases," doctoral dissertation, Dept. of Electrical Engineering, Univ. of Florida, Gainesville, Fla., 1990.

36. S.Y.W. Su, Y.-H. Chen, and H. Lam, "Multiple Wavefront Algorithms for Pattern-Based Processing of Object-Oriented Databases," *Proc. 1st Int'l Conf. Parallel and Distributed Information Systems*, IEEE CS Press, Los Alamitos, Calif., 1991, pp. 46-55.

37. A.M. Alashqur, *A Query Model and Query and Knowledge Definition Languages for Object-Oriented Databases*, doctoral dissertation, Dept. of Electrical Engineering, Univ. of Florida, Gainesville, Fla., 1989.

38. A.M. Alashqur, S.Y.W. Su, and H. Lam, "A Rule-Based Language for Deductive Object-Oriented Databases," *Proc. 6th Int'l Conf. Data Eng.*, IEEE CS Press, Los Alamitos, Calif., 1990, pp. 58-67.

39. M. Guo, *Association Algebra: A Mathematical Foundation for Object-Oriented Databases*, doctoral dissertation, Dept. of Electrical Engineering, Univ. of Florida, Gainesville, Fla., 1990.

40. S.Y.W. Su, M.S. Guo, and H. Lam, "Association Algebra: A Mathematical Foundation for Object-Oriented Databases," *IEEE Trans. Knowledge Data Eng.*, Vol. 5, No. 5, Oct. 1993, pp. 775-798.

41. G. Copeland and S. Khoshafian, "A Decomposition Storage Model," *Proc. ACM Int'l Conf. Management of Data*, ACM Press, New York, N.Y., May 1985, pp. 268-279.

42. H. Lam, et al., "A Special Function Unit for Database Operations within a Data-Control Flow System," *Proc. Int'l Conf. Parallel Processing*, Penn State Press, University Park, Pa., 1987, pp. 330-339.

43. P. Valduriez, "Join Indices," *ACM Trans. Database Systems*, Vol. 12, No. 2, June 1987, pp. 218-246.

44. L. Bic and R.L. Hartmann, "AGM: A Dataflow Database Machine," *ACM Trans. Database Systems*, Vol. 14, No. 1, Mar. 1989, pp. 114-146.

45. E.W. Dijkstra, et al., "Derivation of a Termination Detection Algorithm for Distributed Computation," *Information Processing Letters*, Vol. 16, No. 5, June 1983, pp. 217-219.

46. S.-T. Huang, "Detecting Termination of Distributed Computations by External Agents," *Proc. 9th Int'l Conf. Distributed Computing Systems*, IEEE CS Press, Los Alamitos, Calif., 1989, pp. 79-84.

47. J.L. Peterson and A. Silberschatz, *Operating System Concepts*, 2nd ed., Addison-Wesley, Reading, Mass., 1985.

48. A.S. Gorur, *Implementation of a Query Processor on a Multiprocessor Network*, master's thesis, Dept. of Electrical Engineering, Univ. of Florida, Gainesville, Fla., 1991.

49. S.S. Bhethanabotla, "Design and Implementation of a Distributed Object Manager," master's thesis, Dept. of Electrical Engineering, Univ. of Florida, Gainesville, Fla., 1992.

7

The Datacycle Architecture: A Database Broadcast System

T. F. Bowen, G. Gopal, T. Hickey, G. Herman, K.C. Lee, V. Mak, W.H. Mansfield, Jr., and J. Raitz

Bellcore
Morristown, New Jersey

ABSTRACT

Our research on the Datacycle architecture is motivated by a set of business requirements that force us to consider how to achieve, in a single architecture, the goals of high-performance transaction processing, a powerful and flexible query-language capability, and high levels of concurrent access to a single database by multiple applications. A strength of the Datacycle approach is that it allows independent structuring and scaling of processing resources, both for processing individual queries (intraquery parallelism) and for overall throughput (intertransaction parallelism). The key to realizing this approach is a high-speed, on-the-fly, data-filtering operation, which supports both expanded information-retrieval functionality as well as conflict resolution for management of changes to database contents. In this paper we describe the experimental research prototype implemented at Bellcore and a set of test applications using the system. The process of experimentation forced us to identify and overcome a number of key engineering and implementation issues, and provides a better understanding of the value of this approach to database architecture.

7.1 INTRODUCTION

Beginning with Codd's proposal of the relational model for databases[1] and the subsequent work on System R,[2] two largely distinct lines of research began on architectures for database systems. Research on *high-performance transaction processing*[3,4,5] emphasized database interactions that include both reads and writes, strict enforcement of the transaction model, high levels of concurrency and throughput, and low response time. While transaction processing does not require use of a relational database model, an increasing number of high-performance systems support both transaction semantics and a relational interface to data.[6] A second area of research has emphasized response-time performance in processing *queries* expressed using the relational model. This work has emphasized various approaches to improving functionality and performance for complex queries such as JOINs—efficient algorithms, exploitation of processing parallelism, and database-specific hardware architectures to improve performance.[7-10] Performance metrics for complex queries seldom include multiprogramming level and throughput.

Our research on the Datacycle architecture is motivated by a set of business requirements that force us to consider how to achieve, in a single architecture, the operating characteristics of both of these traditional lines of research—transaction semantics, functionality, application independence, and throughput. Within telecommunications and other industries, the contents of databases are increasingly viewed as corporate assets. The costs of maintaining these assets across the complex of database and application systems in which they reside are substantial; reduction of costs of data storage and administration are major goals. Additionally, increased flexibility of access to data to support new applications also has financial value to the business enterprise. However, constraints of existing database technology limit the ability of users to realize their model of a single image of corporate data supporting multiple performance-critical applications. MCC's BUBBA[11] project is one attempt to address transaction processing and query processing in a common architecture.

The Datacycle project[12-14] is an exploration of how technology trade-offs affect database system architecture, functionality, and performance. This work can be viewed from both the query-processing and transaction-processing perspectives. Viewed in terms of query processing, our experimental research prototype of the Datacycle architecture is a *database machine*, with hardware and architectural support for a powerful and flexible query-language capability and efficient execution of complex queries. For example, it employs on-the-fly hardware filters to provide content-addressability,[15] and allows application of significant processing parallelism to exploit intraquery parallelism in query execution. Additionally, advanced capabilities in the filter hardware permit queries involving manipulation of attributes on full database scans, including multidimensional range queries, distance queries, fuzzy queries, and database triggers. As an experiment in *high-performance transaction processing*, the Datacycle prototype has architectural features that support efficient coupling of many processing subsystems to achieve very high transaction throughput, and allows physical distribution of these subsystems over a wide geographic area. Thus, a strength of the Datacycle approach is that it allows independent structuring and scaling of processing resources, both for query-processing performance as well as for throughput. The result is a unique combination of functionality and performance to support complex information-management applications:

(1) As in most database systems based on the relational model, the interface between application and database system is application-independent. This feature allows the same information to be used simultaneously by different applications.

(2) Unlike traditional relational databases, however, the Datacycle approach does not require application-dependent optimization of internal data structures, like indices, to achieve adequate performance. This approach allows a new application to access an existing database without modifying or rebuilding the database to improve performance.

(3) The Datacycle approach provides additional functionality, including multidimensional range queries, distance queries, and fuzzy queries, but, again, without the use of special data structures and without severe performance degradation.

(4) The architecture provides direct support for database triggers, which are persistent queries that return results whenever items of interest appear in the database.

(5) Flexible transaction management is a key feature of the Datacycle architecture. This allows information-retrieval applications to specify independently the type of consistency guarantees they require (if any) when reading the database while database updates are occurring simultaneously. And, for database applications that both retrieve information and modify information, transaction management ensures that the resulting database will be consistent.

(6) Finally, the Datacycle architecture scales to achieve very high levels of throughput. For applications that are retrieve-only, the number of simultaneous requests that can be made of the database is essentially unlimited. Thus, this approach can support high-volume mass-market applications.

In this paper we describe Datacycle architecture and its implementation and operation in an experimental research prototype, including a set of test applications implemented using this system. This process of experimentation has forced us to identify a number of the key engineering and implementation issues that must be addressed to realize the Datacycle approach, and has uncovered several capabilities of the architecture that were unanticipated at the onset of the research project. Section 7.2 reviews the principles of operation of the Datacycle architecture and provides an overview of the system prototype. Section 7.3 provides a detailed description of the design of the VLSI data-filter hardware. Query processing in this architecture is described in Section 7.4, and transaction processing is described in Section 7.5. Section 7.6 provides a description of a set of directory applications that have been implemented on the system prototype. Section 7.7 describes extensions to the architecture, including a VLSI design for text filtering and an analysis of the use of a conventional digital-signal processor to replace the custom VLSI datafilter. Section 7.8 concludes with an assessment and discussion of the Datacycle approach.

7.2 AN OVERVIEW OF THE DATACYCLE ARCHITECTURE

7.2.1 System Model

The Datacycle system model (Figure 1) comprises an arbitrarily large number of *access managers* acting on a single large set of shared data items. The access managers perform operations on the data on behalf of applications, including simple retrieval and update operations, complex searches, and support for persistent queries that function as database triggers. The entire set of data items is maintained in a central subsystem called the *storage pump*. There is no requirement that all data items in the storage pump be logically related; the data items may comprise multiple, independent databases. Data items are made available to the many access managers by repetitive broadcast of the entire contents of the databases stored in the pump, similar to the proposed distributed shared-memory system described by St. Amand.[16] The broadcast stream is filtered on-the-fly by custom VLSI *data filters*[17] within the access managers; in our research prototype, data filters (described in Section 7.3) are essentially custom microprocessors whose architecture and instruction set are optimized for synchronous, high-speed search. The presence of the entire database contents on the broadcast channel and the ability to filter database contents on-the-fly provide opportunity for direct selection of records based on the values of any attributes or combination of attributes, eliminating the need to store and maintain indices.

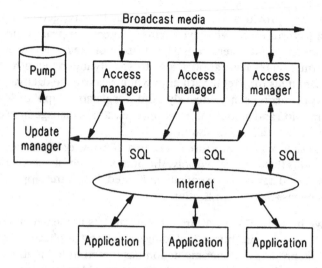

Figure 1.   Datacycle architecture.

A query or transaction submitted by an external application executes within a single access manager; a transaction may read data items, and may attempt to write data items, without knowing where else in the system the data items may be in use. Attempts to write to the database occur when an update transaction in an access manager attempts to commit. Using the upstream network, the access manager sends the update request to the record *update manager*, which executes a nonconflicting subset of the update requests received in a cycle. The update manager guarantees that the contents of the database appearing in a single broadcast cycle are consistent. The access manager subsequently monitors the contents of the broadcast stream to determine if the update attempt was successful, and notifies the host. The system as a whole provides efficient mechanisms that allow a transaction to obtain its readset and ensure that, overall, the set of read-only and update transactions that complete successfully will be serializable. Thus, the system maintains consistency and achieves serializability without requiring access managers executing the transactions to communicate directly with each other.

Realization of this model is based on architectural support for a *consistent predicate-read* operation that can be executed on a common database with an essentially unlimited degree of parallelism. The predicate-read operation is implemented in the data-filtering hardware that monitors the broadcast stream. This operation is fundamental to the architecture, in that it both supports the generation of readsets for many database queries in parallel, and performs the predicate-level set intersection required to validate the readsets and writesets of transactions that attempt to commit concurrently. So, unlike past approaches to database machines, while the Datacycle approach is based on database-specific hardware, the same hardware information-filtering mechanism is central to both query processing and to transaction processing.

7.2.2 The Datacycle Prototype

We have implemented the Datacycle system model in an experimental research prototype. From the perspective of applications accessing it, the Datacycle prototype appears as a database server with a structured-query-language-based interface. In the prototype configuration, applications executing on UNIX or VMS access a Datacycle server over the Bellcore Internet. Applications interact with the prototype using American National Standards Institute SQL, with the addition of data-manipulation primitives providing nontraditional functionality, which we discuss further in Section 7.4. Database contents are defined and managed solely in terms of the relational schema and the values of attributes of individual tuples; no distinction exists between "indexed" and "nonindexed" attributes.

The storage pump is implemented using dual-ported, banked RAM, allowing uninterrupted cycling of data onto the broadcast channel while simultaneously installing updates into the database. The pump is modular; a single triple-eurocard board contains either 32 or 128 megabytes of storage for database contents. Access to pump storage is controlled by the record-update manager, which also handles validation of update requests. The update manager is implemented using INMOS transputers[18] that control access to pump contents and validate proposed updates, to ensure the consistency of the database. Transputers are commercially available microprocessors that are used throughout the prototype because the four on-chip 20-Mbytes-per-second serial communications links allow convenient reconfiguration of the network of transputers to meet evolving project needs. Also included on the pump board is a VLSI data-filter and supporting circuitry.

The read-only port of the pump memory drives the transmission interface for the broadcast channel, which is either a 13-megahertz 32-bit unidirectional backplane (for local distribution) or a 420-Mbytes-per-second serial optical interface (for long-haul distribution of database contents). The effective broadcast rate of data on both channels is 52 Mbytes per second; a 32-Mbyte database stored within a single pump board will appear on the broadcast channel once every 0.6 seconds. Databases whose volume and/or access-time requirements are beyond the capability of a single pump module are supported through multiple pump modules and additional multiplexing of the broadcast channels. The Datacycle architecture imposes no limit on the number of pump modules and broadcast channels comprising a single system, so in theory there is no limit to database size. In a large system, a single-selection operation could require filtering all broadcast channels; this requirement implies that the database-storage and database-search costs scale linearly with database size. A practical solution to improve search efficiency is to provide structure to the database, using simple indexing criteria to assign tuples to specific channels. The use of a single-index structure could reduce filtering to a single channel, but only for that indexed attribute. A grid-file structure could be used to index data based on a number of attributes, and could reduce the search to a set of channels. This structure provides a more economical large-database configuration.

Data items appear on the broadcast channel as records, structured sequences of attributes that may include both data values as well as record-status attributes (for example, time-stamps, logical record IDs) used for data management. Other bit sequences present on the channel delineate broadcast cycle (BEGIN CYCLE) and tuple (BEGIN RECORD) boundaries. The set of data items present in each broadcast cycle is guaranteed to be consistent; the requirement that each full broadcast of the database contain a consistent snapshot of the database is fundamental to the transaction-management techniques described in Section 7.5. Enforcement of this guarantee is the responsibility of the update manager, which must introduce a complete nonconflicting subset of proposed changes to the database into pump storage during each broadcast cycle.

Attached to the broadcast channel are one or more access managers. Each prototype access manager comprises a commercial transputer board and a custom triple-eurocard board containing three data-filter chips, six transputers supporting real-time control of the datafliters, RAM, and FIFO memory. The access manager provides the interface between the Datacycle system and external applications, translating database queries into primitives to

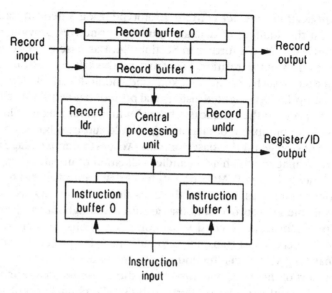

Figure 2.   Data-filter architecture.

control the data-filter chips, scheduling use of filtering hardware, compiling query responses, and passing results back to the host computer, as we describe in Section 7.4. Software in the access manager, working cooperatively with that in the update manager, is also responsible for transaction management.

7.3 VLSI DATA-FILTER

Because both the query-processing and transaction-management strategies depend critically on the efficiency and functionality of the data-filtering operation, exploration of technology alternatives for this operation was a major emphasis of the prototyping project (see the work of Matoba[19] and Lee[20] for a full discussion). Several alternative approaches were considered, including systolic arrays,[21] linear comparator arrays,[22] comparator-with-memory approaches,[23] and both general-purpose and custom microprocessors. The approach chosen was that of a custom microprocessor with an instruction set optimized for synchronous, high-speed search against a structured input-data stream. From our analysis, we concluded that this approach would achieve the required combination of predicate-evaluation operations (Boolean, arithmetic, and movement primitives), dynamic programmability, and I/O and instruction-execution speed necessary to support the high-speed data broadcast. Designed using commercial silicon compiler tools and fabricated in 1989 in 2-micron complementary metal-oxide semiconductors, the resulting data-filter comprised 91,000 transistors in a 475-mils square and achieved a clock rate of 18 megahertz. At this rate, the filter executed 18 million primitive predicate-evaluation instructions (Section 7.3.2) per second, with a search throughput of up to 72 Mbytes per second.

7.3.1 Data-Filter Architecture

The data-filter architecture supports four basic tasks: loading queries to be applied to database contents, loading data (records) from the broadcast stream, executing queries against the records, and outputting data that satisfies a query's requirements. Figure 2 illustrates the architecture of the prototype data-filter. Each record transmitted on the broadcast

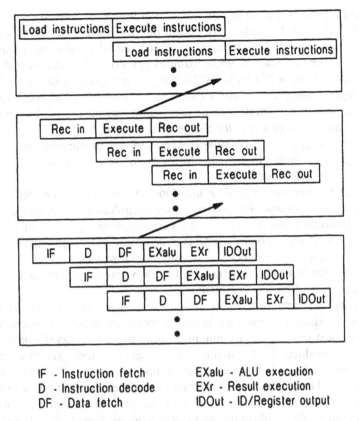

IF - Instruction fetch   EXalu - ALU execution
D - Instruction decode   EXr - Result execution
DF - Data fetch   IDOut - ID/Register output

Figure 3. Data-filter pipeline.

channel is loaded over a 32-bit input port into a *record buffer* on the data-filter chip, where it can be examined to see if it satisfies one of possibly several queries assembled in one of the filter's *instruction buffers*. In our prototype, a physical record may be up to 128 bytes in length, and each instruction buffer holds up to 32 data-filter instructions, each of which operates on four bytes of the buffered record (discussed in Section 7.3.2). Each instruction in the buffer may be associated with a different query, based on a tag called a *query ID*. Records that satisfy one of the queries in the active instruction buffer are output to off-chip FIFOs over a 32-bit output port; simultaneously, the ID or IDs of the queries satisfied by this record are output to a second FIFO, again with a 32-bit port. This latter data path is also used to output summary data stored in registers in the central processing unit; summary data may include sums or counts computed across multiple database records. Multiported cache memories on the chip support double-buffering of instructions and target records, enabling fully overlapped input and output operations.

This architecture reflects a conscious choice of strict synchronization over loose synchronization among query loading, data loading, query execution, and data unloading. This choice affects all aspects of the data-filter design. Strict synchronization, a characteristic of pipeline parallel processing, requires tasks to coordinate at periodic intervals, when data or work is passed between stages in the pipeline. Figure 3 illustrates the pipeline hierarchy in the data-filter. In the data-filter, there are two high-level pipelines: one between the instruction buffers and the central processing unit, and one including the record buffers, the central processing unit, and the record- and register/ID-output function.While the central processing unit executes queries in one instruction buffer for a given cycle, the batch of queries for the next broadcast cycle are loaded into the second buffer. When the BEGIN CYCLE framing pattern on the broadcast channel is detected, the data-filter immediately begins execution on the new queries, while loading begins on queries for the following cycle. Similarly, appearance of the BEGIN RECORD pattern on the broadcast channel triggers the data-filter to begin loading record buffer 1 with record R+1 from the broadcast channel, to start the central processing unit to execute instructions against record R in record buffer 0, and, if a query match was detected for the previous record, to start to output record R−1 from record buffer 1. The record pipeline shifts again when the next record boundary is detected. Thus, query execution in the data-filter is strictly synchronized with both record arrivals and broadcast-cycle boundaries.

The design alternative—loose synchronization—implements a producer/consumer paradigm, where tasks queue work for their neighbor regardless of relative processing speeds. Arriving records would queue for access to the central processing unit, which in turn would queue work (records and/or computed data) to be unloaded from the filter. Similarly, new queries would be queued for execution by the central processing unit. Synchronization would occur only when a queue becomes full or empty; then, one of the stages must suspend until space or work becomes available.

Architecturally, strict synchronization eliminates the need for large record–buffer memories and the sophisticated access–control logic necessary to manage a system that operates statistically and must be designed to minimize buffer overflows. On the other hand, strict synchronization introduces hard real–time requirements for task execution. In particular, since there is no provision for halting database broadcast in the Datacycle architecture, query execution and data unloading must complete in the broadcast time of one record.

In the design of the data–filter chip, we chose to use strict synchronization of record loading, query execution, data unloading, and query loading. It appeared that commercially available memories and programmable logic devices required for a loosely synchronized design would not support desired performance. The smaller buffers permitted by strict synchronization allowed record-buffer memory to be implemented internally within the data-filter. Coupled with on-chip record-loading and data-unloading logic, this choice resulted in greater record-loading bandwidth, faster record-data access, shared record access, and a compact and straightforward subsystem design. However, this choice led to special requirements for the implementation of query execution in the central processing unit of the data-filter, as well as for the design of the supporting hardware and software in the access manager (discussed in Section 7.4).

7.3.2 Data-Filter Query Execution

Viewed as the heart of the data-filtering process, query execution includes the Boolean, arithmetic, and data-manipulation operations performed by the query against the contents of the record buffer. In our data-filter design, strict synchronization requires that all queries in the active instruction buffer be executed against the contents of the record buffer in one record-arrival time. During design exploration, we found that the arithmetic logic unit execution time in the central processing unit was the limiting factor in data-filter performance. In the final design, the central processing unit implemented a six-stage pipeline of instruction-fetch, instruction-decode, data-fetch, ALU-execution, result-execution, and ID/register output (Figure 3).

Predicting the execution time of a sequence of instructions in a commercial microprocessor is difficult because of the potential for pipeline conflicts in the architecture. Con-

Mode	Operations	Conditions	Addressing Modes
System	begin,nop, end	NA	NA
Boolean	pusha, anda, ora, fanda, fora, sanda, sora	true, eq, gt, gte,lt,lte,ne	memory/pattern
Arithmetic	add, sub, neq, inc, dec, nadd, ndec, ones, zeros, equ, not, and, andc	true, eq, gt, gte, lt, lte, ne, hit	register/register, memory/register, register/pattern, memory/pattern

Figure 4.   Instruction set summary.

flicts due to branching, address dependencies on preceding computations, and the need to simultaneously fetch program and operand data can result in processor-execution delays. Accordingly, we sought to design the data-filter to eliminate pipeline conflicts, resulting in a more complex chip architecture but with simplified control and predictable execution performance. For example, instruction and record-data accesses are performed on separate buses. The data-filter has no branch instructions, although instructions can be executed conditionally based on the settings of flags. Addressing modes are very basic, supporting only immediate, register, and direct addressing (within the record buffer).

Like the architecture and control structure of the data-filter, the instruction set that it supports is geared towards search efficiency. An overview of the instruction set is shown in Figure 4. In most ways, the data-filter is a reduced instruction-set computing (RISC) processor; that is, it has a small number of instructions, very few addressing modes, a fixed instruction format, and constant-length instruction execution. In one way, however, the data-filter is a complex instruction-set computer (CISC) processor; its instruction set is highly complex and specialized.

Certain of the data-filter's instruction set (Figure 4) is standard, such as basic arithmetic operations that allow for on-the-fly aggregation operations such as *count, sum*, and *maximum*. But even these basic instructions are enhanced to support conditional execution based on the result of a previous comparison. More important, however, are the complex Boolean test instructions that compare four bytes of the buffered record to a four-byte pattern. Each of these instructions performs multiple primitive functions in a single cycle. An extreme example of this feature is the SANDA instruction, which masks and compares a word of the record to a pattern, *ands* the result to a Boolean flag, tests the flag and, if true, requests that the record and query ID be output.

7.3.2.1 Boolean Instructions

The primary objective of the data-filter is to provide efficient predicate-based record selection. Records that satisfy the query predicates become outputs. Accordingly, Boolean instructions in the data-filter instruction set allow the specification of predicate criteria to be used for record selection. The basic format of the select query is:

SELECT attribute-list **FROM** relation **WHERE** Boolean Predicate **FOR ID**

For example, the query, "What Indian restaurants are in New York?" may be written in the relational algebra as

```
SELECT * FROM rest
WHERE (type = 'Ind') and (location = 'NY')
FOR 1.
```

Design of the instruction set to realize this selection predicate directly affects search performance. For example, this query might be implemented in a general purpose processor as:

```
addr0: cmp @relation, #rest
       jneq addr1
       cmp @type, #Ind
       jneq addr1
       cmp @location, #NY
       jneq addr1
       mov hit, #1
addr1: . . .
```

There are three comparisons corresponding to each of the comparisons in the select clause, with each followed by a branch instruction, requiring execution of seven instructions in the worst case.

To improve execution efficiency, the data-filter Boolean instructions speed up the selection operation through the use of the Boolean accumulator A that accumulates the Boolean result pertaining to one query. There are three basic operations that can be done on the Boolean accumulator: PUSHA, which *pushes* a Boolean value to A; ANDA, which *and*s another Boolean value to the value in A; and ORA, which *or*s another value to the value in A. In addition to the three basic operations, four operations on A are defined in order to tie together the truth values pertaining to one query. FANDA and FORA are like ANDA and ORA but are used for final instructions pertaining to one query. These two instructions turn on the Hit flag, which can be used as a condition for the arithmetic instructions discussed in the next section. SANDA and SORA are also used for final instructions; these turn on the Ghit flag, which causes the output of the current record.

The basic format of a Boolean mode instruction is:

OPr(OPa(**MEM**, Pat, Mask), **ID**).

where OPr is the operation on accumulator A just discussed. This one instruction specifies three operations to be executed in sequence: a comparison, a test on comparison result, and an operation between the result and the accumulator A. The data-filter first compares the word at MEM (Mask) with Pattern, and, if the comparison flags (LT, GT, EQ) satisfy the flag pattern specified by OPa, the filter sets the Boolean value to be true. Finally, the instruction performs the OPr operation on this Boolean value.

A typical select query in SQL compiles into multiple data-filter instructions, one instruction for each of the attribute comparisons. For example, the selection query previously presented may be

```
PUSHA (EQ (relation, 'rest', 1111b), 1).
ANDA (EQ (type, 'Ind', 1110b), 1).
SANDA (EQ (location, 'NY', 1100b), 1).
```

Thus, the data-filter executes the selection query in only three machine cycles.

7.3.2.2 Arithmetic Instructions

The second objective of the experimental data-filter prototype is to support aggregation operations such as *count*, *sum*, and *maximum*. Adding this capability to the filter offloads higher-level software from retrieving and scanning large amounts of data, and supports many of the nontraditional query types discussed in Section 7.4.3.

Aggregate operations are implemented in the data-filter by providing conditional-assignment instructions to accumulate results. A conditional assignment is conventionally implemented by a comparison instruction followed by a branch instruction followed by an assignment instruction. However, this approach can be inefficient due to pipeline breaks. Hence, the data-filter provides an instruction mode that performs assignment based on a condition code. This type of instruction, together with the Boolean instructions previously discussed, allows numeric operations to be carried out without pipeline breaks.

The basic format of the arithmetic mode instruction is given by:

```
OPalu(Cond, M1, M2, M3).
```

The semantics of the instruction are: if the condition specified by Cond is true, carry out the ALU operation OPalu on two operands M1 and M2 and store the result into M3. The condition can be true (unconditional), hit (set by Boolean instructions), and one of six combinations of three ALU flags, *less-than*, *greater-than*, and *equal*. M1 can be a memory address or a register, M2 can be an immediate operand or a register, and M3 is a register.

The main loop of the counting query "How many people live in San Francisco?" is compiled as:

```
PUSHA(EQ(relation, 'peop', 1111b), 2)
FANDA(EQ(town, 'SF', 1100b), 2)
INCB(Hit, null, r1, r1).
```

A sum query can be formed by replacing the increment operation with an add operation on the summing attribute, for example, salary, with the sum register (r1):

```
ADD(Hit, salary, r1, r1).
```

A maximum query can be formed by replacing the increment operation with a compare operation on the maximizing attribute, for example, age, with the maximum register followed by a conditional assignment of the maximizing attribute to the maximum register (r2):

```
SUB(Hit, age, r2, r15)
EQUA(GT, age, r15, r2).
```

Two additional instructions must be added to the above examples of data-aggregation programs to cause output of the calculated value when the cycle boundary is reached.

Operations on the accumulator A can be extended so that the accumulator can be set or cleared, based on application-specific condition flags for linking computation results of added functional components. For example, a string-search unit described in Section 7.7 can be added to the data-filter as a functional component. The result of a string-search operation (finding a pattern in the input stream) can be kept in a condition code and used to set or clear the accumulator A.

7.4 QUERY PROCESSING

Realizing complete query-processing functionality in the Datacycle prototype requires a hardware and software system that receives and translates user requests from the user-in-

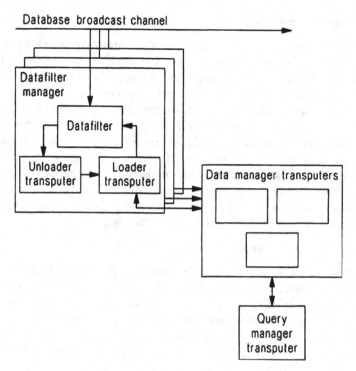

Figure 5.   Access manager.

terface language (SQL) into data-filter instructions, coordinates use of data filters, assembles the resulting query responses, and passes results back to the host computers. These functions are performed in the access manager (Figure 5).

A wide variety of single-table selection operations consistent with SQL standards are supported, and SQL extensions have been implemented for more complex operations involving spatial relationships and imprecise predicates (see Section 7.4.3). Due to constraints in the original very-large-scale-integration data-filter design (such as the lack of local memory for storing temporary results) multitable operations often involve multiple database scans. For instance, JOIN operations can involve many database-scan cycles depending on JOIN selectivity, the size of the tables, the number of broadcast channels, and the lack of additional selection predicates. In Section 7.7.2 we discuss a second access-manager design based on digital signal processor technology that avoids these constraints and can perform very efficient multitable selections. Both access-manager designs are consistent with the overall Datacycle architecture.

7.4.1 Access Manager Overview

The access manager provides access to the contents of the database in support of transactions submitted by applications. The prototype access manager provides processing parallelism in support of four aspects of query processing. First, multiple processors and associated memories are available to allow decomposition of complex queries like JOINs into parallel operations (for example, sorting and merging). Second, the access-manager processing network is expandable to permit multiple broadcast channels to be searched in parallel or to increase the search parallelism applied to a single broadcast channel. Third, this processing network allows parallelism in simultaneously managing the data-filter instruction buffers and retrieving output data from the data-filter. This feature permits maximizing the access-manager I/O throughput while meeting the query-scheduling requirement of synchronizing instruction loading with cycle boundaries. Finally, selection predicates from multiple queries are executed in a single data-filter against database contents in a single broadcast cycle with apparent simultaneity, as we described in the previous section.

The first three types of parallelism are supported by a network of INMOS transputers and associated RAM. In the Datacycle prototype, an access manager is composed of two types of circuit boards, which may be configured to provide the desired level of processing capability and access to the broadcast channel. One board type is a commercial product including four INMOS transputers, each with up to 4 Mbytes of dedicated RAM. These transputers run the software for the query manager and data manager (described in the following section). The transputer board serves as the interface between the access manager and the host computer's UNIX operating system. The second board, called a *data-filter controller*, was designed at Bellcore for experimental use in the system prototype. This board includes six transputers, each with 4 Mbytes of RAM, up to three VLSI data filters, associated FIFOs, and synchronization logic. Each pair of transputers controls a single data-filter, which is responsible for executing query predicates against the 52-Mbytes-per-second data stream. Results from filtering the data stream are stored in the FIFOs, which can be emptied by the transputers at a sustained rate of approximately 230 Kbytes per second.

The fourth type of parallelism is supported by the data-filter itself, which can execute multiple queries concurrently, since its instruction buffer is larger than the number of instructions required for typical queries. Also essential to concurrent query execution is the ability to associate output data with the queries causing the output. The data-filter provides this capability by outputting query IDs in parallel with data.

7.4.2 Access Manager Software Architecture

The software architecture for the access manager consists of a *query manager*, a *data manager*, and one or more *data-filter managers*, each of which controls a single data-filter. The query manager receives database *read* and *write* requests and transaction-control commands from applications in SQL. Database read requests are parsed, compiled, and assembled into data-filter instructions, using the query manager's knowledge of the database schema. If a schema requires a database record longer than the 128 bytes supported by the data-filter hardware, the logical schema is mapped into a physical schema where a long record is represented by a sequence of 128-byte records associated by a common logical ID attribute in each. The query manager handles the schema conversion in a way transparent to the application; from the application perspective, no distinction exists between "normal" and "long" records in the database. Once compiled, the set of instructions associated with a query is passed to the data manager. Processing of transaction control and database write requests are described in Section 7.5.1.

The data manager is responsible for routing the assembled data-filter instructions through the network of transputers to the appropriate data-filter managers, and for collating the results to be returned to the query manager. The data manager maps the logical data schema to the physical data placement on the broadcast channels and routes the translated high-level query to the specific data-filter manager that can filter the appropriate data channels. Knowledge of application workload characteristics can be exploited to utilize filtering resources more efficiently, increase query-processing throughput, and reduce response time by partitioning the database intelligently across the multiple broadcast channels. The data manager can use this data-placement information to route queries only to the filters attached to the appropriate channels. In the simple case when the entire database is broadcast on one channel, the query manager does not require the external data-manager functionality, and can route the query to a single data-filter module, which applies the predicates against the database for one complete cycle.

The data-filter manager performs the actual loading of instructions to, and unloading of results from, a data-filter. Each data-filter manager executes on the two transputers that control a particular data-filter—the loader and the unloader. The data-filter loader accumulates and batches the set of instructions generated from multiple queries and loads the batches into the data-filter for execution. The instruction-loading protocol ensures precise scheduling of the loading of instructions with respect to cycle boundaries. The data-filter loader schedules instruction loading to maximize the number of queries concurrently executed by the data-filter. The data-filter executes the contents of its instruction buffer against the database for that cycle and returns, in separate FIFOs, three output streams. The record stream contains the records output by the instructions. The ID stream contains the IDs of instructions causing record output. The register stream contains units of data smaller than records that were read or calculated by the instructions. The data-filter unloader collates records and IDs and sends the results back to the query manager. The records returned by the data-filter manager constitute the results of applying a predicate against the entire database in one cycle. The guarantee that records were obtained from a single cycle, coupled with the fact that all updates are applied atomically to the database logically between cycles, provides the crucial primitive underlying the Datacycle architecture—the consistent predicate read.

While the data-filter was designed to remain strictly synchronized with the broadcast channel, and processes queries against records as fast as the records arrive (52 Mbytes per second), transputers can unload selected records from the output FIFOs at only 230 Kbytes per second. Consequently, the output FIFOs can overflow if the supplied search predicate produces too much data-filter output, either because the selectivity is too high or because the selected records are grouped closely together on the broadcast channel. If FIFO overflow is detected, the executed instruction set is decomposed into multiple instruction sets, which are re-executed separately. The problem of determining how to decompose an instruction set so that FIFO overflow for each portion is unlikely is similar to the problem of developing an optimal query plan that is dependent on data distributions and data skew.[24] The on-the-fly aggregation primitives in the data-filter permit efficient determination of data-distribution information that is specific to the current instruction set. The number of record "hits" and the uniformity of the distribution of selected records across the database cycle can be determined in a single scan of the database. This data-distribution information can be used to determine the optimal number of database cycles or data-filter managers for a specific query. If a transaction issues a query that must be executed across multiple broadcast cycles to prevent overflow, then the resulting readset is no longer guaranteed to be consistent. If a guarantee of readset consistency is required, the query manager must use the multicycle certification algorithm described in Section 7.5

FIFO overflows are not the only reason why a query may require more than one cycle for execution. Queries that select logical records whose sizes are greater than one physical record also require more than one database cycle. The query manager uses the database schema to detect that a query may select a logical record whose size is greater than one physical record. Then the query manager prepares a set of instructions that, instead of causing output of the selected records, causes projection of the record-identifier attribute of the selected records. In subsequent cycles, instructions derived from the projections are executed to cause output of the previously identified records. For efficiency, the projections are not passed to the query manager; rather, they are processed by the data-filter manager.

7.4.3 Advanced Query Capabilities

The combination of full database scan, high-speed filtering, and on-the-fly arithmetic capability allows the Datacycle architecture to support information-retrieval capabilities that, using conventional approaches, are very difficult to achieve with an acceptable level of performance. Three classes of retrieval capabilities in the Datacycle prototype are particularly important to information-retrieval applications. The first is a powerful *associative-search* capability. The second is a *fuzzy-query* capability. The third is efficient support for database *triggers*.

7.4.3.1 Associative Search

Unlike conventional database systems that use predefined indexes on a *few* attributes for efficient query execution, the Datacycle architecture supports a wide class of search operations based on Boolean and arithmetic functions that operate on the contents of *any* attribute. Because comparisons can involve any attribute, the associative-search property implements a fully *content-addressable database*. In addition, the data-filter's Boolean comparison operations permit a variety of wildcard capabilities that violate typical indexing operations in conventional database systems. Thus, the Datacycle architecture permits a greatly expanded set of functions that are not efficiently supported in traditional database-management systems. Furthermore, these capabilities require no special data structures to improve search efficiency. For example, if attributes X and Y are defined to represent longitude and latitude in a database of customer information, then the query

SELECT * FROM whpg **WHERE** ((X CLOSEST X') and (Y CLOSEST Y'))

is a proximity query that returns the database object (tuple) in the database whose location is closest to location (X',Y'). In this case, the *and*ing of two or more terms involving the closest operator is true when the sum of the differences between the attribute value and the constant in each term is minimized. A proximity query is compiled into a set of data-filter instructions that is subsequently applied to records appearing on the broadcast channel, and that calculates the distance between all (X,Y) values for records in the database and the reference location (X',Y'). In the current prototype, such a query is processed in two broadcast cycles of the database; on the first cycle, the ID of the tuple with the minimum distance is identified, and on the second cycle, the tuple is retrieved. Complex retrieval requests like "Find the closest pharmacy to St. Luke's Hospital" are mapped into a sequence of SQL statements:

SELECT * FROM whpg **WHERE**((business classification = '**PHARMACY**') and (latitude **CLOSEST** 39237775) and (longitude **CLOSEST** 9083789))

In this example the numbers 39237775 and 9083789, which were obtained by a previous query, are the latitude and longitude of Saint Luke's Hospital.

The query manager compiles the critical subquery to identify the tuple ID for the correct pharmacy, on the basis of latitude and longitude, into the sequence of data-filter instructions shown in Figure 6. Note that the Boolean comparison of the content of the business-classification attribute in the relation 'whpg' with the string 'pharmacy' is compiled into a four-byte Boolean predicate evaluation of the substring 'PHAR' against the first

```
fanda(eq(relation name, 'BGNR',f),1)
equb(hit, 0, '0fffffff',r(1))
equb(hit,0,'00000000',r(2))
sub(true,latitude,39237775,r(3))
nega(lt,r(15),'00000000',r(3))
sub(true,longitude,9083789,r(4))
nega(lt,r(15),'00000000',r(4))
nop
add(true,r(4),r(3),r(3))
equa(true,r(1),r(5),r(5))
pusha(eq(relation name,'whpg',f),1)
anda(eq(business classification,'PHAR',f),1)
fanda(eq(business classification+4,'MACY',f),1)
equa(hit,r(3),r(5),r(5))
nop
sub(true,r(1),r(5),r(5))
equa(lt,record identifier,'00000000',r(2))
sub(true,r(5),'00000000',r(5))
equa(lt,r(3),'00000000',r(1))
fanda(eq(relation name,'ENDR',f),1)
equb(hit,0,queryID,r(0))
equa(hit,r(2),r(0),r(0)).
```

Figure 6.   Assembly language for a spatial query.

four bytes of the attribute *and*ed with the evaluation of 'MACY' against the second four bytes of the attribute.

7.4.3.2 Fuzzy Queries

Queries using distance calculations are representative of a larger set of selection operations that perform arithmetic transformations on one or more attributes. For example, the Datacycle architecture permits straightforward implementation of fuzzy-logic queries on a precise database.[25-27] Fuzzy logic provides a way to use imprecise terms, such as *near*, *tall*, and *recent*, in database queries and filtering operations. The imprecise terms define fuzzy sets in which records are placed based on their degree of membership. A value between zero and one provides a measure of the possibility that a record belongs in a set based on its attribute values. In general, a fuzzy query can be formulated by defining a membership function that calculates the degree of membership that a tuple has in a fuzzy set. This membership function maps attribute values into the range *zero to one* and subsequent database fetch operations return tuples in sorted order of membership function value (best match first).

We have implemented fuzzy-query capabilities that include both static and relative types. Static queries refer to queries that define fuzzy-set membership based directly on the attribute values. For example degrees of membership in the set *old* may be defined to have nonzero values starting at age = 60. We identify static membership functions in the query grammar with an IS operator.

SELECT tuple **WHERE** Age **IS** old

returns all tuples in the fuzzy set defined by the membership function *old*.

For relative queries, fuzzy terms are defined statistically relative to information in the database. For example a relative definition of *old* may be defined as having nonzero values starting at the 80th percentile of the range of ages. Relative membership functions are identified in the grammar using a RIS operator. For example,

SELECT tuple **WHERE** Age **RIS** old

returns all tuples defined by the membership function (Relatively) *old*.

Using a relative fuzzy term, a single definition of old can be used to distinguish *old* retirees or *old* preschoolers, even though both sets are present in the same table. A Datacycle system can respond correctly to this query by dynamically determining the age statistics of preschoolers and transforming *old*(relative) to *old*(static) for preschoolers. Thus, a single definition of old can be used in queries selecting old people, old computers, old e-mail, etc., and can process attributes where time is specified in years, months, days, minutes, or microseconds.

A major advantage of fuzzy queries results when fuzzy logic is used in the predicate to combine the fuzzy sets. Queries to identify stocks that have *high* trading volumes and *low* profit-to-earnings ratios would perform a fuzzy-set intersection operation over the sets (*high*, *low*) and return records "closest" to this ideal specification, jointly meeting both criteria.

Because appropriate search structures are so difficult to build, both fuzzy and proximity queries typically require examining many records in the database. Conventional databases are unable to examine individually each record in a large volume of database records in a reasonable time, because each examination may require disk access to fetch the record. In a large database such queries can involve thousands of I/O operations and hence is very inefficient. The Datacycle architecture is very efficient at exhaustive search, and, since the data-filter can perform some of the mathematics required for evaluating fuzzy and proximity queries, the prototype can process them quickly. By combining the ability to do on-the-fly aggregation with fuzzy logic, the Datacycle architecture allows very efficient processing of both static and relative fuzzy queries.

7.4.3.3 Database Triggers

Database triggers are persistent queries that, for example, can continuously monitor a database for the appearance of relevant new information, or that can return a result whenever a predicate describing a database state of interest becomes true. Such queries are important in implementing information-filtering applications, which involve continuously evaluating information relative to a profile of interest established for individual users or applications (for example, see Loeb's work).[28] The Datacycle architecture readily supports continuous filtering queries based on such triggers by allowing a query to be active continuously in an access manager, applying an evaluation predicate against each record in each broadcast cycle of the database. This approach to implementing information filtering, based on customized user profiles, scales to support very large numbers of simultaneous profiles, because additional filtering capacity is provided simply by replicating access managers.

Monitoring a stream of stock-market trade information for utility stocks that have a high activity and high recent price change is one example where the combination of triggering and fuzzy-query processing would be advantageous. In this example, a statistical definition of *high* would be scaled independently to the range of utility-stock activity and price changes. The filtering query can be left active in the access manager, constantly adjusting the filter's definition of *high* to the current market situation.

7.5 TRANSACTION PROCESSING

A major goal of the Datacycle project has been to realize an architecture for transaction processing in which throughput scales as processing resources are added. Scaling by replication of database contents is limited, because the concurrency-control overhead of maintaining the consistency of the replicas eventually saturates the system. A priori knowledge of data-access patterns may permit partitioning of database contents and transaction streams into noninterfering subsets that can be managed by different processors independently, but this approach results in a system whose performance is highly application-dependent. The Datacycle approach avoids both replication and application-dependent partitioning and maintains a single, logically centralized database. Scaling of transaction throughput is based on the ability of access managers to execute independently a consistent predicate read of the database. This capability supports scaling of read-only transactions through the use of additional access managers to access database contents. It also allows for decentralized detection and recognition of conflicts among read/write transactions and permits implementation of full, predicate-based, concurrency control.

Transaction management in the Datacycle prototype is based on optimistic concurrency control[29] using the private workspace model,[30] which provides a suitable framework for shortlived, low-conflict transactions. The architecture is not inherently coupled to this transactional model and could support other models. For each transaction, the query manager creates a private workspace that persists for the duration of the transaction. The private workspace contains all read predicates, the records obtained for each, and records created and/or deleted by the transaction prior to committing. In this way, the private workspace maintains a private view of the database that reflects those changes that have been made locally. When the transaction reaches its commit phase, the workspace manager certifies that the transaction will serialize with all transactions that have successfully committed since the local transaction began or that may be attempting to commit concurrently with the local transaction. The procedures for certifying a transaction vary based on whether or not the transaction performed any writes.

7.5.1 Read-Only Transaction Certification

A read-only transaction that has obtained its readset within a single broadcast cycle is guaranteed to be serializable, because of the consistent predicate-read operation, and succeeds immediately. A read-only transaction whose readset is obtained across multiple cycles must be checked to ensure that the readset is not corrupted by transactions whose effects appeared in the database while the local transaction's readset was acquired. To allow these read transactions to be certified locally at an access manager, the update manager maintains three logs: a global log of the details of update transactions that have been accepted and installed in the past (the *transaction history* log), transactions that have been accepted but whose effects have not yet appeared in the database (the *accepted transaction* log), and update transactions that are proposed, but not yet certified (the *proposed transaction* log). These logs are maintained as distinct database relations in the pump in a history section, which is broadcast at least once every cycle along with the contents of the database. The access manager can certify multicycle read transactions by searching the history section for records that satisfy the original readset predicates and whose creation or deletion timestamp is greater than the time at which generation of the original readset began. This query should result in the null set, indicating that the readset has not changed. If the query results in other than the null set, the transaction must be aborted, or must attempt to recover by acquiring a currently consistent readset.

7.5.2 Update-Transaction Certification

Certification of update transactions requires the same detection of readset corruption as required for read-only transactions as well as the detection of read/write conflicts for transactions that commit concurrently. At transaction commit, the items in the private workspace are compiled into a transaction log and sent to the update manager to begin the global certification process. The log submitted by a given transaction includes the read predicates used, the readset obtained, the set of records deleted, and the set of records created by the transaction. The timestamp of the oldest uncommitted transaction present in the access manager is also piggy-backed onto each submission. The update manager uses the piggy-backed transaction-timestamp information for garbage collection on the history log.

Implemented centrally within the update manager, the Datacycle prototype certifier checks each submitted transaction to ensure that its readset is not corrupted by transactions in the history or accepted logs. It then checks the current set of proposed transactions for mutual interference. Successful transactions are moved from the proposed log to the accepted log and their changes are subsequently installed (atomically) into pump memory. Appearance of the successful transaction within the accepted log notifies the access manager that the transaction has been accepted.

The current prototype certifier considers only schedules in which the serial-equivalent order of transactions is the same as the time order in which the transactions committed. Thus, certain serial-equivalent schedules that allow added concurrency by reordering already committed transactions are not permitted. The implemented certifier thus achieves time complexity that grows as the $\log_2$ (rather than as the square) of the number of transactions in the history.

7.5.3 Levels of Database Consistency

The contents of the three logs, and the processing required of the certifier, depend on the level of consistency requested by a transaction. The level of consistency defines what conflicts the certifier detects, and thus the complexity of the certification process. ANSI defines three levels of consistency to be maintained by a database-management system: Level 0-prohibit dirty reads; Level 2-prohibit dirty reads and guarantee repeatable reads; and, Level 4-prohibit dirty reads, guarantee repeatable reads, and guarantee no phantom records.

The requirement for Level-4 consistency arises from the use of predicates to access the database. For example, if transaction T1 issues a predicate read "for all records where $x = 10$," and T2 creates new records with $x = 10$ between the time of T1's read and T1's commit, these new records are phantom records from T1's perspective, violating Level-4 consistency. (Level-2 consistency is not violated, since the actual records read by T1 remain uncorrupted.) As a concrete example of the need for Level-4 consistency, consider a transaction that is trying to purchase the lowest-priced airline ticket between two destinations. After the transaction finds the lowest-priced ticket, but before it purchases it, a new ticket of even lower price may become available. If this happens, the transaction should abort without purchasing the original ticket. Deciding whether phantom records should actually cause the transaction to abort requires knowledge of application semantics; however, unless the Level-4 consistency requirement is supported, there is no mechanism to inform an application of the potential anomaly. The Datacycle prototype certifier allows each transaction to request the level of consistency that it requires.

Level 0 and Level 2 require similar computational complexity, while achieving Level 4 is substantially more costly. Consistency checking for both Levels 2 and 4 is supported by the Datacycle prototype. Level-2 consistency checking is implemented by storing the entire history of accepted transactions as a sorted structure of the writesets, permitting efficient comparison with records in the committing transaction's readset. To certify a transaction, the structure is searched for each record in the transaction's readset, and if none are found, the records in the transaction's writeset are added to the structure and the transaction is accepted. To permit easy garbage collection of the history, a separate structure containing a copy of the logs of committed transactions, sorted on commit time, is maintained. Transactions can thus be selected for deletion in $O(\log_2 n)$ operations.

Conceptually, Level-4 certification is similar to Level 2. However, since the readset of a committing transaction is expressed as a predicate, the required full scan of the history is prohibitively expensive using standard algorithms. In the Datacycle prototype, predicate-level certification is performed efficiently using the same basic building block as for generation of the original readset—the consistent predicate-read operation. The certifier has one or more data filters to monitor the history portion containing the three logs. The readsets (specified in terms of predicates) of the committing transactions are loaded into these data filters, which perform the full scan of the history efficiently in one cycle. If any record in the history section makes a predicate true, then a conflict with either a real or a phantom record has been detected. The Level-4 certifier scales well to handle additional throughput by growing the number of data filters. In fact, the certification function can be performed in the same access manager that executed the transaction.

The use of the broadcast log has a second important application in the Datacycle architecture. The availability of the log at a remote site, combined with the presence of a redundant, or shadow, pump and update manager at that site, allows the shadow pump to roll forward one database cycle behind the master pump. This operation forms the basis for recovery in the architecture.

7.5.4 Transaction Throughput

Transaction throughput in the Datacycle architecture is determined by two factors: the potential processing bottleneck in the central update manager, and the effects of inter-transaction interference when transactions attempt to commit. The number of read-only transactions that can execute concurrently in the Datacycle architecture scales without limit, since access managers can be added independently to provide the resources necessary to execute additional transactions, and read-only transactions do not need to communicate directly with the update manager. Update throughput is potentially limited by the centralized update manager. Performance measurements taken in the current prototype demonstrate that the current update manager can perform Level-2 certification for approximately 300 single-record-update transactions per second. Level-4 certification is performed in hardware, and certification throughput is limited only by the number of data filters available. The use of broadcast logs allows the certification process to be totally decentralized to the access managers executing the transactions, allowing, again, the ability to scale the certification throughput incrementally by providing additional access managers. Only the creation of the update transaction logs and the actual installation of the changes in the database must be done by the centralized update manager.

Certification throughput measures the rate at which the system can process commit *attempts*. The rate at which multicycle read and update transactions actually *succeed* depends on the rate of intertransaction interference. Optimistic concurrency-control methods are particularly vulnerable to transaction failure due to readset interference. In comparison to traditional implementations of optimistic control, the Datacycle approach can reduce intertransaction conflict probabilities in two ways. First, conflicts are detected at the record (rather than page) level. Second, the Datacycle approach can avoid major causes of database *hotspots*.

Hotspots in general tend to limit concurrency of transaction executions. The common causes of hotspots are summary data (for example, teller and branch balances in a debit/credit application), tree-structured data access, and large granularity of locking or conflict detection.[31] The second and third factors do not apply in Datacycle architecture, and the data-filter capabilities provide an efficient technique to deal with the first. Since the data filters support on-the-fly aggregation operations, summary data can be calculated on demand within a single cycle. To support frequent updates of hotspots, for example, incrementing and decrementing a branch balance, the update values can be appended to the log and used in calculating the appropriate balance.

7.6 MULTI-APPLICATION DIRECTORY DATABASE

To demonstrate the Datacycle prototype in an application setting, an advanced directory-services database was designed and implemented using the Datacycle prototype as a database server. This directory context was chosen to illustrate a typical telecommunications scenario where multiple applications require access to a common database concurrently, with stringent performance requirements, and using a large variety of data selection criteria. Traditionally, database architectures to support directory services have been highly tuned to support high-throughput, low-response-time access on a severely restricted set of search keys; even when common data are used by two applications, a separate database implementation is usually required for each application. Updates are typically applied in batch, offline, since the physical layout of the database must be reorganized to retain the highly optimized access characteristics. Operations-support databases are employed to keep track of changes to the database, which are then periodically downloaded to the systems optimized for the particular queries generated by various applications.

Ideally, the database architecture for such applications should support very high throughput-read accesses that are both flexible and efficient, while allowing simultaneous updates, obviating the need for application-specific implementations and maintenance of data replicated in multiple systems. Such an architecture could also facilitate more rapid development and deployment of new applications requiring access to data stored in a database designed before the application was conceived.

The schema for the multi-application directory database, summarized in Figure 7, includes traditional white-pages information (surname, given name, telephone number, street number, and so forth), latitude and longitude coordinate information for each street address, plus a variety of other attributes associated with each user. Figure 7 summarizes the schema from a user viewpoint. Many of the user-level attributes are actually composed of multiple database attributes. The number in parentheses next to the attribute name indicates how may database attributes comprise it. A total of 55 different database attributes are associated with a tuple in the directory relation. Maximum size of a tuple is 384 bytes. The database supports selection of records based on any attribute or attribute substring, and any combination of attributes (Boolean, range, even selections based on sums and differences of attribute values within a record). The database schema is stored in a file that is read sequentially when the prototype is initialized; thus, dynamic schema changes are not possible. It would, however, be possible to support dynamic schema changes by storing the schema information in the storage pump and broadcasting it periodically to access managers. The access managers would then always have access to the most current schema information and could use triggers to detect when the schema changes.

Relation Name (1)	Interexchange Carrier (1)	Business Location Code (1)
Logical Record Length (1)	Business Name (4)	Business Organization Code (1)
Physical Record Index (1)	Business Classification (1)	Custom Feature List (5)
Record Identifier (1)	Business Telephone Number (2)	Credit Card Number and PIN (3)
Name and Title (5)	Fax Telephone Number (2)	Electronic Mail Address (1)
Residence Address (5)	Cellular Telephone Number (2)	User Text (3)
Latitude and Longitude (2)	Personal Communications Service Telephone Number (2)	Service Class (1)
Residence Telephone Numbers (2)	Schedules for all Telephone Numbers (8)	

Figure 7.   Directory database schema summary.

In general, response time is independent of the nature of a query, and the system can be engineered to support an essentially arbitrarily large number of queries concurrently. No storage overhead is required for indices; fully indexing this database could increase the storage requirements by a factor of 25 for a typical commercial relational database.[32]

The demonstration application supports queries that would be difficult to realize on a conventional system but are of particular value in directory applications; many would require a full scan of the database. For example, the Datacycle prototype supports proximity queries between arbitrary points in an n-dimensional space. "Find the telephone numbers for all physicians within two miles of 445 South Street," and "Call the closest pharmacy to St. Luke's Hospital" (described in Section 7.4) are both supported in the prototype. The combined arithmetic and Boolean modes of the data-filter, together with the full database scan, provide efficient execution of these queries in the Datacycle prototype.

In addition to query functionality, the prototype supports concurrent updates to attributes. One of the demonstrated applications is a personal communicator service that updates the telephone number at which a person can be reached as he or she roams over various domains spanning geographically distributed areas. Full transaction-semantics are also supported in the prototype.

7.7 ONGOING RESEARCH

While the Datacycle prototype is quite robust, it does not realize the full functionality of the architecture, and implementation continues as part of the research process. For example, fault tolerance based on shadow pumps and the use of the broadcast log has not been incorporated. Scalability has been demonstrated only to a limited extent. Multiple broadcast channels, requiring an intelligent data-manager module meeting the real-time requirements associated with synchronizing across the multiple channels, have not been implemented. JOIN queries are not supported by the access-manager software. Data-placement algorithms (equivalent to grid files or extensible hashing) can be used to improve search efficiency, but these are also not implemented. In all of these cases where open questions remain, paper designs exist.

We have also continued to address the question of efficient searching of a high-speed information stream. Specifically, we have considered two issues. First, what is an effective strategy for searching unstructured information (for example, text)? Second, does a custom data-filter remain the best choice for structured search in the Datacycle architecture?

7.7.1 VLSI String-Search Accelerator

While string searching is one of the basic operations in many areas of nonnumeric processing, such as text retrieval in database applications, searching for arbitrarily positioned strings using our prototype data-filter is extremely cumbersome and inefficient. The problem of string searching is to find all occurrences of a p-character pattern, P, constructed from a vocabulary of m distinct characters, in an s-character data string, S. The pattern P may also contain *don't care* characters. For typical applications, $p << s$ and $m << s$. Since the size of the data string is usually very large, sequential search via general purpose processors is prohibitively slow. To expedite the search, numerous hardware-based solutions to string searching have been proposed and implemented. As fast software string-searching algorithms[33, 34] are based on finite state automata, hardware realizations of FSA pattern matching were investigated by Haskin.[35] FSA requires precompilation of the patterns, and processes the data string one character at a time. Although precompilation of the pattern eliminates the need to compare each character of the data string to every pattern character, the sequential character-at-a-time processing severely limits the search rates of these systems. Several papers[22, 36-38] have proposed using comparator arrays to perform pipelined pattern matching directly without precompilation of the patterns. Multiple patterns are compared concurrently to the data string to achieve higher throughput. However, the search rate is still limited by the sequential processing of the data string. In the systolic array approach,[36] data and pattern characters are routed in opposite directions. At any given clock cycle, only half of the cells in the array can perform meaningful computation; therefore, half of the physical hardware is actually wasted. In other studies,[22, 37, 38] pattern characters are pre-loaded into the comparator cells. Each character of the data string is broadcast into all cells serially, and comparison results are generated by all cells simultaneously. Since a string-search operation on text database exhibits very low selectivity, comparisons beyond the first few characters of the pattern are usually unnecessary. Thus, most of the comparisons with the last few characters of the pattern are redundant.

To reduce the number of redundant comparisons and to increase the degree of effective parallelism in the pattern-matching problem, both ALTEP[39] and an algorithm we have designed utilize a data-parallel, pattern-serial scheme in which pattern characters are broadcast and compared to a block of the data string in parallel. While ALTEP is a cellular processor optimized for regular expression comparisons with microprogrammed control, ours is a VLSI filter optimized for variable-length text processing with hardwired control. The decoupling of query resolution from the primitive match operation simplifies the structure of the VLSI filter so that it can be implemented compactly, and is hence more efficient.

7.7.1.1 The DPPM Algorithm

Let S[1:n] be the data string of n characters to be searched and Pat[1:p] be the pattern of p characters. The data string is divided into blocks of b characters each and searched a block at a time. Let Blk[1:b] be the current data block of size b characters. Basically, the DPPM algorithm serially broadcasts each pattern character to a block of the data string. If the pat-

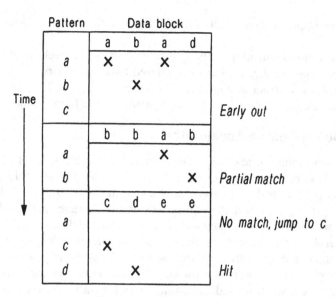

Figure 8.   DPPM example.

tern character matches with any of the characters in the block, the next pattern character
is broadcast in the next comparison cycle. If at any cycle, no match is found between the
current pattern character and the data block, and if no partial match is carried over from
the previous block, the data block is discarded and the search continues with the next
block. A partial match occurs when $Pat[i]$, $i < p$, matches with the last data block character $Blk[b]$. This partial match information is stored and used in the next block to continue
the search by comparing $Pat[i + 1]$ to the first data block character $Blk[1]$.

The DPPM algorithm can be illustrated best using a simple example. Suppose a search
for the pattern "abcd" in the data string "abadbbabcdee" is conducted. Figure 8 shows the
operation of the DPPM algorithm using a block size of 4. The first block, containing the characters "abad," is first loaded into the comparator array. When compared to the first pattern
character "a," two matches are detected. The second pattern character "b" is then broadcast and compared to the characters to the right of the matched characters in the previous
cycle; that is, "b" is compared to the second and the fourth characters in the block. Since a
match is detected again at the second character, a comparison of the third pattern character "c" with the third character in the block is necessary. This time, no match in the block
is observed; thus, the current block is discarded and the search continues with the next
block. This early mismatch-detection mechanism avoids broadcasting and comparing the
fourth pattern character "d" to the current block, since this comparison is redundant .

The next block contains the characters "bbab." The pattern compares successfully up to
the second character "b." At this point, the end of the block is reached. There is a possibility that the pattern may span the block boundary. DPPM remembers this partial match
information and continues the match in the next cycle. Since there is no other match in this
block, the current block is also discarded. The third block contains the characters "cdee."
The first pattern character "a" has no match with the block. At this point, DPPM recalls there
was a partial match in the previous block up to the second pattern character; therefore, it
jumps to the third pattern character "c" and continues the partial match from the previous
block. Finally, a hit or an occurrence of the pattern is detected with the fourth pattern character "d." Although not shown in this example, the DPPM algorithm can also detect mul-

tiple occurrences of the pattern even if they overlap, and no backtracking is required to detect all occurrences.

7.7.1.2 VLSI Design

Figure 9 shows the circuit-block diagram of the DPPM engine design. Before the actual search operation, the pattern, pattern length, and *don't care* positions are first loaded into their corresponding registers. The data string is buffered and read one block at a time to the block register. The comparator array performs the actual comparison between the pattern character and the data block. The results of the comparator array are ANDed with the mask to form T. The DPPM engine integrates the mismatch detection and the partial match propagation mechanisms by combining the Vin register (partial match information from previous block) with the old register (match results of the previous comparison cycle) to form the mask for each comparison cycle. The first bit of the mask is from Vin[i], and the last (b-1) bits are from the first (b-1) bits of T in the previous cycle. The last bit of T is stored into Vout[i]. Each time a new data block is read, the first (p-1) bits of Vout are loaded into the last (p-1) bits of Vin. The first bit of Vin is always set.

The sequence controller controls the operation of the DPPM engine by generating the value, i, which is used to index the pattern, don't care, Vin, and Vout registers. By monitoring the values of T, the content of the Vin register, and the pattern length, the sequence controller decides for each cycle one of the following three actions:

1. Compare the next pattern character with the current block.
2. Jump to a pattern character to continue the partial match from previous block.
3. Discard the current block and continue the search with the next block.

Step 1 is taken if this is not the last pattern character and the content of T is nonzero (match(es) detected in the current cycle). If T is zero, then the index of the next pattern character to be used for comparison is determined by a priority encoder, which encodes the first nonzero bit in the Vin register after masking off the first $(i-1)$ bits of the Vin register using a linear shift register. Step 3 is taken if the last pattern character is reached, or if T is zero and there is no more partial match propagation from the previous block (early out).

The sequence controller also generates a "last character" signal when the last pattern character is reached. This signal is used by the hit-detection unit, which checks the values of T to report any hit in the search. The priority encoder produces the encoded addresses for all hit positions in the current block.

The critical path of the circuit is from the pattern register, through the comparator and AND arrays, to the priority encoder. Using 2-micron complementary metal-oxice semiconductors, the comparison cycle time is about 50 nanoseconds for a block size of 1,000. This cycle time includes the broadcasting delay of 6 ns. If 1.2-micron CMOS is used, the cycle time will be approximately 33 ns. The chip area of the DPPM engine for a block size of 128 is roughly 200×100 mil^2.

7.7.1.3 Performance Evaluation

The DPPM algorithm can be evaluated best by simulating its operation on a real text database. Under such an environment, we can estimate its performance, and can also gain insights into its behavior. The database chosen for this simulation experiment consists of the Associated Press wire news articles on August 2, 1988. The total size of this news article database is 4.4 Mbytes. All uppercase characters in the database were converted to lowercase; case-insensitive pattern matching was used in the experiment. The test patterns cho-

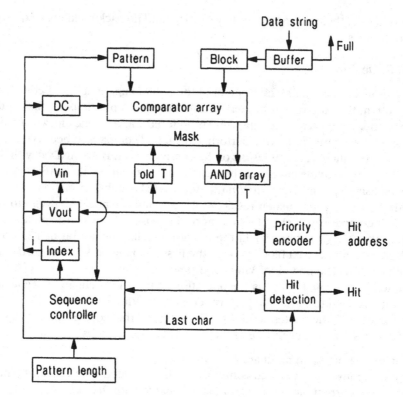

Figure 9.   DPPM engine.

sen for this simulation experiment are the 100 most frequent words in American English that are at least five characters long.[40] The pattern lengths vary from five to 10 characters, with an average of 5.88 characters.

Figure 10 shows the average number of comparison cycles per block, C, measured at different block sizes. Although the pattern characters are serially compared to the data block, early mismatch detection allows the algorithm to search the next block as soon as a mismatch is detected. This feature is especially effective at smaller block sizes, where the probabilities of matching the first few characters of the pattern are low. Without early mismatch detection, C is equal to the average pattern length, in this case, 5.88. At larger block sizes, the probability of finding the pattern in the block is higher; thus, the value of C also increases. As the block size is increased, the value of C approaches the average pattern length asymptotically.

Using 50 ns as the comparison cycle time, Figure 11 shows the search rates at different block sizes. Recall that increasing the block size requires proportionately more comparators on chip. At a block size of 16, the search rate is 212 Mbytes per second. This rate matches the predicted optical-disk-transfer rate of 200 Mbytes per second. At a block size of 128, the search rate reaches 1 Gbyte per second. This rate is sufficient to handle existing memory bandwidth of supercomputers as well as data input from optical-fiber transmission systems in future communication networks.

7.7.1.4 Extension and Integration

Instead of comparing the pattern characters serially to the data block as in the DPPM algorithm, multiple pattern characters can be compared to the data block simultaneously in

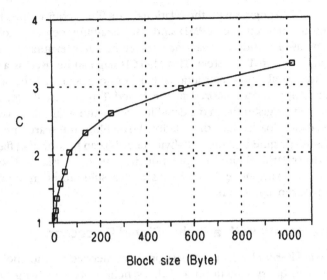

Figure 10. Average number of comparison cycles per block.

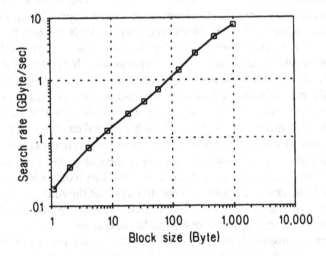

Figure 11. Search rates at different block sizes.

a multiple-pattern, multiple-data (MPMD) algorithm. This approach reduces the number of comparison cycles required per block and thus results in a higher search rate. Since multiple pattern characters can be grouped into a word with proper length (for example, four characters long for a 32-bit processor), the MPMD engine can be integrated easily with the relational data-filter described in Section 7.3, so that the search operations can be performed on both formatted and unformatted data within a single data-filter.

The MPMD engine uses a two-dimensional array of comparators to perform multiple steps of the DPPM algorithm in parallel. Pattern characters can be loaded and compared in parallel to the input data block. The partial-match traces propagate through the comparators in diagonal direction and terminate at the V registers for partial matches and T registers for matches. The whole parallel-comparison operation can be implemented in one or more pipeline stages.

Integrating the MPMD engine with the relational data-filter requires interfaces to pass the control information between the MPMD and the data-filter central processing unit. A MATCH flag can be used to indicate that one or more matches terminated at the current input data block (indicated in T register). This MATCH flag can be used as a condition code for Boolean predicate-evaluation instructions. Furthermore, since all the state information of the string-search operation is stored in the V and T registers, these registers can be mapped as a part of the register file in the data-filter. Since the string-search operation is performed while the data is loaded into the relational data-filter, the search results for each input record (text is also segmented into 128-byte records) can be stored in flags and registers and forwarded to the relational filtering operation in a pipelined fashion. The relational data-filter can then use and manipulate directly the search results stored in the condition codes and in the general-purpose registers.

7.7.2 Database Search with a Digital Signal Processor

Our original data-filter architecture was strongly influenced by the choice of strict synchronization between query execution and the synchronously arriving broadcast-record stream. The data-filter architecture and instruction set guaranteed that, even in the worst case, every instruction in the instruction buffer could be executed before the next record arrived, so that input buffer overflow cannot occur. For synchronous search, we concluded that the data-filter architecture achieves about a factor of 8 improvement in efficiency over a general-purpose microprocessor implemented using comparable technology.

Recently, however, we have re-evaluated that design decision. The re-evaluation has three motivations. First, while the data-filter operates synchronously with the broadcast channel, the problem of FIFO overflow in the access manager downstream from the data-filter required us to deal with the recovery from a condition in which a query could not complete its read-set in a single broadcast cycle. These recovery techniques could also be used to recover from input record-buffer overflow conditions in a loosely coupled datafilter architecture. Second, executing all the instructions comprising a single query (the worst case) occurs very rarely, because most records in the database do not satisfy the query. As in the case of the DPPM string-search processor, early detection of a query "miss" can avoid execution of unnecessary instructions and dramatically improve average utilization of the ALU. Finally, improvements in the speed and density of memory technology made the large, fast, off-chip buffers required by the loosely synchronized architecture reasonable to consider.

Figure 12 shows a possible new architecture for the data-filtering subsystem based on a commercial digital signal processor. A DSP was chosen because it is specifically designed for real-time embedded applications, with its architecture and instruction set geared towards low-level data manipulation, data movement, and arithmetic computation. A large dual-ported memory is used to implement a circular record buffer, managed by sophisticated load-control logic, allowing simultaneous access to record data by the DSP. Unlike the current Datacycle architecture, where the functions of record loading and query execution are strictly synchronized, the DSP architecture supports loose synchronization of loading and execution. Serial link interfaces with direct memory access capability provide the ability to concurrently load queries as well as off-load summary data and selected records. Fast static memory is used for general-purpose needs: program and data storage, the temporary storage of records for certain queries (for example, spatial queries), and the buffering of selected records and projected attributes to be sent to the query manager.

For many relevant applications, the number of records of interest is small. Loose synchronization between record loading and query execution allows the processor to use

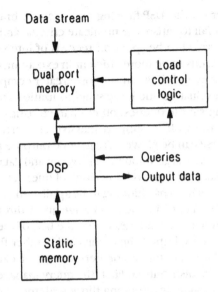

Figure 12. DSP filter subsystem architecture.

longer execution times against records of interest, making up time against records that do not satisfy the query predicates. In short, the performance of the DSP architecture is proportional to the average, as opposed to the worst-case, execution-path timing. This is a significant advantage over the data-filter where processing must complete within a single record-broadcast time, especially when short record-broadcast times might preclude the offering of certain functions, like multiplication, altogether.

Branching and bus conflicts in the DSP execution pipeline are significant concerns because they consume precious clock cycles. Ironically, branching also provides the means of leveraging DSP throughput. For example, a technique in evaluating Boolean expressions is that of short-circuit evaluation (similar to early mismatch in the DPPM algorithm), where encountering a false predicate in the sequential evaluation of conjunctive predicates eliminates the need to evaluate further predicates. With its branch capability, the DSP can implement short-circuit predicate evaluation, reducing the average time to identify records of interest. This capability allows additional time to be allocated for more complex query processing or greater query concurrency.

An analysis of short-circuit evaluation suggests that, for maximum effectiveness, predicate tests should be ordered so that the most restrictive tests are evaluated first. Certain orderings are intuitively obvious—for example, phone number before last name before relation name; others could be decided through statistics or heuristics. Quantitative analysis, on the assumption that predicate ordering is monotonic from most restrictive to least restrictive, reveals that queries having up to seven predicates and selectivity less than 1 percent will average less than two predicate evaluations per record. In contrast, the data-filter must evaluate all query predicates.

To compare the data-filter and DSP-filtering architectures, we can evaluate performance for two kinds of queries: complex queries, which contain several predicates and require extensive computation (for example, fuzzy queries), and simple queries, which output records based on one or two predicates. While we estimate that a new data-filter design using 0.8-micron technology would evaluate predicates six to eight times faster than a current DSP processor, this advantage is mitigated by the DSP's ability to perform short-circuit predicate evaluation. Moreover, in the DSP-filtering architecture, branch capability eliminates processing of records that fail to satisfy the predicate criteria, and loose synchronization allows the processing time saved to be spent on records of interest. For these reasons, the DSP-filtering architecture tends to be more efficient in executing complex queries than the architecture of the data-filter, and thus can support greater complexity.

Although short-circuit evaluation and loose synchronization are not significant factors in the efficiency of executing simple queries, other characteristics of the DSP-filtering architecture potentially allow the DSP to support massive concurrency in executing simple queries. Specifically, the DSP can be viewed as a general-purpose processor with a standard instruction set, having access to large amounts of program and data memory. Algorithms can be devised that take advantage of a priori knowledge of query characteristics and allow optimization techniques such as hash partitioning to be applied to query execution in the DSP.

To illustrate the use of hash partitioning to leverage query throughput of simple queries, we use credit-card validation as an example, where the task of the database system is to retrieve a record (if it exists) based upon the credit-card-number field of the record. The algorithm makes use of *hashing*, a computation performed on a data element that maps data elements to bins in a uniform distribution. First, the query manager compiles lists of credit-card numbers into a large hash table, grouping those with the same hash value in the same bin. Next, this table is loaded into the DSP, where, during execution, the DSP applies the same hash function to the credit-card-number field of incoming records, using the hash value as an index into the vector table. Obtaining the list of credit-card verification numbers from the hash table, the DSP individually compares the current record's credit-card number to each number in the list. If a match occurs, the current record is output. In this manner, the throughput leverage gained is proportional to the number of entries in the vector table. By partitioning the verification queries, only those queries are executed that have a chance at matching against the current record.

Another notable use of hash partitioning in the DSP architecture is in implementing the JOIN operation. Implementing JOINs in the data-filter is inefficient; current algorithms are extremely sensitive to the number of records in the JOIN relations or the number of unique JOIN attribute values. Conversely, the DSP JOIN algorithm using hash partitioning is relatively insensitive to relation size and the number of unique JOIN attribute values, and no assumptions are made about the ordering of records or relations in the database. While we do not describe the algorithm here, it is similar to the simple hash JOIN method described by Mishra.[41]

In summary, a filtering architecture based on the DSP is attractive because of characteristics that allow for increased flexibility, functionality, and, in many cases, performance over the data-filter architecture. Loose synchronization and branch capability permit average execution time instead of worst-case execution time to determine performance. Throughput is leveraged for high-volume applications that submit homogeneous sets of simple queries. The costs of custom data-filter chip design, maintenance, and evolution are eliminated by choosing a commercially available processor. On the other hand, a DSP-filtering architecture places great demand on the intelligence of the query manager, requiring much greater complexity to determine optimized execution strategies, manage concurrency, and predict execution timing. These issues and others relating to the query manager software in a DSP-filtering architecture remain an open research topic. Alternatively, reimplementing the original data-filter in newer technology, with significantly larger record and instruction buffers, and with the text-search capabilities described in Section 7.7.1, is an approach still with merit. Whether the initial and continuing costs of a custom architecture are worthwhile depends on the applications for which such a system will be used.

7.8 SUMMARY

The Datacycle architecture attempts to satisfy many goals simultaneously: support for high-performance transaction processing, support for a powerful and flexible query language, and support for very high levels of concurrent access to a single database by multiple applications. The Datacycle approach to meeting these diverse goals is to apply hardware technology to achieve a different set of performance trade-offs that enable multiple, performance-critical applications to share a single physical database. Key to realizing this approach is the on-the-fly data-filtering operation, which supports query-processing functionality and conflict resolution for high-throughput transaction processing.

The use of custom architectures and hardware for database systems is a subject of controversy. Custom designs can generally achieve greater performance in a particular task, but suffer economically because the initial design cost must be recovered from the single database application, rather than the many applications that may incorporate a general-purpose component like a microprocessor, or a general-purpose computing system. A critical issue in assessing the practicality of a custom design is the trade-off between design effort, the resulting improvement in performance and functionality, and the general applicability of the resulting system. In these terms, we believe that the Datacycle approach provides an unusually versatile system architecture that addresses an acute set of acute application needs not met by conventional approaches.

ACKNOWLEDGMENTS

We would like to acknowledge the following people who have worked on the Datacycle project and the directory-services application: Doug Arnett, Munir Cochinwala, Dorothy Deluca, Robert Fleischman, Prabakhar Krishnamurthy, Ravi Masand, Irene Monaghen, John Ostuni, Chung-li Tsai, and Abel Weinrib.

REFERENCES

1. E.F. Codd, "A Relational Model for Large Shared Data Banks," *Comm. ACM*, Vol. 14, No. 6, June 1970, pp. 377–387.
2. M.M. Astrahan, et al. "System R: A Relational Approach to Data Management," *Computer* Vol. 12, No. 5, May 1979, pp. 42–48.
3. K.P. Eswaran, et al., "The Notions of Consistency and Predicate Locks in a Database System," *Comm. ACM*, Vol. 19, No. 11 Nov. 1976, pp. 624–633.
4. J. Gray, et al., "One Thousand Transactions Per Second," *Proc. IEEE COMPCON*, IEEE CS Press, Los Alamitos, Calif., 1985, pp. 96–101.
5. G. Jackson, "Oracle TP1 Benchmark Methodology," Oracle Corp., Part Number 19753–0788, Belmont, Calif., 1988.
6. Tandem Database Group, "Non-Stop SQL, A Distributed High Performance, High Availability Implementation of SQL," *Springer-Verlag Lecture Notes in Computer Science on High Performance Transaction Systems*, D. Gawlick, M. Haynie, and A. Reuter, eds., Springer-Verlag, New York, N.Y., 1987, pp. 60–104.
7. D.J. Dewitt, "Direct: A Multiprocessor Organization for Supporting Relational Database Management Systems," *IEEE Trans. Computers*, Vol. 28, No. 6, June 1979, pp. 395–406.
8. E. Ozkarahan, *Database Machines and Database Management*, Prentice-Hall, Englewood Cliffs, N.J., 1986.
9. D.K. Hsiao, *Advances in Database Machine Architectures*, Prentice-Hall, Englewood Cliffs, N.J., 1983.

10. D.J. DeWitt, et al., "The Gamma Database Machine Project," *IEEE Trans. Knowledge and Data Eng.*, Vol. 2, No. 1, Mar. 1990, pp. 44-62.

11. H. Boral, "Parallelism in Bubba," *Proc. IEEE Int'l Symp. Databases in Parallel and Distributed Systems*, IEEE CS Press, Los Alamitos, Calif., 1988, pp. 68-71.

12. G.E. Herman, et al., "The Datacycle Architecture for Very High Throughput Database Systems," *Proc. ACM SIGMOD*, ACM Press, New York, N.Y., 1987, pp. 97-103.

13. G.E. Herman and G. Gopal, "The Case for Orderly Sharing," *Springer-Verlag Lecture Notes in Computer Science on High Performance Transaction Systems*, D. Gawlick, M. Haynie, and A. Reuter, eds., Springer-Verlag, New York, N.Y., 1987, pp. 148-174.

14. T.F. Bowen, et al., "A Scalable Database Architecture for Network Services," *Proc. 8th Int'l Switching Symp.*, 1990, pp. 45-51.

15. H.-O. Leilich, et al., "A Search Processor for Data Base Management Systems," *Proc. 4th Conf. Very Large Databases*, IEEE CS Press, Los Alamitos, Calif., 1978, pp. 280-287.

16. J. St. Amand, "A Common File Approach to Data Processing," *Proc. Trends and Applications: 1978 Distributed Processing*, 1978, pp. 78-83.

17. K.C. Lee, et al., "VLSI Accelerators for Large Database Systems," *IEEE Micro*, Vol. 11, No. 6, Dec. 1991, pp. 8-20.

18. *Transputer Databook*, INMOS Corp., Consolidated Printers, Berkeley, Calif., 1989.

19. T. Matoba, et al., "A Rapid Turnaround Design of a High Speed VLSI Search Processor," *Integration: The VLSI Journal*, Vol. 10, 1991, pp. 319-337.

20. K.C. Lee and G.E. Herman, "A High Performance VLSI Data-Filter," in *Database Machines and Knowledge-Base Machines*, M. Kitsuregawa and H. Tanaka, eds., Kluwer Academic, Norwell, Mass., 1988, pp. 251- 268.

21. H.T. Kung and P.L. Lehman, "Systolic (VLSI) Array for Relational Database Operations," *Proc. ACM SIGMOD*, ACM Press, New York, N.Y., 1980, pp. 105-116.

22. T. Curry and A. Mukhopadhyay, Realization of Efficient Non-Numeric Operations through VLSI," *Proc. VLSI '83*, North-Holland, Amsterdam, The Netherlands, 1983, pp. 327-336.

23. P. Faudemay and P. Valduriez, "Design and Analysis of a Direct Filter Using Parallel Comparators," *Proc. 4th Int'l Workshop Database Machines*, Springer-Verlag, New York, N.Y., 1985.

24. C.A. Lynch, "Selectivity Estimation and Query Optimization in Large Databases with Highly Skewed Distributions of Column Values," *Proc. 14th Conf. Very Large Databases*, Morgan Kaufmann Pub., Palo Alto, Calif., 1988, pp 240-251.

25. W.H. Mansfield and R.M. Fleischman, "A High Performance Ad-Hoc Fuzzy Query Processing System for Relational Databases," *North American Fuzzy Information Processing Society Workshop*, Kluwer Academic, Norwell, Mass., 1992, pp. 496-505.

26. V. Tahani, "A Conceptual Framework for Fuzzy Query Processing- A Step toward Very Intelligent Database Systems," *Information Processing & Management*, Vol. 13, 1977, pp. 289-303

27. L.A. Zadeh, "Fuzzy Sets," *Information and Control*, Vol. 8, 1965, pp. 338-353.

28. S. Loeb, "Architecting Personalized Delivery of Multimedia Information," *Comm. ACM*, Vol. 35, Dec. 1992, pp. 39-47.

29. H.T. Kung and J.T. Robinson, "On Optimistic Methods for Concurrency Control," *ACM Trans. Database Systems*, Vol. 6, No. 2, June 1981, pp. 213-226.

30. I. Gold and H. Boral, "The Power of the Private Workspace Model," *Information Systems*, Vol. 11, No. 1, 1986, pp. 1-7.

31. G. Welkum, "Enhancing Concurrency in Layered Systems," *Springer-Verlag Lecture Notes in Computer Science on High Performance Transaction Systems*, D. Gawlick, M. Haney, and A. Reuter, eds., Springer-Verlag, New York, N.Y., 1987, pp. 200-219.

32. *Oracle RDBMS Database Administrator's Guide*, Version 6.0, Chapter 16, Oracle Corp., Belmont, Calif., 1990, pp. 18-19.

33. R.S. Boyer and J. Moore, "A Fast String Searching Algorithm," *Comm. ACM*, Vol. 20, Oct. 1977, pp. 762-772.

34. D.E. Knuth, J.H. Morris, Jr., and V.R. Pratt, "Fast Pattern Matching in Strings," *SIAM J. Computing*, Vol. 6, June 1977, pp. 323-350.

35. R.L. Haskin and L.A. Hollaar, "Operational Characteristics of a Hardware-Based Pattern Matcher," *ACM Trans. Database Systems*, Vol. 8, Mar. 1983, pp. 15–40.

36. M.J. Foster and H.T. Kung, "The Design of Special Purpose Chips," *Computer*, Vol. 13, Jan. 1980, pp. 26–40.

37. A. Halaas, "A Systolic VLSI Matrix for a Family of Fundamental Search Problem," *Integration: The VLSI Journal*, Vol. 1, Dec. 1983, pp. 269–282.

38. K. Takahashi, H. Yamada, and M. Hirata, "Intelligent String Search Processor to Accelerate Text Information Retrieval," *Proc. 5th Int'l Workshop Database Machines*, Kluwer Academic, Norwell, Mass., 1987, pp. 440–453.

39. D. Lee, "ALTEP–A Cellular Processor for High-Speed Pattern Matching," *New Generation Computing*, Vol. 4, Sept. 1986, pp. 225–244.

40. H. Kucera and W. Nelson-Francis, *Computational Analysis of Present-Day American English*, Brown Univ. Press, 1967.

41. P. Mishra and M.H. Eich, "JOIN Processing in Relational Databases," *ACM Computing Surveys*, Vol. 24, No. 1, Mar. 1992, pp. 63–113.

8

Industrial Database Supercomputer Exegesis: The DBC/1012, The NCR 3700, The Ynet, and The Bynet

Felipe Cariño Jr., Warren Sterling, and Pekka Kostamaa

Teradata Advanced Concepts Laboratory
El Segundo, California

ABSTRACT

This chapter provides an in-depth examination of the DBC/1012 architecture and components from the board-level to the software. A comprehensive treatment of the following DBC/1012 issues is provided: (1) data fragmentation, partitioning, and distribution; (2) data access strategies; (3) the relational database intermediate language and query plan generation; (4) performance issues as they relate to parallel execution schemes and intra-query parallelism; and (5) the broadcast sort/merge Ynet interconnection network used for message-passing that enables linear system growth.

Also analyzed are interconnection networks topologies, and the relative benefits and issues relating to each topology. Then our next-generation interconnection network, the Bynet, is examined. We conclude our interconnection network analysis by comparing the Ynet and Bynet. Finally, we describe and analyze the NCR 3700, our next-generation database computer, emphasizing: (1) the architecture; (2) board-level multiprocessing and expected performance gains; (3) strategies and expected benefits derived from using RAID disk arrays; and (4) our new bidirectional, multistage, high-bandwidth, point-to-point Banyan topology Ynet interconnection network, the Bynet.

8.1 INTRODUCTION

The DBC/1012[1] is a multiple-instruction, multiple-data relational[2] database computer[3,4] based on a loosely coupled, share-nothing[5] architecture. Various industrial and academic database machine systems have been documented in the literature, including VERSO,[6] SABRE,[7] RDBM,[8] DBMAC,[9] BUBBA,[10] GAMMA,[11] DDC,[12] ABRE,[13] FDS-R,[14,15] SDC,[16] Hitachi IDP,[17] NTT RINDA,[18] Mitsubishi GREO,[19] and the European Declarative System.[20] General-purpose computer systems that run relational database systems, such as nCUBE, Kendall Square, and VAXCluster, can also be used as database machines.

Our commercial competitive edge and marketplace success has been a result of the almost linear scalability of the DBC/1012 when adding extra processor boards. The DBC/1012 leverages the latest advancements in microprocessor and disk technology, coupled with a proprietary broadcast sort/merge Ynet[21] interconnection network, to apply parallel database processing to very large real-world applications. The DBC/1012 business case and customer case studies are documented[22] concerning the use, fusion, and analysis of real-world decision support applications.[23] These business case studies provide examples of DBC/1012 applications that could not run efficiently on other platforms.

Interconnection networks are an extremely important element of parallel computer systems. Various architectures, strategies, and issues arise as a consequence of the interconnection network topology chosen with a parallel system. We later provide a brief analysis pertaining to interconnection network topologies, and introduce our next-generation interconnection network, the Bynet, designed by Robert McMillen and Cam Watson.[24] The Bynet is a newly designed, higher-bandwidth, point-to-point (and broadcasting), bidirectional interconnection network. A comparative analysis between the Ynet and Bynet features, capabilities, and philosophy is also presented.

The NCR 3700 (originally described as the P-90)[22] is our next-neration parallel-processing computer, succeeding the DBC/1012. It builds on the knowledge obtained from ten years of DBC/1012 commercial experience. The NCR 3700 has the potential to become a UNIX mainframe; however, this chapter will emphasize its use as a database supercomputer. The salient technical differences between NCR 3700 and the DBC/1012 are that the NCR 3700 (1) uses the new Banyan Ynet (Bynet) interconnection network, (2) uses RAID disk arrays connected to multiple processor modules for fault tolerance and performance benefits, (3) uses tightly-coupled microprocessors in each processor module to provide more CPU power, and (4) uses the UNIX SVR4 operating system, as opposed to a custom Teradata operating system.

The rest of this chapter is organized as follows: Section 2 contains an in-depth description and analysis of the DBC/1012 and Ynet interconnection network; Section 3 contains a description of interconnection network topologies and related issues—we introduce the Bynet and compare it to the Ynet; Section 4 contains an analysis of diverse interconnection network topologies; Section 5 contains an exegesis of our next-generation NCR 3700 system; Section 6 presents our conclusions and observations on industrial database parallel supercomputer systems.

8.2 DBC/1012 ARCHITECTURE AND COMPONENTS

Teradata Corp. developed the DBC/1012 (Figure 1) based on a parallel share-nothing architecture.[5] The DBC/1012 processor boards communicate via the Ynet, which is a proprietary broadcast interconnection network. The Ynet interconnection network is used for message passing and data routing between the processor boards, and has built-in intelligence to sort/merge values. The DBC/1012 is a fault-tolerant database supercomputer based on the latest microprocessor and disk technology. The DBC/1012 runs a relational DBMS designed to execute efficiently on a parallel platform and, more importantly, to be linearly expandable from three to 1024 processor modules. A general purpose UNIX application processor has been added to the DBC/1012. The application processor facilitates migrating complex database client-applications from heterogeneous platforms over to a single central server processor within the DBC/1012.

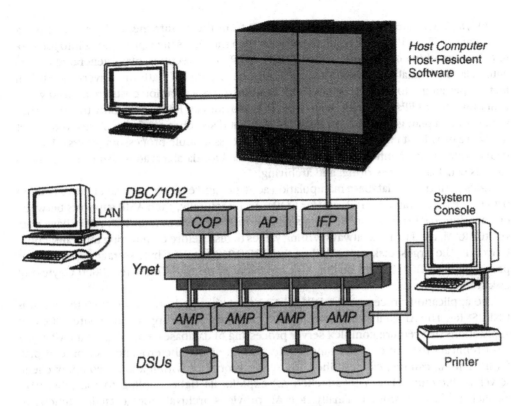

Figure 1. DBC/1012 architecture.

The DBC/1012[22] was the first general-purpose industrial database supercomputer to effectively run a relational DBMS that could handle large commercial applications. The DBC/1012 is comprised of two types of processor modules: external host communication (IFPs, COPs, APs), and internal relational database manipulation modules (the AMPs), which internally communicate via the Ynet. The internal function and DBC/1012 configuration strategies are described below.

Interface processor boards manage the communication and dialog between user transactions on mainframes and the DBC/1012. Architecturally, each IFP board has a channel interface controller, a CPU, and two high-speed Ynet interfaces for fault tolerance. Communication processors are functionally IFP-equivalent except that COPs manage the communication and dialog between users on a ubiquitous combination of (mini) computers, workstations, or PCs, and the DBC/1012. Architecturally, each COP incorporates a local area network adapter, a CPU, and two high-speed Ynet interfaces (for fault tolerance). Each IFP can simultaneously manage the communication and execution of up to 120 concurrent user sessions. The mainframe host resident software that communicates with the IFPs is responsible for evenly distributing the user-session workload among the IFPs. The COP and IFP module boards are almost identical except for special logic to handle channel and LAN connections. The COP is designed to support industry standard networks and protocols, such as Ethernet, FDDI, Token Ring, TCP/IP, ISO/OSI, XNS, and X.25 (with the AP). A master COP assigns and redistributes user sessions to other COPs to ensure an even distribution of the workload. Unlike the IFP, a master COP performs the session dispatching and assignment, since there is no central host-resident software coordinator.

DBC/SQL statements are received by an IFP from the mainframe, or by a COP from a workstation. The IFP or COP resident software then translates the SQL requests into *pseudo-database machine operations*, called *STEPS*. STEPs are execution plans generated to execute relational database operations efficiently on a parallel platform. Diverse statistical metrics pertaining to table sizes, table indexes, and query execution costs are utilized while generating the STEPs execution plan. DBC/SQL provides an EXPLAIN facility that describes the execution plan generated. An IFP/COP resident dispatcher sends the STEPs using Ynet hardware broadcast capabilities to the database access module processors (AMPs). The IFP high-performance channel connections are also used for database administration functions such as data loading, re-storing, and archiving.

AMPs perform the database manipulation activities and execute in parallel the execution plan (STEPs) generated by IFPs and/or COPs. Architecturally, each AMP supports between one and four data storage units, using a storage module devices interface. AMPs have non-volatile RAM, used to avoid always writing values to disk before committing the transaction. Currently, the largest disk supported on the DBC/1012 has 2.5-Gbyte storage capacity, thus providing the DBC/1012 an on-line disk capability of up to 8 Terabytes (8000 Gbytes) of disk storage.

The application processor is a DBC/1012 Ynet-connected processor module that runs UNIX SVR4. The AP facilitates designing and creating a single application source of client applications that require complex server processing of database data. Without an AP, users must replicate the server processing application on diverse heterogeneous frontend platforms. The AP can be best described as a server processor within a more complex client-server architecture. The Ynet-attached AP exploits its tight-coupling to the DBC/1012 parallel database computer. Finally, the AP provides archival storage facility functions, which completely frees user applications from using a mainframe.

8.2.1 Ynet Interconnection Network

The Ynet[1] is a 6-MByte-per-second tree topology broadcast interconnection network for the DBC/1012, with sort/merge capabilities built into its logic to enhance performance. This section focuses on a Ynet description and analysis. The next section covers interconnection network issues, describes our next-generation interconnection network, the Banyan Y-Net (Bynet), and examines the design and performance issues related to both the Ynet and Bynet—especially Ynet saturation issues.

The Ynet is the global communication mechanism used to send messages between the IFP, COP, AMP, and AP processor boards. The Ynet performs message-passing in its hardware logic, thus reducing the broadcast costs and software complexity. The Ynet capabilities are used for global semaphores to coordinate AMP processing. The IFPs/COPs generate execution plans (STEPs) that are broadcast via the Ynet to all the AMPs. Only the AMPs involved in executing the STEPs accept the execution plan message; other AMPs ignore the messages contained in their mailboxes.

The Ynet automatically generates a dynamic grouping of the participating AMPs, thus reducing subsequent message-passing to the AMPs involved in the transaction. The STEPs may contain commands to do data redistribution between AMPs. The redistributed data are transmitted and coordinated using the Ynet. The Ynet logic automatically produces a sorted result set when all tuples are Ynet-merged. As the AMPs retrieve the pertinent data values from the DSUs, each AMP puts its lowest-valued tuple on the Ynet, and the Ynet selects the lowest-valued tuple from among all the current values to pass to the requesting IFP/COP or AP. The net result is that the tuple values are sort/merged by the Ynet as they are returned to the originating processor module requestor. Empirical internal studies show that the interconnection network is a strategic component that the software can exploit for the efficient use of parallel processing.

8.2.2 Data Declustering and Access Strategies

The DBC/1012 declusters relational tables based on hashing. The hashing function is applied to the table's primary index and the tuples are assigned to 3643 buckets. This hash partition strategy (horizontally) fragments the table.[25] The fragments are evenly distributed among the AMPs, and thus enhance parallelism.[26] Primary index searches will always generate an execution plan that hashes to the correct AMP. Data-skew problems are currently handled via table normalization strategies and secondary indexes. The NCR 3700 described in Section 5 has 64-K hash buckets that are distributed and stored on RAID disk arrays.

8.2.3 Parallel STEP Execution Example

Figure 2 pictorially shows how a four-way join is executed by the Teradata database on the DBC/1012. This example uses a 4-AMP DBC/1012 for explanation purposes, but the parallel execution plan would be the same if the DBC/1012 had 400-AMP boards with associated attached disks. The Teradata database uses table index information, row and specific attribute information, row redistribution estimates, and cost formulas, to generate a query execution plan. As previously stated, the DBC/SQL EXPLAIN facility can be used to see the execution plan generated.

A pictorial version of the execution plan is time-plotted in the diagram. Each box describes the operations that are performed (in parallel) at each time interval (RET stands for retrieve). Maximum system efficiency depends on the user queries that are executing at the time. The Teradata database algorithms were designed for global system efficiency, as opposed to executing a single-user, single-query efficiently. Single-query operations are rare, but these can run efficiently on the DBC/1012 by choosing a good database schema and indexing scheme.

The DBC/1012 relational database software collects and maintains table statistics. The table statistics include the number of tuples, and number of unique attribute values. DBC/SQL does not allow duplicate tuples, a practice that prevents some problems.[27] Joins use a "greedy" algorithm (with one table lookahead), table statistics, and index information when choosing a join and data-redistribution plan.

A DBC/SQL EXPLAIN facility, which shows the execution plan generated for a query, provides valuable information when performance-tuning a database schema, defining indexes, and refining queries. Intra-query parallelism that enhances response time is achieved by concurrently dispatching and executing the individual STEPs on the AMPs. For example, when executing an n-table join on each AMP, it is possible to process all n tables concurrently.

8.2.4 DBC/1012 Hardware and Software Fault Tolerance

The DBC/1012 IFP/COP-to-AMP configuration mix is a function of its intended use. An on-line transaction processing (OLTP) application with short-running transactions and high communication requirements will have a higher number of IFPs than a decision support (DSS) configuration. DSS configurations should have more DSUs per AMP than for OLTP. The number of AMPs is configured as a function of the throughput requirements.

System software considerations limit the number of IFPs and COPs in a DBC/1012 to be less than or equal to the number of AMPs. Fault tolerance is achieved by a combination of

```
SELECT  L_ORDERKEY,SUM(L_EXTENDEDPRICE *(1-L_DISCOUNT/100)), O_ORDERDATE
FROM  CUSTOMERS, ORDERS, LINEITEM, TIME T1, TIME T2
WHERE  C_MKTSEGMENT  = :SEGMENT
  AND  C_CUSTKEY  = O_CUSTKEY
  AND  L_ORDERKEY  = O_ORDERKEY
  AND  O_ORDERDATE  = T1.T_TIMEKEY
  AND  ((T1.T_WEEK  <  :WEEK
  AND  T1.T_YEAR  = :YEAR)
  OR  T1.T_YEAR  <  :YEAR)
  AND  L_SHIPDATE  = T2.T_TIMKEY
  AND  ((T2.T_WEEK  >  = :WEEK
  AND  T2.T_YEAR  = :YEAR)
  OR  T2.T_YEAR  >  :YEAR)
GROUP BY  L_ORDERKEY, O_ORDERDATE
ORDER BY  2 DESC, 3 ASC;
```

Relative table sizes

Table name	Number of rows
CUSTOMERS	75,000
ORDERS	750,000
LINEITEM	3,000,000
TIME	2,000

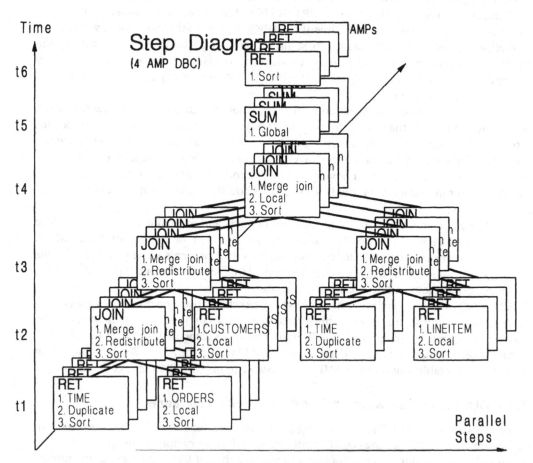

Figure 2.   Example DBC/SQL (macro) and STEP execution plan picture.

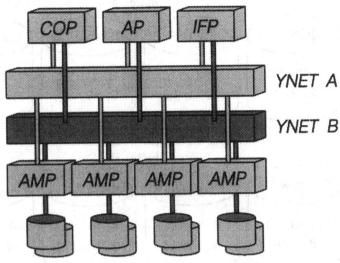

Figure 3. Fault-tolerant Ynet diagram.

hardware and software. Every DBC/1012 processor board (IFP, COP, AMP) has two separate Ynet connections (Figure 3). While operational, both Ynets are used for message-passing.

At table creation, there is an option to specify that a FALLBACK (duplicate table copy) is to be maintained. In addition, the user can specify BEFORE and/or AFTER image logging. The fallback copy is accessed whenever the primary copy becomes unavailable, thus providing data redundancy as well as hardware redundancy. Like the primary table data, this fallback copy is also distributed among the AMPs in the system. However, the fallback copy of each row is stored on a different AMP from the one on which the primary copy is stored. This distribution ensures that a fallback copy of the stored data remains available on other AMPs if an AMP should fail.

Furthermore, the Teradata database has the notion of a "cluster." A cluster is a logical grouping and partitioning of data that can tolerate a single AMP failure within the cluster. If two AMPs fail within the same cluster, the system will crash. An IFP failure results in a system restart, and the IFP sessions are recovered on another IFP. For this reason, mainframe DBC/1012s are sold with more than one IFP. The system administrator may provide additional data protection by "clustering" the AMPs into large groups that consist of two to 16 AMPs. In Figure 4, the AMPs are grouped into two clusters of four AMPs.

8.3 INTERCONNECTION NETWORKS ANALYSIS

This section contains a concise analysis of interconnection networks: topology comparisons,[28] parallel database computers,[29] message-passing,[30] and performance models,[31,32] as they relate to the design of the DBC/1012 Ynet and the NCR 3700 Bynet. The loosely-coupled share-nothing MIMD architectures, like the DBC/1012, rely on message-passing for communication. Athas provides an analysis of message-passing in multicomputers, and provides a formal model and analysis on the performance of multiprocessor interconnection networks.[30] This section contains a description of our next-generation interconnection network, the Bynet. This description is followed by a Bynet and Ynet comparison, and

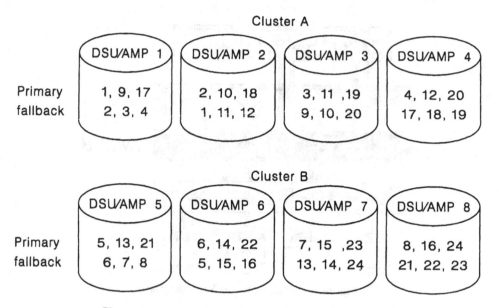

Figure 4.   Distribution of data with clustered AMPs.

an analysis of interconnection network topologies. We conclude with a survey of other interconnection networks.

8.3.1 The Bynet Description and Comparison to Ynet

The Bynet[24] is being designed for our next-generation database computer, the NCR 3700, which is described in the next section. The Bynet (Figure 5) is a scalable multistage interconnection network that supports broadcast, multicast, and monocast messages. It is internally comprised of 8 × 8 crossbar (Figure 7) switch nodes. The NCR 3700 has processor module assembly boards that support two optical fiber connections to the Bynet. Each Bynet has a full-duplexed 10-MByte-per-second bandwidth per PMA connection. Each PMA has a total of 10 MBytes-per-second throughput available per Bynet; hence, two BYNETs per PMA provide 20 MBytes-per-second throughput.

The Bynet is architected to interconnect up to 4096 NCR 3700 PMAs; thus, the maximum monocast throughput is 40 GBytes per second per Bynet, minus contention. Both simulation and hardware analysis of a 64-processor module configuration exchanging 4-KByte messages at random indicate that the sustainable throughput is about 67 percent of the maximum.

```
Bynet CAPACITY = (Number PMAs * 10 MBytes/second) -Contention
Theoretical System Maximum: 40GB = (4096 * 10MBytes/second) -
Contention
```

The Bynet, unlike the Ynet, allows multiple monocast messages on the network. The Bynet is based on Banyan topology, whereas the Ynet is a true broadcast network that allows only one kind of monocast or broadcast connection at a time. Unlike the Ynet, as processor boards are added to a Bynet-based system, the capacity of the network scales up. Another feature of the Bynet is its automatic configuration. The Bynet is designed such that the cabling of the network can be done fairly arbitrarily. During system installation, the

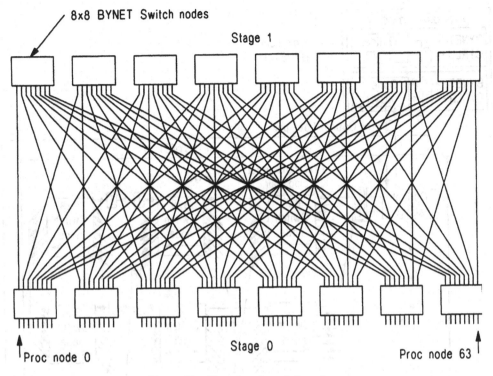

Figure 5.   **Bynet network topology.**

Bynet and diagnostic hardware automatically sense the network cabling and configuration. It is still important, however, to use a systematic method in installing the system.

The Bynet monocast messages are two-way communication links established between two PMA processors. The requesting PMA processor communicates on a high capacity forward channel, while the responding processor can reply using a lower capacity backchannel (Figure 7).

The Bynet supports both blocking and non-blocking protocols.[33] The former are used for broadcast circuits; deadlocks are avoided by routing the circuit to a single crossbar port in the center of the network. The latter are used for monocast circuits to increase throughput (up to a factor of two over blocking) and to minimize the system performance degradation when a single processor module becomes a hot spot.

Another key difference between the Bynet and Ynet is the automatic fault detection and reconfiguration found on the Bynet. Both the Bynet and Ynet are configured as dual systems. If one of the networks fails, the other can take over the whole system load. This du-

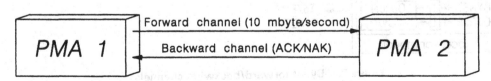

Figure 6.   **Bynet switch nodes.**

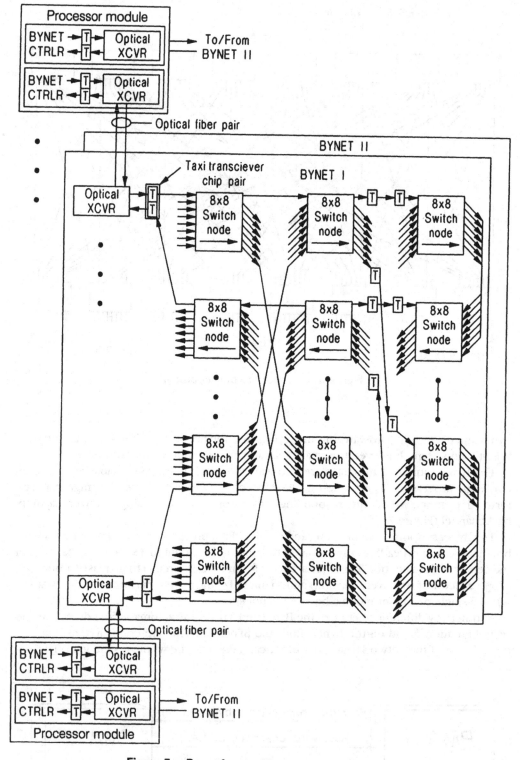

Figure 7.   Bynet forward/backward channels.

ality reduces the network capacity by 50 percent. Each Bynet is designed to be fault tolerant. If a switch node or optical link in the Bynet fails, the network can be reconfigured around the failure, such that only a portion of the network capacity is lost. The Bynet will also detect congestion in the switch nodes, and the load balancing hardware will automatically reroute the network traffic to less-utilized parts of the network.

8.4 INTERCONNECTION NETWORK TOPOLOGIES

The following illustrations and discussion[12,29,30,32] describe interconnection network topologies and performances. Figure 8 pictorially shows the topology for 2D-Mesh, Hypercube, Crossbar, BANYAN, and the Bynet.

Table 1 is a qualitative comparison of network topologies. Table 2 provides a quantitative practical comparison using 64 nodes as an example. SDC-OMEGA,[16] EDS-DELTA,[20,34] MESHNET,[35] and iPSC/860-PARAGON[36] are other interconnection networks that have been designed since the survey was written.[29] Our description above shows the thought processes and rationale behind the Bynet design choices.

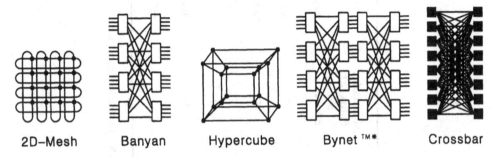

2D–Mesh   Banyan   Hypercube   Bynet ™*   Crossbar

* Bynet based on 8x8 switch nodes; picture uses 4x4 nodes.

Figure 8.   Interconnection network topologies.

Table 1.   Interconnection topology comparison [5].

Topology	Number Physical Circuits	Effective Throughput Messages/Sec	Alternative Paths (per Network)	Scalability	Expandability
2D-Mesh	POOR	POOR	FEW	NOT LINEAR	INCREMENTAL
HyperCube	GOOD	GOOD	FEW	NOT LINEAR	PREDETERMINED
CROSSBAR	NOT PRACTICAL BEYOND 32 NODES		NONE	LINEAR	NONE
BANYAN	BEST	BETTER	NONE	LINEAR	INCREMENTAL
BYNET™	BEST	BEST	MANY	LINEAR	INCREMENTAL

Table 2. Interconnection topology comparison [5].

Topology	Number Physical Circuits	Max Theoretical Throughput Messages/Sec	Alternative Paths (a) per network	Scalability	Expandability	Packaging
2D-Mesh	$f(n) = \sqrt{n}$ $f(64) = 8$	1M	3	Not Linear	Incremental Sqrt(n nodes)	Easy
HyperCube	$f(n) = \dfrac{2n}{Log2n}$ $f(64) = 21$	6M	5	Not Linear	Pre-Determined	Easy
Crossbar	$f(n) = n^2$ $f(64) = 4096^b$	$4B^b$	0	Linear	None	Not Feasible
BANYAN	$f(n) = n$ $f(64) = 64$	8M	0	Linear	Incremental (1 node)	Not (c) Feasible
BYNET™	$f(n) = n$ $f(64) = 64$	16M	7	Linear	Incremental (1 node)	Easy Modular

(a) Optimistic Analysis. (b) This size crossbar is not feasible to build. (c) Not feasible for large system

8.5. NCR 3700—THE NEXT-GENERATION DATABASE COMPUTER

NCR 3700 has been designed based on DBC/1012 experiences and lessons. It uses recent technology advancements in hardware and software. The software design, utilizing new developments in parallel operating systems and parallel relational database algorithms, exploits the NCR 3700 architecture, Bynet, RAID5 storage, and board-level multiprocessing. As for the DBC/1012, the NCR 3700's primary goal was to scale CPU and I/O utilization linearly as the systems grows. Architecturally, at a high level of abstraction, the NCR 3700, like the DBC/1012, is an MIMD loosely-coupled, shared-nothing computer system.

The NCR 3700's (Figure 9) basic building blocks are processor module assemblies. The NCR 3700 has a single processor type, the PMA, that is logically and functionally equivalent to AMPs, IFPs, COPs, and APs on the DBC/1012. Each PMA has a processor board that has four tightly-coupled industry-standard processor units. The first PMA generation uses quad 50-MHz Intel 80486 CPUs and 512 MBytes of memory. Each CPU has an on-chip 8-KByte cache and a second level 256-KByte cache. The channel and network attachments are through the MCA bus connected through Bynet interface controller board. There are plans to replace the PMA 80486-based processor board with Pentium microprocessors.

The PMA is composed of six boards (Figure 10): processor board (PB), memory board (MEM), Bynet interface controller board (BIC), SCSI-2 host adapter board (SHA), power

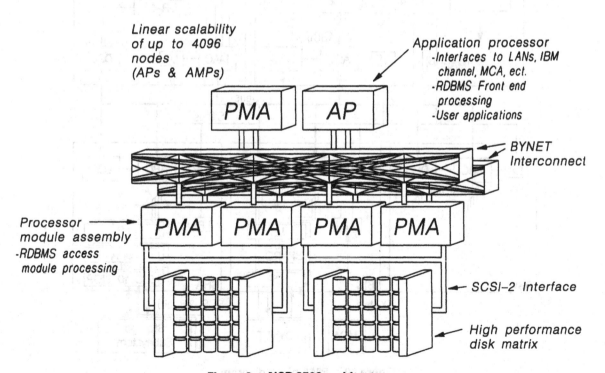

Figure 9. NCR 3700 architecture.

board (PWR), and a board reserved for future functional expansion use (RSV). The six PMA boards share a memory bus, called the JDBus. The JDbus is capable of 200 MBytes per second of peak performance. The PMA status is continuously monitored by a separate processor diagnostic subsystem. The most salient acronyms within Figure 10 are: address bus chip (ABC), data bus chip (DBC), line buffering (LB), and the SPARC, which runs the Bynet interface software. The PMAs are connected to disk arrays through a standard SCSI-2 interface. The disk array has dual access paths, including dual controllers. The data are stored on the disk array using RAID logic, which can survive a single disk failure. The disk array can be configured with hot spares that are used to reconstruct the data of a failed drive. The initial disk array matrix is built using 1.6-GByte drives. Although this chapter uses the term "disk array," it actually is a logical disk matrix configured six deep and five wide. This arrangement provides an unformatted capacity of 48 GBytes per array. Future matrices will have more disks for a planned unformatted capacity of 99 GBytes.

The operating system running on this hardware platform is an enhanced UNIX SVR4 to support parallel processing. Teradata's relational database software was ported to the new platform and enhanced to take advantage of the new hardware and operating system features. This system will increase Teradata's lead in the decision support database market. Furthermore, significant software advances improve the on-line transaction processing capabilities on the new platform. For example, a new hashing algorithm partitions data into

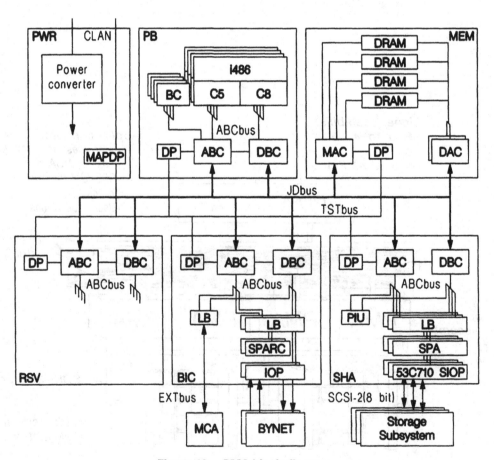

Figure 10.   PMA block diagram.

Figure 11. NCR 3700 clique configuration examples.

64-K hash-buckets and intelligently distributes the data among the disk arrays. Disks within the disk arrays will be assigned to virtual AMPs running on the PMAs. The database software exploits RAID disk arrays.[37]

An NCR 3700 clique configuration consists of two or more PMAs fully connected to one or more disk arrays. Figure 11 shows three sample cliques: 2 PMAs to 1 disk array, 3 PMAs to 2 disk arrays, and 4 PMAs to 2 disk arrays. Although there is no logical (or physical) restriction concerning mixing many clique configurations, there are practical (software) limits to using a system with more than two clique configurations. NCR 3700 cliques are meant to be configured for performance and reliability purposes. Nonetheless, heterogeneous clique (diverse PMA-to-RAID ratio) configurations are being modelled and studied, to better understand their role and performance metrics in real-world applications.

8.5.1 NCR 3700—Unix/NS Operating System

The database kernel on both the DBC/1012 and the NCR 3700 rely on the operating system functions to exploit parallelism. The DBC/1012 uses the Teradata operating system (TOS), while the NCR 3700 operating system Unix/NS is based on Unix SVR4. The Unix/NS operating system extensions are conceptual abstractions for creating virtual processors, virtual resources, dynamic grouping, and message-passing among the dynamic groups that allow the database to manipulate objects globally. What this means in our shared-nothing architecture is that various entities can take a global system view, and let the database exploit the conceptual abstractions that support dynamic groups, global semaphores, process migration, and other related abstractions. In this section we describe the conceptual abstractions used by Unix/NS, such as Virtual Processor (Vproc), Virtual Disk (Vdisk), and the Segment System. These conceptual abstractions evolved from TOS to exploit the tightly-coupled parallelism within an NCR 3700 PMA. Unix/NS supports the concept of a Trusted Parallel Application. The Teradata database is a specific TPA application that runs on the system. Other TPAs can run concurrently on the NCR 3700, provided they execute in their own separate domain. Table 3 shows the conceptual hierarchy from the TPA to the physical resources.

Vprocs can be grouped and assigned to perform a common function. For example, the Vprocs on IFPs perform communication interface and parsing functions, and the AMPs Vprocs perform database operations that retrieve data from the disks. On NCR 3700s, the PMAs are used both as IFPs and AMPs. A Vproc is typed and has a unique Vproc ID. Resources are attached to the Vprocs and identified via the VID. Only tasks within a Vproc such a VIFP/VAMP can share resources. Table 4 shows the DBMS TPA hierarchy.

The Unix/NS Vproc concept creates the notion of a global virtual dedicated parallel machine executing processes. The NCR 3700 has a configuration file that contains the num-

Table 3.   Conceptual Unix/NS hierarchy.

Concept	Concept Explanation
Trusted Parallel Application	Collection of Virtual Processors (Vprocs)
Virtual Processor	Collection of Tasks
Tasks	Collection of Unix Processes
Physical Resources (a)	Memory Segments, Files, Mailboxes, Monitors, etc.

ber of Vprocs (VIFPS or VAMPS), clique configuration, TPA execution space information, and external interface (LAN, Channel) information. As mentioned in the previous section, clique configuration is a function of cost, reliability, and performance requirements. Vprocs enable parallel database operations on RAID disk arrays using a single thread. The Vproc concept (within a clique) is also used for process migration for load-balancing, or when a PMA within the clique is inoperable. The Unix/NS operating system has a special Vproc PMA to aid Unix in performing its internal system management functions.

Globally distributed objects are memory-resident, and are shared by all Vprocs. Unix/NS ensures that they always start at the same address, thus enabling process migration. GDOs use locking to maintain information integrity. The NCR 3700 Unix/NS extends the traditional Unix operating system by providing a segment system (SEGSYS) that enables Vproc processes to share memory space, files, and battery-backed memory. All NCR 3700 RAM has a ten-minute battery backup, whereas on the DBC/1012 only NVRAM survives restarts. This feature can be thought of as a software NVRAM that can flush its RAM values to disk before going down. The Teradata database software exploits this software NVRAM option. SEGSYS uses locking, and a deadlock-prevention mechanism, to maintain information integrity. The actual database is a collection of SEGSYS segments stored on virtual disk space, that is, distributed and placed on different PMAs. The FALLBACK (internal duplex database option) and clique configuration determine how the segments are distributed and updated. As updates occur, they are written to the battery-backed RAM and later to a peer-PMA in the clique.

Unix/NS high level communication concepts and facilities used to process transaction requests are shown in Table 5. Vprocs communicate via mailboxes attached to channels. A logical grouping of the Vproc-group performs diverse operations to satisfy a request. Multicast is achieved by having a channel with multiple mailboxes. A combination of these constructs, together with a Vproc number, is used for message addressing. Messages can be sent to a channel, mailbox, or Vproc-group, which means all logically attached structures also get the message. Semaphores are used to coordinate tasks, and work is scheduled by using priority number and a (Unix) spawn-level. As work flows through the system the priority and spawn-levels are modified to ensure total system usage and fairness.

Table 4.   DBMS, a special TPA hierarchy.

TPA	VPROC	Vproc Tasks	Shared Resources
DBMS	Virtual IFPs	Parser, Dispatcher, Session Control	Segment, Files,
	Virtual AMPs	AMP Worker Tasks	Mailboxes, Monitors

Table 5. Unix/NS communication concepts and facilities.

Unix/NS Concept	Concept/Facility Description
CHANNEL	Logical Channel between Vprocs
MAILBOX	Queues incoming messages and waiting processes
VPROC-GROUP	Collection of Vprocs doing work for a Transaction
MESSAGE	Sent to <Channel, Mailbox, or Vproc-Group>
SCHEDULING	Composed by <Priority & Spawn-Level>
TRANSACTION ID	Composed by <Host ID, Host Session ID, Request ID>

8.6 CONCLUSIONS AND OBSERVATIONS

Ten years of DBC/1012 experience have shown that the ability to run very large applications on a scalable parallel database computer was the enabling technology that allowed business enterprises to move from data processing to information processing. This chapter described the DBC/1012 and Ynet interconnection network products that have been used by modern enterprises. The DBC/1012 commercial experience[22] demonstrates that analysis, synthesis, and fusion of raw data can be profitably metamorphosed into a strategic asset. We analyzed interconnection network topologies in order to explain some of the rationale and thought processes used while designing the Bynet. Finally, we described our next-generation computer, the NCR 3700. The NCR 3700 has Unix mainframe market possibilities not explored in this database-oriented chapter. As a future database computer,[38] the NCR 3700 has great potential to expand the information paradigm from alphanumeric to include multimedia data.

REFERENCES

1. P. Neches, "Hardware Support for Advanced Data Management Systems," *Computer*, Vol. 17, No. 10, 1984, pp. 29–40.
2. E. Codd, "A Relational Model for Large Shared Data Banks," *Comm. ACM*, Vol. 13, No. 6, June 1970, pp. 377–387.
3. E. Babb, "Implementing a Relational Database by means of Specialized Hardware," *ACM Trans. Database Systems*, Vol. 4, No. 1, Mar. 1979, pp. 1–29.
4. D. Hsiao, "Data Base Machines are Coming, Data Base Machines are Coming!," *Computer*, Vol. 12, No. 3, 1979, pp. 7–9.
5. M. Stonebraker, "The Case for Shared-Nothing," *IEEE Data Engineering Bulletin*, Vol. 9, No. 2, 1986, pp. 4–9.
6. F. Bancilhon, et al., "VERSO: A Relational Backend Database Machine," in *Advanced Database Machine Architecture*, D. Hsiao, ed., Prentice-Hall, Englewood Cliffs, N.J., 1983, pp. 1–18.
7. G. Gardarin, et al., "SABRE: A Relational Database System for a Multimicroprocessor Machine," in *Advanced Database Machine Architecture*, D. Hsiao, ed., Prentice-Hall, Englewood Cliffs, N.J., 1983, pp. 19–35.
8. H. Schweppe, et al., "RDBM—A Dedicated Multiprocessor System for Database Management," in *Advanced Database Machine Architecture*, D. Hsiao, ed., Prentice-Hall, Englewood Cliffs, N.J., 1983, pp. 36–86.
9. M. Missikoff and M. Terranova, "The Architecture of a Relational Database Computer Known as DBMAC," in *Advanced Database Machine Architecture*, D. Hsiao, ed., Prentice-Hall, Englewood Cliffs, N.J., 1983, pp. 87–106.

10. H. Boral, et al., "Prototyping Bubba, A Highly Parallel Database System," *IEEE Trans. Knowledge and Data Engineering*, Vol. 2, No: 1, Mar. 1990, pp. 4-24.

11. D. DeWitt, et al., "The Gamma Database Machine Project," *IEEE Trans. Knowledge and Data Engineering*, Vol. 2, No. 1, Mar. 1990, pp. 44-62.

12. B. Bergsten, et al., "A Parallel Database Accelerator," *Proc. Int'l Parallel Architectures and Languages Europe Conf.*, 1989, pp. 397-412.

13. R. Lorie, et al., "Adding Intra-Transaction Parallelism to an Existing DBMS: An Early Experience," *IEEE Data Engineering Newsletter*, Vol. 12, Mar. 1989.

14. M. Kitsuregawa, M. Nakano, and M. Takagi, "Query Execution for Large Relations on Functional Disk System," *Proc. IEEE 5th Int'l Conf. Data Engineering*, IEEE CS Press, Los Alamitos, Calif., 1989, pp. 159-167.

15. M. Kitsuregawa, M. Nakano, and M. Takagi, "Performance Evaluation of Functional Disk System," *Proc. IEEE 7th Int'l Conf. Data Engineering*, IEEE CS Press, Los Alamitos, Calif., 1991, pp. 416-425.

16. M. Kitsuregawa, et al., "The Super Database Computer (SDC): System Architecture, Algorithm and Preliminary Evaluation," *Proc. IEEE 25th Hawaii Int'l Conf. Systems Sciences*, IEEE CS Press, Los Alamitos, Calif., pp. 308-319.

17. K. Kojima, S. Toriji, and S. Yoshizumi, "IDP— A Main Storage Based Vector Database Processor," *Proc. 5th Int'l Workshop Database Machines*, Springer-Verlag, New York, N.Y., 1987.

18. T. Satoh, "Acceleration of Join Operations by a Relational Database Processor," *Proc. 2nd Int'l Symp. Database Systems for Advanced Applications*, World Scientific, River Edge, N.J., 1991, pp. 243-248.

19. M. Kitsuregawa, et al., "Implementing of LSI Sort Chip for Bimodal Sort Memory," *Proc. IFIP TC 10/WG 10.5 Int'l Conf. Very Large Scale Integration*, 1989, pp. 285-294.

20. C.J. Skelton, et al., "EDS: A Parallel Computer System for Advanced Information Processing," *Proc. 4th Int'l Parallel Architectures and Languages Europe Conf.*, Springer-Verlag, New York, N.Y., 1992, pp. 3-18.

21. P. Neches, "The Ynet: An Interconnection Structure for a Highly Concurrent Data Base Computer System," *Proc. 2nd Symp. Frontiers of Massively Parallel Computation*, IEEE CS Press, Los Alamitos, Calif., 1988, pp. 429-435.

22. F. Cariño and P. Kostamaa, "Exegesis of DBC/1012 and P-90—Industrial Supercomputer Database Machines," *Proc. 4th Int'l Parallel Architectures and Languages Europe Conf.*, Springer-Verlag, New York, N.Y., 1992, pp. 877-892.

23. W. Inmon, *Database Machines and Decision Support Systems: Third-Wave Processing*, QED Information Sciences, Inc., Wellesley, Mass., 1991.

24. R. McMillen, C. Watson, And D. Chura, "Reconfigurable, Fault Tolerant, Multistage Interconnection Network and Protocol (The ByNet)," Patent Filed May 1991, Allowed Dec. 1993, Grant Pending.

25. M. Kitsuregawa, S. Tsudaka, and M. Nakano, "Parallel GRACE Hash Join on Shared-Everything Multiprocessor: Implementation and Performance Evaluation on Symmetry S81," *Proc. IEEE 8th Int'l Conf. Data Engineering*, IEEE CS Press, Los Alamitos, Calif., 1992, pp. 256-264.

26. A. Papachristidis, "Dynamically Partitionable Parallel Processing: The Key for Cost-Efficient High Transaction Throughput," in *Database Machines and Knowledge Base Machines*, M. Kitesuregawa and H. Tanaka, eds., Kluwer Academic, Norwell, Mass., 1987.

27. E. Codd, "Fatal Flaws in SQL, Part 1," *Datamation*, Vol. 34, No. 16, 1988, pp. 45-48.

28. O. Frieder, "Multiprocessor Algorithms for Relational-Database Operators on Hypercube Systems," *Computer*, Vol. 23, No. 11, Nov. 1990, pp. 13-28.

29. D. Hsiao, "Impact of the Interconnection Network on Parallel Database Computers," in *Database Machines and Knowledge Base Machines*, M. Kitesuregawa and H. Tanaka, eds., Kluwer Academic, Norwell, Mass., 1987.

30. W.C. Athas and C.L. Seitz, "Multicomputers: Message-Passing Concurrent Computers," *Computer*, Vol. 21, No. 8, Aug. 1988, pp. 9-34.

31. L. Bhuyan, Q. Yang, and D. Agrawal, "Performance of Multiprocessor Interconnection Networks," *Computer*, Vol. 22, No. 2, Feb. 1989, pp. 25-37.

32. J. Hromkovic, et al., "On Embedding Interconnection Networks into Rings of Processors," *Proc. 4th Int'l Parallel Architectures and Languages Europe Conf.*, Springer-Verlag, New York, N.Y., 1992, pp. 53-62.

33. J. Duato, "Improving the Efficiency of Virtual Channels with Time-Dependent Selection Functions," *Proc. 4th Int'l Parallel Architectures and Languages Europe Conf.*, Springer-Verlag, New York, N.Y., 1992, pp. 636-650.

34. R. Holzner, et al., "Design and Simulation of a Multistage Interconnection Network," *Proc. Joint Conf. Vector and Parallel Processing*, Springer-Verlag, New York, N.Y., 1990.

35. P. Osmon, et al., "The TOPSY Project: A Position Paper," *Proc. 4th Int'l Parallel Architectures and Languages Europe Conf.*, Springer-Verlag, New York, N.Y., 1992, pp. 97-112.

36. Intel Corp., "Paragon XP/S Product Overview," Intel Corp., Santa Clara, Calif., 1991.

37. D.A., Patterson, G. Gibson, and R.H. Katz, "A Case for Redundant Arrays of Inexpensive Disks (RAID)," *ACM SIGMOD*, ACM Press, New York, N.Y., 1988, pp. 109-116.

38. D. DeWitt and J. Gray, "Parallel Database Systems: The Future of High Performance Database Systems," *Comm. ACM*, Vol. 35, No. 6, June 1992, pp. 85-98.

9

A Massively Parallel Indexing Engine Using DAP

Nigel Bond and Stewart Reddaway

Cambridge Parallel Processing
Reading, UK

ABSTRACT

This chapter describes how the massively parallel DAP was used to resolve a performance crisis with Reuters Historical Text Service, a free-text retrieval service covering millions of documents and thousands of clients. Reuters is just one victim of the information explosion—the rapid world-wide increase in both information generators and consumers accessing a historically and geographically expanding mountain of text. Rather than attempting to locate texts by scanning, the sheer volumes involved favor an indexing approach. To guarantee universal access to new material this index needs to be centralized and so needs to support high thoroughput. To meet growing demand Reuters needed more horse-power than current serial hardware could deliver. DAPText provides a unique solution based on the combination of massive parallelism and novel system architecture. The key idea is to separate the index server from the data store. Sophisticated data management brings high compression and performance, while rich functionality allows complex queries to be posed. The index server uses a conceptual entity-attribute matrix to (here) link words with documents, though the associative approach has much wider applicability.

9.1 INTRODUCTION

A science writer is researching a story on heavy-metal contamination of subterranean aquifers. He remembers having read several articles contrasting toxic industrial wastes with natural leaching from mineral-rich rocks, but he does not have the exact references.

He would like to find all articles written within the last three years that contain the word *rock* and the phrase *heavy metal*.

However, he really is not interested in the track record of Iron Maiden or any other "heavy metal" rock group, so he would like to exclude the music press and any article categorized as *musical*, or containing the words *play*, *playing*, *player*, or *players*.

The above is an example of a *free-text retrieval query*. Free-text retrieval is, in turn, an example of a more general problem: *searching by content*.

This chapter concentrates mainly on free-text retrieval. The work described here was undertaken by Cambridge Parallel Processing (and its predecessor, Active Memory Technology) on its massively parallel computer, the DAP (Distributed Array of Processors). The development was aimed at radically improving the performance of Reuters' Historical Text Database Service (Textline). However, the lessons learned and algorithms developed are widely applicable to many other similar (and not so similar) database requirements.

Section 2 briefly examines the general issues. Section 3 discusses the requirements for the development. Section 4 describes how massive parallelism, in the shape of a 4,096-processor DAP, has been combined with a novel software solution, known as DAPText, to overcome the processing bottleneck. Section 5 relates the spectacular performance achieved by the DAP to the statistical assumptions adopted, given that the relative difficulty of two queries can vary by three orders of magnitude. In Section 6 the discussion is broadened to consider future enhancements to the functionality currently offered, and how the underlying algorithms may be applied to more general data.

9.2 FREE-TEXT RETRIEVAL

With modern technology, free-text retrieval can be achieved in one of two ways: scanning or indexing. With a text-scanning system, for each query every document in turn is searched to see if it satisfies the search criteria. Virtually all the processing occurs at query-time, and it is well suited to searching a small but highly volatile population of documents. While there have been great advances in string matching, the scanning approach becomes impracticable for historical information systems running into millions of documents, supporting thousands of queries per hour. That kind of capacity is needed increasingly by such applications as:

- news archives,
- legal case-law,
- medical case-histories,
- bibliographies,
- databases of scientific papers,
- patents,
- regulations and standards.

As information technology pervades all aspects of society, new text databases are being set up every year, and existing ones are expanding, often at an accelerating rate. These large archival databases almost invariably use the second approach to free-text retrieval, namely inverted indexing. Rather than checking each document against each query, documents are inverted by maintaining a list for each word of all documents that contain it (see Figure 1). If we subsequently want to find a document containing three separate words, we merely have to inspect their lists to see which documents are common to all three. With inverted indexing much of the work occurs as documents are being added to the index, with the result that subsequent queries benefit twofold: less processing of much less data.

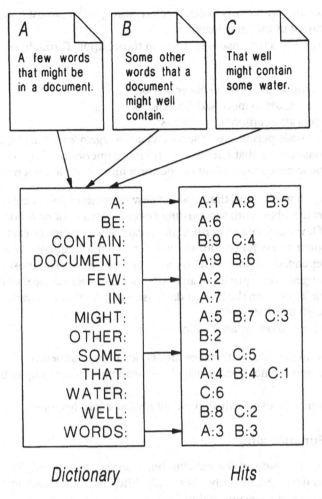

Figure 1. Inverted indexing—example.

There are many software systems and packages available to support the growing needs for Text databases. Some, like the LEXIS system, are attuned to the specific requirements of a particular market, in this case the legal profession. Popular examples of more general free-text retrieval systems include BRS Search, BASIS Plus, and CAIRS. Such systems typically allow searching on both the actual text and also added keywords or assigned characteristics. Initially, they merely return a count of the number of "hit" documents (and sometimes of the individual search terms). If the number of hits is too few or too many, the search may be refined and resubmitted. The list of documents may then be examined (usually by title) and one or more selected for retrieval and detailed perusal of its complete text.

9.3 A CUSTOMER WITH A PROBLEM

Reuters' Historical Text System already provided a free-text retrieval service giving a large (and growing) client base access to a large (and growing) database of news articles, covering a wide range of sources. Based on a large VAX cluster, the service was fast reaching saturation despite the retrieval code having been replaced by custom-optimized assembly code.

It had "hit the ceiling" with conventional architectures, and a radical boost was needed in order to keep abreast of the increasing load.

The primary need was for a major increase in throughput. Throughput affects a number of factors:

- Higher throughput gives rise to faster response.
- Faster response leads to more satisfied clients.
- Satisfied clients attract more new clients.
- Economies of scale permit lower service charges, again attracting higher usage.
- Faster response means that clients perform more queries per hour.
- Faster response encourages clients to perform more complex queries.

A secondary need was for real-time update: new documents added at any time should instantly become retrievable. With the existing system, addition of new documents was performed using off-line machines to periodically create new versions of each database. These new versions would be switched into the live service at a frequency that differed among databases and depended on how "hot" their documents were. The most up-to-the-minute database was changed every quarter of an hour (and some were done six-hourly), so the average inversion delay even on the hottest database was 7.5 minutes. Availability would typically lag by some 30 to 60 minutes.

Real-time update also brings implications:

- Faster access to new material makes the service more competitive.
- This attracts new clients, particularly those needing to react to up-to-the-minute information.
- Such clients may be especially dependent on fast query response.

9.3.1 Query Functionality

Any upgrade had to support the existing functionality unchanged. Re-education of the client base was undesirable; the only discernible difference at the user interface should be a dramatic improvement in response time.

We will now examine that functionality in more detail. Queries are essentially Boolean in nature: the occurrence of a word in a document is a Boolean property dividing the population of documents into the "haves" and the "have-nots." By combining query terms in a Boolean expression, we progressively partition this population to form the desired subset.

Boolean operators include <and>, <or>, plus the negation operator <without>, (represented respectively by plus, comma, or minus). The phrase operator <then> (invoked by just a space) restricts matches to words appearing consecutively. Truncation is supported, a trailing asterisk being used to indicate an implicit <or> between all words beginning with that stem.

Additional keywords are held for documents under a number of different headings. These are characteristics, added to documents, that are used to help categorize them. A qualifier appended to the query term shows which keyword section applies.

The scope of the user's search may be restricted in two ways. He or she may specify a date-range, most commonly expressed relative to the present time, for example, "in the last three months." There is also a mechanism for selecting only documents of particular "types"; the mechanism is used to control which classes of document sources a user wishes (or is allowed) to search. In Reuters' Historical Text database, the type of each document is determined by its source.

Our opening example illustrates all of these functional requirements. We can restate it as the following query:

Query: ROCK <and> [HEAVY <then> METAL] <without> [PLAY :truncated <or> MUSIC :keyword]

Sources: all but: MUSIC

Date-range: since: 1 Sep 89

9.3.2 Target Requirements

The approximate target requirements for the development were set at:

(1) Documents: at least 10 million
(2) Average document size: 2 Kbytes
    hence database size: 20 Gbytes of plain text
(3) Peak Addition rate: 10 K per day
(4) Client base: several thousand
(5) Query throughput: 50 queries per second
(6) Average inversion lag: under 1 second
(7) Average response time: under 0.1 second
(8) Uptime: 168 hours per week (that is, 100 percent)

Moreover, to protect the new investment, there had to be an upgrade path well beyond this level.

9.4 PARALLELISM TO THE RESCUE

The above targets exceeded the performance of the current system by a factor of about 200. It had become painfully clear to the customer that conventional systems were quite unable to deliver this kind of performance; the only way forward was to exploit massive parallelism.

To this end a pilot project was established to use the 4096-processor DAP to achieve this speedup. Following the successful conclusion of this project, the DAP is now being used online to support the Reuters service. Three earlier papers describe aspects of this work.[1,2,3]

Other massively parallel systems, such as the Connection Machine, have been applied to free text retrieval,[4,5,6] and their scoring and ranking approach is compared with the current work.[1] Their initial implementation showed impressive performance, so long as the index data could fit wholly within memory. Their more recent disk-based systems tend to suffer from interprocessor communication load (despite hardware assistance), a problem that escalates as the number of processors is increased.

9.4.1 The DAP

The DAP machines are massively parallel single-instruction, multiple-data computers manufactured and distributed by Cambridge Parallel Processing.[7] The DAP 500 consists of a 2-dimensional array of 32 × 32 simple processing elements that work in concert under the control of a central master control unit. In the larger DAP 600 series used for this application, the array is 64 × 64 PEs. As well as communicating with its neighbors in the 2-D array, each PE can address up to a million bits of memory with an aggregate bandwidth of 5.1 Gbytes per second (for the DAP 610C). It has a fast data I/O channel able to sustain a transfer rate of 40 Mbytes per second in each direction with minimal impact on processing.

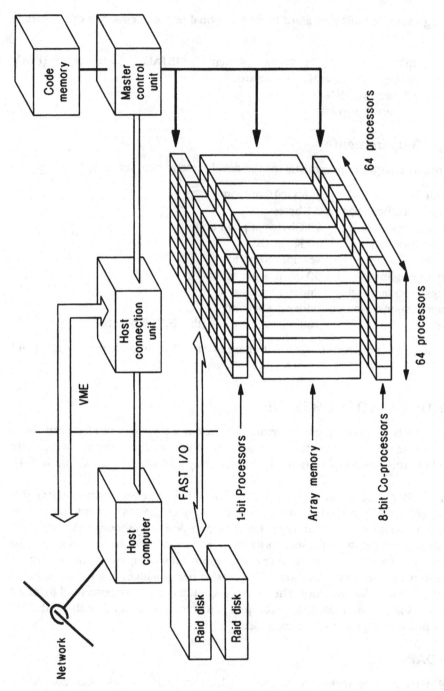

Figure 2. DAP 610 internal structure.

For this application, it is connected to a disk array. Each of the DAP 610C's 4096 PEs actually contains two independent processors: a general purpose single-bit engine and an 8-bit arithmetic coprocessor (see Figure 2).

This combination is rated at 560 megaflops, while for more compact data the performance is considerably more: in one second, it can multiply 2.4 billion 8-bit integers, or carry out a staggering 40 billion Boolean operations. The simple bit-organized architecture allows wide flexibility and economy in the use of both memory and processing, leading to efficient and high-performance algorithms.

9.4.2 The DAPText Solution

From the outset it was recognized that success would depend on a three-pronged attack:

(1) *System design*. The DAP alone was never expected to provide the total solution; we had to establish an appropriate and effective division of labor between it and its surrounding environment.
(2) *Data design*. Obtaining maximum benefit from the DAP architecture depended strongly on the data structures adopted.
(3) *Algorithm design*. The development of new high-performance algorithms would allow the power of the DAP to be harnessed to the full.

9.4.3 System Design

The first task was to undertake a detailed analysis to break the overall problem down into its functional parts and discover just where the processing bottlenecks occurred. This analysis was important because (1) throughput and response time would only improve by tackling elements on the critical path and (2) there was a desire to protect investment in existing hardware.

The complete system was broken into five distinct functional components:

(1) *client handlers*: multiple processes dealing with user interface and screen management,
(2) *query schedulers*: multiple front-end processes that parse a query and select a back-end server to perform it,
(3) *document feeds*: a number of front-end processes that parse a document and then distribute it to all back-end servers for inversion,
(4) *document server*: single central shared-disk subsystem for storage and administration of text originals,
(5) *indexing engines*: one or more back-end servers processing queries and inversions received from the various front-ends.

Of these five functions, it was only the last that needed the power of parallelism. Even given the increase in throughput, the existing hardware could still cope with the remaining functions, since all the most onerous tasks had been delegated to the indexing engine.

This condition leads to a clear division of responsibility for data, with the document server managing several hundred small requests for individual plaintext documents every second, while the inverted index data is being separately maintained by the indexing engine (see Figure 3).

By integrating the tasks of inversion and query processing within the same functional unit, this design also neatly sidesteps the need to switch inverted databases repeatedly in order to gain access to the next set of documents. So the power-house of the new system is a group of DAP-based indexing engines forming a "farm" that can grow painlessly as more power is needed.

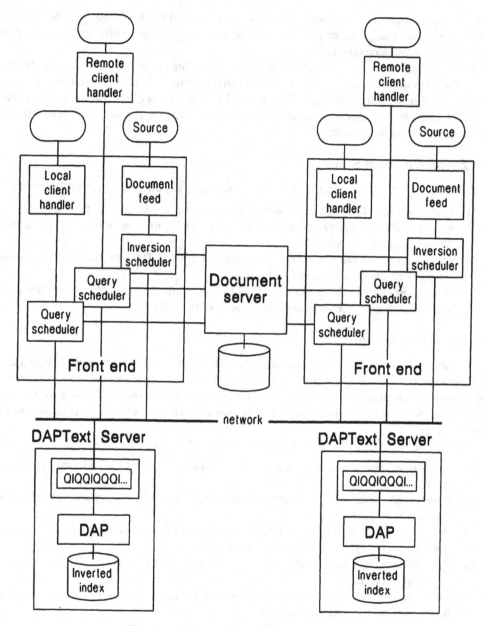

Figure 3. DAPText functional structure.

9.4.4 Data Design

As illustrated in Figure 1, inverted indexing requires a dictionary indexing into a set of lists of references to occurrences of each word. On conventional architectures, free-text dictionaries typically use tree-structured digraph chains. A dictionary of up to a million terms, such as this system demands, may not fit readily within memory. Just to look up a word may then require several disk accesses as the structure is traversed to locate the reference list. The lists themselves comprise sets of 8- to 12-byte {document:word-position} references, resulting in an average index size up to 50 percent bigger than the plaintext originals. Word positions are only needed in order to resolve phrases. The majority of queries do not involve phrases, so it is worthwhile separating out the document-hits from the positional information.

On a database of 10 million documents, the Zipf's-Law distribution[8] predicts at least six orders of magnitude difference between the hit-rates of the most popular and the rarest words (see Figure 4). The space occupied by the index data of different dictionary words will therefore differ widely. However, that same law says that the lower the hit-rate, the greater the number of different words that crop up, so the space requirements of each logarithmic hit-rate band are broadly comparable.

Index data storage cost of a word is the product of three quantities: the hit-rate, the total number of documents in the database, and the space needed to record each occurrence. For simple Boolean selection, repeated ocurrences within a document can be ignored; we merely need to record that that document has been "hit." (See below for discussion of phrases).

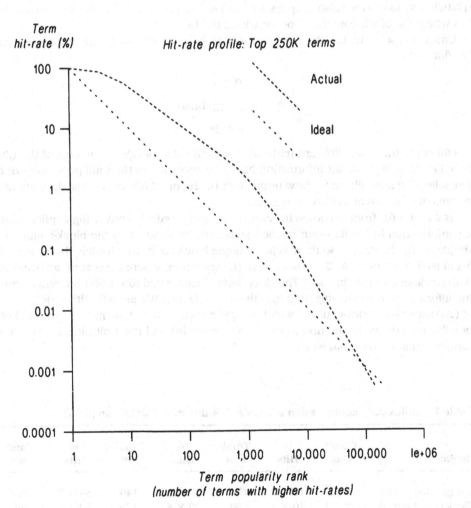

Figure 4.   Zipf's law.

Our first goal is to minimize the number of bits/hit by using a fully dense set of document numbers; in our case 24-bit Docnos will support a population of up to 16 million.

An ideal Zipf's-Law distribution predicts that exactly half the words in any dictionary will ever occur in a single document, and in practice we find that around 40 percent are indeed unique. List encoding is best for this very large number of rare words, although at 24 the bits/hit is large. However, for the more common words, straightforward list encoding can be improved considerably. At a 25 percent hit-rate the 24 bits can be reduced to 4 by using a bit-mapped representation (see below).

9.4.4.1 Compression

If we examine any ordered list of document numbers, we observe that at high hit-rates the leading bits rarely change. This fact shows that they contain a high degree of redundancy. We can improve the encoding efficiency if we can remove some of this redundancy.

By breaking our (2^n) Docno range into (2^p) blocks each of (2^q) documents (where $n = p + q$), we are able to represent actual hit documents as relative block-offsets using just q bits/hit, so long as we also keep a set of (2^p) individual ($q + 1$)-bit block-counts, to point out where the block boundaries occur within the list.

Under this scheme, the storage cost for each hit on a word with hit-rate (r) is given in bits/hit by:

$$q + \frac{(q + 1)}{r \times 2^q} \text{ bits/hit}$$

Obviously there are different trade-offs for each value of (q), as the cost of the (2^p) × ($q + 1$) bits of block-count information has to be spread over the total population of hits. The following table illustrates how terms with 10, 20, or 30 hits on a trivial database of 128 documents each favor a different regime.

As we vary (q) from (n) down to zero, we are progressively converting explicit address-ing information in the lists into implicit positional information in the block-counts. For a simple list (q) equals (n), so there is just a single block-count (the list-length) for the single list of n-bit references. At the other end of the spectrum, where (q) is zero, we are dealing with single-document "blocks." The "lists" have degenerated to zero-bit references, and all the information has now migrated into the block-counts. We are left with simply a vector of ($2n$) single-bit "block-counts," which we call a bitmap. In between, there are (n-1) other possible encodings. In addition to the 24-bit simple list and the 1-bit bitmap, we use two further regimes: 16-bit and 8-bit.

Table 1.   Index data compression example: 128-document database (n = 7).

Regime	Count Bits	10 Hits	Total Bits	20 Hits	Total Bits	30 Hits	Total Bits
List (p = 0,q = 7)	0 × 8	10 × 7	<70>	20 × 7	140	30 × 7	210
Block (p = 3,q = 4)	8 × 5	10 × 4	80	20 × 4	<120>	30 × 4	160
Bitmap (p = 7,q = 0)	128 × 1	10 × 0	128	20 × 0	128	30 × 0	<128>

Although the compression algorithms used in DAPText are based on the above approach, details differ slightly to take advantage of changes of hit-rate over time, and to obtain further processing efficiencies:

(1) *24-bit*: This is the straightforward list-encoding, used for rare words occurring only once in every 50,000 or more documents.

(2) *16-bit*: This regime uses lists of 16-bit offsets within 64K document blocks. The compression crossover to the 8-bit regime comes at about 160 hits per block (0.25 percent), so we only need 8-bit counts.

(3) *8-bit*: The 64K document block is treated as 256 separate sub-blocks, each having its own smaller count field.

(4) *Bitmapped*: Here the whole block is represented by a simple vector of 64K bits. The theoretical crossover to bitmapped is at just over 12 percent, although practical limitations lead to a rather lower crossover.

The optimum compression regime is determined individually for each block of 64K documents. The trade-offs between the various regimes are illustrated graphically in Figure 5.

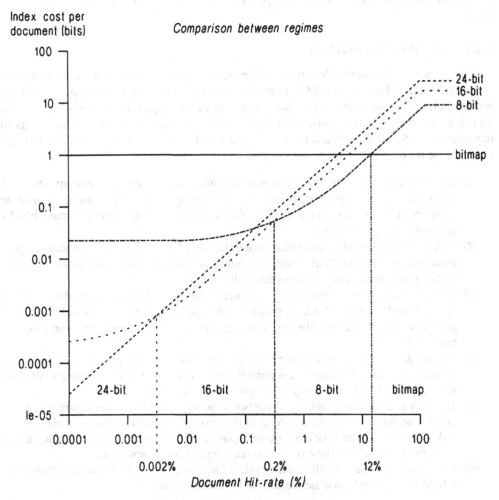

Figure 5. Compression trade-offs.

In rating compression efficiency, it is easy to be misled: the two extreme encodings offer two very different reference points. Contrasted with an equivalent full bitmap, the compression ratios look dramatic:

- 8-bit compressed term (0.4 percent hit-rate): 19.4 x
- 16-bit compressed term (0.006 percent hit-rate): 875 x
- 24-bit compressed term (0.0001 percent hit-rate): 41667 x

Compared with the space needed for the equivalent 24-bit list, the maximum scope for compression is only 24 times, so the figures are more modest:

- bitmapped term (30 percent hit-rate): 7.2 x
- 8-bit compressed term (0.4 percent hit-rate): 1.87 x
- 16-bit compressed term (0.006 percent hit-rate): 1.3 x

The above compression figures are for "hit" data. To allow phrases to be matched, text data is also indexed on word "position" within the text. This adds 16 bits per word occurrence; there may, of course, be several occurrences of a word in one document. Positions are observed to need about twice the space of "hit" data. Together they total around 22 percent of the plaintext size, a seven-fold improvement over some more traditional data structures.

9.4.4.2 Disk Data Organization

A key consideration in the design was to prevent the performance being limited by disk accesses. The DAP FastDisk is a RAID configuration (redundant array of inexpensive disks) with peak transfer rate of 16 Mbytes per second, and an average transfer latency of around 25 mS. These characteristics encourage the use of a few relatively large transfers, so as to minimize the effects of the fixed latency overheads. To achieve that, the following techniques were used:

(1) Date-ranging is an important element of most queries, and the documents most often searched are the most recent. This has prompted the use of *publication-date* as the primary sort key for documents. This allows us to only retrieve as many blocks as the date-range demands.

(2) It also allows the most recent blocks of index data for every term to be retained permanently in memory. With enough memory for several months of index data, the majority of queries avoid disk accesses altogether.

(3) The same efficient compression techniques are used for the index data both in memory and on disk. This maximizes the number of memory resident blocks, and minimizes the space that the rest occupies on disk (and hence the time taken to transfer it).

(4) Phrases are used only in a minority of queries. Only phrases require word-position information, so by holding that separately from (but adjacent to) document hit-data, we can choose to fetch it only when phrases are involved.

(5) The data was originally held as a number of separate databases on separate disks. A query that was asked to scan several of these smaller databases had to make several disk accesses. Under DAPText, these separate databases are unified, reducing the number of accesses at the expense of retrieving more index data.

(6) Depending on word length, the index data for multiple words invoked by truncation is held contiguously, and hence can be fetched together.

9.4.5 Algorithm Design

Three predominant factors influence the design of effective algorithms for the DAP:

- Bulk processing is cheap.
- Flexible word length saves both space and processing costs.
- Relative costs of operations differ markedly from conventional machines.

The simple PE means that simple Boolean operations are several orders of magnitude faster than complex floating-point operations. These factors often lead to DAP algorithms that differ radically from those used on a more conventional architecture.

We will now examine a few of the more unusual algorithms employed in DAPText.

9.4.5.1 Dictionary Look-up

When words are sorted into dictionary order, their lengths often vary. To perform proper comparisons, shorter words have to be padded out with spaces. As we have seen, some 40 percent of the words in the dictionary will only occur once. To avoid excessive waste of space in the dictionary (as distinct from the index data it references), DAPText uses a family of dictionaries, each dealing with words falling in a separate length-range. One such dictionary may handle words of six letters or less, while another might deal with those of length 10 to 15. Separate dictionaries are also used to hold the various classes of keywords and other characteristics.

In any dictionary there is usually a fairly dense coverage of the first couple of letters, while those that follow are progressively sparser. This property allows us to divide the dictionary terms into heads and tails. We maintain a table with an entry for every possible 12-bit head (4096 entries), that shows where its tails are to be found. The tails are close-packed into a separate table, along with the pointers to the individual terms' index data.

When a term is looked up, its head is used to index directly into the dense head-table, which tells us which section of the tail-table we need to examine. We then associatively match the tail across this section, to discover (if it is present) where its index data is to be found. This associative mechanism automatically yields multiple matches on right-truncated terms.

This dictionary organization is both space-efficient and rapid to use, since the associative stage can match up to 4K entries at once in parallel.

9.4.5.2 Bitmaps

Within a list, each document is represented explicitly by its address, while in a bitmap it is identified entirely by position. Boolean combination of terms on conventional serial architectures is best achieved by arithmetic comparisons between entries on lists. However, the DAP architecture is ideally suited to performing Boolean operations between large parallel arrays.

For this reason, on the DAP the inverted index of "hits" is viewed as an enormous Boolean matrix, with a column for every document and a row for every term in the dictionary. (In its general canonical form, this is termed an entity-attribute matrix and is effectively just a gigantic tick-list that can be used to record the presence or absence of any arbitrary set of attributes against any arbitrary set of entities.)

When we invert a fresh document, we are (conceptually) adding a new column to the right-hand end of this matrix, with a tick against all of the words and keywords it contains. For query processing, we are (conceptually) getting hold of the 10-megabit row representing each of the terms, and performing appropriate parallel Boolean operations between them. In practice, so as to take advantage of date-ranging and reduce working space requirements, we only process one block of 64K documents at a time, expanding compressed index data into vectors 64K bits long.

9.4.5.3 Counting and Extracting Hits

With a conventional serial machine, queries would be processed by fetching hit-lists for the various terms, restricting them to references falling in the required date-range, and then merging and checking for coincident references. The end result would be a hit-list that could be passed straight back to the user. The hit-counts for the individual terms and the final survivors are simply the lengths of these restricted hit-lists. In DAPText, we are combining term bitmaps to produce a resulting bitmap of survivors. It is by no means trivial either to count the hits or to convert them to a list of addresses that we can pass back to the client.

The first task is achieved on the DAP by a highly parallel algorithm that can count at a rate of 8 billion bits per second. When it comes to the second task, we do cheat a bit when many hits result. There seems little point (1) in wasting time extracting hundreds of hits, (2) into a buffer that would need to be dynamically extensible to accommodate them, (3) which would then cause congestion being sent back to a user, (4) who is in any case likely to have little interest in reviewing such a large number of documents. In fact, the user's most likely course of action is to refine and resubmit the query without examining even a single hit. The most recent 100 hits are generally more than enough. If a user does actually ask for the 101st, the user's query is automatically resubmitted, with instructions to skip the first 100 and send the next 100 hits instead.

9.4.5.4 The 8-Bit Expand

Statistical analysis of term distributions within queries shows that search terms in the 8-bit compressed band occur frequently. The 8-bit expansion code therefore has a strong bearing on query performance. (Compression is not as critical; it is only done when the index is built).

Within each 64 K document block, the 256 counts first have to be used to tease apart the sublists of 8-bit addresses. Bits must then be set in each 256-bit sub-block of the bitmap according to its own set of addresses. Using a parallel algorithm, DAPText performs this complex rearrangement an order of magnitude faster than a serial implementation could achieve.

9.4.5.5 Temporary Inversion

DAPText supports retrospective or prospective addition of documents at a time that differs from their publication date. This means that as the conceptual entity-attribute matrix is always ordered by publication date, fresh columns will not always be simply appended to the right-hand end, but will sometimes be inserted into it at an arbitrary point.

Documents are sometimes either withdrawn or replaced by new editions. This will require removing an existing column from an arbitrary point anywhere in the matrix. Such insertions and deletions will tend to change the alignment of columns with respect to block boundaries, affecting the position of all subsequent hits on all terms in all dictionaries (and maybe even changing their compression regimes)—not the kind of task to be undertaken every time a document is added!

DAPText gets around this problem by adding documents in two stages. The initial temporary inversion abandons publication-date ordering in favor of simple concatenation at the right-hand end of the matrix. We then merely have to record extra hits on the rows representing the terms that actually occur in the new document. These extra hits, together with the new document's publication-date and source-type, are held in a memory region that is periodically checkpointed. Brand new words (that is, those not found in any dictionary) are recorded in other special tables, which are searched associatively on every query to allow typical queries to hit newly added documents. A special map is maintained in memory to mark any "dead" documents that have been designated for removal or replacement. This mark acts as a filter on every query to effectively censor them.

9.4.5.6 Shakedown

As we have seen above, the work required to insert or delete a single document from the stable index is daunting, and not to be undertaken lightly. The various additional tables are able to support our temporary inversion strategy, but only up to a point. There comes a time when the whole index needs to be taken offline and completely rebuilt.

This process of combination is aptly termed a *shakedown*, and may typically be performed on each DAPText server in turn for every 25,000 to 50,000 documents added. The exact amount of work involved depends on the earliest change to the assignment of document numbers; only documents to the right are shuffled. The work can be summarized by the following flow:

(1) Use the tables of publication dates and types for the latest documents, together with the dead document list and knowledge of the date-type partitioning among the stable documents, to form a mapping from old to new document numbers.

(2) For every term, expand all blocks to bitmaps; shuffle and repack their bits according to the predetermined mapping; recompress each new block appropriately; keep a running total for every block of the total size of all index data; continue until all done.

(3) Comparing the block totals with the amount of memory available, decide on the limit (the "horizon") for memory-resident index data; for every term, carve off the index data for all blocks since the horizon; build it into the memory image under construction; continue until all done.

When shakedown is complete, the newly prepared memory image can be loaded and the server brought back online. It will then receive any inversion requests that have been queued up while it was offline, to bring it up to date with the other server(s). As we have seen, the work involved depends on how disordered the new additions are, but trials show that for this application, it will typically take about an hour.

9.5 PERFORMANCE METRICATION

A major design problem was accurately defining the requirement. Many aspects of the workload could exert a profound influence on both the approach used and the throughput achieved. Unfortunately, few reliable statistics existed. As well as guiding design decisions, a secondary need for such system statistics was to provide a reliable basis for calculating, demonstrating, and verifying the performance improvement achieved. Reasonably accurate estimates were needed for such parameters as:

(1) Document Characteristics:
peak addition-rate

average growth trend
words and other indexing terms per document
word-length distributions
shared-stem fan-out
hit-rate distributions
repetition of words in documents
(2) Query Characteristics:
peak query-rate
query-rate profile
average number of terms
usage of truncation
usage of phrases
date-range profile
type-selection profile
user expectations of response-time vs. complexity

Even where figures were available or predicted, it was accepted that many would change. Some of them involved feedback; it was likely that many query characteristics were primarily determined culturally by the response rate that clients actually experienced. By providing a large boost in performance, we would materially alter that culture.

This shortfall of information was addressed in four ways:

- analysis,
- metrication,
- adaptation,
- progressive prototyping.

Analysis of a breakdown by term hit-counts of one of the dictionaries gave insights into many of the gross statistics, such as the size and composition of the dictionary, and the hit-rate distribution, confirming, for example, that different regions adhere approximately to Zipf's Law. A transaction monitor was built and plugged into the existing system for a couple of months, to capture a large cross-section of queries (some 200 K). Analysis of these queries yielded important information on some of the query characteristics, such as the variability of query complexity, and profiles of date-range.

Many other parameters were more elusive. To accommodate these properties, and to support future applications, a fair degree of flexibility was designed-in. There are very few hard-and-fast limits frozen into DAPText; wherever possible the data structures have been designed to adapt dynamically to differential growth patterns. A wide range of nested counters and timers were fitted to the pilot code, to measure how often different paths were taken, and how much processing they required. The information so obtained gave invaluable feedback during development, allowing optimization effort (and occasionally a complete change of algorithm) to be applied where it was most needed.

9.5.1 Workload Statistics

Metrication also made it possible to build an empirical mathematical model of the performance, from which the behavior could be extrapolated to full scale operation, and the effects of different operating conditions predicted. This performance model incorporated several sets of system parameters:

- Operational parameters could be preset, such as the number of indexing engines, their memory size, document addition-rates, and overall database size.
- Query characteristics were empirically derived by running the captured set of 200K user queries.
- Bulk statistics of documents, dictionaries, and volumes of index data were extrapolated from over a quarter of a million user documents.

It is interesting to note a few of the statistics that emerged:

(1) Queries:
  average terms/query: 2.2
  average documents scanned: 1 M
  queries needing disk: 25 percent (with assumed memory size)

(2) Documents:

	Hits only	*Hits*+Positions
Index data (bytes/document):	150	450
compared with average 2K document size:	7.5 percent	22.5 percent
compared with average 3K STATUS index:	5.0 percent	15.0 percent

9.5.2 Performance Achieved

On the basis of these observed statistics, the following processing performance is obtained using two DAPs:

Peak query rate: 46 queries per second
Inversion lag: 0.5 seconds per document

Relative to existing system:

Query performance   × 230 (was 0.2 per second)
Reduction in inversion lag   × 900+ (was 7.5 min at best)

This query rate applies when most queries do not need disk; that is, sufficient DAP memory is available in relation to the average number of documents scanned.

9.6 FUTURE DIRECTIONS

There are many possible extensions to the functionality of DAPText. This section presents some ideas for future enhancement, but these have yet to be demonstrated in a practical implementation.

9.6.1 Proximity Functions

DAPText stores word positions for all its documents. Currently these are only used for the <then> operator, to resolve phrases such as "ACID <then> RAIN." Additional proximity functions could readily be added. For example:

- "CHIEF <near> POLICE" (where <near> might be pre-set to mean <within 2 words of>)
- "<leads> PRESIDENT" (where <leads> might imply <mentions within the first 50 words>)

9.6.2 Left-Truncation

By using associative-matching techniques, DAPText could be readily adapted to efficiently match a trailing stem. Although such matches would tend to be scattered throughout the dictionary, leading to more disk accesses, subsequent processing would be just as fast as for right-truncation. This feature is important for languages such as German that often combine words to form new ones.

9.6.3 Concepts

Attributes that characterize the semantic content of a document (rather than just the words used to express those ideas) are sometimes called *concepts*. Added keywords are an example of concepts. Judicious editorial assessment is needed in reducing a document to the underlying set of concepts. This task is being attempted increasingly by artificial-intelligence preprocessors, although some degree of human intervention is generally still required.

Concept-based retrieval carries both benefits and dangers. It can provide high accuracy and recall, even on documents of diverse languages. It can also be used to access nontext objects, such as pictures, diagrams, or even recordings. Using concepts, it is far easier to build thesauri and taxonomies that the user can then explore to broaden or narrow down the queries. If the concept base is the only index, it will be many times smaller than a free-text inverted index, because it takes several words to express each idea. If we construct a thesaurus that translates words to concepts, users can still supply free-text terms, which will then get mapped down onto the core concept base.

The danger of concept coding is that it is tedious, time-consuming, and only as good as the editorial process; assignment of concepts is often borderline, arbitrary, or just plain wrong. For reliable recall, it is probably best to use both full free-text and concept indexing. Where indexing is restricted to free-text only, a words-to-concepts thesaurus is still useful. It can be applied in reverse, to expand user-supplied concepts into a number of free-text terms or phrases.

9.6.4 Grammatical Roots

The English language is far from systematic. While a right-truncation such as COMPUT* can successfully match COMPUTE, COMPUTER, COMPUTING, COMPUTATION, COMPUTABLE (and probably a few more), simple truncation is of little help in finding articles on, for example, running or swimming. By providing *thesaurus links* in the dictionary structure, we can associate variations such as SWAM or SWUM with their common grammatical root, SWIM. Even for more regular forms, these grammatical links would help to locate CONSERVE, CONSERVING, and CONSERVATION, without pulling in references to CONSERVATIVE or CONSERVATORY also. Other links (maybe implemented as rules-plus-exceptions) would be used to join singular and plural forms, or to provide dialect translation, for example, between English and American spellings.

9.6.5 Scoring

Often when trawling through a text database, the size of the catch cannot be known in advance. Another problem with pure Boolean expressions is their sheer complexity for large numbers of terms, especially where the user is still interested in documents containing only some of the given set. In both these situations it is desirable for a retrieval system to apply some sort of scoring system to rank documents by degree of relevance, the top scorers being returned first for examination. Under such scoring systems the contributions of hits can be assessed in a number of ways. The simplest mechanism merely counts how many of a given set of scoring terms occur in the document. Applying various weightings, calculations can be made progressively more sophisticated, involving:

(1) *Repetitions of a term*: More weight is attributed to a term mentioned often in a document.

(2) *The "importance" of each particular word or concept:* Recorded against each term in the dictionary is a measure of how specific and narrow that term is. This measure controls its contribution to the score. A variation on this method allows the user to specify at query time the weight to be applied to each of the scoring terms.

(3) *The "importance" of each particular word or concept within the context of each document:* Each document is awarded (at inversion time) individual relevance weightings on a series of terms that improve the accuracy of scored retrievals involving them.

9.6.6 Relevance Feedback

This much-vaunted technique could also be described as "query-by-example." Having first selected and reviewed a core set of documents, the user tags some as "good" examples of the sort of document being sought. Some of the rest may also be dubbed "counter-examples." In the simplest variant of this technique, the system collects a small number of well-focused terms from the good examples and a similarly narrow set from the counter-examples, and formulates a query requiring all of the former but none of the latter. This next batch is reviewed and the cycle is repeated until the required degree of accuracy and recall has been achieved. More usually, relevance feedback is based on scoring. A large number of scoring terms (for example, 100 or more) are selected from the two sample sets and given positive or negative weightings depending on how often they occur in the examples or counter-examples. Relevance feedback can be a powerful and sophisticated refinement tool. It works best when the user already has one or more fairly relevant examples.

9.6.7 Storing Numbers

There are two distinct ways in which the entity-attribute matrix can be employed to store numeric information for every entity. If there is a small domain of possible values, or few actual values are in practice encountered, then we can build up a family of rows, each denoting one of these values. Every entity has a "tick" against one of these values. Together, these rows form an enumerated set. However, in most cases numbers will be stored in binary. One approach is to treat each bit as a separate term; for positive integers this is an efficient method of storing arbitrary precision numbers, as only the bit-positions actually used appear in the index data. A separate sign flag allows the same encoding to be used for negative integers as well.

9.6.8 Using Numbers

In order to handle numeric selection criteria we need to deal with both of these representations. Suppose we wish to select from a personnel database all individuals with HEIGHT >72 (inches). The numeric attribute HEIGHT would probably be held as an enumerated set, especially as it forms a normal distribution with few samples outside the range 50 to 80. A Boolean-expression generator would compare the *cut-point* (72:73) with the dictionary details of the enumerated set, and form an expression involving the smaller subset of terms. For example, (comma means <or>)

$$(\text{height}_{73}\,,\ \text{height}_{74}\,,\ \ldots\ ,\ \text{height}_{79}\,,\ \text{height}_{80}\,,\ \text{height}_{85}\,)$$

(This assumes that we could tell from the dictionary that the tallest individual yet logged was 85 inches, and there were no others over 80 inches.)

Suppose, additionally, we are interested in those individuals with PAY >= 12,000. Here we are more likely to be dealing with binary numbers. Although it is possible to translate this criterion into a logical expression involving the bits in the binary set, it is easy on the DAP to reassemble the expanded bit vectors into a numeric vector and apply the necessary arithmetic comparison efficiently in parallel. These techniques not only offer efficient numerical processing, but they are also space-efficient; in essence, we are throwing away all the zeroes in our data.

9.7 CONCLUSION

The world is witnessing an information explosion. More and more information generators are trying to satisfy more and more information consumers. Compounded with this expansion, information is being collected and disseminated over a progressively wider geographic base.

While the trend is to devolve and distribute both data and processing outward to the user's desk, that strategy is only appropriate for stable databases that are not too large. Applications providing prompt access to rapidly changing data suffer major problems in keeping multiple distributed databases current. The solution is to allow a worldwide client base to dial into a single centralized database, but that needs considerable horsepower. The development of DAPText has demonstrated that massively parallel processing has a vital role to play in overcoming the performance bottleneck of existing serial architectures.

The principles we have established in DAPText are by no means limited to free-text retrieval. In its general form our inverted index is an entity-attribute matrix that can be used to record the presence or absence of any arbitrary set of attributes against any arbitrary set of entities. Given the proposed extensions to accommodate numbers, DAPText will become the basis for a powerful general-purpose database engine.

REFERENCES

1. S.F. Reddaway, "High Speed Text Retrieval from Large Databases on a Massively Parallel Processor," *Information Processing and Management*, Vol. 27, No. 4, 1991, pp. 311–316.
2. S.F. Reddaway, "Very Large Text Databases: Applying Massively Parallel Processing for Very Fast Retrieval," *Proc. Advanced Information Systems, AIS91*, Learned Information, Oxford, England, 1991, pp. 31–37.
3. S.F. Reddaway, "Text Retrieval on the AMT DAP," in *The Design and Application of Parallel Digital Processors*, IEE Conference Publication No. 334, London, England, 1991, pp. 105–111.
4. C. Stanfill and B. Kahle, "Parallel Free-Text Search on the Connection Machine System," *Comm. ACM*, Vol. 29, No. 12 Dec. 1986, pp. 1229–1238.
5. C. Stanfill, R.Thau, and D. Waltz, "A Parallel Indexed Algorithm for Information Retrieval," *Proc. 12th Int'l Conf. Research and Development in Information Retrieval*, ACM Press, New York, N.Y., 1989.
6. C. Stanfill, "Partitioned Posting Files: A Parallel Inverted File Structure for Information Retrieval," *Proc. 13th Int'l Conf. Research and Development in Information Retrieval*, ACM Press, New York, N.Y., 1990.

7. D.J. Hunt, "AMT DAP: A Processor Array in a Workstation Environment," *Computer Systems Sci. and Eng.*, Vol. 4, No. 2, 1989, pp. 107–114.

8. H.P. Zipf, *Human Behaviour and Principle of Least Effort*, Addison-Wesley, Cambridge, Mass., 1949.

10

The IFS/2: Add-on Support for Knowledge-Base Systems

Simon Lavington

Department of Computer Science
University of Essex
Essex, England

ABSTRACT

Knowledge-base systems use a spectrum of programming paradigms and information models, drawn from database and artificial-intelligence technology. In this chapter we identify underlying generic tasks in terms of operations on data structures such as sets, relations, and graphs. We introduce an applications-independent formalism for the representation of knowledge-base data and a repertoire of whole-structure operations on this data. An add-on active memory unit, known as the IFS/2, is described. This unit uses single-instruction, multiple-data parallel hardware to achieve associative (that is, content-addressable) storage and processing of sets, relations, and graphs. The IFS/2 allows natural data parallelism to be exploited. Performance figures are given for a prototype IFS/2 hardware add-on unit.

10.1 MOTIVATION

Throughout the last 40 years of computer design, there has been a history of successful innovations which take the form of add-on performance accelerators. For example, hardware floating-point units, address-translation units (for virtual-memory management), graphics units, and "smart" disk controllers have all in due course proved cost-effective for their target applications domains. Eventually, many such units have become integrated into the main computational platform rather than remaining optional extras. In each case, success has come only after general agreement about standard interfaces and functionality.

In the field of database support, the ICL content-addressable file store[1] is an early example of an add-on performance accelerator which was then re-engineered and (since the early 1980s) integrated into every Series 3 ICL mainframe. Where SQL has been accepted as a standard, relational database machines such as the NCR/Teradata DBC 1012,[2] described in this book, are now regarded as add-on performance accelerators. It is now time for manufacturers to be thinking ahead to the possibility of providing add-on hardware support for information models richer than the relational.

For knowledge-base systems and AI applications—perhaps best summarized collectively as smart information systems—the approach to performance accelerators is subject to some debate. Research trends have been toward special-purpose computers, rather than add-on units to conventional computers. Developments have tended to focus either on particular language paradigms or on particular knowledge-representation formalisms. Examples of the former are the PROLOG and LISP machines;[3] examples of the latter include Production Rule machines, such as DADO,[4] and semantic network machines such as SNAP.[5] Designers of (declarative) language machines have generally tried to accomplish computational speed, for example, as measured in logical inferences per second via an append benchmark, and have given lower priority to any ability to handle the large amounts of data occurring in practical knowledge-base systems. The knowledge-representation family of machines has produced some interesting technical innovations but, regrettably, little market take-up. This is no doubt partly because smart information systems themselves are not yet in widespread use. Thus, the Connection Machine, originally intended to support semantic networks,[6] has since been equipped with floating-point capability and sold to the scientific and engineering community. Furthermore, the AI community employs a variety of knowledge-representation formalisms so that machines which only perform cost-effectively on a single formalism or a single declarative language may find it hard to gain acceptance. Finally, very few AI-oriented machines provide easy migration paths from conventional data-processing platforms. In short, the prerequisites mentioned in the first paragraph (that is, agreement on standard interfaces and functionality) do not yet exist.

However, the challenge certainly does exist. Smart information systems are strategically important, but run slowly on conventional computers, and their software is too complex. Can we design hardware support, preferably in the form of an add-on unit, that will solve the twin problems of slow and complex software?

In this chapter we outline the top-down functional requirements of smart information systems in terms of generic activities, and propose an appropriate novel architecture that supports these activities. The philosophy behind this architecture is to exploit the natural parallelism in whole-structure operations, via an *active-memory* add-on unit that both stores and processes structures such as sets, relations, and graphs. The whole-structure operations are then made available to high-level programmers as convenient data-processing primitives. We describe a prototype hardware add-on unit known as the IFS/2. We present the IFS/2's low-level command interface, higher-level programming environments, and the performance of the prototype IFS/2 when compared with conventional software.

10.2 THE NATURE OF SMART INFORMATION SYSTEMS

We define smart information systems, or knowledge-base systems, as computer applications that incorporate nontrivial data-manipulation features, such as the ability to adapt, deal with dynamic heterogeneous information, or carry out inferencing. We use the term *inferencing* to include related techniques of reasoning and deductive theorem-proving. Practical examples of smart information systems include deductive databases, management information systems, expert systems, AI planners, and intelligent information retrieval. More generally, such applications deal primarily with large amounts of complex symbolic (that is, nonnumeric) data, usually describable in terms of sets, relations, or graphs.

The phrase *usually describable* begs comment. For a given knowledge-manipulation task, the programmer makes a choice of practical data structures and processing strategies. This choice depends partly on the knowledge representation adopted and partly on the computational platform (hardware and software) available. There are many representational schemes, not all of which, unfortunately, have a formal basis. Examples include relational, object-oriented, and frame-based schemes; production rules, clausal logic, semantic nets, neural networks, and nonstandard logics (for example, for belief systems). With the exception of neural networks and some higher-order logics, the commonly used schemes can easily be described in terms of the super-type relation, which is taken to include operations on sets, relations, and graphs.

Notions of knowledge representation often go hand-in-hand with processing strategies but, here again, it is believed that relational processing is generally of relevance. For example, marker-propagation algorithms can also be expressed as relational operations such as closure and intersection; also, some well-known matching algorithms in production-rule systems can either be expressed in terms of tree traversals or in terms of flatter relational operations.[7]

In spite of the above arguments in favor of a relational approach, relational processing is a paradigm that some AI programmers do not find convenient. Particularly, AI programmers often use lists to represent sets (because of a language culture?). At some level of detail, sets and lists are of course interdefinable. However, the set is the more fundamental mathematical notion. Since ordering, and indeed graphs and trees, can be represented in the relational paradigm, we promote a relational or set-based approach to the generic data structures encountered in all information systems. The strong pragmatic argument in favor of this common approach is that it promotes practical formalisms and architectures that may serve a very wide spectrum of applications, extending from conventional databases to the more advanced cognitive systems. Standard interfaces and convenient software migration paths are thus facilitated.

10.3 FUNCTIONAL REQUIREMENTS

Abstracting away from choice of programming language, and so forth, the important generic activities in knowledge-base systems may be grouped under four somewhat overlapping functional headings:

- representation and management of knowledge,
- pattern recognition,
- inference,
- learning.

Actually, pattern matching is often an important component of all four activities (not just the second one), an observation to which we return later. The data structures over which pattern matching could be required are, as argued previously, relational in flavor. This condition allows us to call upon the accepted notions of tuple and set, as the common building-blocks from which all relevant data types may be constructed. It also promotes a focused debate on the desirable repertory of data-manipulation primitives for smart information systems.

The functional requirements of smart information systems can be described abstractly in terms of operations on sets. Any novel architecture that aims to support smart information systems has to have three attributes: (1) a practical memory scheme for the low-level representation, accessing, and management of large amounts of set-based information; (2) a strategy for carrying out set manipulations rapidly, for example, by exploiting inherent parallelism; and (3) an agreed procedural, or possibly task-based, interface whereby the set operations may be presented to the high-level programmer as convenient data-processing primitives.

For (1), the memory system should ideally organize its accessing and protection mechanisms around the concept of logical (rather than physical) sets or objects of varying granularity. That is to say, technology-dependent physical storage boundaries and mappings should be decoupled from the shape and size of the logical objects as seen by an information system's software. Similarly, the maintenance of structural relationships between objects should be decoupled from physical addressing details. These requirements may be seen to be consistent with the properties required of a persistent object manager.

For (2), it would be advantageous if the set manipulations were to be carried out as whole-structure operations on sets referred to by system-wide logical names; this procedure would once again help to decouple software from details of physical location or physical size. It could also remove from programmers any obligation to think about parallelization strategies.

For (3), there exist a few high-level languages, such as SETL[8] and SQL, that already offer relational processing primitives. These languages should enjoy *direct* hardware support from the candidate novel architecture. This support may be presented via a task-based, or transaction-based, interface. Users whose applications are better served by other languages, for example, PROLOG or LISP, should be able to call upon a readily understandable, general-purpose, set-based procedural interface to the novel architecture. This interface might conveniently take the form of a collection of C library procedures.

Returning to general functionality, the nature of both pattern matching and set operations implies the comparison (often in *any* order) of a collection of data elements against one or more interrogands. These comparisons also constitute the basic action of an associative (that is, content-addressable) memory. An associative memory has exactly the required properties of decoupling logical access from physical addressing, as required in attribute (1) above. Associative access is therefore seen as a desirable property in an architecture that supports smart information systems. It is shown in Section 10.7 that the IFS/2 provides a cost-effective mechanization of large volumes of pseudo-associative memory. However, before going into details of the IFS/2 hardware, it is necessary to consider the desirable low-level representation of tuples and tuple-sets in an associative memory, and to be more precise about the pattern-matching capabilities of such a storage system, especially as it will be required to handle variables as well as ground data.

10.4 THE IFS/2 REPRESENTATION OF TUPLES AND SETS

We require a semantics-free set-based formalism for low-level storage, suitable for use by a wide variety of knowledge-representation schemes. The scheme used by the IFS/2 is now introduced. The basic elements of the IFS/2 formalism is a universe, D, of (atomic) objects, Ai. The objects comprise the members of two infinite sets and one singleton set:

- C, the set of constants (that is, ground atoms);
- W, the set of named wild cards (that is, an abstraction of the variables of logic programming languages);
- ∇, the unnamed wild card (that is, an individual distinct from all the members of the other two sets).

Thus:

$$D = \{C1, C2, \ldots\} \{W1, W2, \ldots\} \{\nabla\}.$$

Within this formalism, the symbol A will be used to denote an (atomic) object of unspecified kind (see below).

A word should be said about ground atoms. These may represent actual external entities such as a numerical constant or a lexical token. They may also represent some higher-level <type> information, or an abstract entity including a <label>. The notion of a <label> as a shorthand name for a tuple is mentioned again later. In general, tuples, tuple-sets, and graphs may be given names that are themselves constants. Thus, the fields of a tuple may represent structures (nested to *any* depth) constituting a mechanism for accommodating general constructor functions, structure mappings, and some higher-order features. Conventions for the representation of null, or incomplete, information are the responsibility of higher-level information models; ground atoms and the unnamed wild card may be used as appropriate. Similarly, closed-world (or otherwise) assumptions are properly left to the information modeler and/or higher-level language designer. For example, a ground atom in a tuple can be assigned for mapping the value of that tuple onto the set {*true, false, undefined*}.

Having established the IFS/2's domain of objects, information is represented as sets of tuples composed from this domain. For this representation, the IFS/2 supports a *make-tuple* constructor. In general, tuples may be of any length, although there are some IFS/2 practical limitations mentioned later. Tuples may consist of any choice of component atoms. The *i*th tuple thus has the general format:

$$T_i = <A_{i1}, A_{i2}, A_{i3}, \ldots, A_{im}>,$$

where $A_{i1}, A_{i2}, \ldots, A_{im} \in D$. The *m* atoms are often referred to as the attributes or fields of the tuple. The scope of a wild card atom is the tuple and its extensions. If a tuple is required to be referenced within another tuple (or within itself, in self-referential systems), then a ground atom can be used as a <label>. This gives a straightforward method for representing structured information. It is up to the higher-level knowledge modeler to ensure <label> uniqueness, and to enforce a strict (for example, Gödel-number) or congruence semantics. In other words, we see no theoretical reason for singling out <labels> for special treatment at the lowest level of information representation (but see Lavington's work[9] for comments on efficiency).

Tuples may be grouped into tuple-sets, via an IFS/2 make-tuple-set constructor, according to typing and semantic information. The tuple-set is the basic unit of IFS/2 information from the memory-management viewpoint (that is, paging and protection). Obviously, logical tuple-sets of varying granularity can be described, down to the single tuple, thus suggesting a mechanism for memory management, as discussed briefly in Section 6.

Practical use of the IFS/2 make-tuple and make-tuple-set constructors, and other data-manipulation facilities, is discussed in Sections 8 and 9. Facilities naturally exist for creating, deleting, modifying, and retrieving the tuples that constitute a knowledge base. Retrieval is achieved as a result of pattern-directed searching. As mentioned in Section 3, searching or matching activity lies at the heart of many operations on relational structures. Because of its importance, we now consider in some detail searching over tuple-sets. Of particular interest is the handling of variables (that is, wild card atoms).

10.5 A FORMALIZATION OF SEARCH

Pattern-directed search is conceptually a single function with three arguments: the interrogand, the matching algorithm to be used, and the tuple-set to be searched. Its result is in general another tuple-set (being a subset of its third argument). Operationally, the search proceeds as follows. Each member of its third argument is compared with the interrogand, which is itself a <tuple>; if they match, as determined by the matching algorithm, then that tuple appears in the output set. There are many possible varieties of matching algorithm, including nearness matching as implied by neural-network paradigms, using a metric such as Euclidean distance or Hamming distance. For the purposes of this chapter, we confine ourselves to matching in the context of the supertype *relation*.

In the IFS/2, the matching algorithm may specify

- a search mode (see below);
- a compare-operator, that is, logical or arithmetic versions of =, ≠, >, ≥, or ≤;
- a compare mask, to inhibit a part or the whole of one or more fields from taking part in the comparison.

For information systems containing variables, unmasked equality is generally the most relevant type of compare operator and mask. Various modes of search are possible, depending upon whether unnamed and named wild cards are given their full interpretation or are treated as if they were constants. We call these two cases *interpreted* and *uninterpreted*. Furthermore, atoms in the interrogand and/or in the stored tuple can be interpreted or uninterpreted. There are thus 16 possible modes of search (not all of which turn out to be useful). Five of the more obvious modes are:

(1) *Identity matching*: Bit-patterns are compared, regardless of the kind of atom (that is, wild cards in both interrogand and stored tuple are uninterpreted).
(2) *Simple matching*: Unnamed wild cards in the interrogand are interpreted, as in conventional content-addressable memory.
(3) *One-way matching (F)*: Both kinds of wild card in the stored tuple are interpreted; this search mode is similar to the functional programming paradigm.
(4) *One-way matching (D)*: Both kinds of wild card in the interrogand are interpreted (the database paradigm).
(5) *Two-way, or unifiability, matching*: All wild cards are interpreted.

The IFS/2 supports all the above modes. In Section 9 we give an example of a C procedure that allows a programmer to specify a particular search option.

10.6 AN ARCHITECTURAL FRAMEWORK FOR ACTIVE MEMORY

Having presented an abstract view of the IFS/2's internal storage conventions, we now discuss the development of a practical architectural framework. The previous two sections suggest that an appropriate memory scheme for smart information systems consists conceptually of a very large table for holding the variable-length tuples of Section 4. Furthermore, this table should be accessed associatively (that is, by content), according to the pattern-directed search modes described in Section 5, to yield resultant tuple-sets. These tuple-sets may then be subject to further processing, for example, via a relational join operation, during which there is much inherent parallelism. How can we exploit this condition by performing parallel processing?

Current parallel architectures differ in the way that processor-store communications are organized. There is a range of possibilities. At one extreme there is the shared-memory design, in which several processors share access to, and communicate via, a single memory (for example, Encore Multimax). At the other extreme there is the fully distributed design, in which each processor only has access to its own local memory, and processors communicate directly with each other (for example, the European Declarative System.)[10] The big issue for each of these machines is likely to be the strategy for distributing both data and work among nodes, in order to achieve an acceptably scalable performance for nontrivial information systems.

One perceived advantage of distributed-memory designs is that the overall store bandwidth is increased linearly as more processors are added to the system. However, when handling large data structures, the overhead of interprocessor communication often outweighs the delays caused by contention in a shared-memory design. An alternative approach is to reduce the store bandwidth requirement and access contention by making a shared memory more active as a unit, instead of being passive. The I-Structure store introduced by Arvind[11] is a step in this direction. Instead of holding an array in the dataflow graph itself, Arvind proposed that it be held in a separate store that is capable of performing array-update operations in response to commands that are primitive to the source language. Extending the I-Structure notion somewhat, we might envisage a physically bounded region of memory which contains all shared data and the means (*methods*) for performing operations upon that stored data. If used in a multiprocessor environment, the shared memory would accept one command (or one packet of commands) at a time.

Using the regular form of representation for symbolic data described in Section 4, it is possible to imagine an active form of memory that is capable of performing whole-structure operations such as set intersection in situ. This capability yields several advantages. The store-bandwidth requirement is considerably reduced, since only high-level commands and printable results cross the processor-memory interface. Given the regular format, an efficient single-instruction, multiple-data approach can be taken to exploit the fine-grain parallelism available in the majority of required operations (see discussion below). The need for a mapping from backing store formats (for example, files) to more efficient RAM representations is eliminated. The architecture provides a natural framework for the notion of data persistence.

In the spirit of Arvind's I-Structure store, the IFS/2 is an add-on active memory unit which both stores and manipulates the data structures used by knowledge-base systems. In addition to the general functional requirements of symbolic applications discussed in Section 3, there are several, more specific, operational features that are desirable, including persistence, support for garbage collection, concurrent-user access, and so forth.

Object-based persistent languages, for example PS-algol,[12] allow data structures created in RAM to survive longer than the programs that created them. From an architectural point of view, the most important attribute of a persistent object store would appear to be the ability to access objects of various sizes without requiring a priori knowledge of their physical location or cardinality.

As mentioned previously, this ability implies the isolation of software from physical addressing, so that names used for objects at the applications-programming level are carried through to the storage level, regardless of memory technology. This *universal naming* may be mechanized by some form of one-level associative (that is, content-addressable) memory. In particular, the IFS/2 arranges that the tuple-sets of Section 4 are all held in one very large associatively-accessed table. When retrieving information from this table, the atoms in an interrogand are the same bit-patterns as the named atoms used by an applications programmer.

In an associative memory, some of the problems of garbage collection are reduced because physical slots that become vacant can be reused without formality (physical location is irrelevant to data retrieval). A more intriguing problem is how to manage data movement (that is, *paging*) within a hierarchy of associative units. This problem is related to protection (that is, locking). We have presented in detail a scheme for memory management known as semantic caching, which uses descriptors similar to the tuple interrogands of Section 4 to identify logical tuple-sets of varying granularity.[13] The IFS/2 will employ relatively straightforward logical tests on descriptors, to determine whether a particular tuple-set is wholly, partly, or not at all contained in the fast cache section of an associative-memory hierarchy.

There are several examples of the application of CAM techniques to symbolic processing. At the disk level, there are database machines such as Teradata.[2] At the other extreme, there are special-purpose very large scale integration chips such as PAM.[14] We know of no affordable CAM technology that will offer the flexibility to store large quantities of tuple-sets of a variety of formats, as implied by the general data-type representation proposed in Section 4. Relying on disk alone tends to push the processing of data structures back into the locus of computational control (that is, a CPU), which goes against the philosophy of whole-structure processing and the active memory. In the next Section we describe the IFS/2's prototype SIMD hardware, which offers direct support for a useful range of primitive operations on data structures in the context of an associatively-accessed, one-level, active-memory unit.

10.7 IFS/2 HARDWARE DESIGN

The first technical challenge in designing the IFS/2 was to devise a modularly-extensible associative-memory cache that would provide several tens of megabytes of content-addressable storage at semiconductor speeds. An approximation to this goal has been achieved by employing groups of simple SIMD search engines (essentially comparators), each with its own bank of dynamic RAM. This technology was first used in our Intelligent File Store project, IFS/1.[15] The first production IFS/1 knowledge-base server went into operation at a customer site in December 1987, with 6 megabytes of pseudo-associative memory and typical search times as follows:

- 38 microseconds (no wild cards in interrogand),
- 244 microseconds (one wild card),
- 2 milliseconds (two wild cards),
- inserting a tuple took between 38 and 76 microseconds,
- deletion took between 4 and 38 microseconds.

Although the IFS/1 appeared as a fully parallel associative table to programmers, we call the technique *pseudo-associative* because search times increase as the number of wild cards in the interrogand increases. This increase occurs because the IFS/1 uses hardware hashing to limit the area of SIMD search; the more unknown fields in the interrogand tuple, the less hashing information is obtainable, and so more hashing bins have to be searched. Note, however, that there is no concept of key (or index) fields; associative access is also independent of tuple-ordering.

For the new IFS/2 unit, we have adapted the IFS/1 SIMD technology to suit the active-memory concept introduced in the previous section. The SIMD associative memory is now more flexible. It is used both as an associative cache to the IFS/2 associatively-accessed disks and as associative buffers for the whole-structure relational operations on tuple-sets. The basis for this approach to relational processing was investigated via a hardware test-bed.[16] The number of relational buffers can be arranged dynamically to suit the particular sequence of (relational algebraic) commands being executed by the IFS/2, as explained later. Thus, the IFS/2's SIMD search engines are used both for pattern-directed search and for the element-by-element comparisons inherent in most set and graph primitives. In this way, whole-structure operations, or even packets of operations, are performed *in situ* and *in parallel* without intermediate transfer of commands or data between the IFS/2 and its host computer.

Figure 1 gives an overall view of the prototype IFS/2 add-on unit. Connection with the host computer, typically a Sun workstation, is via a standard SCSI channel. The IFS/2 is based on modularly-extensible nodes, each node containing a transputer-based node controller, a group of SIMD search modules, and an SCSI disk. The prototype shown in Figure 1 has three nodes, each containing nine megabytes of associative cache and a 720-Mbyte associatively-accessed disk. Each nine megabytes of cache is arranged as three double-Euro-sized printed-circuit boards, each containing three banks of DRAM and three search engines, connected by a local 32-bit wide bus to its node controller. This 32-bit bus is memory-mapped into the node-controller's address space. Apart from the four SCSI channels, all other interconnections in Figure 1 are transputer links.

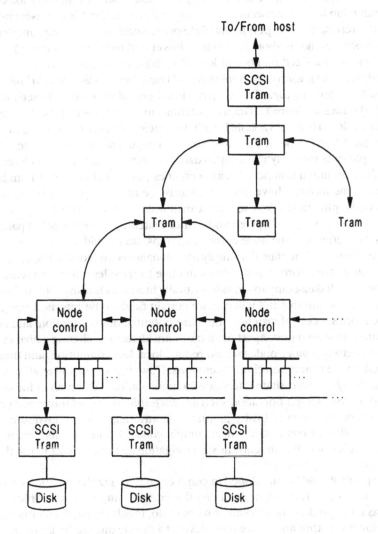

Note: TRAM stands for "transputer plus RAM". Each TRAM consists of either a T425 or T801 transputer plus up to 4 Mbytes of DRAM.

Figure 1. The prototype IFS/2.

The node controllers in Figure 1 are T425 transputers, each with 2 Mbytes of local RAM and operating at a clock speed of 25 MHz. The external-access time to the group of SIMD search engines, which depends partly upon bus characteristics and search logic but principally on the 80-nanosecond DRAM employed, is set at 160 nanoseconds. The blocks labeled TRAM in Figure 1 each consist of an off-the-shelf small daughter-board containing a T801 transputer and 4 Mbytes of local RAM. The SCSI TRAM modules are similar off-the-shelf modules containing a transputer-based SCSI controller and local buffering.

Apart from the SIMD search modules themselves, the only other section of tailor-made (as opposed to bought-in) logic is a hardware hasher subunit attached to each node controller. The byte-manipulation facilities in the T425 transputer's instruction set are somewhat limited, and it was found that a software Occam routine for deriving a hash value from a tuple-field was taking about 10 microseconds. Our hardware hasher, consisting of nine programmable array-logic chips and two programmable read-only-memory look-up tables, can do the same job in 40 nanoseconds, that is, well within the 160-nanosecond SIMD access time. (Interestingly, an experimental field-programmable gate arrays implementation of this same hasher design is about four times slower and four times as costly).

The IFS/2 employs a fixed number of logical hashing bins (usually 512, but variable for experimental purposes). Each search module in Figure 1 contains a *vertical slice* of all 512 hashing bins. After deriving logical hashing-bin numbers, all data is distributed *horizontally* across all SIMD nodes in Figure 1. (Graph operations may vary this distribution strategy; see below). Since tuples may be of variable length, this means that corresponding tuple-slots on all search engines have to be of the same length. The actual division of a search module DRAM into tuple slots varies dynamically as data is inserted or marked as deleted.

Choice of the optimum number of search engines per node in Figure 1 is an interesting compromise. As mentioned above, the basic hardware data-comparison time for 32 bits is 160 nanoseconds, plus time taken to read a match-status line, and is independent of the number of search engines (n) at a given node, since matching is done in SIMD parallel across all n engines. For reference, the node-controlling transputer could do the same single-word comparison in about half the time if it simply had 80-nanosecond local DRAM and no search engines to control. Therefore, it is not cost-effective to have less than two search engines per node. The overall data-comparison rate naturally increases linearly with n. However, all tuples that match the interrogand will require certain fields to be returned along the common bus; the more successful matches, the more potential bus contention, and hence possible degradation in search rate. Apart from cost considerations, sharing a given number of search engines between more nodes would reduce local bus contention, and therefore potentially speed up the simple searching operations. However, the diadic relational algebraic operations such as *join* necessitate internode communication, an argument for keeping the number of nodes low. Graph operation such as *reachable_node_set* introduce yet another set of considerations. For very bushy graphs, it is advantageous to distribute the graph among several nodes. In contrast, the data comparisons for thin chainlike graphs are best confined to a single node. We are currently investigating all these effects in the three-node, 27 search-engine IFS/2 prototype.

One other point should be mentioned in connection with graph operations that are nondeterministic in nature. The task of detecting the end of computation is difficult, because each node has an unpredictable amount of work to do, involving unpredictable amounts of communication with other nodes. We have devised a simple internode hardware *busy* line, which greatly simplifies the controlling Occam firmware. This feature will be more fully reported elsewhere.

The IFS/2's total associative memory may store tuples from many tuple-sets, having various formats and belonging to various users. Each declared tuple-set is given a unique *class_number*; all stored tuples in that set are preceded by a system control word containing the class number, a byte-count giving the length of the tuple, and a free/occupied marker. Predictions of search times are complicated, because they are data-dependent. As detailed in our previous work,[17] the time for a simple match (see Section 5) for class c depends upon

- average number of hashing bins to be searched,
- average number of tuples in class c per search engine per bin per node,
- average number of expected matching tuples per search engine per bin per node,
- average number of tuples not in class c per search engine per bin per node,
- average number of responders (fields) per bin per node,
- communication time taken to return each responder.

Actual times for sample data are given in Section 10, together with IFS/2 performance figures for relational and graph operations.

The following points of implementation detail should be mentioned about the prototype IFS/2.

(1) At present, up to 2^{16} distinct tuple-sets (or *classes*) can be accommodated. Each tuple-set format can specify up to 128 fields. Each field is represented by 32 bits, so that longer or shorter fields have to be modeled accordingly (see point 2 below). Remember that a mask can be specified at search time (See Section 5).

(2) Variable-length *lexemes*, such as ASCII character strings, are mapped into fixed-length 32-bit internal identifiers. In the old IFS/1, associative memory was provided to do this conversion by hardware.[18] At present, we do the conversion in host software. In due course, we will use some of the IFS/2's SIMD search engines to give hardware assistance to lexical token conversion.

A photograph of the prototype IFS/2 is shown in Figure 2. It is difficult to attach an accurate cost to the IFS/2 as an add-on unit, but it is estimated to be about two to three times the cost of an average workstation. As is shown in Section 10, the overall effect of adding an IFS/2 to a standard workstation could be to speed up smart information systems by perhaps one or two orders of magnitude.

10.8 THE HIGH-LEVEL LANGUAGE VIEW OF THE IFS

The IFS/2's tuples and tuple-sets may be manipulated by the standard operations associated with the supertype *relation*. These operations would be expected to include:

1) *Operations on data of type set*:
   member, intersect, difference, union, duplicate removal, subset;
2) *Operations on data of type relation (a subtype of set)*:
   insert, delete, select, project, join, product, division, composition;
3) *Aggregate primitives for sets/relations*:
   cardinality, maximum, minimum, average, sum, count, count unique;
4) *Graph operations*:
   transitive closure, find component partitions, find reachable nodes/edges, find shortest path, test for subgraph matching, test for connectedness, test for cycles.

Ideally, all these kinds of primitives would already be embedded in a well-used persistent programming language. This ideal language would support efficiently both database and AI paradigms. Since no such utopian language yet exists, we have to work through the more traditional software conventions. For example, there are at least three products that com-

Figure 2. A three-node IFS/2 prototype, connected via a SCSI channel to a Sun Sparc workstation. Each IFS/2 node currently consists of 9 Mbytes of semiconductor associative storage based on an array of SIMD search engines, backed by a 720-Mbyte associatively accessed disk. The 3 x 9 Mbytes are used both as associative cache and for the associative processing of structures such as sets, relations, and graphs. The architecture is modularly extensible.

bine logic programming and relational database technology. Megalog (formerly Kb-Prolog)[19] is a good example.

As mentioned previously, few programming languages based on higher-level set primitives exist. Perhaps SETL[8] is the best example. SETL has been used with good effect for software prototyping, but runs inefficiently because its higher-level primitives normally have to be mechanized by inappropriate (that is, von Neumann) architectural support. Nevertheless, SETL demonstrates that set and relational primitives find acceptance among software implementers.

Of course, SQL may be regarded as the best way of presenting relational operations as far as databases are concerned. We are currently implementing an SQL front-end to the IFS/2. This has a tailor-made interface to the IFS/2, based on a relational algebraic tree representation of each SQL statement. The package of database actions (*selection*, *join*, and so forth) implied by each SQL statement is transmitted as a tree structure across the SCSI interface from the host (see Figure 1). As this stage, only algebraic query-optimization has been performed. Once the relational algebraic tree has entered the IFS/2, Occam firmware carries out IFS-specific optimizations and the SIMD search engines are employed to perform the set of low-level actions implied by the original SQL statement. Note that intermediate (that is, temporary) results are held in associative buffers within the IFS/2. Note also that the standard SQL commands *create_index* and *drop_index* are irrelevant to the IFS/2, and are not supported. We plan to extend the relational, packet-based, interface to support Datalog and recursive queries, by incorporating iteration constructs and graph primitives. The graph primitives are based on the repertory described in the next section.

IFS/2 front-ends to other languages may use a general-purpose C procedural interface. For example, we are developing an IFS version of an OPS5-like production-rule system called CLIPS.[7] The general-purpose C procedural interface upon which other front-ends are built is now described.

10.9 IFS/2 LOW-LEVEL PROCEDURAL INTERFACE

The IFS/2 procedural interface at present consists of 42 C library procedure calls. These procedure calls, available on a host computer, communicate with the actual IFS/2 hardware via the SCSI channel as shown in Figure 1. The 42 commands are grouped as follows:

(1) five for housekeeping (for example, opening and closing the IFS/2);
(2) three for tuple descriptor management, allowing structures to be declared and destroyed; these cause entries to be inserted in or deleted from a Tuple Descriptor Table administered by IFS firmware;
(3) three for inserting and deleting tuples and pattern-directed search over sets of tuples;
(4) five for handling character strings or similar lexical tokens; these strings are converted into fixed-length internal identifiers;
(5) five for label management; these commands help in particular with fast label dereferencing;[9]
(6) seven for relational algebraic operations;
(7) 14 for graph operations that support deductive databases.

By way of example, the following is the procedure call for the IFS/2's main pattern-directed search command (see group 3 above):

```
ifs_search(matching_algorithm, code, cn, query, &result),
```

where:

- *matching_algorithm* specifies one of the search modes of Section 5;
- *code* specifies three parameters for each field in the interrogand, namely a bit-mask, a compare-operator ($=$, $>$, and so on), and whether this field is to be returned in the responder-set;
- *cn* is the tuple-set identifier (or *class-number*), specifying the tuple-set to be searched;
- *query* holds information on the interrogand, in the form of a tuple-descriptor giving the characterisation of atoms (see Section 4) and the actual field values;
- *&result* is a pointer to a buffer in the host that contains information on the result of the search.

This buffer contains a header giving (1) a repeat of the *query* parameter, (2) the descriptor of the responder tuple-set (including a new class-number allocated to it by the IFS/2), and (3) the cardinality of this responder tuple-set. In the software simulator version of the IFS/2, the header is then followed by a buffer containing the first n fields of the responder-set itself; in the actual IFS/2 hardware, the responder-set is held in the unit's associative memory, according to the active memory's default of treating all information as persistent.

When manipulating persistent structures, for example, via the active memory's relational algebraic operations (group 6 above), the IFS/2 procedural interface builds on the existing C file-handling syntax. This procedure is illustrated by the following fragment of host C program. We assume that three structures called Alf, Bill, and Chris are being manipulated, and that each structure is stored as a single base relation. Of these structures, let us assume that Alf already exists in the IFS/2's persistent associative memory, that Bill is to be created during the execution of the present program, and that Chris is the name we wish to give to the result of joining Alf and Bill. In other words:

$$\text{Chris} : = \textit{join} \ (\text{Alf, Bill}),$$

according to specified, compatible join fields. The following program fragment assumes that the types IFS_ID, IFS_BUFFER, and IFS_TUPLE are defined in the included library file *ifs.h*; the last two are structures and the first is a 32-bit integer holding a structure's <class-number>. Assume that we already know from a previous program that the <class-number> of Alf = 1. The program loads tuples from a host input device into the new structure Bill, and then performs the required join:

```
#include "ifs.h"
main()
{
        IFS_ID          Bill,
                        Alf = 1,
                        Chris;
        IFS_BUFFER      *Bill_buf;
        TUPLE           t1;
        Bill = ifs_declare(<type>);
        if ((Bill_buf = ifs_open_buf(Bill, "w")) ! = NULL);
        {
                while ( <there are more tuples to be written> )
                {
                        <set t1 to next tuple>
                        ifs_write (Bill_buf, t1);
                }
                ifs_close _buf (Bill_buf);
                Chris = ifs_filter_prod (Alf, Bill, <join
                parameters>); /* the join command */
        }
}
```

ifs_filter_prod is a generalised relational command which has the following C procedural format:

```
        ifs_filter_prod (cn1, cn2, expr e, expr_list el)
```

This procedure forms the cartesian product of tuple-sets cn1 and cn2, then filters the result by (e, el) as follows:

expr and *expr_list* are structures defined in the header file *ifs.h*. A structure of type *expr* represents an expression constructed from the usual Boolean and arithmetic operators. The third argument in *ifs_filter_prod* should represent a Boolean expression; the fourth should be a list of integer-valued expressions that define the contents of the output relation. These two arguments together specify a combined *selection* and *projection* operation, which in IFS/2 terminology we call a *filter*. The various relational *join* operations are special kinds of *ifs_filter_prods*.

It is important to note that all *ifs* commands in the above program fragments are sent down a communications-link to the IFS/2 active memory unit, where they cause hardware actions that proceed independently of the host CPU. The result is a reasonably direct route between a relational primitive and its corresponding hardware support.

The full repertory of relational algebraic commands in group (f) are:

- *ifs_filter,*
- *ifs_filter_union,*
- *ifs_filter_diff,*
- *ifs_filter_prod,*
- *ifs_filter_div,*
- *ifs_calc.*

The last command implements the usual aggregate operations (summing, averaging, and calculating maximum and minimum values) over a given column of a given relation.

As far as graph operations are concerned, the repertory of possible commands is quite extensive.[9] For the present, we have concentrated on those primitives that are useful for supporting deductive databases (including certain recursive queries). In addition to three procedures concerned with declaring graphs, the following commands are supported:[20]

- *transitive closure,*
- *reachable node set,*
- *reachable edge set,*
- *nth wave nodes,*
- *nth wave edges,*
- *check path,*
- *relation composition,*
- *check cycles,*
- *check cycles in a subgraph,*
- *waveset edges 1,*
- *waveset edges 2.*

In general, graphs are materialized from base relations, an entry in a graph descriptor table giving the recipe for constructing the graph from fields selected from one or more base relations. For example, the set of nodes reachable from a given node may be obtained via the procedure call:

```
ifs_reachable_nodes (gn, start_node, &result)
```

where

- *gn* is a graph number identifying an entry in the GDT that gives the recipe for constructing the graph from base relation(s),
- *start_node* is the value representing the start node,
- *&result* gives the class-number of the resultant set (held within the IFS/2).

10.10 IFS/2 PERFORMANCE

The IFS/2 project is still in the development stages, so the results presented below must be regarded as preliminary. Some idea of the basic search capabilities may be obtained from the following figures, which relate to the storage of a single relation (class) consisting of 276,480 three-field tuples. This curious cardinality was arrived at by arranging for the IFS/2's associative cache to be divided into 512 logical hashing bins, and limiting each bin on each of 27 search modules to hold a maximum of 20 tuples. Tuples were generated synthetically so that the values hashed evenly over all bins. Thus, the total number of tuples was (27 × 512 × 20), = 276,480. Each field for this synthetic data was a 32-bit integer. Each tuple is preceded by a 32-bit system-control word giving class number, and so forth. Thus, the total volume of data was (276,480 × 4 × 4) = 4.4 Mbytes. This volume left more than 23 Mbytes of search-module capacity for the associative relational algebraic buffers.

For this 276,480 tuple relation, the following times were observed:

- insert a tuple: 339 microseconds,
- member: 117 microseconds on average,
- delete a tuple: 113 microseconds,
- search with one wild card: 688 microseconds (no responders).

The above times, and indeed all the IFS/2 figures quoted in this section, were for a version of the prototype which had its 32-bit word SIMD search time set to 200 nanoseconds, rather than the more up-to-date value of 160 nanoseconds that we currently use (see Section 7).

It is interesting to compare the IFS/2's search rates with another SIMD architecture, namely the AMT DAP510.[21] This distributed array processor has a 32 × 32 array of one-bit processing elements, each equipped with a one-bit-wide memory of up to 1 megabit. The DAP would conveniently store a relation as *layers* of 1024 tuples. Coincidentally, it happens that the time for a DAP to inspect all 1024 three-field tuples is about the same time as it takes the IFS/2 to inspect one tuple (a little over 10 microseconds). Thus, for small-cardinality relations the DAP and the IFS/2 return similar search times, since the IFS/2 is able to narrow its area of search via hardware hashing. As may be expected, the IFS/2's performance relative to the DAP gets progressively worse as the number of wild cards in an interrogand is increased.

The potential of the IFS/2 hardware is perhaps better illustrated by evaluating the time taken to do a relational join, when compared with several commonly-used software systems. All the software systems were normalized to a technology roughly comparable with that of the IFS/2's hardware, the nearest easy equivalent being a Sun Sparc workstation running at a clock rate of 24 MHz and having 16 Mbytes of RAM.

For the tests, two equal-sized relations of various cardinalities were joined. Each relation's arity was 3, each field being a 32-bit integer. The integer values, which were unique, were chosen so that the output cardinality after the join was about 10 percent of the input relations' cardinality. This simple synthetic benchmark is being used as part of an analysis of several novel architectures.[22] Basically, two joins are performed, as follows:

$$\text{Test (a):} \;\; R \bowtie S \qquad\qquad \text{Test (b):} \;\; R \bowtie S$$
$$3 = 1 \qquad\qquad\qquad\qquad 3 = 2$$

The following software systems were evaluated against the IFS/2 hardware:

(1) a general-purpose C program,
(2) MEGALOG (formerly known as KbProlog),[19]
(3) Quintus PROLOG,
(4) Kyoto Common LISP,
(5) the INGRES relational DBMS,
(6) another well-known relational DBMS (labelled X in Figure 3 for reasons of commercial confidentiality).

Previous work discusses the source code for each of these programs.[22] The average of elapsed times for join tests (a) and (b) are plotted in Figure 3 for each of the six software systems, when running on the same workstation. The six sets of results are seen to span about four orders of magnitude in performance. Note that the C, MEGALOG, INGRES, and X Systems, when taken individually, each gave approximately equal runtimes for join tests (a) and (b), indicating that for this simple benchmark the indexing strategies for these four programs were not sensitive to the position of the join fields. However, tests (a) and (b) gave runtimes that differed by three orders of magnitude in the case of LISP and two orders of magnitude in the case of PROLOG. For example, Quintus PROLOG yielded the following runtimes, measured in seconds:

Input relation cardinality,n	join test (a)	join test (b)
1,000	0.1 seconds	18.867 seconds
3,375	0.317	219.284
8,000	0.767	1,231.317
15,625	1,483	too long for comfort
27,000	2.533	too long for comfort
42,875	3.867	too long for comfort
64,000	6.100	too long for comfort

In Figure 3 we have plotted the average of the times (a) and (b), in the case of Quintus PROLOG and Kyoto Common LISP.

Figure 3 shows elapsed times in seconds versus relation cardinality (that is, number of tuples in each input relation), plotted on a log/log scale. Besides the six software systems, we plot two sets of results for the IFS/2 hardware: the 27 search-module machine of Figure 1 and an IFS/2 containing an infinite number of search modules.

Ferranti International has recently announced a memory-resident PROLOG database management system written in C, known as the Ferranti Prolog Database Engine.[23] This greatly enhances the database performance of Quintus PROLOG, producing join results similar to those of the IFS/2 in Figure 3.

As far as conventional software is concerned, Figure 3 supports the general view that the common AI implementation languages are unlikely to be efficient at manipulating structures containing realistic volumes of data. In contrast, the MEGALOG system appears to perform very well.

It is seen from Figure 3 that the IFS/2 hardware may be expected to perform join operations between two and 5,000 times faster than conventional software. Note that the times given in Figure 3 for the IFS/2 hardware are known to be capable of improvement; the prototype design is currently being refined.

It is also appropriate (but more onerous) to measure the join performance of the IFS/2 against that of other add-on hardware accelerators. In previous work we showed that a prototype IFS relational algebraic processor comfortably outperformed a prototype (but now discontinued) Ferranti relational processor.[23] We have now begun measuring the IFS/2's performance against a more recent accelerator, the White Cross 9010 deskside database server, announced in November 1992.

In summary, the following general observations may also be made about the IFS/2:

(1) For small relations, the IFS/2 hardware may not be efficient. The break-even point between IFS/2 hardware and conventional software depends on the nature of the whole-structure operation and the particular software system being evaluated. For

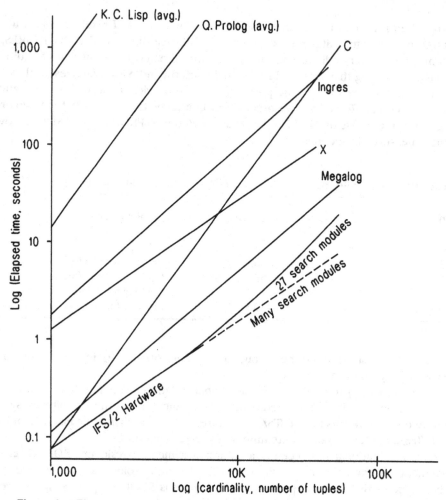

Figure 3. Elapsed times for the *join* benchmark, plotted on a log-log scale for values of n ranging from 1,000 to 64,000.

example, Figure 3 shows that the hand-coded C program performs joins faster than the IFS/2 hardware for relations smaller than about 1,000 tuples. The crossover points for the other software systems of Figure 3 lie below 100 tuples. These conclusions are in line with our measurements of the IFS/2 when supporting the CLIPS Production Rule System.[7] The IFS/2 may speed up production systems by three orders of magnitude if the number of initial facts is greater than about 10,000.[7] Conversely, use of the IFS/2 actually slows down performance for production systems having fewer than about 100 initial facts.

(2) For the particular join tests of Figure 3, there is no advantage in having more than 27 search modules in the IFS/2 hardware for cardinalities under about 3,000 tuples. Above that size, the IFS/2 performance curve can be kept linear by adding more search modules.

10.11 CONCLUSIONS

To be cost-effective, hardware support for knowledge-based systems must not only offer raw performance improvements. It must also reduce overall software complexity and be capable of easy integration with conventional hardware and software standards. In this chapter, we have identified frequently used generic tasks within knowledge-based systems, and then moved responsibility for these tasks to add-on hardware. The super-type *relation* is shown to underpin the important generic tasks. The IFS/2 is a performance accelerator for the super-type *relation*.

In order to preserve applications- and language-independence, we have developed a scheme for the low-level representation of information based on the well-understood notions of *tuple* and *set*. These, together with a formalization of pattern-directed search, form the basis for the IFS/2's repertory of whole-structure operations on sets, relations, and graphs. The operations have been presented to applications software through C-library procedures and a standard SCSI interface.

A rather better task-based interface is under development, as mentioned in Sections 3 and 8. This work should lead to the definition of an Abstract Machine that may provide a useful target both for applications programmers and for developers of future hardware.

The IFS/2 hardware uses SIMD-parallel techniques to achieve associative (that is, content-addressable) storage and processing of structured data. This hardware strategy enables the parallelism inherent in operations such as pattern-directed search to be exploited automatically. The design is modularly-extensible, and makes much use of off-the-shelf components such as transputers. The cost-per-bit of the IFS/2's associative storage is not much more (perhaps five times more) than conventionally addressed linear memory. The IFS/2's architecture conforms to the principle of *active memory*, by means of which logical objects of varying granularity are managed and manipulated in a manner that requires no knowledge of physical addressing on the part of host software. Performance figures for the IFS/2 prototype indicate that speedups in the range 10 to 100 times over conventional software are readily achievable. Work is in hand to develop the prototype in a number of directions, particularly to produce useable higher-level language interfaces, extend the repertory of graph operations, allow more flexibility in choice of field formats, implement hardware support for lexical token conversion, understand better the optimal distribution of SIMD search engines among nodes, refine the low-level Occam firmware, and conduct realistic performance analysis and benchmarking against commercially acceptable workloads.

ACKNOWLEDGMENTS

It is a pleasure to acknowledge the contribution of all other members of the IFS team at Essex. Particular mention should be made of Neil Dewhurst, Jenny Emby, Andy Marsh, Jerome Robinson, Martin Waite and Chang Wang. The work described in this chapter has been supported by the UK Science and Engineering Research Council, under grants GR/F/06319, GR/F/61028 and GR/G/30867.

REFERENCES

1. V.A.J Maller, "Information Retrieval Using the Content-Addressable File Store," *Proc. IFIP-80 Congress*, North-Holland, Amsterdam, The Netherlands, 1980, pp. 187-192.
2. J. Page, "High Performance Database for Client/Server Systems," in *Parallel Processing and Data Management*, P. Valduriez, ed., Chapman and Hall, London, 1992, pp. 33-51; pp. in this book.
3. P.M. Kogge, *The Architecture of Symbolic Computers*, McGraw-Hill, New York, N.Y., 1991.
4. S.J. Stalfo and D.P. Miranker, "DADO: A Parallel Processor for Expert Systems," *Proc. IEEE Conf. Parallel Processing*, IEEE CS Press, Los Alamitos, Calif., 1984, pp. 92-100; pp. in this book.
5. D. Moldovan, W. Lee, and C. Lin, "SNAP: A Marker-Propagation Architecture for Knowledge Processing," *IEEE Trans. Parallel and Distributed Systems*, Vol. 3, No. 4, July 1992, pp. 397-410.
6. W.D. Hillis, *The Connection Machine*, MIT Press, Cambridge, Mass., 1987.

7. S.H Lavington, et al., "Hardware Support for Data Parallelism in Production Systems," in *VLSI for Neural Networks and Artificial Intelligence,* J. Delgado-Frias and W. Moore, eds., Plenum Press, New York, N.Y., 1994, pp. 231–242.

8. R.B.K. Dewar, E. Schonberg, and J.T. Schwartz, *High-Level Programming: An Introduction to the Programming Language SETL,* Courant Institute of Math. Sciences, New York, N.Y., 1983.

9. S.H. Lavington, et al., "Exploiting Parallelism in Primitive Operations on Bulk Data Types," *Proc. Conf. Parallel Architectures and Languages Europe,* Springer-Verlag Lecture Notes on Computer Science 605, Springer-Verlag, New York, N.Y., 1992, pp. 893–908.

10. C.J. Skelton, et al., "EDS: A Parallel Computer System for Advanced Information Processing," *Proc. Conf. Parallel Architectures and Languages Europe,* Springer-Verlag Lecture Notes in Computer Science, No. 605, Springer-Verlag, New York, N.Y., 1992, pp. 3–18; pp. in this book.

11. Arvind, R.S.Nikhil, and K.K. Pingali, *I-Structures: Data Structures for Parallel Computing,* MIT Lectures in Computer Science (CSG Memo 269), Mit Press, Cambridge, Mass., 1987.

12. Persistent Programming Research Group, *PS-algol Reference Manual,* 4th ed., Persistent Programming Research Report No. 12, Dept. of Computing Science, Univ. of Glasgow and Dept. of Computational Science, Univ. of St Andrews, Glasgow, Scotland, 1987.

13. S.H. Lavington, et al., "Hardware Memory Management for Large Knowledge Bases," *Proc. Conf. Parallel Architectures and Languages Europe,* Springer-Verlag Lecture Notes in Computer Science, Nos. 258 and 259, Springer-Verlag, New York, N.Y., 1987, pp. 226–241.

14. I. Robinson, "A Prolog Processor Based on a Pattern Matching Memory Device," *Proc. 3rd Int'l Conf. Logic Programming,* Springer-Verlag Lecture Notes in Computer Science, No. 225, Springer-Verlag, New York, N.Y., 1986, pp. 172–179.

15. S.H. Lavington, "Technical Overview of the Intelligent File Store," *Knowledge-Based Systems,* Vol. 1, No. 3, June 1988, pp. 166–172.

16. S.H. Lavington, J. Robinson, and K.Y. Mok, "A High Performance Relational Algebraic Processor for Large Knowledge Bases," in *VLSI for Artificial Intelligence,* J. Delgado-Frias and W. Moore, eds., Kluwer Academic, Norwell, Mass., 1989, pp. 133–143.

17. S.H. Lavington, et al., "A Modularly Extensible Scheme for Exploiting Data Parallelism," *Applications of Transputers 3,* IOS Press, Amsterdam, The Netherlands, 1991, pp. 620–625.

18. C.J Wang and S.H. Lavington, "SIMD Parallelism for Symbol Mapping," in *VLSI for Artificial Intelligence and Neural Networks,* J. Delgado-Frias and W. Moore, eds., Plenum Press, New York, N.Y., 1991, pp. 67–78.

19. J. Bocca, et al., *KB-Prolog User Guide,* European Computer Industry Research Centre, Munich, Germany, 1990.

20. N.E.J. Dewhurst, S.H. Lavington, and J. Robinson, *DDB Graph Operations for the IFS/2,* Internal Report CSM-169, Dept. of Computer Science, Univ. of Essex, Essex, England, May 1992.

21. S. Reddaway, "High-Performance Text Retrieval with Highly Parallel Hardware," *Proc. UNICOM Seminar on Commercial Parallel Processing,* UNICOM Seminars Ltd., London, England, 1992, pp. 61–66.

22. A.J. Marsh and S.H. Lavington, *A Synthetic Join Benchmark for Evaluating DBMS/KBS Hardware and Software,* Internal Report CSM-173, Dept. of Computer Science, Univ. of Essex, Essex, England, July 1992.

23. B.L. Rosser, J.M. Bedford, and C.R. Dobbs, *The Ferranti Prolog Database Engine,* Ferranti International Report No. ASP/AI/REP/68, Cwmbran, Wales, Sept. 1992.

11

EDS: An Advanced Parallel Database Server

L. Borrmann,[†] F. Hutner,[†] S.R. Leunig,[††] M. Lopez,[†††] M.J. Reeve,[††††] C.J. Skelton,[††] and K.F. Wong[††††]

[†]Siemens AG, Munich, Germany
[††]ICL, West Gorton, Manchester, UK
[†††]Bull S.A., Gieres, France
[††††]ECRC, Munich, Germany

ABSTRACT

The increasing volume of data processed by today's information systems, together with the growing demands of highly sophisticated information-processing functionalities, are overstretching existing database management systems. Many applications are either too complex for today's DBMSs or too large to be handled by them. Although some DBMSs claim to be able to cope with the complexity and size, the execution performances are too sluggish to be considered practical. The European Declarative System project (ESPRIT-II EP2025) is aimed at improving this situation. Its prime objective is to develop an advanced large-scale parallel database server for building business information systems. Parallel technology is widely employed in the EDS server. Parallelism is exploited at the hardware, operating-system, and database-processing levels. Moreover, EDS supports an advanced database query language, ESQL (an extension of the standard structured query language) and provides features for manipulating objects and abstract data types, as well as the capability to handle recursive views and rules. These features make the EDS database server suitable for a continuum of database applications ranging from online transaction processing (OLTP) applications, which feature simple queries, to management support systems characterized by queries with low and medium complexity. In this paper, the different levels of parallelism exploited in the EDS server and the advanced functionality supported by ESQL are described.

11.1 INTRODUCTION

Information-technology users are encountering performance bottlenecks as they extend their applications to encompass more users and more of the critical operations. As a consequence, there are growing demands for both performance and system capability in information-processing systems. At present, there are many application areas (for example, business and CAD) where the requirements of applications outstrip the continuing growth in the performance and capability of the underlying information-processing system. Attempts have been made to increase performance by simply using faster processors. This strategy, however, cannot scale up with the increasing size and complexity of the applications. The prime objective of the EDS (European Declarative System) project is to develop a high-performance advanced database server to circumvent the aforesaid predicament.

EDS is a 57 MECU project supported by the European Commission, DGXIII, under the ESPRIT-II (European Strategic Programme for Research and Development in Information Technology) initiative, and involves the collaboration between Bull (France), ECRC (pan-European), ICL (UK), Siemens (Germany) and a number of European industrial and research organizations. EDS will provide a fully integrated parallel platform to meet the increasing performance and programming demands in information technology.

The demands for high-performance information systems is ever increasing. Business-information processing is one of the target application areas of EDS. One application area that is much concerned in EDS is online transaction processing. Many business applications employ OLTP technology and demand very high transaction rates to cope with the large number of customers. A forecast provided by the marketing divisions of the EDS industrial partners states that the transaction rate of a typical OLTP system will grow by a factor of 10 over the next five years. However, based on the current trends, this growth rate will not be matched by the performance growth rate of today's mainframe computers.

In addition, the profile of the transaction load is changing as management-support queries and queries over knowledge bases (including rules) are added to the existing, largely clerical, workloads. Although very complex queries, (for example, in knowledge management,) will contribute little to throughput demands, medium-complex queries, (for example, in online decision-support systems,) will certainly demand significant throughput.

The advanced EDS database server is designed to support a continuum of database applications ranging from OLTP-like (simple) queries to queries of low to medium complexity. It will deliver up to 10 times the performance of conventional mainframes expected in the mid-90s. In particular, for OLTP applications, over 12,000 transactions per second are predicted.[1] To achieve this target, parallel technology is extensively used on all levels of the EDS database server, including the employment of a distributed-memory multiple-instruction, multiple-data architecture for hardware level parallelism, a parallel operating system, and a parallel database executive to exploit both interquery and intraquery parallelisms.

EDS also addresses the greater programming demands of information technology. Structured query language is widely used for database applications and can be found in almost all existing commercial products. Notwithstanding its many desirable high-level program constructs, SQL lacks some advanced functions (for example, objects with complex structures, multistatement queries, abstract data types, deductive capability, and so forth); as a result, the scope of application of conventional relational databases is restricted.

The EDS database system, the "golden core" of the EDS server, is designed to provide advanced functionalities by incorporating extensions to SQL. The query language under development, ESQL (Extended SQL), is a strict superset of the SQL standard. It is, therefore, upward-compatible for existing database applications. Furthermore, the SQL extensions will make the EDS server also suitable for tomorrow's advanced applications.

To further widen the application spectrum of EDS, two parallel artificial-intelligence programming languages, namely ElipSys (a parallel logic programming language) and parallel EDS Lisp, are supported by the EDS server. Complementary to ESQL, these languages are designed to solve very complex queries typically found in knowledge-base applications.

This paper presents an overview of the parallel architecture of the EDS advanced database server. In the next three sections of this chapter, the parallel architectures of the EDS hardware, operating system, and database system are described, respectively. A description of the advanced capabilities provided by the database query language ESQL follows in Section 5. In Section 6 the simulated OLTP performance of the EDS database server is reported. Finally, in Section 7, the conclusion of the paper is given.

11.2 PARALLEL EDS MACHINE

A major goal of the EDS machine is to provide a high-performance parallel-hardware platform for advanced database applications. A number of design issues were considered in reaching this goal:

(1) *Scalability*. The EDS machine had to be scalable from a few to several hundred processors. Therefore, a common bus or a physically shared memory was not viable. For this reason, EDS adopts a distributed-memory, MIMD parallel-computer architecture.

(2) *Design effort and price/performance ratio*. Standardized interfaces and off-the-shelf components were used wherever possible during the development. As a result, the EDS machine can be upgraded easily to account for future technology advancements, for example, the existing main SPARC processor on the processing element module can be replaced by a next generation SPARC processor that can offer higher performance. However, no well-suited standard components were available for the interprocessor-communication network, so the network-switching element and the network interface unit to the processing element were specially built as semicustom chips (see next section for the descriptions of the PE and the NIU).

The EDS database server functions as an accelerator for a host computer. The basic building blocks of the EDS machine[2] are processing elements (PE), where application programs and system software run. By adding PEs a range of machine sizes of increasing performance can be produced. Also, specialized functional elements can be added to the system to perform specific functions, for example, a diagnostic element (DE) that carries out diagnostics, low-level debugging and monitoring; a host element (HE) that provides the interface to the user; and optionally an I/O element (IOE) that provides local disk access (see Figure 1). All elements communicate via the high-bandwidth multistage interconnection network that can accommodate up to 256 of them (PEs and specialized functional elements) in total. Plate 1 shows the fully installed EDS prototype system.

In the following subsections, the functions of the PE, the specialized functional elements, and the communication network are described.

11.2.1 Processing Element (PE)

The PE contains four basic components, as shown in Figure 2. The processing unit (PU) is the main processor where primarily application programs and the operating system kernel run. It is connected to the store unit (SU) via a local bus. The system support unit (SSU) is an additional processor that mainly controls communication. However, these processors can also operate in a symmetrical multiprocessing mode on each single PE, where only the communication control tasks need to be fixed to the SSU and all other processes can be scheduled freely to any one of the two processors.

The PU and the SSU are both standard reduced instruction-set computing processors from the SPARC family delivering about 26 million instructions per second each. The SSU

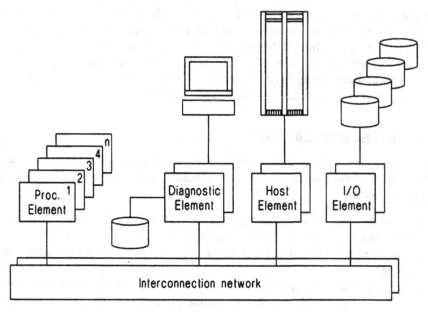

Figure 1. The hardware architecture of the parallel EDS machine.

is tightly coupled to the network interface unit (NIU) to allow for very fast control transfer. This coupling also frees the local memory bus from the direct-memory-access control traffic. The PU is a complete, commercially available processor module that integrates an instruction unit, a floating point unit, a cache controller, a memory management unit, and also some cache RAMs. This integration allows the exchange of the PU with newer, faster SPARC processors without any hardware changes. Such compatible, faster processors are currently appearing in the market.

The store unit (SU) is a a two-way interleaved dynamic memory with a size of 64 megabytes (extendible up to 4 gigabytes). It has error-checking-and-correction logic that can tolerate and correct single-bit fails and recognize multibit fails. The EDS virtual memory scheme is also supported by the SU. There is a tag bit associated with every 128-byte portion of the memory, holding information whether this "sector" is locally valid or not. Thus,

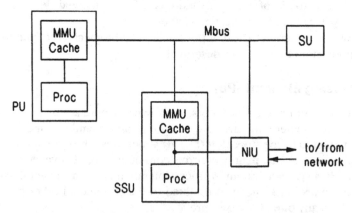

Figure 2. The EDS processing element (PE) architecture.

it is possible to copy only a 128-byte sector, instead of a whole memory page of 4 kilobytes, from a remote node in case of a nonlocal memory access.

The NIU provides the interface between the local memory bus and the network. It serves as a direct-memory-access unit under SSU software control. Provided with the necessary parameters (physical address, number of bytes) it arbitrates on the memory bus and transports data from the network to the SU and vice versa, performing the necessary data format conversions.

11.2.2 Specialized Functional Elements

Besides the PEs, the EDS machine can have varying numbers of specialized functional elements (see Figure 1). They form the links to the "outside" world.

(1) The host element (HE) connects the EDS system to the host computers. A wide range of host machines from ICL, Bull, and Siemens will be supported. HEs are host-dependent, so the architecture of an HE varies between different types of host computers.

(2) The diagnostic element (DE) provides a route for initial software loading, alternative access paths to other elements under fault conditions, and an engineering tool for fault analysis.

(3) The input/output element (IOE), an optional element, provides additional mass storage devices. Normally information storage is provided directly by the SU on the PEs.

11.2.3 Communication Network

The EDS communication network[3] provides the functionality imposed by the database execution models and achieves high global throughput and low latency, to avoid performance degradation due to communication overhead. It is suitable for a wide range of load profiles and distributions, expected from various workloads. Its topology is a multistage interconnection network. The network offers up to 256 full duplex channels with a bandwidth of 20 Mbytes per second in each direction. It is built of very-large-scale-integration semicustom chips, each forming an 8x8 crossbar switch with 32 independent packet buffers. By detailed simulation it was shown that for a full-size network a throughput of more than 3 Gbytes per second can be maintained without saturation. Figure 3 shows the EDS DElta interconnection network.

The EDS network is a packet-switched network with variable packet size. A packet consists of 16 header bytes, up to 128 bytes of data, and 2 more bytes for error detection. The switch operates on the *virtual cut-through* scheme, which adds the advantages of circuit switching to the packet-switching mode; that is, the network has a very low latency as long as the total communication load is low.

Figure 3 shows the network configurations for a smaller system with only two stages and a large configuration. The latter even provides some redundancy in the middle stage of the network, thus adding resilience features to the machine.

At the application layer, the EDS network facilitates inter-PE communication. There are two means in which two PEs can communicate: (1) message passing, by explicit transfer of user-specified data from a source PE to a destination PE and (2) virtual store copying, by accessing virtual shared data physically stored on another PE. Message passing is made available to users by a set of operating-system primitives. The store-copying mechanism is transparent to users and is designed for supporting the virtual shared-memory mechanism in the EDS operation system (see Subsection 11.3.1.2).

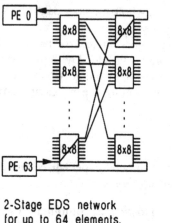

2-Stage EDS network
for up to 64 elements.
The communication path from
PE63 to PE0 is also shown.

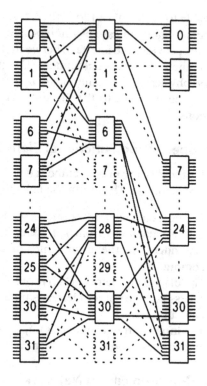

3-Stage extended EDS network
for up to 256 elements.

Figure 3.   The EDS interconnection network.

11.3 EMEX—THE EDS OPERATING SYSTEM

The EDS operating system, EMEX, is the common platform for the EDS parallel database, as well as for two other parallel-programming language subsystems supported by the EDS server, namely, ElipSys[4] and EDS Lisp[5] (see references for more information about the two systems). As such, it is a crucial element of the overall EDS system architecture.

As an operating system for a parallel machine, EMEX offers novel features to support parallel programming, such as built-in support for virtually shared memory. Additionally, EMEX provides a full Unix SVR4 interface on each node. This enhancement was achieved by enriching Chorus/MiX,[6] a microkernel-based implementation of SVR4, by another subsystem for parallel-programming support.

The parallel-programming interface of EMEX is called PCL (Process Control Language). PCL was designed within the EDS project after the requirements imposed by its main "customers," that is, the EDS database and programming language subsystems. Nevertheless, PCL is by no means limited to support them only, as shown in a study that implemented a parallel C++ programming interface (PARC++, an extension of PRESTO) on top of PCL and EMEX.

In the following sections the concept behind PCL and its Chorus-based implementation are described, followed by a description of the additional operating-system facilities supported by EMEX. These facilities include host and file I/O, naming service, and dynamic linking and loading.

11.3.1 Basic Concepts of PCL

Besides some minor additional functions, PCL covers three important areas:

- the process model,
- the store model,
- the communication model.

The communication model provides primitives for explicit, synchronous and asynchronous, message passing. These primitives are customized to run on the EDS parallel hardware. The process models and store models[7] are widely hardware-independent and provide abstractions and primitives for process control and memory management. These two are closely related but can be used independently of the communication model.

11.3.1.1 The Process Model

The PCL process model is an extension of the two-level model of Chorus or Mach. In these two-level models, there are threads and tasks, or actors. A thread is a process, without a private memory context. Multiple threads can coexist in the same virtual-address space. A task (Mach) or actor (Chorus) is a set of threads with the enclosing memory context. Conventional Unix processes can be regarded as single-threaded actors in this model. This two-level model renders concurrency within a monoprocessor or multiprocessor, but is insufficient for parallel programming in the distributed-memory architecture of the EDS machine. For this reason, in the PCL process model a four-level hierarchy is used:

(1) The *thread* is a lightweight process that can share an address space with other threads. It is directly mapped onto a thread of Chorus.

(2) A *team* is a set of threads within a common virtual-address space on a single processing element. Thus, threads of a team share a physical memory, and a coherent cache. A team is implemented by an actor in Chorus.

(3) *Tasks*, as the third level, were introduced that can span multiple PEs. A task in PCL is a set of teams, each on a different PE. The remarkable thing about tasks is that teams of a common task use *virtually shared memory* (see below), and that the address space of those teams is managed in a consistent manner by the system. An abstraction like the PCL task is not provided by either Chorus or Mach, and is implemented by the PCL process and memory manager.

(4) A *job* is a group of multiple tasks that cooperate within a parallel application, or a user session. Jobs cannot be created by other jobs but only by a privileged instance in the system (for example, the EDBS's Session Manager—see Section 4).

When a new team is created from an existing one, it will automatically inherit all the memory segments of its parent by either copying (like a Unix fork), or by virtual sharing. In PCL, virtual sharing is the default case, and will be used for the text and the data segments. For all other segments, it is a user decision whether to apply copying or sharing. This inheritance mode is fixed at segment-creation time and does not change throughout the life of a segment. Compared to child processes in Unix, the teams of a task are much more closely coupled. When a team creates a new segment, it will become visible for all teams of the task. As an (extended) equivalence of Unix fork, task creation is provided. Sharing or copying can be achieved here, too, but once a new task is created, it is independent of its parent. Figure 4 shows an example of a two-team task with seven threads, running on a 3-PE EDS machine.

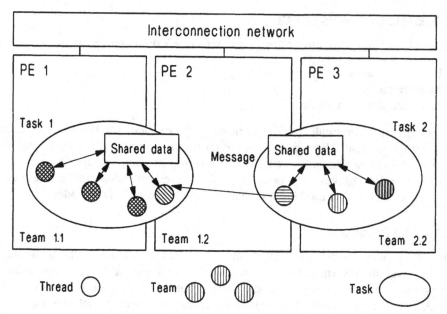

Figure 4.   Example of PCL process model.

Other than in Chorus, there are no empty tasks in PCL. An initial team and thread is created automatically for convenience, and when the last thread of a team terminates, the team itself (and maybe even the task) will be deleted also. Likewise, stack creation and collection is handled automatically by the system.

11.3.1.2 The Store Model

Virtually shared memory has been mentioned previously; it is an underlying feature on which the process model is based. Virtual sharing (see Figure 5) is achieved using a caching approach; that is, a page of memory can be replicated over several PEs in the EDS machine

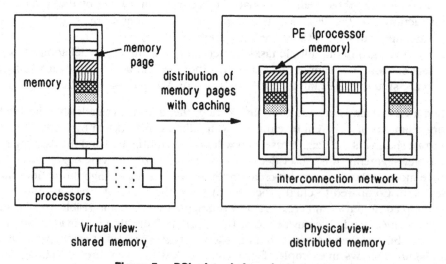

Figure 5.   PCL virtual shared memory.

to speed up read access. Page copying and management are triggered by page faults, and handled in a dedicated process, called a *mapper*, which is a server in the Chorus kernel. The hardware-supported store-copying mechanisms, described in Section 11.2.3, facilitate efficient page copying.

Replication of pages inevitably raises a coherency problem when pages are being updated. PCL implements multiple protocols to solve this problem. The best-known scheme is strong ordering, which makes it necessary to restrict page access to multiple readers or a single writer. This approach[8] offers strong coherency, as in a bus-based shared memory system. The mapper ensures that, at any given time, either write access to a single PE or concurrent read accesses to multiple PEs are possible.

Performance improvements can be achieved by moving to a weaker coherency model,[9] thus reducing blocking effects due to teams competing for page access. In the current system, multiple readers and a single writer can proceed concurrently. The updates being made by the writer are not immediately visible to a reader. Visibility is undefined until a coherent view is explicitly restored. The coherent view can be established by either readers or writers using dedicated system functions like *dsmFlush()* or *dsmGuaranteeVisibility()*. These coherency-control functions are not inserted by the user; instead, they are automatically generated by the EDS programming-language systems (that is, ESQL, ElipSys or EDS Lisp).

In EMEX, multiple coherency schemes can coexist, each in a separate mapper if desired. The user can choose among the available models at segment-creation time, and can thus use the appropriate scheme according to the way the data item is used.

11.3.1.3 The Communication Model

The communication model in EMEX provides a uniform message-passing mechanism between threads, regardless of whether the threads are local or remote to one another. Message passing is achieved through communication ports. A port is an object to which messages may be sent and from which messages may be received. A unique identifier (that is, port-id) is associated with a port. Each port has a set of connections and each connection has a set of send-endpoints and a receive-endpoint. Each endpoint is identified by a handle and owned by a unique team. There is only one receive-endpoint per port, which is common to all connections and is established at the time of port creation. A connection endpoint is owned by the team that established the endpoint; any thread of the same team may therefore make use of it.

The physical communication means that between a sender and a receiver endpoints are transparent to the users; it is determined by the locations of the ports. If a send-endpoint is on a different PE to the receive-endpoint, messages must be sent via the interconnection network. If the send-endpoints and receive-endpoints are on the same PE, but in different teams, messages can be sent by store copying. In certain circumstances, if the send-endpoints and receive-endpoints are on the same PE and in the same team, messages can be sent by pointer passing.

Two types of port are supported in PCL: ordered and non-ordered. An ordered port guarantees delivery of messages in the chronological sequence in which they are presented at a send-endpoint. As a result, messages from different threads sent using the same send-endpoint are interleaved; similarly, messages sent from different send-endpoints to the same receive-endpoint are also interleaved. For a nonordered port, messages are not delivered in a guaranteed sequence; thus, any message discarded at the receive-endpoint can be retransmitted out of sequence.

Furthermore, PCL provides both synchronous and asynchronous message passing. A synchronous send blocks the sender thread until the message has been delivered successfully into a user buffer at the receive-endpoint (or until the transmission has failed). An asynchronous send blocks the sender thread only until the message has been queued for transmission.

11.3.2 PCL Subsystem Implementation

EMEX is based on Chorus. To support the aforesaid PCL operation models, a number of components have been added to the standard Chorus system:

- a message-passing component,
- a process manager,
- a memory manager,
- multiple mappers,
- a system manager.

These components can be added to Chorus in various ways. As mentioned previously, an EMEX mapper is an abstraction of Chorus. Besides a default mapper responsible for disk paging, an arbitrary number of mappers can be present in the system. Each memory segment is assigned to a dedicated mapper via a capability that includes the server-port address of the mapper. When page faults occur, the kernel will send messages (remote procedure calls) to the responsible mapper, using a published and well-defined interface. This interface includes functions like *pullIn()* (get a page of data), *pushOut()* (swap a page of data out), or *getAccess()* (get further access right, for example, write access).

The memory manager and the process manager are supervisor actors connected to the system-call interface (trap interface) of Chorus. (Currently, the process manager is part of the kernel, but this is to be changed to enhance portability.) This means that certain system calls generated by a user process will not be handled by the kernel itself, but by the respective manager process. Other than with the mapper interface, no message passing is involved here, but the handler is entered via a direct subroutine call.

The complete set of additional components can be regarded as the PCL subsystem. Effectively, it extends the functions of Chorus by those defined in PCL, similarly to the Unix subsystem of Chorus. The implementation of PCL is thus a good example of how a microkernel can be put into use.

11.3.3 Additional Operating-System Facilities

In the EDS server, the presence of a Unix subsystem on each PE is optional. The decision to incorporate a Unix subsystem in EDS was influenced by the large number of existing Unix-based applications. The EMEX Unix subsystem will make the EDS server readily usable by such applications.

The support of parallel programs via PCL is independent of Unix. It was thus necessary to provide for certain facilities conventionally available in Unix systems without being part of the EMEX kernel. These additional facilities are:

(1) *Host and file I/O.* The EMEX file server supports a minimal set of facilities to enable applications running on the EDS machine to interchange data with a remote machine and to create, re? i, write, and destroy files on a remote Unix file system. This function is built upon the message passing as described above. In general, all I/O except trace messages will be implemented by remote procedure call.

(2) *System Manager.* The system manager provides users with an interface to load EMEX applications and to access system information. It uses the file server for host communication, and the EMEX loader to load applications. The system manager also provides for *name binding* in the distributed environment, thus enabling other programs to know about the port-ids of available servers.

(3) *EMEX loader and linker.* This component supports dynamic loading of executable files, as well as dynamic linking to load and exchange code objects at runtime. Load objects are in Unix-compatible format. The mechanisms used are similar to the mechanisms used in SunOS, but with a more powerful programming interface.

11.4 EDBS—THE PARALLEL EDS DATABASE SYSTEM

The aims of the EDS database system, EDBS, are to provide an order of magnitude improvement in performance compared to mainframes for commercial OLTP workloads, and advanced functionality (object-oriented and deductive features) to extend database support to a wider range of applications. Moreover, an important design target is the provision of a flexible and extensible database system that can be easily enhanced to provide more advanced facilities over time. In order to achieve these objectives a number of design strategies are being used.

(1) Parallelism available in the base EDS system is being exploited. In particular, EMEX has been specially designed to support a high-performance parallel-database system. A large stable RAM is assumed, which will to hold the persistent data, including across-system breaks. The prototype EDS hardware will not provide a stable RAM, but the design of the database system assumes its existence.

(2) The database system will be based on standard relational database technology extended to provide object-oriented database and deductive database facilities.

(3) The programming interface will be via an extended version of the language SQL (ESQL).[10] In particular, the language will provide a rich and extendible type system based on abstract data types, where the methods can be defined in various programming languages, in complex objects with object sharing by combining the ADTs with object identity, and in the equivalent of a DATALOG deductive capability (see Section 5).

(4) A RISC-like approach is taken in compiling ESQL queries to native machine code.

(5) The query compiler optimizer has been designed to be extensible to allow the system to evolve.

Figure 6 shows the overall architecture of EDBS. EDBS is split into three main components: the request manager (RM), which compiles database commands into native machine code; the data manager (DM), which provides the runtime facilities required to execute those commands; and the object manager, which provides the shared object store. In addition to them, interface to the hosts is provided by the session manager (SM). The SM provides the mechanism by which an application starts a database session. It creates an instance of each of the the RM and the DM for each database session. The SM-host communication makes extensive use of standard RPC techniques. (Work on the session manager has not been fully developed; its discussion is omitted here.)

In this section the operation principles and the architectures of EDBS are described. The section is structured as follows: (1) the operation principles behind EDBS (that is, the EDBS execution model) are described in the next subsection; (2) three subsections give descriptions of the individual EDBS components (that is, the RM, DM and object manager); and

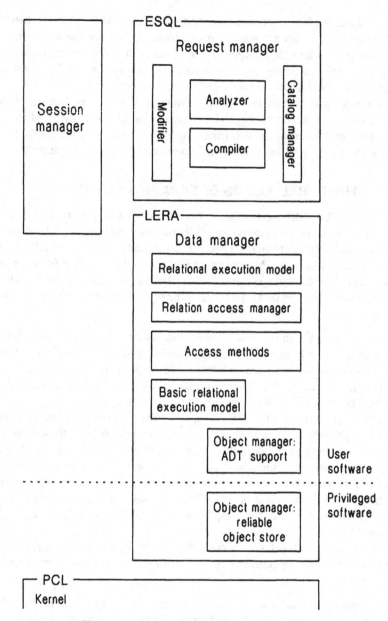

Figure 6.   The EDBS system architecture.

some issues relating to integrating between the EDBS and the EDS platform are outlined at the end of the section.

11.4.1 EDBS Parallel-Execution Model

11.4.1.1 Basic Operation Principles

Declustered store

   Database relations are declustered (also referred to as horizontal fragmentation) using a criterion applied to one or more of their attributes. When a relation is declustered, the whole relation is partitioned into a number of relation fragments, and these fragments are stored on different PEs. Common criteria for declustering are *hash*, *range* or *round robin*. For example, in Figure 7, relations R and S are declustered into a set of *n* fragments using criterion H. The set of PEs where a relation is stored is the *home* of that relation. In practice, the number of home PEs for a relation is a function of the relation size and access frequency.[11] Depending on the query, an operation involving a relation may take place on one or more home PEs.

Parallel database operation

Inter-operation and intra-operation parallelism.   Data declustering and pipelining are the basis for parallel-database execution. By splitting an operation into instances and having each operation instance executing on a home PE, intra-operation parallelism is achieved. In addition, another form of parallelism, namely inter-operation parallelism, can be exploited. This parallelism is achieved by having multiple operations executed simultaneously. (From a different point of view, an operation that exploits intra-operation parallelism is equivalent to single-instruction, multiple-data execution, and a set of operations is performed in multiple-instruction, multiple-data fashion under inter-operation parallelism.) In essence, data declustering facilitates the important parallelization concept of "performing database operations locally where the data are." Operations are sent to the homes of their operands; thus, the communication costs can be significantly reduced. Due to the dynamic

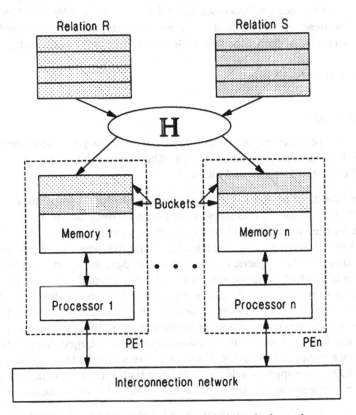

Figure 7.   Parallel storage model: data declustering.

nature of the data set, it is sometimes necessary to re-decluster a relation in order to increase parallelism. This operation is more likely (and much simpler) to apply to intermediate relations rather than to permanent base relations.

Pipeline parallelism.   Pipelining (sometimes referred to as streamlining) exploits temporal parallelism during data transfer between two database operations. When a database operation produces some data and these data are consumed by another database operator rather than materialized, a pipeline (or a stream) can be set between them for data transfer. (The former is the producer and the latter the consumer.) In this case, the consumer operation can start as soon as the data is produced.

Operation placement.   The parallelization of an operation is achieved by first decomposing an operation into instances and then placing them onto the relevant home PEs for local execution. For example, given a relation R that is declustered on n PE, the operation *Select(R)* is equivalent to the union of n sub-operations, *Select(Ri), where i* = 1..n. Each individual sub-operation (or instance) can be performed in parallel on node i.

Dedicated parallel operations.   The aforesaid parallel-database operation techniques form the basis of all shared-nothing database computers, such as Bubba,[12] Gamma,[13] Grace, and Teradata DBC1012.[14] However, it is worth noting that EDS adopts a homogeneous architecture (where all PEs are identical) similar to the Bubba and Gamma architectures. On the other hand, Grace and DBC1012 have a heterogeneous architecture consisting of special-purpose processing modules. Some examples are the Processing (P-), the Memory (M-), the Communication (C-), and the Disk (D-) modules of Grace and the Interface Processor (IFP); the Communication Processor (COP); and the Access Module Processors (AMP) of DBC1012. In these machines, database operations are performed in parallel using dedicated processors, that is, the P-Modules of Grace and the AMP of DBC1012.

11.4.1.2 Implementing Issues

Data declustering

In practice, there are two types of data in EDBS: temporary and permanent. The permanent data are held as objects managed by the EDS object manager and the temporary data are held in the volatile EMEX virtual memory.

Permanent data.   The direct storage model[15] is used for the implementation of the permanent relations. This model was chosen because it allows efficient access to the conceptual relations for the most important access patterns. One of the advances in EDBS has been the development of a cost model,[16] used to determine the degree of parallelism available in a database and the profile of queries; with this knowledge, the optimal declustering of (that is, the number of PEs for) a relation can, in turn, be determined. Unfortunately when a permanent relation is created, there is only very little information available and it is insufficient to derive the cost model. As a temporary measure the *TABLE* command has been extended to allow the user to indicate the degree of fragmentation of the relation, and even the physical PEs to be used for the relation. In the longer term it is envisaged that the database would be periodically reorganized using metrics from the relations and the access patterns in the cost model. EDBS also supports indexes associated with relations to improve the efficiency of access. These indexes are purely local to the individual relation fragments.

Temporary data.   The direct storage model is also used for the intermediate or temporary relations used in queries. The logical distribution of the temporary data (that is the number of fragments and their association with other relations) is determined at compile time, while the runtime system determines the mapping of the fragments to the physical PEs. This distribution gives rise to a better opportunity for load balancing than can be obtained with the permanent relations, whose placement is relatively static.

Data-flow and control-flow separation

Another attribute of the EDBS execution model is the separation of the control flow from the dataflow operations, allowing the global synchronization necessary for the semantics of a query program to be separated from the purely local low-level synchronization that occurs at the level of the local operations. This attribute gives rise to a number of compiler optimization techniques. For example, where messages are sent to a subset of a home the *WAIT* control operator will only wait for control signals from those home PEs that have been activated; otherwise, without such a control operator, all the home PEs, even the ones that do not contain any interesting data for the execution, would need to wait for a termination signal (for example, *End Of Stream* of all dataflow) when the database operation is completed. The latter is excessive; it occupies unnecessary resources, which leads to a degradation in system throughput.

Simple operations

The EDBS execution model has been designed to support the RISC-like approach for query compilation. In this approach the basic database operations of the system are chosen to be a small set of simple operations so that high performance can be achieved by optimizations performed by the compiler. A simple operation simplifies the realization of a number of compiler optimization techniques; for example, in the area of local data access:

(1) Data operations are restricted to accessing only local data. In this situation, the operations no longer suffer from variable latencies that would have been caused by delays due to remote data access. As a result, unnecessary inter-PE synchronizations are avoided and a predictable performance characteristic is ensured for the operations.

(2) For situations where the compiler knows in advance that only local communication is necessary for a query, it can plant local transfer operations in the final execution code. This communication can be implemented as procedure calls or coroutines, thus avoiding the overheads of a general message-handling facility.

Alternative implementations

At the implementation level, the distributed store based EDBS execution model maps nicely to the distributed-memory EDS machine. Nevertheless, the EDBS execution model is purely a logical one and other alternative implementations are possible. An example of an alternative implementation is the DBS3 parallel-database system developed on a Encore MULTIMAX shared-store multiprocessor.[17]

11.4.2 Request Manager—the EDBS Query Compiler

The programming interface to EDBS is ESQL (see Section 11.5). The role of the request manager (RM) is ESQL-query compilation. Internally, in the RM an ESQL query is processed in various stages. The resulting execution program is based on an intermediate algebraic language, LERA (Language for Extended Relational Algebra).[18] The LERA program is then executed directly by the data manager (see Figure 6).

The RM follows a compilation approach with sophisticated query optimization and parallelization processes that work on a representation of the query in terms of LERA. Compared to a relational query optimizer, the EDBS optimizer is complicated by three factors.

(1) LERA has higher expressive power than relational algebra (ADT functions and predicates, nested operations, fixpoint operations).
(2) The parallel-execution system of the data manager (see Section 11.4) offers a wide range of execution strategies that are difficult to abstract.
(3) The required ability of efficiently optimizing both repetitive (OLTP) and ad hoc (decision-support) queries implies that the optimization time, and therefore the optimization algorithm, must itself be controllable.

To cope with the above difficulties, the optimization process is divided into three activities. First, the query rewriting (logical optimization) activity[19] consists of a simplification and partial ordering of LERA operations in order to make the optimization problem tractable. In particular, complex recursive queries are transformed using the Alexander method; a simpler method, based on transitive closure, is used to handle linear recursion. Second, an operation-selection activity identifies those operations in the LERA program warranting optimization. For each of them, an operation-optimization activity is triggered. The operation optimizer makes use of extended relational query-optimization techniques, such as join ordering and fixpoint optimization. Furthermore, the design of the optimizer is extensible so that new optimization algorithms and access methods can be easily accommodated. This extensible feature enables the optimizer to cater to a wide range of possible execution strategies. Finally, in order to achieve the performance objectives mentioned above, the cost function used is a combination of response time and total time, thus enabling a controllable trade-off between the transaction's response time and global throughput. Similarly, the operation-optimization algorithms are also controllable so that, when optimization time matters, a trade-off between optimization time and execution time can be achieved.

The execution semantics of an optimized LERA program is a centralized one but the program contains annotations, produced by the optimizer, about distribution decisions (indicating where the operations should be executed) and about the parallel algorithms that should be used to execute the operations. The parallelizer uses these annotations when translating the LERA program from a centralized semantics to a parallel semantics. To cope with its complexity, the parallelization process is performed in two phases.

(1) The *abstract parallelization* phase generates the programs for the global algorithms associated with the relational operations, produces the communication schemes to facilitate the required data transfer between these operations, and determines a parallel execution schedule.
(2) The *control parallelization* phase introduces the control operators[20] (that is, synchronization, termination detection, and so on) required to implement the execution schedule.

After parallelization, the LERA program undergoes a code-generation phase that produces the executable code to be run in the DM's environment, as explained in Section 11.4. It is worth mentioning that there are two code generators in the EDS database systems; one is designed for EDBS (a distributed store-based system) and the other for DBS3,[15] a shared-memory testbed of EDS. Notice that both code generators accept a common language as input, namely LERA.

11.4.3 DM—An Environment for Parallel Database Processing

The parallel programs generated by the RM are executed in the runtime environment provided by the data manager. The DM consists of four main components.

(1) *Relational Execution Model*. This component provides the basic operations of the execution model. That is, it is a runtime library consisting of the relational operations, operations supporting the ADT, objects and rules, and control operators.

(2) *Relation Access Manager*. This component provides a global abstraction of the relations in the database. It hides the distributed nature of the relations from the operations in Relational Execution Model, and also provides the mechanism for calling the appropriate access methods for the indexes associated with a relation.

(3) *A Set of Access Methods*. The access methods provide the mechanisms for accessing the tuples of a relation. There will be an access method to implement each index associated with a relation. The indexes are used to provide fast methods for accessing the tuples of a relation. The system has been designed to allow new access methods to be easily "plugged in" to the DM.

(4) *Basic Relational Execution Model*. BREM is a parallel-program environment designed to provide abstractions tailored for the efficient execution of RM programs. The abstraction provided by BREM gives the upper levels a much simpler environment to implement their parallel programs.

11.4.4 The Object Manager

The object manager provides basic object storage and manipulation facilities required for the support of EDBS. The functions provided by the object manager are storage of persistent objects, concurrency control to allow sharing of objects, logging, and recovery. The object manager is based on the Arjuna system,[21] with ideas incorporated from the Camelot project and the Choices project.

The object manager has a fairly conventional design and is effectively a set of local object managers, one per PE, which use an optimized 2-phase commit protocol to coordinate transactions. Standard 2-phase locking protocol and logging mechanisms are used for concurrency control and recovery.

The performance of the object manager has been enhanced by taking advantage of the facilities provided by EMEX and the large RAM store on each PE. In particular, the critical parts of the object manager are built with the EMEX kernel and execute in supervisor mode. This feature avoids context switching when object-manager operations, such as taking a lock, are performed. Similarly, the EMEX mapper (see Section 11.3) facilities are used in a simi-lar way as Camelot[22] to support the object manager.

11.4.5 Integrating the EDBS to the EDS Platform

The EDS hardware and operating system have not been designed in isolation, but have been influenced heavily by the requirements of the parallel-database system, while still providing general-purpose computing facilities.

The EDS machine. In addition to its parallel-processing capability the EDS machine has two main features for the support of EDBS: a high-performance message-handling system and a large local RAM store (64 Mbytes capacity extendible up to 4 Gbytes per PE). The message-handling performance is provided by the interconnection network, which gives a high bandwidth, and the SSU-NIU interworking pair (see Section 2.1), which gives a high message rate. The large local RAM store improves database performance significantly.

The EMEX kernel.   The EMEX kernel has a number of features designed to enhance the performance of EDBS.

(1) *Message-passing communication*. The EMEX communication system provides a reliable, ordered stream of data transfer between two interconnected data operators. Moreover, the asynchronous send facility enables continuous tuple processing immediately after an intermediate-result tuple is sent, making data transfer transparent to the EDBS. As a result, higher concurrency is achieved in the system, which in turn can increase the data-processing throughput, one of the major design targets of the EDS database server.

(2) *Store copying*. The EMEX communication system can also transmit data directly from the sender's buffers and deliver them directly into the receiver's buffers. This feature has several beneficial effects: it removes two data transfers, it avoids the complications of a large kernel buffer pool, and it opens the message-passing resources for different jobs, thus avoiding interference between different users' work. Furthermore, the use of the SSU-NIU interworking pair (see Section 11.2.1) for the message handling significantly reduces the number of context switches in the processing unit.

(3) *Threads*. An EMEX thread is a lightweight operating-system process and avoids the high overheads of a conventional heavyweight task or process for small units of work. This low overhead is particularly useful in EDBS for supporting the idea of simple database operations. Simple operations are the basic requirement for achieving the RISC-like approach for compilation and optimization.

(4) *Scheduling*. EMEX provides preemptive scheduling with priorities between tasks. Time slicing is used between tasks of equal priority. This type of scheduling is vital for any OLTP system that needs to run applications with different (user) priorities. Threads within a task also have priority-based preemptive scheduling, but all runnable threads are scheduled before the task suspends itself. This scheduling minimizes the number of context switches, in contrast with the scheduling systems of the Chorus system, where threads are the main unit of scheduling.

(5) *External pager technology*. EMEX provides external pager facilities similar to those of Mach[22] and Chorus.

(6) *Distributed tasks*. Although it is not necessary for the performance of the system, the distributed-task concept provided by EMEX has greatly simplified the initialization of the DM. It allows the EDBS to use a standard dynamic loader instead of developing complicated multiprocessor loaders such as those found in some other multiprocessor database systems.

(7) *Supervisor subsystems*. Like Chorus, EMEX allows a special "supervisor subsystem" to be built into the nucleus. It is used by the object manager to provide trap interface to the critical object-manager interfaces, avoiding a context switch to enter a protected environment for the object manager.

11.5 ADVANCED FUNCTIONALITY: COMPLEX QUERY HANDLING

The EDS database subsystem, EDBS, is relational in nature, with extensions to support abstract data types, objects, and deduction capabilities. It therefore implements an extension of SQL called ESQL (Extended Structured Query Language). Database queries in EDBS are specified in ESQL,[10] a query language designed for traditional data-processing applications as well as for nontraditional information-processing applications. ESQL is upward compatible with SQL. The SQL extensions are provided with minimal impact to the existing SQL standards, making ESQL simple to use by SQL users. Also, the additional language features in ESQL enable the language to be used for advanced applications such as computer-integrated manufacturing, computer-aided software engineering, and geographic information systems, as well as for complex decision-support applications.

11.5.1 Abstract Data Types and Objects

While the relational data model only supports values, ESQL supports both values and objects. A *value* is an instance of a basic type or of a user-defined ADT, while an *object* associates a unique object identifier to an ADT value (the object's *state*). An ADT is a new type, together with functions applicable to data of that type. Therefore, ESQL data are divided between objects and values, and only objects may be referentially shared using object identity.

To support complex values, ESQL generalizes the notion of domain with generic ADTs that may be combined at multiple levels. Generic ADTs are higher-order constructors that take types as arguments. The generic ADTs are *tuple, set, bag, list,* and *vector.* By combining objects and generic ADTs, arbitrarily complex objects can be supported.

In the following ESQL type declarations, *Person* corresponds to an object whose state is a tuple of values. *Actor* is a subtype of Person, thus inheriting its nature (it is an object), structure, and applicable functions. Actor is a specialization of Person both from the structural point of view (as it has an additional element in the tuple), and from the behavioral point of view (as the new function *Increase_salary* is attached to it). Unlike Person and Actor, which are objects, type *Actors* represents values whose structure is a set of Actor objects. Similarly to Person and Actor, type Actors is an ADT and therefore it is possible to attach functions, such as *Max_salary*, to it.

```
TYPE Person OBJECT TUPLE OF (name Char(30), firstname Char(20));
TYPE Actor SUBTYPE OF Person WITH (salary Numeric);
FUNCTION Increase_salary(Actor, Numeric) RETURNS Actor LANGUAGE C;
TYPE Actors SET OF Actor;
FUNCTION Max_salary(Actors) RETURNS Numeric LANGUAGE C;
```

Tables *Film* and *Actor* are defined below using these ADTs. Note in particular that attribute *actors* in table Film and attribute *actor* in table Actor are both defined on the object type Actors (given that Actors is itself a set of Actor). This definition allows Actor instances to be shared between these two tables, thus reducing data redundancy and enforcing the underlying referential integrity constraint. In EDBS, although objects can be created (within an ESQL procedure) independently from any table, they will not persist unless they are attached to (referenceed by) a table's attribute; that is, tables are the only persistency roots.

```
CREATE TABLE Film (filmnum Num, title Char(50), actors Actors,
producer Person);
CREATE TABLE Actor (actor Actor, films Films);
```

In order to query and update the corresponding database, ESQL provides facilities such as the possibility of ADT method calls in SQL statements, the manipulation of shared objects by using a functional notation, and the manipulation of nested objects through nested statements. Data manipulation in ESQL is more regular than in SQL, much in the way of SQL2. The following statement illustrates some of these features. *Extract* and *Getfield* are generic functions delivering an object's status (that is, a value) and a tuple's component, respectively. Note that the join condition is expressed using function *Contains* (another generic function) which delivers 1 as its value if the given set contains the given object.

```
SELECT Extract(actor)
FROM Film, Actor
WHERE title = "Pretty Woman"
AND Getfield(actor, salary) = Max_salary(actors)
AND Contains(actors, actor) = 1
```

11.5.2 Recursive Views and Deduction

A deductive capability enables one to abstract in a rule base the common knowledge traditionally embedded with redundancy in application programs. The rule base provides centralized control of knowledge and is primarily useful to infer new facts from the facts stored in the database. ESQL provides this deductive capability as an extension of the SQL view mechanism, including recursive views. This capability gives to ESQL the power of the DATALOG logic-based language using statements already available in SQL.

As an example, consider the definitions of table *Dominates* and of view *Better_than* in the following discussion. Table Dominates records the fact that in a given film actor1 had a more important role than actor2. The view is recursive and corresponds to a classification (partial order) among the actors. Note that it is almost standard SQL2, except that SQL2 does not allow referencing views in a view definition. The EXCEPT statement is used to eliminate cycles.

```
CREATE TABLE Dominates (filmnum Num, actor1 Actor, actor2 Actor)
VIEW Better_than (actor1, actor2) AS (
     SELECT actor1, actor2
     FROM Dominate
UNION
     SELECT B1.actor1, B2.actor2
     FROM Better_than B1, Better_than B2
     WHERE B1.actor1 = B2.actor1
EXCEPT
     SELECT B1.actor1, B2.actor2
     FROM Better_than B1, Better_than B2
     WHERE B1.actor2 = B2.actor1
     AND B1.actor1 = B2.actor2 )
```

11.6 OLTP PERFORMANCE

One of the main application areas for the EDS database server is online transaction processing (OLTP). It is targeted to provide an OLTP-transaction rate of 12,000 transaction per second at 30 percent machine utilization. This performance target assumes the TPC-B[23] operation conditions. These conditions influence the operation behavior of the EDS server and thus affect its performance. Noticeably, during the benchmarking period under TPC-B, 90 percent of the transactions are required to have a residence time of under two seconds, and 85 percent of them are required to be performed locally (that is, access to the branch, teller, account, and history relations are made on the same home PE).

To ensure that the design of the EDS server can meet the performance targets, its OLTP performance is constantly assessed throughout the development stage. This assessment is performed by using the EDS OLTP behavioral-simulation model, which is programmed in very high density language (VHDL).[1] The simulation model is based on some critical baseline performance parameters. These parameters account for the execution times of machine operations, database-processing primitives, network communications, and EMEX primitives, and are always kept up-to-date with the latest measured values. (A list of performance parameters used in the OLTP simulation can be found in the appendix of the reference above.)[1]

The simulated OLTP performance of the EDS server is illustrated in the TPS curve shown in Figure 8. The x-axis shows the system throughput of the system in 1000 x transactions per second (k-tps) and the y-axis the response times. The vertical dotted line between x = 10.0 and x = 20.0 is the 30 percent utilization marker, which is is the expected load of the system on which the 12,000 tps target performance is set. The intersection between the curve and the vertical dotted line shows the simulated performance at 30 percent load. It clearly indicates that the EDS server can meet the 12,000 tps target comfortably; in fact, the actual OLTP performance at this load is simulated to be 16,000 tps (see the x-value where the vertical dotted line crosses the x-axis). This value is higher than any OLTP performance

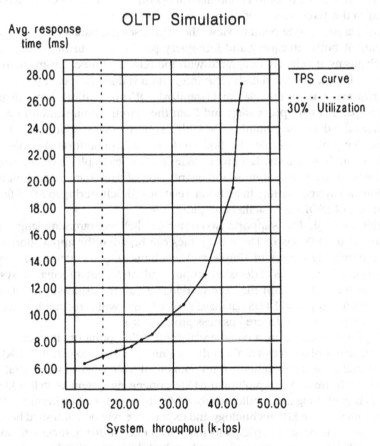

Figure 8. Simulated EDS's OLTP performance.

figures even reported (for example, nCube with 64 PEs, 1073 tps),[24] and it is far higher than the tps ratings of typical conventional database systems running on contemporary mainframes, minicomputers, and PCs; some examples are the IBM 3090 600S (256 tps), DEC VAX 6360 (66 tps), and PC 386 (10 tps).[25]

In addition to OLTP performance assessment, the EDS behavioral-simulation model has also been used to study a number of implementation techniques, for example, parallel logging.[26] Simulation is not the only means for performance evaluation of the EDS system. Direct measurements of both hardware and software components are actively underway. Unfortunately, due to commercial reasons, these measurement figures cannot be presented here.

11.7 CONCLUSION

The design of the EDS database server focused on two main aspects: high performance through different levels of parallelism, and advanced database functionalities through the ESQL query language. They have been described in the preceding sections.

Database processing in the EDS server is done with two main goals in mind: to achieve high performance in terms of both global throughput and execution time, and to be able to tune the system to provide this high performance in OLTP environments, in information-management environments, or in a combination of both. The features of the server that contribute most to the achievement of these goals are as follows.

From the data-processing point of view, the EDBS uses the parallel facilities provided by EMEX to exploit both interquery and intraquery parallelism. Furthermore, the ADT and object mechanisms are closely integrated with the relational mechanisms to avoid system oversizing and interaction overheads. This integration is done in such a way that query-execution performance in purely relational (standard SQL) applications is not degraded.

Related to parallel data processing and from the system administration point of view, ESQL provides the database administrator with a facility to cluster or decluster (partition) relations explicitly over multiple PEs. Both uniform and nonuniform data distribution are supported. A number of data-placement strategies (for example, hashed, range, and so forth) can be used to achieve nonuniform distribution of data. Data placement is an important technique for system tuning. In addition, relations (de)clustering in EDBS facilitates the implementation of ESQL on a parallel computer.

In addition to ESQL, EDS supports two other parallel programming language systems, namely ElipSys[4] and EDS Lisp.[5] These languages can broaden the application spectrum of EDS from the existing targets of simple and medium-complex queries to very complex queries, especially in the areas of decision support and intelligent information systems. Such systems are envisaged to occupy the main workload in future business applications. For this reason, the advanced parallel EDS database server is and will remain a leading-edge technology for both present and future business professionals.

Regarding future work, from a commercial exploitation point of view, EDS is on course to achieve the major objectives set out at the beginning of the project. ICL (UK) is now engaged in the full-scale development of a commercial-scale open-system parallel-database server. Siemens (Germany) is exploiting the EMEX operating system as well as EDS Lisp, and Bull (France) is exploiting the parallel advanced-database system. Furthermore, from the research point of view, the EDS technology and experience will be continued beyond the ESPRIT-II initiative. The project participants have been exceptionally successful in winning a number of ESPRIT-III research projects based on the EDS results. EDS2 is evaluating the EDS system with commercial-scale applications. Intelligent Database Environment for Advanced Applications (IDEA) is continuing the development of the advanced EDS database system. European Parallel Operating System based on Chorus (EPOCH) is extending the work on EMEX to develop an operating system for high parallel performance, system management, and integrity. Application and Assessment of Parallel Programming using Logic (APPLAUSE) is developing large-scale applications using ElipSys to provide a commercial evaluation of the technology. Pythagoras is a followup project based on the EDS performance evaluation activities, and is aimed to produce a performance-evaluation toolkit for advanced information systems.[27]

ACKNOWLEDGMENTS

Thanks are due to the Commission of the European Communities for partially funding the EDS project (ESPRIT-II project number EP2025), and to all the researchers and engineers who have contributed to the project.

REFERENCES

1. K.F. Wong, et al., "Performance Evaluation of an OLTP Application on the EDS Database Server Using a Behavioural Simulation Model," in *Data Management and Parallel Processing*, P. Valduriez, ed., Chapman and Hall, London, England, 1992, pp. 317-350.

2. M.Ward, et al., "EDS Hardware Architecture," *Proc. Joint Conf. Vector and Parallel Processing*, Lecture Notes in Computer Science, LNCS 457, H. Burkhard, ed., Springer-Verlag, Berlin, Germany, 1990, pp. 816-827.

3. R. Holzner, et al., "Design and Simulation of a Multistage Interconnection Network," *Proc. Joint Conf. Vector and Parallel Processing*, Lecture Notes in Computer Science, LNCS 457, H. Burkhard, ed., Springer-Verlag, Berlin, Germany, 1990, pp. 385-396.

4. S.A. Delgado-Rannauro, et al., "A Shared Environment Parallel Logic Programming System on Distributed Memory Architectures," *Proc. 2nd European Conf. Distributed Memory Computing*, Lecture Notes in Computer Science, LNCS 487, A. Bode, ed., Springer-Verlag, Heidelberg, Germany, 1991, pp. 371-380.

5. C. Hammer, et al., "Using a Weak Coherency Model for a Parallel Lisp," *Proc. 2nd European Conference on Distributed Memory Computing*, Lecture Notes in Computer Science, LNCS 487, A. Bode, ed., Springer-Verlag, Heidelberg, Germany, 1991, pp. 42-51.

6. Chorus Systemes, *CHORUS Kernel v3r4.0, Implementation Guide*, CS/TR-91-68, Chorus Systems, France, 1991.

7. P. Istavrinos, et al., "A Process and Memory Model for a Parallel Distributed Memory Machines," *Proc. Joint Conf. Vector and Parallel Processing*, Lecture Notes in Computer Science, LNCS 457, H. Burkhard, ed., Springer-Verlag, Berlin, Germany, 1990, pp. 479-488.

8. K. Li, et al., "Memory Coherence in Shared Virtual Memory Systems," *Proc. 5th ACM Symp. Principles of Distributed Computing*, ACM Press, New York, N.Y., 1986, pp. 229-239.

9. L. Borrmann, et al., "Store Coherency in a Parallel Distributed-Memory Machine," *Proc. Distributed Memory Computing*, Springer-Verlag Lecture Notes in Computer Science, LNCS 487, A. Bode, ed., Springer-Verlag, Berlin, Germany 1991, pp. 32-41.

10. G. Gardarin, et al., "ESQL: An Extended SQL with Object and Deductive Capabilities," *Proc. Int'l Conf. Database and Expert System Applications*, Springer-Verlag, Berlin, 1990, pp. 299-307.

11. G. Copeland, et al., "Data Placement in Bubba," *Proc. ACM SIGMOD Conf.*, ACM Press, New York, N.Y., 1988, pp. 99-108.

12. H. Boral, et al., "Prototyping Bubba, A Highly Parallel Database System," *IEEE Trans. Data and Knowledge Eng.*, Vol. 2, No. 1, Mar. 1990, pp. 4-24.

13. D.J. DeWitt, et al., "The Gamma Database Machine Project," *IEEE Trans. Data and Knowledge Eng.*, Vol. 2, No. 1, Mar. 1990, pp. 4-24.

14. K.F. Wong, "Architectures of Database Machines," *ICL Tech. J.*, Vol. 7, No. 3, May 1991, pp. 584-613.

15. P. Valduriez, et al., "ImplementationTechniques of Complex Objects," *Proc. Int'l Conf. Very Large Databases*, Morgan Kaufmann Pub., Los Altos, Calif., 1986, pp. 101-110.

16. F. Andres, et al., "A Multi-Environment Cost Evaluator for Parallel Database Systems," *Proc. 2nd Conf. Database Systems for Advanced Applications*, 1991.

17. B. Bergsten, M. Couprie, and P. Valduriez, "Prototyping DBS3, a Shared-Memory Parallel Database System," *Proc. 1st Int'l Conf. Parallel and Distributed Information Systems*, IEEE CS Press, Los Alamitos, Calif., 1991, pp. 226-234.

18. C. Chachaty, et al., "A Compositional Approach for the Design of a Parallel Query Processing Language," *Proc. Conf. Parallel Architectures and Languages Europe*, Lecture Notes in Computer Science, LNCS 605, D. Etiemble and J.-C. Syre, eds., Springer-Verlag, Berlin, Germany, 1992, pp. 825-840.

19. B. Finance, and G. Gardarin, "A Rule-Based Query Rewriter in an Extensible DBMS," *Proc. IEEE Data Eng. Conf.*, IEEE CS Press, Los Alamitos, Calif., 1991, pp. 248-256.

20. P. Borla-Salamet, C. Chachaty, and B. Dageville, "Compiling Control into Queries for Parallel Execution Management," *Proc. 1st Int'l Conf. Parallel and Distributed Information Systems*, IEEE CS Press, Los Alamitos, Calif., 1991, pp. 271-279.

21. G.N. Dixon, and S.K. Shrivastava, "Exploiting Type-Inheritance Facilities to Implement Recoverability in Object-Based Systems," *Proc. 6th Symp. Reliability in Distributed Software and Database Systems*, IEEE CS Press, Los Alamitos, Calif., 1987, pp. 107-114.

22. S.Z. Spector, et al., "The Camelot Project," *Database Eng.*, Vol. 9, No. 4, Dec. 1986.

23. Transaction Processing Performance Council (TPC), "TPC Benchmark B," *The Benchmark Handbook*, J. Gray, ed., Morgan Kaufmann Pub., San Mateo, Calif., 1991, pp. 79-117.

24. nCUBE, "nCUBE 2 Supercomputer Running Oracle Parallel Server DBMS Exceeds 1000 Transactions Per Second," news release, July 22, 1991.

25. J. Spiers, "Mapping a 4th-Generation DBMS to a Range of Parallel Machines," in *Parallel Processing and Data Management*, P. Valduriez, ed., Chapman and Hall, London, England, 1992, pp. 53-67.

26. K.F. Wong, "Performance Evaluation of Three Logging Schemes for a Shared-Nothing Database Server," ECRC Internal Report dps/WP/92/001.

27. K.F. Wong, et al., "Pythagoras: Performance Quality Assessment of Advanced Database Systems," *Proc. 6th Int'l Conf. Modeling Techniques and Tools for Computer Performance Evaluation*, Edinburgh Univ. Press, Edinburgh, Scotland, 1992.

12

A Parallel and Distributed Environment for Database Rule Processing: Open Problems and Future Directions

**Salvatore J. Stolfo, Hasanat M. Dewan,
David Ohsie, and Mauricio Hernandez**

Department of Computer Science
Columbia University
New York, New York

ABSTRACT

Rule-based systems have been used extensively by the AI community in implementing knowledge-base expert systems. A current trend in the database community is to use rules for the purpose of providing inferential capabilities for large database applications. However, in the database context, the performance of rule-program processing has proved to be a major stumbling block, particularly in data-intensive and real-time applications. Similar work in the AI community has demonstrated the same problems, mainly due to the predominantly sequential semantics of the underlying rule languages and the lack of facilities to optimize runtime execution performance.

In this paper, we detail the Parulel rule language and its meta-rule formalism for declaratively specifying control of rule execution. We argue that the meta-rule facility provides a means for programmable operational semantics separating control from the base logic of a rule program. This separation allows the potential realization of a wide range of operational semantics, including those of Datalog and OPS5. In previous work, we presented an incremental update algorithm for Datalog and extended it for Parulel. Runtime performance optimization is also studied by way of the technique of copy-and-constrain. We briefly describe extensions of this work to include runtime reorganization as a principle to enhance execution performance after an initial compile-time analysis. These features (incremental update, copy-and-constrain, and runtime reorganization) are being developed within a parallel and distributed environment for execution of Parulel programs targeted to commercial multiprocessors.

12.1 INTRODUCTION

Speeding up rule-based systems has been an active area of research in recent years, with many different approaches being investigated by various researchers[1,2] These approaches include faster match algorithms,[3,4] compilation of rules to imperative form,[5] partitioning schemes to reduce the combinatorics of rule matching, and parallel processing, to name a few. Of these, speeding up rule-based systems through parallel processing is of particular interest as parallel and distributed computing environments have become more common.

Indeed, a number of proposed parallel machine architectures have been designed and developed over the last decade to accelerate knowledge-base systems. A wide variety of such systems can be found in the literature, and some of the latest systems are described in this volume. The reason for this wide variety of proposed machines is simply that no single standard "abstract knowledge-base machine model" exists that covers the widest spectrum of knowledge-base applications. Knowledge-base systems are usually written in high-level "declarative" languages, that is, in a high-level abstract machine formalism. However, there is no one widely acceptable "KBS abstract machine." Typically, the semantics of such machines varies from language and system to language and system. Consider OPS5, Prolog and Datalog.[6,7,8] Each has its alternative semantics, and thus alternative system primitives. (Indeed, each has its rather sizable collection of variants.) Thus, one can find a sizable range of different architectures that are targeted to accelerate the more important primitive operations in each of these formalisms.

In this paper, we shall not propose or describe another new machine architecture, but rather we shall focus on system architecture issues, including language semantics and several desirable environmental subsystems to allow the extraction and implementation of parallelism from a high-level declarative rule formalism. The system we seek to design is intended to be "architecture-independent." This means that the same rule program should be portable from any parallel machine to any other with the aid of analysis and mapping subsystems that require a model of the targeted machine. In time, with experience and performance measurement, design characteristics may be uncovered to allow a single machine architecture to be designed to accelerate the most important elements of the system architecture. The key to success is first to extract the maximum amount of parallelism discernible from the program. This is not an easy task.

To maximally exploit parallelism for the purpose of speeding up rule processing, there are many principal issues that need to be addressed:

(1) A new generation of rule languages with inherently parallel execution semantics needs to be defined. The proposed Parulel rule language, described below, is intended to ameliorate the negative effects on parallel performance of inherently sequential rule languages, such as OPS5.

(2) Rule languages must feature language constructs to easily specify control of rule execution in a parallel environment. A purely declarative specification in rule form of an inference process in many applications must necessarily be controlled, especially in the case of non-monotonic reasoning.

(3) An incremental update algorithm that allows updates to the initial set of facts to be incorporated in an efficient manner is needed. We seek to repair faulty prior inferences as efficiently as possible, rather than discarding prior work entirely and starting over from scratch each time newly arriving information refutes prior assumptions.

(4) An algorithm is required that produces a parallel-processing strategy for a given rule-program and system architecture. An initial distribution, or partitioning, of data and rules among parallel-processing sites must account for system features that vary from machine to machine.

(5) A low-cost runtime facility to reorganize the parallel computation is desired to ameliorate the effects of performance bottlenecks not predictable at compile time.

(6) Rule languages must embed in host parallel and distributed computing environments to coexist with "ordinary" applications and to use native data types. The matching of terms in the antecedent of rules should be generalized to operate over a range of data types, and alternative definitions of *term equality*.

(7) Demonstrations of solutions to these various problems need to be performed on realistic applications (rather than prototypical toy problems embodied by a very few rules) that exhibit realistic behavior of the application environment.

Although this is a rather broad range of issues and concerns, we and many other researchers have made substantial progress in studying them. We seek to extend these solutions, and study other solutions in a fully integrated rule-processing environment implemented within a commercial database-management system. The rule-processing environment under development has come to be called Paradiser (PARallel And DIStributed Environment for Rules). Much of our prior work has been application-driven. We continue this approach by applying our techniques and implemented systems to real-world problems supplied by industrial sponsors. Two such applications are described briefly below. One of these applications has been implemented in OPS5, and in Parulel, the kernel language of the Paradiser environment. The other application demonstrates yet another desideratum for rule languages applied to databases, the generalization of term matching to include the specification of equational theories. This latter issue, although not specific to parallelism, is important and described in the section treating the second application.

A full treatment of each of these issues are well beyond the scope and size limitations of this chapter. Instead, we discuss the incremental update of Parulel programs, and propose new work in the area of optimization with respect to the *copy-and-constrain* technique. Where appropriate we describe the status of our work to give the reader a sense of what has been accomplished in all areas detailed above and what remains to be done.

In short, we seek to develop a complete database rule-processing environment targeted to a variety of commercial parallel and distributed systems. Paradiser will allow the specification of inferential tasks in a high-level rule language, to be applied to large amounts of data primarily stored on disk. Much work in rule processing in the AI community has considered main-memory-based systems exclusively. Next-generation rule systems must necessarily operate over data sets that are much larger than primary store; that is, most of the data is stored externally.

Included in the Paradiser environment are subsystems that:

- compile a rule program into primitive database operations,
- optimize the rule program by way of several techniques to elicit parallelism and distribute the work load of processing the rule program among a number of processing sites,
- map this compiled program onto distributed or parallel hardware,
- reorganize the runtime computation to ameliorate the negative effects of bottlenecks not predicted at compile time.

The proposed system architecture is being developed within a commercial database environment. This design decision is not arbitrary, but based upon reasoned prediction. In our earlier work, we designed and developed a specialized machine architecture to accelerate rule-based systems by way of parallel processing (see the various articles on the DADO machine).[9-14] Since that time a number of commercial multiprocessor systems have become available that appear to provide the necessary hardware and systems software support to run knowledge-base systems effectively. It stands to reason that most if not all of the commerical database-management systems will eventually be fully ported to these multiprocessors.

Thus, in the current state of technology and the commercial marketplace, the implementation of knowledge-base systems should be conducted on generally available multipurpose devices, rather than more specialized hardware designed for the acceleration of a particular class of problems. Realistic experience on such machines will provide invaluable guidance for next-generation specialized devices. In the meantime, current efforts to design such systems provide the opportunity to augment the knowledge we glean from this general experience by identifying useful design concepts and possibly blind alleys to avoid in next-generation systems.

The remainder of this paper is organized as follows. In Section 2, we provide a brief description of our prior work on the DADO multiprocessor, to set the stage for our subsequent discussion. In Section 3, we detail the Parulel rule language and its operational semantics, and the current status of our implementation. Although some in the database community may dismiss a rule language that lacks a semantics based upon formal logic, our view is that Parulel is based upon a formal semantics that is appropriate for real-world applications.

Parulel may be viewed as a generalization of OPS5, a widely used language that has been effective at solving a large number of disparate applications (estimated to be in the thousands). The semantics we define for Parulel are sufficient to formalize criteria to prove the correctness of our incremental update algorithm. In Section 4, we discuss the general problem of incremental update of rule programs and outline our proposed solution detailed elsewhere. The operational semantics of Parulel provides the means of analyzing programs to optimize performance by way of the copy-and-constrain paradigm. Section 5 details the copy-and-constrain technique and proposes a means of automatically optimizing rule programs by way of statistical information gathered by a database-management system. Following in Section 6 we discuss the topic of reorganizing a distributed rule evaluation at runtime by low-cost means. In Section 7, we mention applications to test and demonstrate the language efficacy and the utility of its environment, as well as its runtime performance. Within the context of one of these problems, we discuss another desirable feature, embedding equational theories within the term matching of a rule language. Finally, Section 8 discusses the question of whether or not specialized hardware for knowledge-base systems is a reasonable technological pursuit.

12.2 THE DADO MULTIPROCESSOR

On December 5, 1985 a 1023-processor parallel machine named DADO2 was successfully demonstrated at Columbia University. DADO2 is the first large-scale prototype of a class of machines called DADO, and the fourth of a succession of smaller experimental prototypes. DADO was first proposed in 1980 as a special-purpose parallel computer, attached to a conventional host processor, designed to accelerate a particular class of AI rule-based programming paradigms called *production systems*. PSs have been widely used for the implementation of knowledge-base expert systems. Since that time, we have learned that DADO is suited to the high-speed execution of a large class of problems that we call *almost decomposable searching problems,* of which PSs are but one example. Several specific examples of this class of problems are presently running on DADO2.

DADO is a medium-grain parallel machine in which memory and processing are extensively intermingled. A full-scale version would comprise a large number of processing elements, each containing its own processor, a substantial amount of local memory, and a specialized I/O circuit for high-speed communication. The PEs are interconnected in a complete binary tree. Within the DADO machine, each PE is capable of executing in either of two modes under the control of runtime software. In the first, which is called SIMD (for single-instruction stream, multiple-data stream), the PE executes instructions broadcast by some ancestor PE within the tree. In the second, which is referred to as MIMD mode (for multiple-instruction stream, multiple-data stream), each PE executes instructions stored in its own local RAM, independently of the other PEs. A single conventional host processor, adjacent to the root of the DADO tree, controls the operation of the entire ensemble of PEs. Indeed, DADO is viewed as a hardware accelerator of the host running knowledge-base systems at high speed. When a DADO PE enters MIMD mode, its logical state is changed in such a way as to effectively "disconnect" it and its descendants from all higher-level PEs in the tree. In particular, a PE in MIMD mode does not receive any instructions that might be placed on the tree-structured communication bus by one of its ancestors. Such a PE may, however, broadcast instructions to be executed by its own descendants, provided all of these descendants are in SIMD mode. The DADO machine can thus be configured such that an arbitrary internal node in the tree acts as the root of a tree-structured SIMD device in which all PEs execute a single instruction (on different data) at a given point in time. (This is an oversimplification of DADO2's true operation. DADO2 provides parallel remote-procedure invocation in the style of SIMD processing. The procedures, stored locally within the PEs, operate autonomously and, therefore, may take different amounts of time to complete. Machine-level instructions are not broadcast and executed in lockstep. Rather, addresses of prestored code are broadcast to PEs for local execution. This mode of operation may be regarded as single-program, multiple-data stream execution. This flexible architectural design supports multiple-SIMD execution (MSIMD), whereby the machine may be divided logically into distinct partitions, each executing a distinct task.

The DADO2 I/O switch, which is implemented in semi-custom gate-array technology, has been designed to support rapid global communication. In addition, a specialized combinational circuit incorporated within the I/O switch allows for the very rapid selection of a single distinguished PE from a set of candidate PEs in the tree, a process we call min-resolving. The importance and utility of these operations will be detailed later.

The reader is cautioned not to confuse DADO with DADO2. DADO refers to a class of machines sharing certain architectural principles: tree-structured topology for fast broadcast of data, fast resolution, and a software architecture providing SIMD, MIMD, and MSIMD (or SPMD) modes of operation. The distinctions among members of this family are granularity, storage capacity, and processor functionality at an individual PE. DADO2, succeeding the 15-processor DADO1, refers to a single (expedient) hardware realization of the architecture designed to experiment with parallel execution of AI PS programs. (It should be noted that the suffix "2" refers not to the second invented architecture, but the second hardware realization, or PE design.) Two 3-PE machines, named DADO1$\frac{3}{4}$ and DADO1$\frac{7}{8}$, were constructed to test various nuances of the PE circuit and were used to finalize DADO2's PE design. The DADO4 machine has granularity matched to signal-interpretation tasks, including speech processing. Figure 1 depicts a simplified block diagram of the DADO4 processing element.

DADO2 has demonstrated two very important principles to date: a 1023-processor machine is relatively inexpensive and easy to build, and it works. Indeed, DADO2 was constructed within a university laboratory environment with relatively modest support. What DADO2 also teaches is that knowledge-base software is harder to parallelize than previously suspected. In operation, a rule-based program repeatedly executes the following cycle of operations:

- *Match*: For each rule, determine whether the left hand side (LHS) matches the current database of facts. All matching instances of the rules are collected in the *conflict set* of rules.

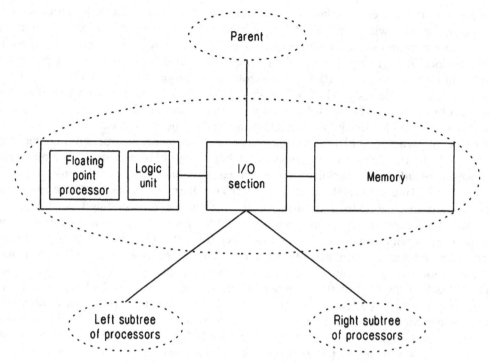

Figure 1.   Simplified block diagram of the DADO4.

- *Select*: Choose exactly one of the matching rules according to some predefined criterion.
- *Act*: Add to or delete from the database all assertions specified in the right hand side (RHS) of the selected rule.

One of the simplest reported algorithms (named the *full-distribution algorithm*) for PS execution on DADO works by distributing a single rule to each of the available PEs. Data are broadcast in turn to all PEs, which match them against the stored rule, saving those that match some condition element of the LHS of their rule. Rules whose LHSs are thus fully matched are then "resolved" to determine the single-rule instance to execute. The RHS actions of the selected rule are then broadcast to all other PEs, initiating another match cycle. In effect, the entire rule base is fully distributed into a collection of one-rule rule programs processed in parallel. The question to ask at this point is, precisely what speedup can be achieved for such programs? Much has been written and debated about this very point. The issue centers upon two key observations.

First, the match function itself is executed in parallel by a large number of PEs. In certain measured OPS5 programs, it has been reported that on each cycle a relatively small and stable number of rules must be matched on each cycle of execution. That is, on average, each rule-firing in OPS5 produces new data elements that affect (or are relevant to) the LHS of a small number of rules. This small *affect set*, as it has been called, thus indicates that the number of individual match operations executing in parallel that compute "useful" new matching-rule instances is small. Hence, a large number of invoked parallel procedures compute nothing at all and the utilization of the parallel resources is poor.

The second observation to note is that the variance in processing times for the concurrent match operations can be quite large. That is, the total running time is proportional to the slowest match operation, indicating that utilization of the parallel resources may decrease even further while possibly many PEs wait for the slower PEs to catch up and synchronize for the resolve operation.

We tested a number of OPS5 programs on DADO2 to verify these claims. The programs executed consisted of from 13 to 884 OPS5 rules and from 12 to 528 database facts. Measurements were made of the total time to execute the rule system over a large number of rule-execution cycles. Performance measurements indicated that at best we sped up programs by a factor of 31, and at worst by only a factor of 2. Of particular interest is the performance of the programs that were dominated by data, rather than rules. That is, we measured better speedup for programs that have proportionately more data elements than rules. Realizing only a factor of 31 with 1,023 available processors indicates strongly that much more work is needed than first suspected.

The two observations noted (small affect-set and large variance in processing time between rules) may lead one to the pessimistic view that rule programs, in particular OPS5, can best be accelerated by a small number of parallel processors rather than the large-scale approach taken in the DADO machine. We believe this very point requires further investigation, not from the architectural perspectives, but rather from the perspective of language semantics and parallelization analysis. The Parulel rule language, described next, is an attempt to ameliorate the more inhibiting features of OPS5.

12.3 THE PARULEL LANGUAGE AND META-RULES

Considerable work has already been done in an effort to determine the available parallelism in rule-based programs, and of the speedup to be expected from their execution on parallel machines. Studies of existing OPS5 production-system programs have yielded results indicating that, in fact, a modest amount of parallelism is available in the current generation of "sequential" rule-based languages.

There are a number of reasons why rule-based expert systems are slow performers. Often, rule languages are so high-level that all data-structure manipulation is the sole responsibility of the rule interpreter and is inaccessible to the application programmer. Thus, rule interpreters would, in general, efficiently implement the best data structures for the task only by chance.

To make matters worse, the execution semantics of the rule interpreter may not be precisely what is needed by the application. Matching of all rules against the entire set of data on every cycle, for example, may not be the best strategy. Thus, the rule interpreter may execute a number of operations that turn out to be superfluous, whereas an imperative language implementation might bypass these operations entirely.[15] Therefore, running such systems in parallel may execute these superfluous instructions more quickly, but ultimately it buys nothing.

Furthermore, many of the studied AI rule-based systems typically involve rule sets operating upon small amounts of data. The Rete[3] match algorithm was invented with this in mind. Executing rule-based systems with massive databases has not been a topic of wide study in the AI community, but is, of course, of central importance in the database community. Much has been learned from work in large knowledge-base systems research, yet little has been done regarding parallelization of these systems.

Lastly, although rule-based formalisms appear at first glance to be highly parallel by virtue of their declarative expression, closer inspection reveals that too often sequentialities are programmed into the rule base to force desirable sequences of rule-firings. These sequentialities are represented by *control elements* that serve to activate or deactivate rules as these elements are added to or deleted from the working memory. What is lacking is a means to express parallel operations within a rule set effectively, rather than the present state of affairs that seems to encourage purely sequential thinking.

By way of summary, AI rule languages such as OPS5 are tuple-oriented; an instance of a rule matches a small number of individual data items, rather than, say, a set-oriented rule language that may match a large set of data items. Since the act of firing an OPS5 rule produces a small number of changes to the working memory, the number of subsequently affected rules is also small, thus limiting the amount of work to be performed in the parallel match. Without a large amount of possibly concurrent work to perform, speedups under parallel execution are thus not realizable.

Since we believe that parallelizing a sequential formalism has been only moderately successful, we posit that the approach of defining an inherently parallel rule language may well produce better results in the long term for many applications. Parulel is based on this idea. We do not attempt to maintain the semantics of OPS5's conflict-resolution scheme based on *recency*, where prior work on instance-level parallelism and concurrency control seems to focus. Instead, we provide a means of expressing preferences within a set-oriented semantics. The earliest work in this direction was reported over a decade ago in the form of controlled rule languages[16,17] and meta-control by way of meta-rule formalisms.[18] These two early techniques are related in that they provide a means to express the control of execution of an underlying "nondeterministic" formalism. Although parallelism and non-determinism are distinct concepts, they share some intellectual kinship. Hence, the approach of explicitly controlling nondeterminism, we believe, can be extended to form the basis of controlling parallelism.

Another synergistic path is parallelizing the rule base to gain efficient parallel performance by removing unnecessary sequentialities. One example of this is the *copy-and-constrain* technique (a data-reduction technique) that has been demonstrated to elicit much more parallelism from a rule set than was previously believed possible.[19,20]

We suspect that several well-known reported studies[21] produced disappointing results in parallelizing rule sets solely because of unnecessary sequentialities encoded in those rule sets. These studies have unfortunately concentrated on just a few sample OPS5 programs executed under the RETE match algorithm. We believe it is unfortunate that these few programs have gained notoriety, and are regarded as representative of most AI rule-based programs. It is unknown whether all of the tasks the reported OPS5 programs solve can be better solved with alternative implementations that admit more parallelism than the few programs have exhibited. However, we were able to acquire some of these programs and have demonstrated that indeed significant performance improvements are possible by using a different match algorithm (Miranker's TREAT,[4] for example) and modifying the programs to remove sequentialities.[20]

In fact, what our studies indicate is the success of language designers in removing the parallelism from the problem in order to allow the efficient execution of the resulting encoding on a sequential machine. The main question to be answered by our work is, can a language designer have equal success in preserving the parallelism of the problem in its encoding? If so, can the parallelism so maintained be exploited in the efficient execution of the problem on a parallel machine? Initial results we have obtained indicate not only that this can in fact be done, but that the effect can be dramatic both in the amount of parallelism in the encoding and in the expressiveness of the language and hence its ease of use.

There are two main places that the parallel language designer may look to exploit parallelism in the encoding of a problem. The first is what is typically called *data para-*

llelism, which can be defined as the parallelism available when a large number of the same or similar objects have a common operation performed on them. An example would be a database query operation, where the large number of similar objects would be the records of the database and the operation might be some update or selection operation. One initial experiment we conducted proved very encouraging. By adding a simple data-parallel operation to a rule language, we have seen an order of magnitude increase in the potential parallelism of one small expert system with 13 rules and 64 working memory elements.[22]

The other potential source of parallelism is that of *control parallelism*, which can be defined as being a branch in the flow of control at which a number of alternate paths may be taken, each of which moves the current state of the computation closer to a solution. The classic examples of control parallelism are those of multiple rule-firing in production systems and *and* and *or* parallelism that arise frequently in such applications as logic programming and other goal-directed reasoning.

It is well known, however, that if the problem being solved admits little or no parallelism in any solution, then no amount of parallel processing in any language on any parallel machine will produce fast parallel solutions. However, if the problem does admit parallelism, it is foolish that it not be exploited.

Our current research involves discovering a set of constructs that increase the expressiveness of rule-based languages as well as the choice of execution semantics, while at the same time increasing the available parallelism. The expressiveness of a language is one of those qualities of a good programming language for which, unfortunately, no generally agreed-upon formal metric exists. The available parallelism, on the other hand, is something that we can measure quantitatively. Therefore we will use it as the measure of the usefulness of the constructs we might choose to add to a rule language and the appropriateness of the parallelization strategies employed.

Here we briefly describe the execution semantics and structure of Parulel.[23] The syntax of Parulel is derived from OPS5, but its operational semantics is closer to Datalog in several respects. Specifically, in Parulel, all instantiated rules that have been processed by a programmable *conflict resolution* phase are fired in parallel. If the actions of rules specify database updates, that is, additions or deletions, numerous tuples can be added or deleted in one cycle as in set-oriented processing. In contrast, OPS5's semantics essentially enforces a *tuple-at-a-time* behavior. The programmable conflict-resolution strategy in Parulel is realized via meta-level rules. After filtering the conflict set of instantiations with the meta-level rules, the remaining rule instances can be fired in parallel, realizing set-oriented database updates.

The discussion of Parulel is developed in the context of AI research on rule languages. In AI parlance, Parulel consists of the usual *production memory* of rules and a database of facts called *working memory*. Each rule is a named object consisting of a *left-hand side* of conditions to be tested against the working memory, and a *right-hand side* of actions (deletions or insertions of facts) performed on the working memory. More specifically, the LHS of a Parulel rule consists of a conjunction of positive or negative condition elements in the OPS5 style, which are matched against the WM elements. If there is a match, the pattern variables are consistently bound in the positive condition elements. If the LHS is satisfied, the actions specified on the RHS are executed. These actions consist of deletions, insertions, or modifications of WM elements.

As mentioned earlier, Parulel is not based upon a formal logic-based semantics. The generalized operational semantics of Parulel is captured in the following iterative procedure.

procedure PARULEL_SEMANTICS

(1) Start with the database consisting of the input D. Initialize the evaluation iteration count $IC = 0$.
(2) (Match) Determine S, the set of rule instances with respect to the current database. If this set is empty, stop.
(3) (Redact) Let S' be the subset of S consisting of all the instances which survive the application of redaction meta-rules.
(4) (Act) Execute the RHS operations of the set of instances in S', in parallel. Increment IC by 1. Go to 2.

end {procedure Parulel_SEMANTICS }

To complete the definition of the operational semantics, we must define what happens in the case where a fact in S' is both added and deleted. If the redact phase fails to specify what to do in the event of multiple actions on the same tuple, then the action performed is chosen non-deterministically.

In Parulel, checking and eliminating conflicts among rule instances is expressed through redaction meta-rules. The redaction meta-rules, formulated by the programmer, specify which instantiations of rules should be removed from the conflict set. Thus, the meta-rules act as an instrument for resolving inconsistencies implicit in the original rule set as execution progresses. There are a number of advantages to using meta-rules. First, we need no added runtime synchronization or concurrency control, eliminating the associated overhead, but rather the same mechanism used for rule evaluation is applied to the redaction meta-rules. Second, the declarative specification of conflict resolution in meta-rule form provides a means of efficiently determining appropriate actions to be performed during incremental update. Finally, Parulel's meta-rules attempt to push the primary desiderata of rule programming, that is, declarative specification, into the realm of "control." Thus the operational semantics, or conflict-resolution strategies, can themselves be declaratively specified. (A specific example of this feature is provided in the context of the ALEXSYS program described in the section on applications.)

Thus, one of our goals for Parulel is to define a base rule-language architecture that can be programmed declaratively to exhibit the declarative and operational semantics of any rule language desired, including Datalog and OPS5.

For concreteness, we provide the following example stylized rule set written in the OPS5 notation of LHS → RHS.

P_1: $A(x_1, y_1), A(x_2, y_2),$
$\quad x_1 \neq x_2, y_1 + y_2 < c$
$\quad \rightarrow$
$\quad -A(x_1, y_1), -A(x_2, y_2), B(x_1, x_2).$

P_2: $A(x_1, y_1), A(x_2, y_2), A(x_3, y_3),$
$\quad x_1 \neq x_2 \neq x_3, y_1 + y_2 + y_3 < c$
$\quad \rightarrow$
$\quad -A(x_1, y_1), -A(x_2, y_2), -A(x_3, y_3), C(x_1, x_2\, x_3).$

In the first rule, P_1, we wish to find the set of pairs of distinct tuples from the A relation (in OPS5 terminology, we seek pairs of working-memory elements of the class A) satisfying the requirement that the sum of their second attributes is bounded by a constant, c. In the second rule, P_2, we likewise find triples of tuples satisfying the same condition on their second attributes. Executing the rule instances forms new relations, B or C, composed of the first attributes of the tuples matching one of the rules. However, notice that some individual tuple from the A relation may appear in multiple instances of either rule, or both.

Suppose that in our stylized application, we have two requirements that must be met. Namely, an individual tuple from the A relation cannot be used more than once (and hence we need to remove all instances in which it appears except for one) and that the particular instance in which it is used is a *preferred* instance by some arbitrary criterion. Here, for pedagogical reasons, let us assume that instances of P_2 that match a tuple dominate those instances of P_1 in which it also appears; that is, when we may fire either P_1 or P_2 matching overlapping data, we prefer to fire P_2. We can capture this preference by the redaction meta-rule M_1 shown below. Notice that the names of the rules, P_1 and P_2, are written as predicate symbols and that the predicate symbol, A, is written as a term. The redaction meta-rule M_2, also shown below, handles the case of redacting instances of the same rule in which a tuple is used multiple times. Further, notice that we retain the instance that matches the pair of tuples which has the *maximum sum over all pairs*. The other instances are redacted from the conflict set. Thus, we may specify control by meta-rules not solely on the basis of rule names or a shared datum between rules, but also by *preferences* of matched data.

M_1: $P_1(A(z_1, w_1), A(z_2, w_2)),$
          $P_2(A(z_3, w_3), A(z_4, w_4), A(z_5, w_5)),$
          $z_1 \in \{z_3, z_4, z_5\} \vee z_2 \in \{z_3, z_4, z_5\}$
          $\rightarrow$
          $-P_1(A(z_1, w_1), A(z_2, w_2)).$

M_2: $P_1(A(z_1, w_1), A(z_2, w_2)),$
          $P_1(A(z_1, w_1), A(z_3, w_3)),$
          $z_3 \neq z_2, w_1 + w_3 > w_1 + w_2$
          $\rightarrow$
          $-P_1(A(z_1, w_1), A(z_2, w_2)).$

Although it seems at first glance that much more programmer responsibility has been levied (particularly if we extend this scheme to the meta-meta level to redact possibly conflicting meta-rules), it is our belief that under parallel-execution semantics, and providing conflict resolution meta-rules, the programmer can be expected to not only think of parallel solutions to problems, but also enjoy actual efficient, parallel execution of the resultant code. In addition, a programmer can modify the execution behavior, that is, the operational semantics, of a rule program without modifying the base logic of the application. This approach provides a uniform language, consisting of rules and meta-rules, to express logic, control, and parallelism.

The reader may object to the introduction of meta-rules on the grounds that implicit database concurrency-control mechanisms and rule-priority schemes may be sufficient, and easier to use, for the expression of control information. Many rule-processing systems, including Starburst,[24] Postgres,[25] and ART,[26] to name a few, use this approach to control rule execution. Such issues are difficult to resolve, since they rely more upon assessments of ease of use of a language feature, and less upon formal argument. However, we posit the following as potential sources of benefit for using meta-rules as a separate body of control information.

First, we note that the explicit separation of control knowledge indeed not only enhances readability of the rule program, but also provides the means of easy modification and automated analysis. As we have reported elsewhere, meta-rules make explicit what re-evaluation is necessary when performing an incremental update of a faulty inference process. Furthermore, the declarative specification of control information allows the base logic of the rule program to be free of obscuring implicit program elements. An OPS5 rule is typically not understandable on its own, without resorting to a deeper analysis of control flow usually represented as "secret messages" threaded throughout a group of rules, or worse, counting symbols appearing in the rule to determine its priority of execution over other rules. When one wishes to alter program behavior, many rules may need to be re-written to effect the necessary change in control information flowing between rule instances during execution. In our scheme, changing the meta-rules implies no change to the base rules.

Second, basing conflict-resolution or rule-sequencing information on a *prioritization of rules* scheme does not address the problem of expressing prioritization of instances of a single rule. Likewise, typical database-concurrency control by way of data locking does not allow for the expression of *preferential locking*. We envision the use of meta-rules to allow the programmer to specify control on the basis of problem semantics. Whether or not the meta-rules exist at runtime as a separately interpreted body of knowledge is debatable. We may, for example, wish to "compile" meta-rules away in terms of more primitive and implicit concurrency control schemes. But the programmer will not see these implementational details.

Thus, we believe that the meta-rule construct provides an interesting and potentially useful means for programmers to declaratively specify complex inferential processes against large stores of information without resorting to procedural mechanisms that may complicate the coding of rule programs.

12.3.1 A Compiler for Parulel

The database of facts in Parulel programs is provided by a relational database-management system, rather than the LISP environment of typical AI rule languages such as OPS5. Compiling Parulel rules into database queries involves generating correct relational expressions that perform arbitrary joins. We have designed a compiler front end that accepts legal Parulel programs and generates data structures that can be interpreted by a *code generator* that generates relational expressions. The generated "code" is embedded within a runtime system that interacts directly with a relational database server.

The basic technique for rule matching is similar to the method used in the semi-naive evaluation of Datalog rules.[27] Our method is augmented to handle negative condition elements and deletions occurring in the actions of rules, and is based upon the TREAT algorithm.[4] (Others have considered quite similar approaches.)[28] Here we present the basic technique, and do not discuss the details when negation is present. Suppose we are evaluating at inference cycle i. For simplicity, we consider the LHS conditions as representing a join over relations $R_1, R_2, \ldots, R_k$. The Δs prefixing relations specified below represent the increment in that relation from the previous iteration, $i - 1$. Relations that are not prefixed denote "augmented" relations; that is, these relations are augmented with the Δs from the previous cycle before participating in the matching process. For positive condition elements and positive Δs (that is, changes to base relations are only additions), the match is the following union:

$$\Delta R_1 \bowtie R_2 \bowtie R_3 \bowtie \ldots \bowtie R_k \cup \quad (1)$$
$$R_1 \bowtie \Delta R_2 \bowtie R_3 \bowtie \ldots \bowtie R_k \cup \quad (2)$$
$$\ldots$$
$$\ldots$$
$$R_1 \bowtie R_2 \bowtie R_3 \bowtie \ldots \bowtie \Delta R_k \quad (k)$$

To compute the join (1) above, for example, we seed the join with ΔR_1, and then compute the join $\Delta R_1 \bowtie R_2 \bowtie \ldots \Delta R_k$ using database query facilities. One of the issues we need to be concerned about is the various indexing schemes that should be used for the different relations.

Another issue is when and how base tables are updated as inference proceeds. The details of the implementation, including various optimization issues, are addressed in one of our Columbia University technical report.[29]

We are also investigating the means of compiling meta-rules into an efficient form, including the possibility of mechanically rewriting the object-level rules in a form that captures the semantics of the meta-level rules. This rewriting would obviate the need for a separate redaction phase after rule matching. Instead, the only instantiations formed would be those that can be fired in parallel, without conflicting with one another. A more detailed treatment of Parulel has been published.[23]

12.3.2 Performance of Rule-Based Systems in Parulel

Hernandez[30] has studied the performance of a suite of benchmark OPS5 rule-based programs reimplemented in Parulel. For each benchmark, the problem-solving strategy used in the OPS5 version was studied and then the program was implemented in Parulel with an eye to preserving the original problem-solving strategy. However, changes were made where necessary to take advantage of the parallel semantics of Parulel. In all cases, metarules were used to either provide the control of execution or remove synchronization points.

The programs that were studied include the well-known benchmarks Waltz, Toru-Waltz, and Tourney.[30] The performance was measured along several significant dimensions. We mention only one of these, namely the comparison of the number of inference cycles needed to solve the task at hand between the OPS5 and Parulel implementations. This comparison is given in the form of an *improvement factor* that indicates the factor by which the number of OPS5 cycles dominate the number of Parulel cycles for the same task. For Waltz, the improvement factor was in the range 5–7 on problem sizes in the range 9–27. For Toru-Waltz, the improvement factor was in the range 7.6–16.6 for problem sizes in the range 5–30. For Tourney, the improvement factor was 31.3. The initial performance results obtained, together with an informal comparison of the results with other multiple rule-firing systems, shows that a large amount of parallelism can be extracted from the Parulel implementation of the programs studied.

12.3.3 Two Related Rule Languages

The reader may possibly note a striking similarity between Parulel and RPL.[31] RPL provides a rule language with programmable conflict resolution expressed by meta-rules. Although there are obvious syntactic differences between RPL and Parulel (RPL requires SQL in the LHS of rules, for example), there are fundamental differences between the two. RPL appears to provide only two mechanisms to express parallelism. The *all* construct dictates that all instances of a rule should be fired. But this is useful only if all instances of a single rule can be fired at once without conflict; otherwise, one has to resort to *fire-one-instance* semantics. Parulel's meta-rules provide the means of redacting unwanted rule instances of the same rule and firing all that remain in parallel. The *firing group* construct of RPL is its second major construct reminiscent of various rule-partitioning schemes in other earlier work.[5] Here the idea of representing *commutative* rules by way of mutually exclusive rule clusters is provided. But no further optimizations are applied, and hence according to Miranker[32] no large gain of parallelism can be expected. Parulel's execution is intended to be optimized by way of copy-and-constrain techniques applied to rules distributed to different processing sites. Likewise, optimizations are certainly to be applied according to rule-interdependence analysis, as described by Ishida.[33]

Besides the issue of parallelism, RPL provides a declarative framework for conflict resolution like that proposed for Parulel. However, it appears that the attributes of the firing groups used for conflict resolution are hard-coded; there is no actual way of accessing the conflict set itself.

Another system related to Parulel is RDL.[34] Although the execution semantics is defined as non-deterministic choice for rule execution, control can be specified separately from the rules by way of a control language based upon regular expressions. An early (dissertation) work[35] defines a rule language controlled by a separate control language based upon regular expressions that specified sequential, repetitive (Kleene star), alternative and permutable (parallel) rule executions. Although useful, the approach had a major problem in practice. Occasionally the control expression being followed required the execution of a rule that had no instantiations. Ultimately, meta-rules were defined to resolve these *control conflicts*, which then quickly subsumed the entire regular-expression language; that is, meta-rules provided sufficient specification of control. As we have noted, there is of course the problem with strict specification of control sequences by way of rule names. It is impossible to specify control on the basis of data matched by rules, nor can one specify control between instances of the same rule. Parulel's meta-rules ameliorate these problems.

It is evident as well that neither of these languages and systems describes any mechanism or language support for incremental update in the context of *random* changes to the base relations while inferencing over the relations. In the following section, we describe the general problem of incremental update and the algorithm for its solution.

12.4 INCREMENTAL UPDATE OF RULE PROGRAMS

Traditional AI rule-based systems, such as OPS5, are composed of a knowledge base consisting of a set of facts, the database, and a set of rules that operate on them. Ordinarily, the database changes only as a result of inference activity being carried out by a rule interpreter that evaluates rules. The initial working-memory facts define what is called the *extensional database*, while the rules define the *intensional database*. The IDB may be regarded as a view on the database, and this view can be either computed dynamically or stored in some fashion. The process of computing the IDB view is equivalent to evaluating the rules in the rule program defining the IDB relations.

AI research in reasoning systems teaches that in many real-world applications, reasoning is necessarily non-monotonic, and a means is required for maintaining the consistency of a deductive process. Assumptions about the truth of certain formulae are initially made only to be retracted later as new information dictates.

In data-intensive applications (such as communication-network management) or financial applications (such as financial securities allocation),[1] the database may change independently of the inference process, and thus a *truth-maintenance* capability is called for to maintain the consistency of the set of derived deductions in the IDB. Consider the mortgage pool allocation expert system, ALEXSYS, described in the section on applications, which seeks to allocate optimally a number of financial securities to contracts by way of a set of IDB relations, assigning individual securities to specific contracts. Suppose the expert allocator computes the IDB view (that is, the allocation of particular securities in the inventory to particular contracts to be filled) periodically, and caches the result until the next round of computation. Suppose it has assumed some fact f during the initial computation of the IDB view (that is, that some security is in inventory) and subsequently a message arrives refuting f (that is, some other agent has removed that security from inventory). The naive approach for incorporating this late-arriving information would be to restart the expert allocator from the beginning, re-evaluating all the rules in the program, and thus reallocating the entire inventory. However, for efficiency, it is often essential to have an inference mechanism that performs only the actions necessary to bring the IDB view to a consistent state *incrementally*, that is, to refresh the view in the light of the newly arrived information, without recomputing the entire set of IDB relations.

Incremental update of rules is also useful for parallel and distributed rule processing in the following sense. When the processors evaluating a single program operate asynchronously, then they may have different views of the database. The general framework we develop for incremental update can be used to synchronize such disparate views. For example, let us consider the copy-and-constrain paradigm for distributed and parallel rule processing[36] (described in detail in the next section). It stipulates that in a distributed- or parallel-processing architecture, each processor evaluates a specialized version of the original rule program, but with less data. The specialized versions are chosen such that their union is equivalent to the original program. The operations of each processor that result from the evaluation (for example, *add_a_fact* or *delete_a_fact*) are transmitted to other processors to derive other inferences.

Suppose that the evaluation proceeds asynchronously. Then it is possible that a processor p_1 that is evaluating at cycle t_1 receives an *add_e* from a processor p_2 that is evaluating at cycle t_2, with $t_1 > t_2$. This means that p_1 has to incorporate e into the database of cycle t_2, an earlier version of the current database. Then the problem it faces is exactly the problem of incremental rule processing: it has to undo the consequences of e at cycle t_2, and redo the consequences of $\neg e$ at cycle t_2, but without backing its whole rule evaluation to cycle t_2. In other words, individual processors need to have the ability to incorporate changes in arbitrary previous iterations. Our algorithm for incremental update works for an arbitrary cycle update, and therefore can be applied to asynchronous parallel and distributed rule processing by copy-and-constrain.

The incremental update of Parulel programs is characterized by an inference process that alternates between two main modes of operation: *normal* and *incremental*. Normal mode evaluation consists of the procedure *PARULEL_SEMANTICS* of the previous section. After the *act* step, we check to determine whether an *interrupt* message has been received, either from some external source or from some other parallel process evaluating some portion of the rule program. If so, an interrupt-handler procedure, *PARULEL_INCR_UPDATE*, is invoked, which incrementally updates the deduced database to a consistent state. Intuitively, the incremental-update stage consists of an *undo* phase and a *redo* phase. The recursive procedure *PARULEL_INCR_UPDATE* is invoked by the inference system as an exception handler on receiving incremental modifications to past assumptions made on the database. The procedure modifies the database, given two sets of operations as arguments, U and R, that have to be incorporated at some past evaluation iteration i. Each set contains positive and negative facts. The set U represents a collection of facts whose addition or deletion (depending on the sign) has to be undone at iteration i. It is called the *undo set*. The set R represents a collection of facts whose addition or deletion has to be incorporated at iteration i. It is called the *redo set*. The details of incremental update for the general case and also for Parulel semantics are detailed in other work.[37-39]

In the case of incremental update under Parulel semantics, the meta-rules dictate those base rules that need to be re-evaluated in order to update the database correctly on any changed fact. Specifying control declaratively by way of meta-rules provides the means of identifying the appropriate subset of instances that need to be reformed. For a language like OPS5, conflict resolution is built in by way of sorting instances according to recency of the facts in the working memory or database. To redo or undo rule-firings in this case would be very difficult. It would be necessary to reconstruct the entire state of the rule matching at iteration i in order to sort all instances properly, as would be done in OPS5 conflict resolution in order to determine the correct *undo* and *redo* sets. If the set of changed facts includes a fact that was not present in the database at iteration i, what recency number should be assigned to this new fact? This number is important to determine the ordering of the instances in which it appears. The declarative meta-rule construct simply abolishes the need to encode the recency numbers of facts, and thus this problem does not exist in Parulel.

We have reported previously the incremental update algorithm.[37] The reader is encouraged to see the work of Dewan et al.,[38] where we reformulate the algorithms in a manner that lends itself to rigorous treatment for the purpose of proving correctness. We have formalized the proof to accommodate a variety of operational semantics, including those of Datalog, OPS5 and Parulel.

The performance of the incremental update algorithm under Parulel semantics has been measured. In one test case, incremental update is shown to correct an inference process far more efficiently than simply restarting the process from the beginning. In another test case, quite the opposite is found. Thus, incremental update is an important and desirable system feature to be applied judiciously in the appropriate context. The details of measured performance and a deeper analysis of the results of that performance appear in work by Ohsie et al.[39]

12.5 COPY-AND-CONSTRAIN

The essence of the copy-and-constrain technique[36] and its variants (for example, data reduction),[40-42] is to "rewrite" the rule system in such a way that individual rules that require more processing than the "average" rule are replaced by a number of copies of the rule in question with additional distinct constraints appearing in each copy. The effect of this transformation is to preserve the same computation as that of the original rule, but to provide the opportunity to match the copy-and-constrain rules in parallel. The total effect is that a number of rules representing a *hot-spot* rule can calculate more quickly the same instances in parallel.

The technique can be applied to each rule in the program, producing a number of constrained versions of the original program. In earlier work,[43] we found that as more hot-spot rules undergo the copy-and-constrain technique, greater parallelism and faster execution is achieved, with varying degrees of performance gains being observed for different programs. The potential speedup of matching a single hot-spot rule by applying the copy-and-constrain technique can be seen as follows. Let rule r be:

$$r : C_1 \land C_2 \land \ldots \land C_n \rightarrow A_1, \ldots, A_m \ n, m \geq 1$$

where the C_i, $i = 1 \ldots n$ are conditions selecting a subset of the database tuples, and where $A_j, j = 1 \ldots m$ is a set of m actions (updates to the database). Let $R(C_i)$ denote the tuples selected by C_i. The work, $W(r)$, to process r is bounded by the size of the cross product of the tuples selected on the LHS of r:

$$W(r) \leq |R(C_1)| \times |R(C_2)| \times \ldots \times |R(C_n)|$$

Suppose we choose to copy-and-constrain rule r on condition C_i to produce k new conditions $\{C_i^1, C_i^2, \ldots, C_i^k\}$, and k new replicas of r, $\{r^1, r^2, \ldots, r^k\}$, where each replica has C_i replaced by $C_i^l, l = 1 \ldots k$, on the LHS. If the new conditions are chosen such that

$$|R(C_i^l)| \approx \frac{|R(C_i)|}{k}, l = 1 \ldots k, \cap_{l=1}^{k} R(C_i^l) = \emptyset, \text{ and, } \cup_{l=1}^{k} R(C_i^l) = R(C_i),$$

then

$$W(r^1) \approx \ldots \approx W(r^k) <\approx |R(C_1)| \times \ldots \times (\frac{|R(C_i)|}{k}) \times \ldots \times |R(C_n)| \approx \frac{W(r)}{k}$$

For appropriately chosen conditions, each of the k replicas require $\frac{1}{k}$th the amount of work as the original rule r to process, forming the same set of instantiations. If the replicas are processed in parallel, the evaluation of r has been sped up by a factor of k. Clearly, we can apply this technique to all rules in a program P, producing k new programs $P^1, P^2, \ldots, P^k$ such that the number of instances formed by matching the rules of the original program P is identical to the union of the instances formed by matching the k constrained programs $P^1, P^2, \ldots, P^k$.

Suppose for concreteness that C_i is a selection of a large number of physical objects, represented by a relation with *name*, *color*, and *shape* attributes, and that the domain of the color attribute is {RED, GREEN}. We can construct two new condition elements, in two copies of a rule (one replacing the selected value of the color attribute with RED, the other replaced by GREEN), and assign the two distinct rules to distinct processors. These two copy-and-constrain rules may be matched in parallel, and the set of instantiations is exactly the disjoint union of the instantiations of the original rule. If a small finite domain of attribute values is not known *a priori* (as in the example with RED and GREEN objects), two variations on the technique are possible. The first is *hash partitioning*. Suppose that, in the above example, the domain of the color field is not {RED, GREEN}, but is some (possibly infinite) domain D. If there is an easily computable hashing function, we can split $R(C_i)$ into k partitions over the range of the hash function and assign each of the k partitions to a separate processor, along with a suitably constrained version of the rule r. In the best case, again, the processing time for the match phase of r is divided by k, the number of partitions, by way of concurrent queries operating on a large number of small relations. The second variation of the basic technique applies when the domain is a totally ordered set: we can simply divide it into disjoint subranges.

Continuing with the above example, suppose the domain of the color attribute is some range of wavelength values of the light reflected by the objects. We can again divide this range of values of the wavelength into subranges and assign each to a separate processor, together with constrained versions of the original rule. This *disjoint-subranges* scheme is a special case of hash partitioning that bypasses the explicit computation of a hashing function.

These three well-known approaches have been exploited in efforts to parallelize ordinary relational queries. Here we provide a fourth scheme for partitioning data based upon clustering. This alternative strategy calls for constraining a rule on the basis of a distance metric defined for the tuples of a relation referenced by the rule. The underlying relations are partitioned into clusters around several *centroids*. Every tuple whose distance from one of these centroids is lower than a specified threshold is placed in the corresponding cluster. (This technique is discussed further in the section describing applications.)

The copy-and-constrain approach is not without problems. It may be difficult to determine the tuple attributes that should be constrained and how they should be constrained. Choosing these attributes requires knowledge about the program's behavior, and knowledge about the domain, to decide the best choice of constraints. It should be stressed that, although our prior experimental results depict moderately good performance gains while utilizing the copy-and-constrain technique, we did not attempt to choose the "optimal" constraints. Hence, the programs we studied may be expected to run even faster with additional fine-tuning.

In our current work, we have formulated a strategy to produce automatically copy-and-constrain versions of rule programs written in the Parulel rule language[23,1] by analyzing *system catalogs*. Many commercial database-management systems provide system catalogs that gather various statistics on the database while the database is updated. Thus, statistics on value ranges for various attributes, cardinality of base relations, numbers of distinct values of attributes, and so forth, may be used to produce various schemes for partitioning. The use of such information is detailed in a Columbia University report.[44]

As an initial partitioning scheme, we may, for example, interpolate the frequency distribution of the values of an attribute over its domain as a function by probing random tuples in the base relations, compute the integral of the interpolation function, and partition the range into *buckets* of roughly equal size. These buckets are then appropriately associated with each constrained rule in which the attribute appears. To our knowledge, no published method has been reported to choose an attribute for partitioning automatically. Rule interdependencies complicate matters greatly; for example, if different rules select different tuples from the same base relation, then partitioning must be sensitive to this common dependency to reduce potential data replication. Thus, even though partitioning the data may indicate opportunities for parallelism, it is not clear that the work of evaluating the rule program will actually be distributed.

Recently, several papers[40-42] have investigated the copy-and-constrain technique under the term *data reduction*, introduced independently of our earlier work by Wolfson. Much of this work has focused on syntactic characterization of rule programs that are decomposable in the sense that a copy-and-constrain version of such programs requires no runtime communication. A recent paper by Wolfson, et al.,[45] demonstrates the technique under alternative strategies (that is, alternative tuple attributes and hash partitions) for a simple program solving the single-source reachability problem. An analytical model is given that accounts for machine characteristics, including communication time. Experimental results show modest performance gains over "random graphs." In fact, Wolfson remarks that, for the particular problem studied, parallelism seems bounded by a small constant. This observation demonstrates that the technique is clearly fundamentally limited by the inherent parallelism in the problem (and of course inherent overhead in system architectures). Of course, it is not clear either that the optimal partitioning was selected in any case.

However, there is another possible technique, not considered by Wolfson, that may be used in conjunction with copy-and-constrain. This is motivated by the observation that it may be advantageous to gather statistics at runtime that would be used to produce a better partitioning on subsequent runs of the rule program. If the base relations change slowly from run to run, then gathering statistics on the size of hash partitions and communication loads at runtime can be useful in computing new parallelization strategies and partitioning schemes for subsequent runs. On the other hand, if the base relations change rapidly, such statistics might have limited utility. Note also that runtime statistics may be the only practical way of estimating the distribution of intensional relations.

As noted above, system catalogs may be useful in analyzing the distributions of the base relations, and runtime statistics are useful in describing the distribution of the intensional relations and interrule communication (that is, that amount of communication between interdependent rules that are distributed). Perhaps the same information may be useful at runtime to reorganize the system "on-the-fly." That is, it may be possible to reorganize dynamically the distribution and the partitioning of the program to elicit better performance at runtime, rather than waiting for the next run of the program for a possibly different base relation. Bottlenecks that may arise at runtime and are not predicted at compile time may be avoided, or their effects reduced. Ishida[46] recently reports on a dynamic reorganization scheme that may provide a means of accomplishing this task effectively.

We end this section with a brief overview of an algorithm that utilizes the copy-and-constrain idea for automatically partitioning the database of facts among several processing sites. The algorithm, which we call *bisection copy-and-constrain*,[44] generates a set of replicas of the original program for distribution over a set of processing sites. Previous work considered the distribution of a single rule to a PE, or *clusters* of rules to a PE. The BCC algorithm can support both of these distribution schemes. However, its principal strength is in its ability to distribute constrained versions of all rules in the program, that is, distribute constrained replicas of the entire program, guided by a cost analysis of the rules in the program under a well-defined cost model. The BCC algorithm has two main phases.

In the first phase, BCC attempts to smooth out cost variations among the rules of a rule program P so that all rules are uniform within some parameter λ (lambda uniformity).

λ-uniformity is desirable when the computing environment consists of elements of both parallel and distributed processing. If a processing site consists of multiple processors, we may want to match all the rules in parallel, as in the *full-distribution* parallel algorithm[12] for production-system execution on a tree-structured parallel computer.[9, 47] The natural strategy is to require that each rule be of approximately equal cost to every other rule in the constrained version of the program allocated to that site. Each rule in a λ-uniform version P_u of a program P is roughly equal in terms of cost of evaluation to within the tolerance λ. The other reason why a balanced program is desirable is discussed by Pasik.[20] Basically, many rule-based programs are distinguished by a group of "culprit" rules that dominate the cost of evaluation. The performance of such programs under parallel-execution environments can be improved by copy-and-constrain techniques applied to the culprit rules.

Once λ-uniformity is attained, all the rules in the program are replicated by generating restricting predicates attached to appropriate rules of P_u. In BCC, the rules are constrained such that each constrained version of a rule matches approximately half the data matched by the original. Thus, a constrained version of a program generated by the BCC algorithm will have total cost approximately half of the cost for the program version from which it is derived by the copy-and-constrain method.

The BCC algorithm is similar to bisection search. We iteratively copy-and-constrain all the rules of those constrained versions of the program that have total cost exceeding some desired cost threshold C_d. This effect is achieved by bisecting the range of data matched by each rule in half. Each constrained version P_i is assigned to a processing site. The data "relevant" to a site are also replicated at that site. Note that the restricting predicates that define the program replicas provide strong guidance as to how the master database should be partitioned so that relevant data are available at each processing site (that is, data relevant to some constrained version P_i that resides at processor p, are also available at processor p locally, without a network transfer being necessary). The details of the BCC algorithm appear in a Columbia University report.[44] The algorithm has been formulated but not implemented at the time of this writing.

12.6 RUNTIME REORGANIZATION

In a recent article, Ishida[46] reports on an architectural schema for reorganizing a distributed computation to increase effective throughput and response times. The class of application studied is problem-solving systems represented in rule form.

The key ideas proposed are as follows. An initial rule program together with organizational information is located at a single processing site, and problem-solving requests are issued from some external source (all data are assumed main-memory resident). As problem solving (rule inference) progresses, and additional problem-solving requests are received, some collection of rules, called an *agent*, is decomposed into two independent and asynchronously executed agents.

Initially there is only one agent, the original rule program. Reorganization is demanded when, after the agents have been distributed around a number of processing sites, very high demands are placed upon a small subset of rules. Some agents therefore have more work than others. These "overstressed" agents (we may otherwise call them hot-spots) are determined on the basis of response time rather than on the size of the local database. Whole rules stored within a slow-running agent, and the tuples matched by those rules, are communicated from the parent agent to its newly formed sibling agent. When demand loads decrease, and underutilized resources are detected, two agents can compose into one agent, thus freeing up resources for other agent decompositions that may need these resources. Note that the rule program is not compiled but rather represented declaratively as data that is executed by a rule interpreter.

The organizational information declaratively specifies agent relationships (called *agent-agent knowledge*) as well as rule interdependencies (called *knowledge-agent knowledge*) between the rule sets in related agents. Clearly data is replicated between agents if they share matching data in their respective partitioned rule sets. This organizational information is not compiled but rather is also represented declaratively as data that can be transmitted when agents are composed or decomposed. The organizational information is used to determine how to decompose a single agent and where to send its sibling agent, or where to send an agent that wishes to compose with some other agent. The approach is demonstrated using one test-problem solver, a rule program implementing the Waltz line-drawing labeling algorithm, and good performance is reported in a distributed setting.

The approach is interesting but not without problems. For example, whole rules are migrated among processors as data at runtime, along with the tuples they have matched. Thus, rules are stored explicitly, and are interpreted at runtime, rather than being initially compiled to a more efficient runtime form. In addition, Ishida's work assumes each problem-solving request is entirely independent of other previously received requests. This means that each problem-solving request accesses different base relations (but a common body of organizational information that is memory resident). As described earlier, in many real-world applications incoming requests may simply dictate that prior assumptions used in earlier inferences were wrong, and thus we are faced with the circumstances of incremental update. This observation implies that Ishida's organizational information, appropriate for dynamic repartitioning and distribution, requires augmentation with historical inference information as we have detailed in our incremental update algorithm.[37,38]

We have devised a scheme to extend Ishida's scheme, but one that we believe to be much more efficient, especially in the important case of rule processing in large databases. First, we note that problem-solving requests may not be independent of each other. Our proposed incremental update algorithm can simply be used to allow problem-solving requests to be directly related. Second, we believe there is a simple and efficient means of composing and decomposing agents according to Ishida's scheme based upon copy-and-constrain. This proceeds as follows.

Rather than locating the entire rule program initially at one processing site, each processing site is given an initial copy-and-constrain version according to the scheme outlined in the previous two sections. Each version is simply compiled; no declarative rule base is needed at runtime, nor an expensive interpreter. Then, as bottlenecks are detected and reorganization is called for, new constraint ranges are passed among the distributed agents. Thus, rather than whole rules being communicated, only the new version of an already resident rule needs to be communicated between agents by way of new partition information. Communication requirements, and speed of execution, should be far faster than in Ishida's case.

For example, in Ishida's case, imagine we have an initial agent with two rules and the following tuples stored locally.

> Agent1 :
> $P_1 : A(x), B(x) \rightarrow C(x)$
> $P_2 : A(x), D(x) \rightarrow E(x)$
> with D = {A(1), A(2), B(1), B(4), D(1), D(6)}.

After reorganization, Ishida's system will produce

> $Agent_1$:
> $P_1 : A(x), B(x) \rightarrow C(x)$ with D={A(1), A(2), B(1), B(4) }.
> $Agent_2$:
> $P_2 : A(x), D(x) \rightarrow E(x)$ with D={A(1), A(2), D(1), D(6)}.

Note that the A relation is replicated entirely, and that the reorganization required the communication of rule P_2 , along with all tuples from the A and D relations. (The requisite organizational information is not shown.)

In the scheme we propose, the picture is quite different. Initially, both agents have a copy of the entire rule program, but only the first agent has hash ranges sufficient to match the entire database. The second matches nothing. Thus, we have:

> $Agent_1$:
> $P_1 : A(x),B(x),hash(x) \in \{ even,odd \} \rightarrow C(x)$.
> $P_2 : A(x),D(x),hash(x) \in \{ even,odd \} \rightarrow E(x)$.
> with D = {A(1), A(2), B(1), B(4), D(1), D(6)} and
> $Agent_2$:
> $P_1 : A(x),B(x),hash(x) \in \phi \rightarrow C(x)$.
> $P_2 : A(x),D(x),hash(x) \in \phi \rightarrow E(x)$.
> with D = ϕ.

Upon reorganization in this case, we simply split the range of hash partitions between the two agents, one matching over values that hash to an even number, the other to odd, and send the appropriate tuples. Thus, our reorganized agents will be as follows:

> $Agent_1$:
> $P_1 : A(x),B(x),hash(x) \in \{even\} \rightarrow C(x)$.
> $P_2 : A(x),D(x),hash(x) \in \{even\} \rightarrow E(x)$.
> with D = {A(2), B(4), D(6)} and

> $Agent_2$ ::
> $P_1 : A(x),B(x),hash(x) \in \{odd\} \rightarrow C(x)$.
> $P_2 : A(x),D(x),hash(x) \in \{odd\} \rightarrow E(x)$.
> with D = {A(1), B(1), D(1)}.

This result was accomplished by simply communicating new hash ranges ("odd") and fewer tuples (the "odd" tuples from the three relations). Notice, further, that we did not need to communicate the rules, and thus those rules prestored and appearing in all agents can be "compiled" into faster running code. (In order to change the range of values each compiled rule matches, without requiring the recompilation of the rule, we can simply assert the hash ranges that are then matched by an additional literal added to the rules.)

One other problem with Ishida's approach to system reorganization is the manner in which hot-spot agents are detected. Here he outlines an approach where measurements are made repeatedly to keep track of the response time of each agent. When an agent becomes delayed, and does not meet its preset deadline, the runtime system is signaled to reorganize the computation. Ishida points out that the system parameters must be carefully set (by some ad hoc process) prior to initiating the distributed computation to properly initiate the reorganization cycle at runtime.

An alternative, and clever, means of accomplishing the same task can be found in the work of Massalin.[48] Here a *software phase-locked loop* is used as a fast runtime sensor that measures the I/O buffers of a process. The approach assumes that a process is consuming data from some process, and produces a stream of output consumed by some other process. Such is the case with distributed evaluation of a rule program as outlined above. If either the input buffer or output buffer grows too rapidly, or both are "out of phase" with each other, system reorganization is signaled for the hot-spot process by a phase-locked loop implemented in software. Of particular interest is the fact that this approach is "self-stabilizing." This means that during runtime, the various phase-locked loops attached to the various processes will readjust themselves automatically to balance the I/O behavior of all processes in the global system. No preset schedule is needed at startup. Rather, a runtime schedule is computed on-the-fly. The implementation of this simple scheme is remarkably efficient and has been demonstrated by Massalin to improve operating-system performance by a factor of 2–3 over conventional process-prioritization schemes.

At the present time, we have not formalized this approach, but rather have outlined the approach intuitively. We hope to provide a rigorous treatment of this runtime-reorganization approach in the near future. We next detail the context in which our studies will be conducted, a specific real-world application of rule processing against a database supplied by an industrial collaborator.

12.7 APPLICATIONS

12.7.1 Mortgage-Pool Allocation—ALEXSYS

The first application we mention is the mortgage-pool allocation problem, a combinatorial optimization problem that deals with potentially thousands of data items. One implementation of a system to solve this problem is in operational use at Citicorp. The system, which we call ALEXSYS,[49,1] serves as our testbed for various studies on parallel processing of rule programs. In our work,[1] we present details of the ALEXSYS system and analysis of performance data for an implementation of the system in Parulel. In summary, the results show that while an OPS5 implementation of ALEXSYS requires progressively more inference cycles to complete the allocation task as the size of the data set is increased, the Parulel implementation requires almost a (small) constant number of cycles, which vary little with the size of the data set. Significant improvement was observed both in the number of inference cycles, the number of database actions per cycle, and other relevant metrics, for example, the "efficiency of instance generation (EIG)." The reader is encouraged to see the work for details.[1]

12.7.2 The Merge/Purge Problem and Equational Theories

The recent enactment of the high-performance computing-and-communications (HPCC) legislation demonstrates the deep conviction of many researchers about the promise of large-scale parallel and distributed computing. Orders of magnitude speedup of computing hardware will provide the opportunity to solve computational problems well beyond the reach of today's fastest computers. Concomitantly, many expect that by the end of the decade vast amounts of information stored in diverse databases will be able to be transmitted over high-speed networks, and integrated and coalesced, providing unprecedented new opportunities for acquiring new knowledge. These goals will likely be met but not without significant advances in our understanding of how to build advanced knowledge-base systems that would bridge the semantic gap inherent in diverse sources of information.

The issue is this. Given two or more databases of primarily textual records, representing information about some set of domain entities or concepts, how does one determine whether two records represent the same domain entity? How might one develop an *equational theory* that accurately specifies the logic of when two unequal strings represent the same domain entity?

There are two sources of techniques that may be brought to bear on this problem. Statistical pattern-recognition techniques attempt to classify large sets of data (although usually numerical quantities, symbolic data has been attempted as well)[50] into semantically meaningful clusters of similar data. Likewise, AI learning techniques attempt to learn logic rules to cluster symbolic data into semantically meaningful classifications. We believe the lessons learned from these two areas of research can be applied to multidatabase integration. Specifically, one must explicitly represent and utilize domain knowledge in order to classify raw data in meaningful ways; that is, a knowledge-base approach is a requirement.

The specific instance of this problem we study is called the *merge/purge* problem. Each month large quantities of information are supplied to various organizations and then are merged into existing databases. Some of the information contained in the newly acquired data might be found to be irrelevant or redundant and thus is purged from the database. The fundamental problem is the merge. Data supplied by various sources typically include identifiers, as string data, that are either different or errorful; that is, determining that two records from two databases provide information about the same entity is highly complex. It is evident that our understanding of how to develop efficient means of integrating diverse information sources of very large size is lacking and requires considerable research.

There are two fundamental problems with performing merge/purge: (1) the size of the data sets involved is so large that only a small portion of the data base can reside in main memory at any point in time and (2) the incoming new data is corrupted, either purposefully or accidentally, and thus the identification of matching data requires complex tests; for example, the matching of two data items may require inference. Simple structural matching tests (that is, one field of the data record "equals" another) are not possible in all cases.

Although these problems appear daunting at first glance, merge/purge can be solved with varying degrees of effectiveness and computational efficiency. The typical approach is to sort the data in such a way as to bring in close proximity all records that are likely to be merged together. The comparison of records is then restricted to a small neighborhood within the sorted list. The effectiveness of this approach is based on the quality of the chosen *keys* used in the sort. Poorly chosen keys will result in a poor quality merge; that is, data that should be merged will be spread out far apart in the final sort and hence will not be discovered.

An alternative approach we study is to partition the data sets into independent clusters of records that are within a specified distance to some well chosen *centroid record*. The partitioning is done by choosing a set of records from the database that are highly dissimilar. The other records in the database are then clustered to the record to which they are most similar. The determination of "similarity" of records is based upon knowledge-base distance metrics. The clustered data sets should be both much smaller in size than the entire database, and guarantee that records that should be merged will indeed occupy the same cluster. Thus, borrowing from statistical pattern-recognition techniques, we believe it is possible to partition the data initially in such a way as to reduce the combinatorics of the merging process. Recall our discussion of copy-and-constrain. This is the fourth partitioning scheme under investigation that extends value and hash-range partitioning by way of *similarity metrics.* However, we also need a means of specifying an *equational theory* that dictates the logic of domain equivalence, not simply string equivalence or similarity.

A natural approach to specifying an equational theory and making it practical would be to use a declarative-rule language, which additionally had the capability of resolving arbitrary conflicts manifested via rule instantiations, when they arise. Parulel is ideally suited for fast execution on a multiprocessor. Thus, Parulel can be used to specify the equational theory and conflict-resolution strategies to be employed in the event of unacceptable matches for the merge/purge task. In addition, Parulel extends the usual rule-language semantics by providing LHS predicates. It provides the means of expressing equational theories based on closeness of match by calling on routines in C that compute, for example, distance metrics.

As an example, here is a rule in English that exemplifies one "axiom" of our equational theory relevant to merge/purge:

> Given two records, r1 and r2.
> If the last name of r1 equals the last name of r2,
>> AND the first names differ slightly,
>> AND the address of r1 equals the address of r2
> then r1 is equivalent to r2.
>> Retain the "longer" first name (or both).

In the syntax of Parulel, this rule may be coded as follows. Note that the segment of code included within curly braces denotes the actual conditions under which two records may be considered equivalent:

```
(p first-name-discrepancy
   (parameters ^string-distance-threshold <threshold>) ;obvious
   (data ^id <r1> ^fname <f1> ^lname <l1> ^address <a1>) ;first
      record
   (data ^id { <r2> <> <r1> } ;second record
      ^fname { <f2> <> <f1> ;unequal first name
         $>$ (length <f1>) (length <f2>) ;longer first name
         $<=$ (distance <f1> <f2>) <threshold>} ;closely
            spelled
      ^lname <l1> ;with last name equal to the first record
      ^address <a1>) ;with address equal to the first record
-->
   (delete 3) ;delete the second record
   (modify 2 ^merged-with <r2> ) ) ;and modify the first
      record.
```

At the moment, the approach we have proposed is to derive domain attributes of textual strings by inference represented in rule form. However, if we identify the string *Michael* as an *Anglican male name*, we wish to represent this information explicitly in some fashion for subsequent comparison operations (or for the preliminary clustering phase as described above). The approach we have described accomplishes this by way of merging along with the source records other databases that map names to various attributes. That is to say, *Michael* will appear in some database with the attributes *male* and *Anglican*, as well as other pertinent information, as data to be matched by a rule rather than being explicitly represented in a rule. (The latter approach would lead to an unmanageable number of highly specialized rules.)

Furthermore, we seek to compute the transitive closure of our equational-theory rule base. For example, we may find that record *A* is (provably) equivalent to record *B* through a series of rule inferences, while also finding that B is equivalent to record C, but do not find A to be equivalent to C directly. Hence, we will necessarily execute the rule program iteratively to a *fixpoint* to form the transitive closure. There are clearly two important issues: the number of iterations and the combinatorics of the matching. In the first case, we believe it is unlikely that very many iterations will be needed to reach a fixpoint. This is clearly a function of the data and the number of individual records that are indeed equivalent. Even if there were many, it is likely most if not all will be captured after one iteration. As for the second case, the best we hope for is to form small clusters, making rule evaluation as efficient as possible.

12.8 SPECIALIZED HARDWARE FOR KNOWLEDGE-BASE SYSTEMS

The question we pose is simply this. Are there substantial reasons to design and develop specialized hardware for knowledge-base systems? If so, what system primitives are appropriate to be designed into the hardware that will provide large performance gains for knowledge-base software over conventional general-purpose multiprocessor systems? We believe it is still too soon to determine the appropriate set of system primitives without a large body of acceptable example programs that would serve as the appropriate guidance for system designers. Other researchers have arrived at essentially the same conclusion.[51] Reduced instruction-set computing has succeeded so well because of a well-chosen collection of C programs that have been appropriately analyzed to determine appropriate system primitives to optimize in hardware. What are the best knowledge-base systems that everyone can agree upon as being the best exemplars? Like Monte Carlo simulation, a numerical computation technique that has been the subject matter of intensive studies on parallelization, the body of software called knowledge-base is highly "irregular," and thus the chances of finding an agreeable set of ubiquitous system primitives remains to be seen.

Monte Carlo is a simple and effective idea that has been exploited by many researchers. Each instance of a Monte Carlo simulation, however, bears little resemblance to another, other than following an iterative process of generating points in some n-dimensional space and computing function evaluations and secondary estimators. There is no one Monte Carlo simulation engine. Rather, a wide variety of different systems have been built and used for various versions of Monte Carlo programs. Knowledge-base systems can be viewed as the Monte Carlo of the symbolic computing domain. Both Monte Carlo and KBS systems are domain dependent, and the variability of processing from domain to domain makes it very difficult to find a suitable set of system primitives that cuts across all domains.

However, the same remarks can be made about the RISC model and C programs. The RISC model is highly general and the C programs that have been optimized on the model are also highly irregular. However, C provides a sufficiently restrictive, low-level abstract machine that optimization is quite possible due to the restrictive nature of its operational semantics and a consistent set of runtime locality behaviors exhibited by typical C programs. The semantics of the abstract C-machine are generally agreed upon and stable by the widest community of users. KBS systems, as we have noted earlier, has no single agreed-upon abstract machine.

Some will argue, however, that the best strategy for any community wishing to accelerate its general class of system is to compile the system into a *thread-based* abstract C machine, and then run it on "standard" multiprocessors with RISC engines. This is not a bad strategy; it may not be elegant, but it will probably work well in practice.

In summary, research on KBS machines should certainly be pursued. A wide space of design choices is available and many exciting ideas are naturally being explored. However, until a stable abstract-machine model emerges for knowledge-base systems, it is likely that this line of research will continue to produce a wide collection of variant machine models, each optimized for a limited class of problems.

In our current state of knowledge, we believe effort is better expended on analyzing and extracting more parallelism from existing systems and formalisms to attain higher efficiencies on current-generation hardware systems. Languages like Parulel and its entire programming environment, Paradiser, are an attempt to do just that to the space of applications coded in rule form.

12.9 CONCLUSION

What we have stressed in this paper is that substantial analysis and alternative semantics of KBS languages to elicit more parallelism is crucial for further development of the field. We believe that sequential rule languages "hide" much of the parallelism inherent in the task to be solved by a rule program. Thus, a new generation of parallel-rule languages is an important topic for future research. Our proposed parallel-rule language, Parulel, is based on an inherently parallel-execution semantics involving set-oriented processing, typical of database systems, and relies on redaction meta-rules to control parallelism among rule instantiations. Furthermore, the declarative specification of conflict resolution in meta-rule form provides a means of efficiently determining appropriate actions to be performed during the *redo* and *undo* phases of incremental update. The operational semantics or conflict-resolution strategies can themselves be specified declaratively, separating the logic of a program from its control.

A notable aspect of Parulel as an architecture is the incremental update facility, which we believe every rule-processing facility targeted to databases in realistic environments must provide. This paper describes a provably correct solution that is being developed within a total rule-processing environment. Included in that environment is an optimization facility mapping a Parulel program to a distributed or parallel processing environment. The key techniques under study are focused on automated means of producing efficient copy-and-constrain versions of a rule program based upon compile-time analysis of system catalogs. An interesting possibility exists to provide runtime reorganization by way of low-cost repartitioning of a distributed-rule program.

Furthermore, large scale, realistic applications are pursued in order to provide the widest and most stressful test cases for performance studies. Two such applications have been described, a combinatorial optimization problem and the merge/purge problem. The former provides an interesting vehicle to study the effectiveness of incremental updating of a faulty inference process. The latter demonstrates the need for embedding equational theories into the term-matching phase of rule processing. In addition, merge/purge sets our sites on problems of very large scale, which many predict will be the norm when HPCC-technology developments and wide area-network computing become available.

We posit that research in specialized machine architecture for knowledge-base systems remains an interesting and exciting area, but results will likely produce a wide range of solutions. It is not clear at all which of the proposed machines will have a large impact, mainly due to the shifting requirements of the underlying formalisms they intend to accelerate. Perhaps in a decade the clear winners will be apparent.

ACKNOWLEDGMENTS

The authors wish to thank the New York State Science and Technology Foundation for their support of this work.

REFERENCES

1. S. Stolfo, et al., "Parulel: Parallel Rule Processing using Meta-Rules for Redaction," *J. Parallel and Distributed Computing*, Vol. 13, No. 4, 1991, pp. 366–382.

2. S. Kuo and D. Moldovan, "The State of the Art in Parallel Production Systems," *J. Parallel and Distributed Computing*, Vol. 15, 1992, pp. 1–26.

3. C.L. Forgy, "Rete: A Fast Algorithm for the Many Pattern/Many Object Pattern Matching Problem," *Artificial Intelligence*, Vol. 19, 1982, pp. 17–37.

4. D.P. Miranker, *TREAT: A New and Efficient Match Algorithm for AI Production Systems*, doctoral dissertation, Dept. of Computer Science., Columbia Univ., New York, N.Y., Oct. 1986.

5. D.P. Miranker, et al., "On a TREAT-Based Production System Compiler," *Proc. 10th Int'l Conf. Expert Systems*, EC2, Cedex, France, 1990, pp. 617–630.

6. D. Maier and D.S. Warren, *Computing with Logic: Introduction to Logic Programming*, Benjamin-Cummings, Redwood City, Calif., 1987.

7. S. Abiteboul and E. Simon, "Fundamental Properties of Deterministic and Nondeterministic Extensions of Datalog," *J. Theoretical Computer Sci.*, Vol. 78, No.1, 1991, pp. 137–158.

8. C.L. Forgy, *OPS5 User's Manual*. Tech. Report CMU-CS-81-135, Dept. of Computer Science, Carnegie Mellon Univ., Pittsburgh, Pa., July 1981.

9. S.J. Stolfo and D.E. Shaw, "DADO: A Tree-Structured Machine Architecture for Production Systems," *Proc. Nat'l Conf. Artificial Intelligence*, AAAI, Morgan Kaufmann Pub., San Mateo, Calif., 1982, pp. 242–246.

10. S.J. Stolfo, "Initial Performance of the DADO2 Prototype," *Computer*, Special Issue on AI Machines, Vol. 20, Jan. 1987, pp. 75–83.

11. S.J. Stolfo and D. Miranker, "The DADO Production System Machine," *J. Parallel and Distributed Systems*, Vol. 3, No.2, Aug. 1986, pp. 269–296.

12. S.J. Stolfo, "Five Parallel Algorithms for Production System Execution on the DADO Machine," *Proc. Nat'l Conf. Artificial Intelligence*, AAAI, Morgan Kaufmann Pub., San Mateo, Calif., 1984, pp. 300–307.

13. M. van Biema, et al., "PSL: A Parallel LISP for the DADO Machine," tech. report, Dept. of Computer Science, Columbia Univ., New York, N.Y., Feb. 1984.

14. A. Gupta, "Implementing OPS5 Production Systems on DADO," tech. report, Dept. of Computer Science, Carnegie Mellon Univ., Pittsburgh, Pa., 1983.

15. M. van Biema, *The Constraint-Based Paradigm: The Integration of the Object-Oriented and Rule-Based Programming Paradigms, doctoral dissertation*, Dept. of Computer Science, Columbia Univ., New York, N.Y., Feb. 1990.

16. M.P. Georgeff, "Procedural Control in Production Systems," *Artificial Intelligence*, Vol. 18, No. 2, Mar. 1982, pp. 175–201.

17. S.J. Stolfo, "Learning Meta-Rule Control of Production Systems from Execution Traces," Tech. Report CUCS-10-80, Dept. of Computer Science, Columbia Univ., New York, N.Y., Aug. 1980.

18. R. Davis, "Meta-Rules: Reasoning About Control," *Artificial Intelligence*, Vol. 15, 1980, pp. 179–222.

19. S.J. Stolfo, D. Miranker, and R. Mills. "More Rules May Mean Faster Parallel Execution," *Proc. Workshop on AI and Distributed Problem Solving*, Navy Research Laboratories, Office of Naval Research and National Academy of Sciences, National Academy Press, Washington, D.C., 1985, pp. 101–108.

20. A. Pasik, *A Methodology for Programming Production Systems and Its Implications on Parallelism*, doctoral dissertation, Dept. of Computer Science, Columbia Univ., New York, N.Y., May 1989.

21. A. Gupta, *Parallelism in Production Systems,* doctoral dissertation, Dept. of Computer Science, Carnegie Mellon Univ., Pittsburgh, Pa., Mar. 1986.

22. M. van Biema, D. Miranker, and S. Stolfo, "The Do-Loop Considered Harmful in Production System Programming, " *First Int'l Conf. Expert Systems*, ACM Press, New York, N.Y., 1986, pp. 88–97.

23. S.J. Stolfo, H.M. Dewan, and O. Wolfson, "The Parulel Parallel Rule Language," *Proc. IEEE Int'l Conf. Parallel Processing*, CRC Press, Boca Raton, FL., Vol. II, 1991, pp. 36-45.

24. L. Haas, et al., "Extensible Query Processing in Starburst," *Proc. ACM SIGMOD Intl. Conf. Management of Data*, ACM Press, New York, N.Y., 1989, pp. 377-388.

25. M. Stonebraker and G. Kemnitz, "The POSTGRES Next-Generation DBMS," *Comm. ACM*, Vol. 34, No. 10, Oct. 1991, pp. 78-92.

26. Inference Corp., "ART-IM Programming Language Reference Manual," tech. report, Inference Corp., 1990.

27. J.D. Ullman, *Principles of Database and Knowledge-Base Systems, Vol. 2*, Computer Science Press, Rockville, Md., 1989.

28. C. Sellis, C. Lin, and L. Raschid, "Implementing Large Production Systems in a DBMS Environment: Concepts and Algorithms," *Proc. ACM SIGMOD Intl. Conf. Management of Data*, ACM Press, New York, N.Y., 1989, pp. 404-412.

29. H.M. Dewan, D.A. Ohsie, and S.J. Stolfo, "The Design and Implementation of Paradiser V0.0," tech. report (in preparation), Dept. of Computer Science, Columbia Univ., New York, N.Y., Sept. 1993.

30. M. Hernandez and S.J. Stolfo, "Parallel Programming of Rule Based Systems in Parulel," *Proc. IJCAI-93 Workshop on Production Systems and Their Innovative Applications*, Morgan Kaufmann Pub., San Mateo, Calif., 1993, pp. 3-12.

31. L. Delcambre, "RPL: An Expert System Language with Query Power," *IEEE Expert*, Winter 1988, pp. 51-61.

32. D.P. Miranker and B.J. Lofaso, "The Organization and Performance of a TREAT-Based Production System Compiler," *IEEE Trans. Knowledge and Data Eng.*, Vol. 3, No. 1, Mar. 1991, pp. 3-9.

33. T. Ishida and S.J. Stolfo, "Towards the Parallel Execution of Rules in Production System Programs," *Proc. Int'l Conf. Parallel Processing*, IEEE CS Press, Los Alamitos, Calif., 1985, pp. 568-575.

34. G. Kiernan, C. de Maindreville, and E. Simon, "Making Deductive Database a Practical Technology: A Step Forward," *Proc. ACM SIGMOD Intl. Conf. Management of Data*, 1990, pp. 237-246.

35. S. Stolfo, "Learning Control of Production Systems," *Cognition and Brain Theory*, Vol. 7, No. 1, 1984, pp. 61-88.

36. S. Stolfo, D.P. Miranker, and R. Mills, "A Simple Processing Scheme to Extract and Load Balance Implicit Parallelism in the Concurrent Match of Production Rules," *Proc. IFIP TC-10 Working Conf. on Fifth-Generation Computer Architecture*, Univ. of Manchester, Manchester, England, 1985, pp. 55-65.

37. O. Wolfson, et al., "Incremental Evaluation of Rules and its Relationship to Parallelism," *Proc. ACM SIGMOD Intl. Conf. Management of Data*, ACM Press, New York, N.Y., 1991, pp. 78-87.

38. H.M. Dewan, et al., "Incremental Database Rule Processing in Paradiser," *J. Intelligent Information Systems*, Vol. 1, No. 2, Oct. 1992, pp. 177-209.

39. D. Ohsie, et al., "Performance of Incremental Update in Database Rule Processing," tech. report, Dept. of Computer Science, Columbia Univ., New York, N.Y., 1992. (Also appears in *Proc. 4th RIDE-ADS Conf.*, 1994.)

40. O. Wolfson, "Parallel Evaluation of Datalog Programs by Load Sharing," *J. Logic Programming*, 1992, pp. 369-393.

41. O. Wolfson and A. Ozeri, "A New Paradigm for Parallel and Distributed Rule-Processing," *Proc. ACM SIGMOD Int'l Conf. Management of Data*, ACM Press, New York, N.Y., 1990, pp. 133-142.

42. S. Cohen and O. Wolfson, "Why a Single Parallelization Strategy is Not Enough in Knowledge Bases," *Proc. 8th ACM Symp. PODS*, ACM Press, New York, N.Y., 1989, pp. 200-217.

43. A. Pasik, "Improving Production System Performance on Parallel Architectures by Creating Constrained Copies of Culprit Rules," Tech. Report CUCS-313-87, Dept. of Computer Science, Columbia Univ., New York, N.Y., 1987.

44. H.M. Dewan, "Runtime Reorganization of Parallel and Distributed Expert Database Systems," Ph.D. thesis, Dept. of Computer Science, Columbia Univ., New York, N.Y., September 1994.

45. O. Wolfson, et al., A Methodology for Evaluating Parallel Graph Algorithms and its Application to Single Source Reachability," *Proc. Parallel and Distributed Information Systems (PDIS)*, IEEE CS Press, Los Alamitos, Calif., 1993, pp. 243-250.

46. T. Ishida, L. Gasser, and M. Yokoo, "Organization Self-Design of Distributed Production Systems," *IEEE Trans. Knowledge and Data Eng.*, Vol. 4, No. 2, Apr. 1992, pp. 123–134.

47. T. Ishida and S.J. Stolfo, "Simultaneous Firing of Production Rules on Tree-Structured Machines," Tech. Report CUCS-109-84, Dept. of Computer Science, Columbia Univ., New York, N.Y., 1984.

48. H. Massalin and C. Pu, "Fine-Grain Adaptive Scheduling Using Feedback," *Computing Systems*, Vol. 3, No. 1, 1990, pp. 139–173.

49. S.J. Stolfo, et al., "The ALEXSYS Mortgage Pool Allocation Expert System: A Case Study of Speeding Up Rule-Based Systems," *AI and Business Workshop, AAAI-90*, Morgan Kaufmann Pub., San Mateo, Calif., 1989.

50. C. Stanfill and D.L. Waltz, "Toward Memory-Based Reasoning," *Comm. ACM*, Vol. 29, 1986, pp. 1213–1228.

51. G. Bell, "Ultracomputers: A Teraflop Before its Time," *Comm. ACM*, Vol. 35, Aug. 1992, pp. 27–47.

13

IXM2: A Parallel Associative Processor for Knowledge Processing

Tetsuya Higuchi

Electrotechnical Laboratory
Ibaraki, Japan

ABSTRACT

This chapter describes a parallel associative processor, IXM2, developed mainly for semantic-network processing. IXM2 consists of 64 associative processors and nine network processors, having a total of 256K words of associative memory. The large associative memory enables 65,536 semantic-network nodes to be processed in parallel and reduces the order of algorithmic complexity to O(1) in basic semantic-net operations. We claim that intensive use of associative memory provides far superior performance in carrying out the basic operations necessary for semantic-network processing: intersection, marker-propagation, and arithmetic operations.

13.1 INTRODUCTION

In this chapter, we propose a parallel associative-memory processing architecture, and examine its performance superiorities over existing architectures for massively parallel machines. The parallel associative-memory processing architecture is characterized by its intensive use of associative memory to obtain massive parallelism. The architecture is ideal for processing very large knowledge bases often represented by semantic networks. We have implemented the IXM2 associative-memory processor based on our architecture in order to validate the benefits of our architecture.

Several efforts are underway to develop a very large knowledge base containing over a million concepts.[1-3] Microelectronics and Computer Technology Corporation's CYC[3] and Japan Electronic Dictionary Research Institute, Ltd.'s electric dictionaries[2] are such examples. The basic framework of these knowledge bases can be represented by semantic networks.[4] While notable effort has been made to develop a sound theory on how to *represent* and *develop* VLKB, no significant investigation has been made on how to *process* VLKBs.

The obvious problem of processing VLKB, as opposed to a small or medium-size knowledge base, is its computational cost. Even a simple operation to propagate markers through a certain link would require increasing computing time on serial machines as the size of the network grows. This cost also applies to intersection-search, marker-propagation, and arithmetic operations, which are three basic operations for processing semantic networks.

One obvious way out from this problem is the development of massively parallel machines. There are several massively parallel machines already developed, or currently being developed (SNAP;[5] the Connection Machine).[6] In general, these machines assume one-node-per-processor-type mapping of the semantic network onto the hardware. The underlying assumption is that significant speedup can be obtained due to parallel computing by each processor in a single-instruction, multiple-data manner.

However, the pitfalls of this approach are that (1) processing within each processor is performed in a bit-serial manner and (2) all marker propagation must be done through communication links, a very slow process. This observation implies that current architectures exhibit serious degradation in performance regardless of the fact that these operations look highly parallel for the user who observes the phenomena from outside of the processors. In scientific computings, especially in matrix computing, all processing elements are always active and communictions are limited to neighbor PEs, thus taking full advantage of SIMD parallelism. However, in the semantic network, although most processing can be carried out in a SIMD manner, not all PEs are activated all the time. The number of PEs active at a time varies during processing; it could range from a few PEs to thousands of PEs. All communications need to be performed between distant PEs. Thus, a processing and communication capability of each PE significantly affects overall performance of the system. Unfortunately, for a machine with 1-bit PEs, bit-serial operations and communication hamper high-performance processing.

In this chapter, we propose a new approach to massively parallel computing in order to avoid the problem described above. Our approach is based on intensive use of large associative memories. The IXM2, a machine built based on this paradigm,[7-9] consists of 64 associative processors and nine network processors, interconnected based on a complete connection scheme to improve marker propagation; it provides 256K words of large associative memory. Using an associative memory of this size, IXM2 can perform the parallel processing of 65,536 semantic-network nodes with a processing time of $O(1)$ in basic operations, and only a minimum communication will be carried out between processors.

(Readers may wonder whether the size of 256K words is really a "large" associative memory, compared with sizes of current ordinary memories. However, it should be noted that associative memory circuits are much more complex than ordinary memories; even with the very-large-scale-integration full-custom design, the NTT associative memory chip used in IXM2 machine can implement only 512 words.)

13.2 SEMANTIC NETWORK PROCESSING

This section gives a simple example of semantic-network processing, explaining the three basic operations and discussing the necessity of the parallel processing.

13.2.1 Characteristics of Semantic Network Processing

A semantic network is a form of knowledge representation that uses a *node* to represent a *concept*, and a *link* to represent the *relationship* between two concepts. The most important characteristic is the inheritance mechanism in *isa* hierarchy networks.[10] Because an *isa* link allows the lower concepts to inherit properties from super-classes, more memory

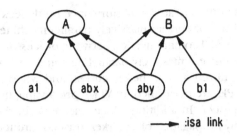

Figure 1.   A semantic network representing two sets.

space can be saved for descriptions of knowledge bases as the knowledge bases become larger. Therefore, the inheritance-network representation used in semantic networks and frame systems is inevitable in developing large knowledge-base systems, such as the CYC project.

In semantic-network processing, three fundamental operations are used intensively: *association*, *set intersection*, and *marker propagation*. These operations are performed efficiently by using *marker bits* assigned to each node of the semantic network. A marker bit is a one-bit flag in which the result of processing is stored.

Now we explain the use of marker bits with Figure 1. Suppose the question, "Which member belongs to both set A and set B?" is asked of the semantic network of Figure 1. To find the solution, an association operation is executed first, to set marker bit 1 of the node A. Next, marker propagation sets marker bit 1 of all the nodes that belong to the hierarchy of node A along the *isa* links, starting from the A node and going downward. These nodes represent members of set A. Similarly, marker bit 2, for members of set B, is set using association and marker propagation. Finally, a set-intersection operation is executed to find the intersection of set A and set B by ANDing marker bits 1 and 2 of each node. Then, the answers are abx and aby.

On sequential computers, these operations become terribly slow as the network size grows larger. Therefore, for example, programmers who have to deal with the intersection of large sets often use heuristics or special-case tactics to avoid computational explosion. However, in order to focus on other aspects of the problem-solving, parallel hardware is required in which set intersection is a trivial operation, as noted by Fahlman.[11] To solve this situation, Fahlman proposes an efficient parallel-processing scheme, NETL. In NETL, by allocating each node or link on a simple PE, association and set-intersection operations can be performed in O(1) for any size of network. In addition, set members can be obtained by marker propagations in the execution time proportional to the depth of the network; a binary tree of one million nodes can be marked in 20 steps. A marker bit on each node can represent a set membership; at any time after it is established, it is available for subsequent processing. On sequential computers, however, if set members are obtained during a search, they must be collected and stored in a list or an array for subsequent processing. These attractions have led to the development of parallel machines such as Connection Machine.

13.2.2 Problems of Current Massively Parallel Machines

The central problem preventing current massively parallel machines from further performance improvement in artificial-intelligence applications is that all PEs are not always active. The number of active PEs at a time range from one to a few thousands. Thus, when relatively small numbers of PEs are active, performance bottleneck often emerges. Specifically, the two characteristics of current massively parallel machines (a bit-serial operation in each processor and bit-serial communication between processors) cause the degradation of performance, because current massively parallel machines assume tasks where most of the 1-bit PEs are highly utilized during the execution, and where local and simultaneous communications among PEs are performed. In VLKB processing, marker propagation is especially tough in this respect. In addition, since one node in the semantic network is mapped to a single PE, any propagation of a marker must go through communication links, resulting in the so-called *hillis bottleneck*. This section reviews problems in current architectures in three basic operations for processing semantic networks: (1) set-intersection, (2) marker-propagation, and (3) logical/arithmetic operations.

The set intersection is a very important operation in AI and is frequently performed to find a set of PEs with two properties. Although set intersection contains SIMD parallelism, there is room for further improvement, because current architecture carries out the intersection in a bit-serial manner by each 1-bit PE.

Marker propagation, however, presents more serious problems. First, propagation of markers from a base node to N descendant nodes requires a sequential marker-propagation operation to be carried out N times at the 1-bit PE of the base node. In addition, the serial link is very slow. Thus, as average fanout (and hence parallelism) increases, current architecture suffers from severe degradation. Second, marker propagations are very slow because all the propagations are performed through the message-passing communications among PEs. Message-passing communications among PEs are slow due to the limited bandwidth of communication lines, the delays caused by intervening PEs in message passing, message collisions, and so on. For these reasons, the marker propagation in the Connection Machine is two orders of magnitude slower than SUN-4, Cray, and IXM2.

13.3 IXM2 ARCHITECTURE

13.3.1 Design Philosophies Behind IXM2

The use of associative memory is the key feature of the IXM2 architecture. Needless to say, IXM2 is a parallel machine constituted from a number of processors. However, the IXM2 attains massive parallelism by associative memory, not by processor itself. IXM2 has only 64 T800 transputers,[12] each of which has a large (4K) associative memory. Instead of having thousands of 1-bit PEs, IXM2 stores nodes of the semantic network in each associative memory. Because each associative memory can store up to 1,024 nodes, IXM2 can store 65,536 nodes in total.

In order to deal with semantic networks larger than 65,536 nodes while maintaining the same performance as the current version of IXM2, IXM2 needs more associative-memory chips. It is possible to implement, on the boards of the same size, twice as many associative memory chips as the current IXM2, resulting in 128K nodes of semantic networks. Also, using RAMs as the secondary storage of semantic networks and swapping them between associative memory and RAM will increase the size of semantic networks, but it causes degradation of performance. However, it should be noted that the current knowledge-base technology could not implement even 64K nodes of semantic network. Possibly the largest semantic network implemented on real machines is 64K nodes in PARKA, but the semantic network is not genuine because the network is generated randomly. The development of large semantic networks seems to be similar to the development of large programs. In developing large semantic networks, much attention has to be paid to multiple inheritance, which causes inconsistent results of inference. The complexity in such inheritance control increases rapidly as the network size grows. "Thesaurus" may be considered to be a much simpler form of semantic network, where only a few relations between words are defined. In the Japan Information Center of Science and Technology (JICST) thesaurus designed for database retrieval, there are 170,000 words. It took seven years to develop. There is no doubt that semantic networks of the same size would require more years and much more effort for the development.

Four major issues have been addressed in the design decision to use associative memory in the IXM2:

- attainment of parallelism in operations on each node,
- minimization of the communication bottleneck,
- powerful computing capability in each node,
- parallel marker propagation.

The term *node* refers to a node in the semantic network, but not necessarily that of a single PE. By allocating nodes of semantic networks on associative memories, association and set intersections can be performed in O(1). Because of the bit-parallel processing on each word of associative memory, these operations can be performed faster than on 1-bit PEs.

Multiple-node allocation on a PE offers a significant advantage in minimizing communication bottleneck. Because a large number of nodes can be loaded in a PE, propagation of markers from a node to other nodes on the same PE can be done by memory reference rather than by communication between PEs. In addition, to deal with marker propagation between PEs, IXM2 employs a full-connection model, in which all processors in a cluster are directly connected. Thus, it decreases the time required for communication between PEs more than other connection models such as nCube or torus. Specifically, the full-connection model minimizes the chance of collision and message-interleaving PEs.

Associative memory has extremely powerful logical and arithmetic computing power. When an operand is stored in each word of the associative memory, a bit-serial operation can be executed to all words in parallel. Massive parallelism offered by this mechanism provides nanoseconds-order execution time per datum.

By use of the parallel write and the search functions of associative memory, multiple marker propagation from a node can be done in parallel, independent of the number of fanouts (O(1)). We call this powerful feature *parallel marker propagation*.

13.3.2 Overall Structure

IXM2 contains 64 associative processors (AP) and nine network processors (NP) for communication. Figure 2 shows an external view of the IXM2 (left), and its structure (right). Eight APs and one NP form a processing module (PM), where eight APs are completely interconnected. In recursive fashion, eight processing modules are also interconnected to each other and to one NP with a connection with the host SUN-4. IXM2 works as an AI coprocessor. The technical summary of IXM2 is described in Table 1.

IXM2 employs complete connection to speed up marker propagation among APs. Marker propagations between two APs have to be done as much as possible between APs that are directly connected; message-path distance in marker propagation must be kept as close to 1 as possible. Although it is almost impossible to establish a complete connection among 64 APs, complete connection among a smaller number of APs is possible. Eight APs are selected as a unit of complete connection. Furthermore, it is possible to keep the communication locality in marker propagation within these eight APs. It is known that a large semantic network can be divided into sub-semantic networks, with dense connectivity

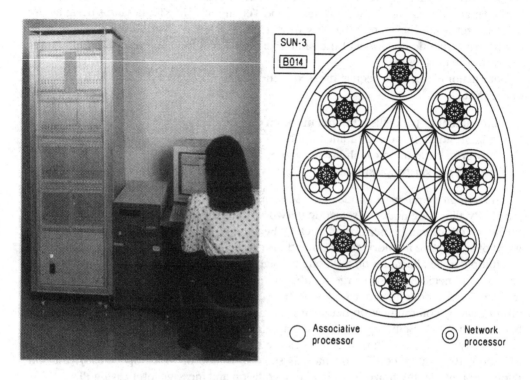

Figure 2.   The IXM2: an external view and its structure.

among the nodes of a given sub-semantic network, but with relatively few connections to the outside sub-semantic network.[14]

Even in a worst-case scenario, where communication locality within a PM is difficult or impossible to maintain (that is, marker passings occur between any pair of the 64 APs), the average message-path distance in the IXM2 interconnection can be kept smaller than that of hypercube and torus, as shown in Table 2. There, marker passings are assumed to occur

Table 1.   IXM2 technical summary.

Associative Processor	T800 Transputer (17.5 MHz), 4 KB on-chip RAM (57ns), 32K X 32 bit SRAM (230 ns), 4 serial link (2.4 Mbytes/sec), 4096 X 40 bit associative memory (375 ns) [17] 4 link adaptors (IMS C012)
Network Processor	T800 Transputer (17.5 MHz), 32K X 32 bit SRAM (230 ns) 2048 X 40 bit associative memory, 16 link adaptors, broadcast up to 16 destination APs or NPs

Table 2. Average message-path distance for IXM2 and other interconnections.

No. of PE	IXM2	hypercube	torus
4	1	1.33	1.33
8	1	1.71	—
16	2.06	2.13	2.13
32	2.54	2.61	—
36	—	—	3.08
64	2.77	3.04	4.03

between each AP and among all other APs in the system, and then the average length of each message-path distance is calculated for different PE sizes.

13.4 PROGRAMMING THE ISM2

Because IXM2 consists of multiple transputers, the programming of IXM2 can be done in Occam2 language.[14] Programs on IXM2 are invoked by the message from the host machine where Prolog, Lisp, and C programs run. These programming interfaces are provided in the IXM2 programming environment.

For the convenience of the development of semantic-network applications, we have developed the knowledge-representation language IXL.[15] In this section, we describe the IXL language and how the IXL programs are executed on IXM2 in parallel with the host machine.

13.4.1 The IXL Knowledge-Representation Language

IXL is a superset of Prolog. It includes special predicates for semantic-network processing in addition to usual Prolog predicates. The additional predicates are shown in Figure 3, and are called *IXL commands*. Using these commands, IXL can perform descriptions, inquiries, and modifications of knowledge bases. IXM2 executes IXL commands for semantic-network processing. The commands are distributed one at a time by the host. Each IXL command is executed in terms of an IXM machine instruction whose execution control is *marker-driven*; the execution sequence is determined by the arrival of markers from other APs.

The IXL interpreter on the host is written in Quintus-Prolog so that Prolog programs can be executed by the interpreter. Therefore, a programmer using the host computer who has experience of Prolog can easily perform parallel processing of semantic networks on the IXM2 machine. For example, suppose that the following statement is entered on the host to obtain all the lower concepts of "bird":

```
?- isa(X,bird),write(X),fail.
```

The IXL interpreter on the host interprets isa(X, bird) as an IXL command and so the command is passed to the IXM2 machine, which finds all the answers of the query command in parallel and sends them back to the IXL interpreter on the host. The IXL interpreter binds the answers to the variable X of isa(X,bird) one at a time whenever the backtracking comes to isa(X, bird).

```
To construct a relation:        To connect nodes by a link:
   assertion (R,X,Y).              link(is_a,X,Y).
   property(R,X,Y).                link(not_isa,X,Y).
To inquire about a link:          link(instance_of,X,Y).
   isa(X,Y).                       link(not_instance_of,X,Y).
   instance(X,Y).                  link(a_kind_of,[X,Y, . . .].Z).
   ako(X,Y).                       link(source,R,X).
   source(R,X).                    link(destination,R,Y).
   destination(R,Y).               link(rule,X,((

To inquire about a relation        asset(R,X,Y):. . . .
   asst(R,X,Y).                     prop(R,X,Y):. . . .
   prop(R,X,Y).                     isa(X,Y):. . . .
                                    instance(X,Y):. . . . )).
```

Figure 3.   The IXL commands.

13.4.2 Semantic Net Processing on the IXM2

In IXM2, data and programs for semantic net processing are allocated as follows:

- A large semantic network to be processed by IXM2 is partitioned into semantic sub-networks and stored in the associative memory of each AP.
- Subroutines to execute IXL commands are stored in the local memory of each AP.

The network processors broadcast an IXL command simultaneously to all the APs. NPs also accept results from each AP and pass them back to the host computer for the IXM2 (SUN-4/260). An IMS B014 transputer VMEbus board is installed in the SUN-4 to control the IXM2, load occam2 programs into the IXM2, collect answers returned from the IXM2, process error handling, and so on.

13.4.3 Execution of an IXL Command

Each AP begins execution of IXL commands using subroutines stored in the local memory. Most operations are performed on the sub-networks stored in the associative memory of the AP. As IXL commands are entered from the host one at a time, the behavior is SIMD at the command level. However, once each AP starts, APs operate independently in MIMD manner (marker-driven). During the execution of an IXL command, APs require no synchronization because of the way the IXM instruction works; an instruction in the subroutine for an IXL command (the instruction is called an IXM machine instruction) specifies a particular marker bit as the qualification for execution and the instruction only becomes executable when the specified marker bit is set. This condition is similar to situations in dataflow (data-driven) computers where the arrival of data initiates the execution of an operation. Because of this MIMD nature, answers are returned to the host via the NPs as soon as they are found.

For example, an IXL command, isa (X, bird), is written with the following IXM machine instructions:

```
ASSOC ( bird , 1 )
MARK ( 1 , isa , 1 )
REPORT ( 1 ) .
```

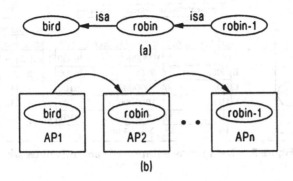

Figure 4. Execution of an IXL command on IXM2.

Each IXM instruction is written in occam2. The first instruction finds the `bird` node and sets marker-bit 1. The second indicates that if a node has a marker-bit 1 set and has *isa* connections, then set marker-bit 1 of the destination nodes connected via the *isa* links. The third instruction returns to the host computer the identifiers of all the nodes which have marker-bit 1 set.

Suppose we have the semantic network of Figure 4 (a) and each node is stored in IXM2's AP as shown in Figure 4 (b).

When the `isa(X, bird)`command is broadcast, then all the APs execute `ASSOC (bird, 1)` but only AP1 has the `bird` node and so only it succeeds in setting marker-bit 1.

Because the marker-bit 1 has been set and an *isa* link exists at the `bird` node, then `MARK(1,isa,1)` becomes executable. Execution of this instruction on AP1 sets the marker-bit 1 of the `robin` node in AP2. This operation is performed by sending a message from AP1 to AP2. Then, AP2 is activated and it executes `MARK(1,isa,1)` to set the marker-bit 1 of the `robin-1` node in APn. The `MARK` instruction is repeated until all the *isa* chains are traversed.

`REPORT(1)` is also executed in AP2 and the identifier of the `robin` node is sent back to the host computer. Thus, executions go on in MIMD mode; IXM2 machine instructions are executed in marker-driven manner to exploit the concurrency in IXL command execution.

13.5 PARALLEL PROCESSING USING ASSOCIATIVE MEMORIES

This section describes how parallel processing is performed on an associative memory. We begin by describing the data representation of a semantic network. Then parallel marker propagation and set intersection are described.

13.5.1 Representation of Semantic Network

The semantic-network representational scheme in IXM2 is strongly node-based. Each node stores information in both associative memory and RAM. Node information stored in associative memory is intended to be processed with the massive parallelism provided by large associative memory (256K words). By this means, the times for association, set-intersection, and marker-propagation operations can be reduced to O(1).

The information in associative-memory words comprises:

- a marker-bit field (28 bits),
- a link field (8 bits),

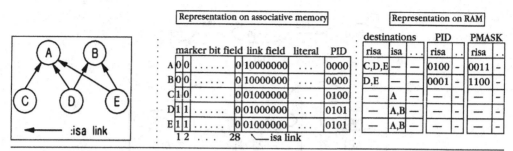

Figure 5.   Data representation of semantic network.

- a parallel marker-propagation identifier abbreviated as *PID* (22 bits),
- a literal field (16 bits).

The marker-bit field stores the results of processing and is used just like a register in microcomputers. There are 28 marker bits in the current implementation.

The link field consists of eight bits; each bit indicates the existence of a primitive link through which the node is connected to other nodes. The four types of primitive links are defined in IXM2 to support basic inference mechanisms in the knowledge-representation language IXL, which is an extended Prolog for IXM2.[15] The primitive links are *isa*, *instance-of* (iso), *destination* (des), and *source* (soc) link. Because the direction of a primitive link must be distinguished, there are eight bits in a link field; from MSB, they are *risa*, *isa*, *riso*, *iso*, *rdes*, *des*, *rsoc*, and *soc*. The "r" signifie s an inverse link. If a node is pointed to by an *isa* link, the node has a *risa* link and the MSB of the link field becomes 1.

The literal field is prepared for a node which is itself a value and is processed by algorithms which exploit the massive parallelism of large associative memories.

The following node information is kept in RAM:

- destination nodes from the node (classified according to the link type),
- eight parallel marker propagation identifiers *(PID)*,
- eight search masks for parallel marker propagation *(PMASK)*.

For example, Figure 5 shows the representation of the semantic network. The node a1 points to the A node via an *isa* link, and the link field of node a1 has '01000000' because the position of '1' in the link field represents that the a1 node has outgoing *isa* links. The destination field on RAM area has 'A' in the *isa* part, because the destination of the a1 node connected by an *isa* link is the A node.

The information for parallel marker propagation such as PID and PMASK are explained in the next subsection.

13.5.2 Marker Propagation

Marker propagation in IXM2 is performed either by a sequential marker propagation or by a parallel marker propagation. A sequential marker propagation is performed by message passing either within an associative processor or among associative processors, using the destination information stored in the RAM area. Parallel marker propagation is performed within an associative processor; it can perform multiple marker propagations from a large fanout node in parallel. (In addition to this parallelism within one AP, parallelism among 64 APs is available.) The rest of this section describes how the parallel marker propagation is performed.

In the network example in Figure 5, marker propagation from node A to a1, abx and aby can be performed using parallel marker propagation. We call the node A a base node and nodes a1, abx, and aby descendant nodes.

The basic idea of parallel marker propagation is to search descendant nodes and write a particular marker bit into them by use of associative memory. The search and parallel write functions are used, specifically to:

(1) assign an identifier to all the descendent nodes of a large fanout node;
(2) assign the same identifier to the large fanout node;
(3) issue (at the base node) the search operation with the identifier to find descendants nodes, and set new marker bits in parallel into descendent nodes just searched.

The identifier in (1) and (2) is a parallel marker-propagation identifier *PID* described earlier. This identifier is provided beforehand by the allocator, and loaded with the network. In the search in (3), a search mask *PMASK*, defined earlier, is used to search only for the bits satisfying the matching.

Using this method, parallel marker propagation is performed in Figure 5 as follows. Suppose parallel marker propagation is to be performed from the A node to a1, abx, and aby nodes. At first, the *PID* and the *PMASK* are retrieved from the SRAM area for the A node: '10' for the *PID* and '10' for the *PMASK*. They are set into the search-data register and the search-mask register of the associative memory respectively, as shown in Figure 6; the hatched bits of the search-mask register show that the bits are not searched. Next, the search operation is executed; the words for a1, abx, and aby node are hit by this search. Finally, the parallel write operation, which is a function of the associative memory, is performed to set a marker-bit 1 at the same time in each of the three words just searched. Similarly, marker-bit 2 of members of set B (nodes abx, aby, and b1) are written using parallel marker propagation.

The data for parallel marker propagations such as *PID* and *PMASK* are prepared by the semantic-network allocator. The allocator recognizes pairs of {a base node, link type, descendent nodes} and gives to each pair a unique identifier (*PID*) and a search mask (*PMASK*). The recognition of such pairs is based on the number of the fanout given to the allocator as a parameter. If the parameter is N, only the nodes with more than N fanout are recognized as the candidates of the parallel marker propagation. For example, in Figure 6, N is 3 and two pairs are recognized: {A, risa, (a1,abx, aby)} and {B, risa, (b1,abx, aby)}.

	marker bit field			link field	literal	PID
A	0	0	......	0 10000000	...	0000
B	0	0	......	0 10000000	...	0000
C	1	0	......	0 01000000	...	0100
D	1	1	......	0 01000000	...	0101
E	1	1	......	0 01000000	...	0101

(a)

SMR ▓▓▓▓▓▓▓▓▓▓▓ 00 ▓▓▓
SDR 00.................0100

(b)

SMR 00▓▓▓▓▓▓▓▓▓▓
SDR 1100.................000

(c)

Figure 6.   Set intersection with associative memory.

13.5.3 Set Intersection

To obtain the intersection of sets A and B we only have to search those words at which both marker-bit 1 and marker-bit 2 are set. Figure 6 (a) shows the status of associative memory after two parallel marker propagations. By setting the search-mask and search-data registers as in Figure 6 (b), the intersection can be found in one search operation. Then, a parallel write operation can be performed to set marker-bit 3 of the abx and the aby nodes. Thus, set intersection can be done in O(1).

13.6 PERFORMANCE EVALUATION

This section discusses the performance of IXM2 in two contexts: basic operations and applications. The IXM2 performance is compared with results from other high-performance machines, such as the Connection Machine (CM-2), the Cray X-MP and the SUN-4/330.

The figures shown below were measured using IXM2, whose clock speed is 17.5 megahertz. In the programs for IXM2, IXM machine instructions are written in occam2. Programs for Cray and SUN are written in C and are optimized with -O4. Programs for CM-2 are written in C* and are optimized. Programs are executed on CM-2, whose PE clock is 7.0 MHz. Execution times have been measured using timers on CM-2 and they show CM busy-time, excluding host-interaction timings.

13.6.1 Basic Operations

13.6.1.1 Association and Set Intersection

Because of the bit-parallel processing in the associative memory, the execution time of the association operation on IXM2 is always 12 μs for any amount of data up to 64K. It is also possible on sequential machines to implement O(1) association time using hashing or indexing.

However, set intersection for large data is very time consuming on sequential machines. Table 3 shows the performance of set intersection on IXM2, CM-2, Cray X-MP and SUN-4/330, where two sets of the same size are intersected.

IXM2 can consistently perform the set intersection in 18μs for any size of data up to 64K; the set intersection is performed in O(1). It is noted that in the case of sematic network larger than 64K nodes, the content of associative memory needs to be swapped with the rest of semantic network stored on SRAM, because IXM2 can process 64K nodes at a time. However, the 64K node size is enough for practical applications of semantic network for the time being, because describing large semantic networks (even for a network of thousands of nodes) is a very hard job. Although CM-2 can also perform the set intersection constantly in 103μs, IXM2 is faster because of bit-parallel associative memory.

Table 3. Execution times of set intersection (μs).

set size	1000	10000	64000
IXM2	18	18	18
CM2	103	103	103
Cray X-MP	1829	7372	39823
SUN-4/330	28998	44332	142827

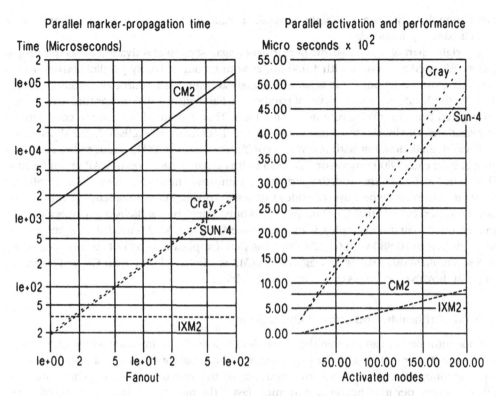

Figure 7. Marker propagation time vs. parallel activation.

Sequential computers become very slow as the data grow larger. It is true even for the Cray, in spite of the indexing algorithm of O(N). Although the Cray is much faster than the SUN-4 because of the vectorization available in the algorithm, there is a difference of three orders of magnitude between IXM2 and Cray in the processing of 64K data.

13.6.1.2 Marker Propagation

Next we compare the performance of marker propagation. First, we compare the time to complete propagation of markers from one node to all descending nodes. The left chart of Figure 7 shows performance by each machine with different fanout from the node. IXM2 is outperformed when only one link exists from the node. However, if an average fanout is over 1.75, IXM2 outperforms the Cray and the SUN-4. (Cray is slower than SUN-4 in marker propagation because of the overhead of recursive procedure calls used in link traverse. Another Cray (Y-MP) was also slower.) If an average fanout is nearly 1, using a parallel machine is not a rational decision in the first place. It should be noted that IXM2 completes propagation at a constant time due to parallel marker-passing capability with associative memory. The parallel-marker propagation by one AP constantly takes $35\mu s$, independent of the number of descendent nodes N. On sequential machines (Cray and SUN-4), computational time increases linearly to the number of fanouts. CM-2 also requires more linear time as fanout increases. This is due to its serial link constraints that markers for each descending node have to be sent in a serial manner. As we have discussed in section 2, CM-2 does not gain advantage of parallelism at each processor. Thus, if average fanout is over 1.75, IXM2 will provide a faster marker-propagation than any other machine. Note that although Cray has a capability of vector parallel processing, its control flow in program is basically sequential.

The right chart of figure 7 shows performance against parallel activation of marker propagation. We used a network with 1,000 nodes with fanout of 10. By parallel activation, we mean that more than one node is simultaneously activated as a source of marker propagation. On the X-axis, we show a level of parallelism. Parallelism 1,000 means that markers are propagated from 1,000 different nodes at a time. Time measured is a time to complete all propagations. Obviously, serial machines degrade linearly to parallelism. IXM2 shows similar linear degradation, but with much less coefficient, because IXM2 needs to fire nodes sequentially at each T800 processor. The data in this graph is based on one AP out of 64 APs. Thus, when all 64 APs are used, the performance improves nearly 64 times. CM-2 has almost constant performance because all nodes can start propagation simultaneously. It is important, however, to note that CM-2 outperforms only when the parallelism exceeds a certain level (about 170 in this example), in case only one AP of the IXM2 is used. This figure would be equivalent to 10,880 with 64 APs, implying that if applications do not require more than 10,880 simultaneous marker propagations, IXM2 is a better choice than CM-2. This tradeoff point, however, changes as average fanout changes.

13.6.1.3 Arithmetic and Logical Operations

Node information can contain the literal field in associative memory when a node is itself a value. This literal field can be processed with bit-serial algorithms for associative memory. Execution time is constant, independent of the number of items. Therefore, the execution time per item becomes extremely fast if the number of data items stored in associative memory is large.

The *less than* operation takes on average $36\mu s$ for the comparison of 32-bit data. This speed seems quite slow when compared with the execution time on sequential computers; for example, it takes $1.25\mu s$ in an Occam2 program run on a T800 transputer at 20 MHz. However, it corresponds to an execution time per datum of 0.56 nanoseconds when each of 64K nodes contains a literal field and is processed in parallel. Although the number of data items available as candidates for the processing is application-dependent, the associative-memory algorithm will surpass the performance on sequential computers if there are at least 100 candidates. The additions for 8-bit data and 16-bit data take $46\mu s$ (0.72 nanoseconds per datum) and $115\mu s$ (1.80 nanoseconds per datum), respectively.

13.6.2 Application

IXM2 applications have been developed for three areas: natural-language processing, knowledge-base processing, and machine learning.

13.6.2.1 Memory-Based Natural-Language Processing

The most active area where IXM2 is used intensively is the natural-language processing, especially a new area called *memory-based machine translation*, or *example-based machine translation*. Carnegie Mellon University and Advanced Telecommunication Research Institute International (ATR) have been using IXM2 for their research independently.

The traditional approach to machine translation has been to rely on extensive rule application. The performances of systems based on this approach are not good because of the serial application of piecewise rules. The performance problem is one of the most serious problems of current MT systems, especially when MT is to be applied to spoken-language translation and other applications that require real-time translation.

The basic idea of memory-based MT systems is to use examples of translation (for example, corpus and pairs of translation in the past) directly in order to carry out the translation. By using this approach on massively parallel computers, the real-time response can be obtained in tasks such as interpreting telephony.

ASTRAL of Carnegie Mellon University is the first memory-based MT system implemented on a massively parallel computer, that is, the IXM2.[16,17] The overall architecture is shown in Figure 8. The memory hierarchy of ASTRAL consists of four layers, represented in semantic networks: a phoneme layer, a phoneme-sequence layer, lexical-entry layer, abstraction hierarchy, and a concept-sequence layer.

Figure 9 shows the example of a phoneme-sequence layer. The figure shows a node for a word 'about' and how the phoneme sequence is represented. The left side of the figure is a set of IXL commands to encode the network in the right side on the IXM2 processor.

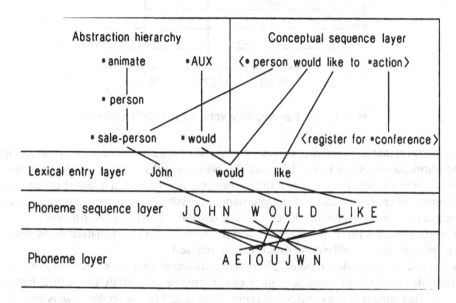

Figure 8.   A semantic network structure for the memory-based parsing.

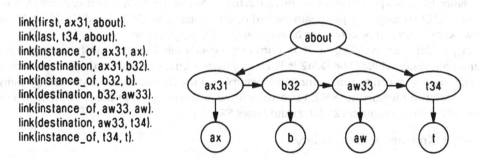

```
link(first, ax31, about).
link(last, t34, about).
link(instance_of, ax31, ax).
link(destination, ax31, b32).
link(instance_of, b32, b).
link(destination, b32, aw33).
link(instance_of, aw33, aw).
link(destination, aw33, t34).
link(instance_of, t34, t).
```

Figure 9.   An example of a phoneme sequence layer and its representation in IXL language.

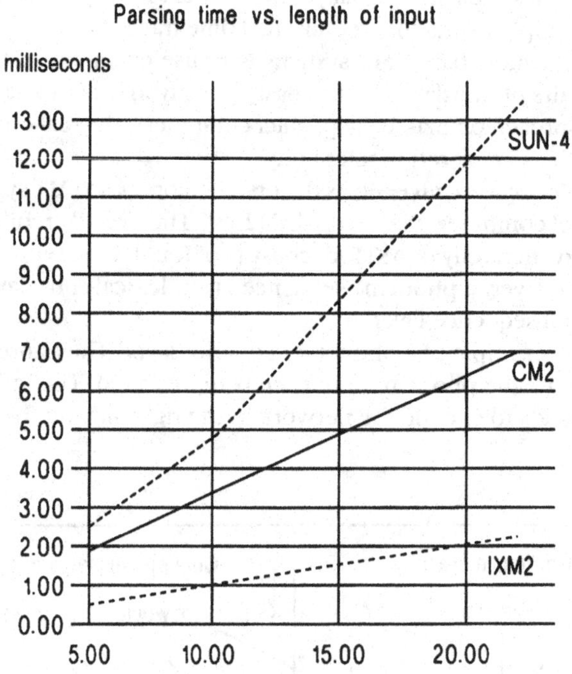

Parsing time vs. length of input

Figure 10. **Parsing time versus input string length.**

Audio input, that is, phoneme, enters into the the phoneme layer and traverses the links to the phoneme-sequence layer. When all the phonemes that form a word enter the network, the word is recognized at the phoneme-sequence layer and a signal is sent to the lexical-entry layer. Thus, when all the phonemes constitute a sentence, a template is recognized at the concept-sequence layer, and it is used for the translation process.

By using IXM2 for these link traverses and the recognition of translation units, the real-time response, that is, millisecond order, can be realized.

In ASTRAL, a network including phonemes, phoneme sequences, lexical entries, abstraction hierarchies, and concept sequences is prepared to translate the natural language sentences that appear in the conference registration task. The vocabulary size is 405 words in one language, and at least 300 sentences in the corpus have been covered. The network has relatively large fanout (40.6).

Figure 10 shows performance of the IXM2, the SUN-4, and the CM-2. Due to a large fanout factor, IXM2 far surpasses processing speed of other machines (SUN-4 and CM-2). SUN-4 is slow because set intersections are heavily used in this application.

In parallel with ASTRAL, ATR is currently developing the example-based machine-translation system (EBMT) on IXM2.[18] Their emphasis is on the target-word selection, where the distance between an input word and examples in the thesaurus are calculated by using the associative memory of IXM2. (The associative processor used in EBMT is the new version with T801 transputer (25 MHz) and faster SRAM.)

13.6.2.2 Knowledge-Base Query

The wine knowledge base was developed, consisting of 277 nodes and 632 links. The sample query elicits wines that belong to Bordeaux wine with the ranking of four stars. Table 4 shows the results on IXM2, CM-2, and SUN-4/330. Although the network is relatively

Table 4. Query processing time (millisec.).

IXM2	CM-2	SUN-4/330
0.8	28.4	3.0

small to take advantage of parallelism, IXM2 performs better than other machines. Maximum parallel activation is 87 in this knowledge base, so that CM-2 would be much slower than IXM2. Also, over 95 percent of computing time by CM-2 was spent on communication to propagate markers between PEs.

13.6.2.3 Genetic-Based Machine Learning

Genetic algorithms are becoming popular as robust and efficient search techniques for AI applications. Genetic-based machine learning is a new paradigm of machine learning using genetic algorithms. GBML is usually implemented in terms of *classifier systems*, which is almost the same structure as the usual production systems. That is, the rule base takes the form of IF-THEN rule and the recognize-act cycles are repeated until the goal is satisfied. The difference from the usual production systems is that the rule base can be "evolved" to the environment by the use of genetic algorithms.

In classifier systems, the matching cycle is the most time-consuming part. Hence, the matching capability of associative memory is essential in implementing calssifier systems that require real-time response. Carnegie Mellon University and Electrotechnical Laboratory have developed a GBML, called GA-1, on IXM2. It has been shown[19] that IXM2 outperforms CM-2 in matching operations.

13.7 DISCUSSIONS

First, the drastic difference of performance in set operation between serial processors (SUN-4 and Cray) and SIMD parallel processors (CM-2 and IXM2) rules out the possibility of serial machines to be used for a large-scale semantic-network processing in which extensive set operations involving over 1,000 nodes are anticipated.

Second, performance comparison in marker propagation indicates that IXM2 exhibits superior performance to CM-2 for many AI applications. IXM2 is consistently faster for processing semantic networks with large fanout, but limited simultaneous node activation. When the average fanout is large, IXM2 has an advantage over CM-2, and CM-2 gains benefits when large simultaneous activations of nodes take place. Let F be an average fanout, and N the number of simultaneously activated nodes in the given task and network. IXM2 outperforms CM-2 when the following equation stands:

$$\frac{T_{CMlink}}{T_{IXMnode}} > \frac{N}{F \times AP}$$

AP is the number of APs used in IXM2, which ranges from one to 64. T_{CMlink} is the time required for the CM-2 to propagate markers for one link from a node. $T_{IXMnode}$ is the time required for the IXM2 to propagate markers from one node to all descending nodes. In this experiment, T_{CMlink} was 800 microseconds (the best value obtained in our experiments; other values obtained include 3,000 microseconds per link), and $T_{IXMnode}$ was 35 microseconds. Of course, this value changes as a system's clock, software, compiler optimization, and other factors change.

The average fanout of actual applications that we have examined (wine database and natural language), were 2.8 and 40.6, respectively. In order for the CM-2 to outperform IXM2, there must be always more than 4,097 (wine database) and 59,392 (natural language) simultaneous activations of nodes. Notice that these figures represent the average "number" of simultaneous activations, not the peak number.

In the wine database, maximum possible parallel activation is 87. In this case, all terminal nodes in the network simultaneously propagate markers. For this task, IXM2 obviously outperforms CM-2. In the natural-language processing, maximum parallelism is 405, in which all words are activated (which is not realistic). Since syntactic, semantic, and pragmatic restriction will be imposed on actual natural-language processing, the number of simultaneous marker propagations would be a magnitude smaller than this figure. Thus, in either case, IXM2 is expected to outperform CM-2, and this expectation has been supported from the experimental results on these applications.

Although the average parallelism throughout the execution would be different in each application domain, it is unlikely that such a large numbers of nodes (4.1K and 59.4K nodes in our examples) continue to propagate markers simultaneously throughout the execution of the application. In addition, when such a large number of nodes simultaneously propagate markers, a communication bottleneck would be so massive that performance of the CM-2 would be far less efficient than speculated from the data in the previous section.

In addition, there are other operations, such as a set operation, logic operation, and arithmetic operation, in which IXM2 has magnitude of performance advantages. Thus, in most AI applications in which processing of semantic networks is required, IXM2 is expected to outperform other machines available today.

13.8 CONCLUSION

In this chapter, we proposed and examined the IXM2 architecture. The most salient features of the IXM2 architecture are (1) an extensive use of associative memory to attain parallelism and (2) full-connection architecture. Particularly, the use of associative memory provides the IXM2 with a truly parallel operation in each node, and nanoseconds-order logical and arithmetic operations.

We have evaluated the performance of the IXM2 associative processor using three basic operations necessary for semantic-network processing: intersection-search, parallel marker-propagation, and logical and arithmetic operations. A summary of results shows:

- Association operations and set intersections can be performed in O(1). IXM2 attains high performance due to bit-parallel processing on each associative memory word.
- Parallel marker propagations from a large fanout node can be performed in O(1) through the use of associative memory, while marker propagation implemented on a sequential computer and CM-2 requires linear time proportional to the number of links along which a marker is passed.
- Arithmetic and logical operations are executed in an extremely fast manner due to the algorithms developed for associative memory. These algorithms fully utilize parallel operations on all words, thus attaining nanoseconds performance in some cases.

Cases where other machines possibly outperform IXM2 has been ruled out, because these situations are implausible in practice. Thus, we can conclude IXM2 is a highly suitable machine for semantic-network processing, a function essential to many AI applications.

Besides the performance of the IXM2, one of the major contributions of this chapter is identification of some of the benchmark criteria for massively parallel machines. While *parallelism* has been a somewhat vague notion, we have clearly distinguished a parallelism in message passing (by a fanout factor) and in simultaneous activation of PEs (by active node number). These criteria are essential in determining which type of machine should be used for what type of processings and networks. For example, we can expect IXM2 to be better on large fanout but not too large simultaneous activations (most AI applications are this type), but CM-2 is better when a fanout is small, but large number of PEs are always active (most scientific computing is this type).

ACKNOWLEDGMENTS

The author gratefully acknowledges the support and the contributions made by Ken'ichi Handa, Tatsumi Furuya, Naoto Takahashi, Hiroaki Kitano, and Takeshi Ogura.

REFERENCES

1. M. Evett, J. Hendler, and W. Anderson, "Massively Parallel Support for Computationally Effective Recognition Queries," *Proc. 11th Nat'l Conf. Artificial Intelligence*, MIT Press, Cambridge, Mass., 1993, p. 297–302.

2. ICOT-JIPDEC AI-Center, *VLKB Project: Preliminary Study*, Japan Information Processing Development Center (JIPDEC), Tokyo, Japan, July 1991.

3. D. Lenart and R. Guha, *Building Large Knowledge-Based Systems*, Addison-Wesley, Reading, Mass., 1989.

4. M.R. Quillian, "Word Concepts: A Theory and Simulation of Some Basic Semantic Capabilities," *Behavioral Sci.*, Vol. 12, 1967, pp. 410–430.

5. D. Moldovan, et al., "SNAP: Parallel Processing Applied to AI," *Computer*, Vol. 25, No. 5, 1992, pp. 39–50.

6. D. Hillis, *Connection Machine*, MIT Press, Cambridge, Mass., 1985.

7. T. Higuchi, et al., "The Prototype of a Semantic Network Machine IXM," *Proc. Int'l Conf. Parallel Processing*, Penn State Press, University Park, Pa., Vol. 1, 1989, pp. 217–224.

8. T. Higuchi, et al., "IXM2: A Parallel Associative Processor," *Proc. 18th Int'l Symp. Computer Architecture*, IEEE CS Press, Los Alamitos, Calif., 1991, pp. 22–31.

9. T. Higuchi, et al., "XM2: A Parallel Associative Processor for Knowledge Processing," *Proc. 9th Nat'l Conf. Artificial Intelligence*, MIT Press, Cambridge, Mass., Vol. 1, 1991, pp. 296–303.

10. D. Touretzky, *The Mathematics of Inheritance Systems*, Morgan Kaufmann, San Mateo, Calif., 1986.

11. S.E. Fahlman, *NETL: A System for Representing and Using Real-World Knowledge*, MIT Press, Cambridge, Mass., 1979.

12. Inmos Ltd., *Transputer Reference Manual*, Prentice-Hall International, Hemel, Hempstead, England, 1988.

13. T. Ogura, et al., "A 20-Kbit Associative Memory LSI for Artificial Intelligence Machines," *IEEE J. Solid-State Circuits*, Vol. 24, No. 4, 1989, pp. 1014–1020.

14. Inmos, *Occam2 Reference Manual*, Prentice-Hall, Englewood Cliffs, N.J., 1988.

15. K. Handa, et al., "Flexible Semantic Network for Knowledge Representation," *J. Information Japan*, Vol. 10, No. 1, 1986, pp. 15–19.

16. H. Kitano and T.Higuchi, "High Performance Memory-Based Translation on IXM2 Massively Parallel Associative Memory Processor," *Proc. 9th Nat'l Conf. Artificial Intelligence*, MIT Press, Cambridge, Mass., Vol. 1, 1991, pp. 149–154.

17. H. Kitano and T.Higuchi, "Massively Memory-Based Parsing," *Proc. 12th Int'l Joint Conf. Artificial Intelligence*, Morgan Kaufmann Pub., San Mateo, Calif., 1991, pp. 918–924.

18. E. Sumita, et al., "Example-Bases Machine Translation on Massively Parallel processor," to appear in *Proc. 13th Int'l Joint Conf. Artificial Intelligence*, Morgan Kaufmann Pub., San Mateo, Calif., 1993.

19. H. Kitano, S. Smith, and T. Higuchi, "GA-1: A Parallel Associative Memory Processor for Rule Learning with Genetic Algorithms," *Proc. Int'l Conf. Genetic Algorithms*, Morgan Kaufmann Pub., San Mateo, Calif., 1991, pp. 311–317.

FURTHER READING

C.C. Foster, *Content Addressable Parallel Processors*, Van Nostrand Reinhold, New York, N.Y., 1976.

Thinking Machines Corp., *Paris Release Note*, ver. 5.2, Thinking Machines Corp., Cambridge, Mass., 1989.

14

An Overview of the Knowledge Crunching Machine

Jacques Noyé

European Computer-Industry Research Centre
Munich, Germany

ABSTRACT

The ambition of the KCM project was to better understand the benefits and limitations of CPU hardware support for Prolog. An experimental approach was taken: a machine, the first desk-top machine to reach one mega-logical inferences per second, was built and the accompanying software developed, including a full-blown incremental Prolog system. This leaves few doubts as to the feasibility of the approach as well as its difficulties. This overview presents the software and hardware architecture of the KCM and gathers evaluation results. The conclusion summarizes the lessons from the experiment.

14.1 INTRODUCTION

The aim of Logic Programming is to provide both a single, simple, and rigorous language and logic, for both expressing and reasoning about problems, as well as actually programming solutions to these problems. The programming language Prolog has been so far the most successful incarnation of Logic Programming. Its success is widely due to the development of a reasonably efficient compiler by D.H.D. Warren,[1] a refinement of which, called the WAM (Warren abstract machine),[2] has become the de facto standard for implementing the language. By itself, however, the breakthrough of the WAM was not sufficient to reach the efficiency of imperative languages such as C. Bridging the gap requires combining advances in compiler and runtime technology, processor design, and parallelism. All three areas have been studied at the European Computer-Industry Research Centre within different projects.

The Knowledge Crunching Machine (KCM) project, started at ECRC in 1987 in collaboration with ECRC's shareholders (Bull, ICL, and Siemens), focused on processor design, while taking advantage of progress made in compiler and runtime technology. The project was motivated by two years of preliminary studies[3-5] that led to the conclusion that the time was ripe for an actual implementation.

The outcome of the project is a single-user, single-task, high-performance back-end processor to be coupled to a UNIX (a registered trademark of AT&T) workstation.[6-9] Although the KCM is dedicated to Prolog, it is not restricted to Prolog and can be seen as a sketch of a tagged general-purpose machine with support for Logic Programming. A complete software environment has been written, including a language-independent kernel and an incremental, Edinburgh-like, Prolog system based on SEPIA,[10] a Prolog system developed at ECRC and targeted to standard UNIX machines. The Prolog system includes a number of advanced features, in particular modules and coroutining.

Four prototype machines were operational in July 1988 and one of the prototypes, with a clock pushed beyond its nominal frequency, was the first desk-top Prolog machine to reach 1 mega-logic inferences per second on deterministic list concatenation. A small series of pilot machines were subsequently built and installed to various academic sites and research institutes by the shareholders.

This overview of the KCM project is organized as follows: Section 2 explains the main design decisions. Sections 3 and 4 present the hardware and software architecture of the KCM. Section 5 gathers evaluation results, including a benefit analysis of the architectural features of the KCM, a performance comparison with ECLiPSe,[11] the successor of SEPIA, running on a SPARCStation II, and a performance comparison with the VLSI-BAM,[12] a recent RISC-based design. We conclude by sketching some important research issues and perspectives. Familiarity with Prolog[13] and the WAM[14] is assumed.

14.2 BASIC DESIGN DECISIONS

14.2.1 A High-Level Architecture

Rationale. The initial and most important design decision was to resort to microprogramming and provide, at the instruction-set level, WAM-like instructions. Evan Tick[15] put forward two main arguments to justify this choice rather than the choice of translating the high-level architecture to a lower-level architecture, for example, one of the emerging RISC (reduced instruction-set computer) architectures.[16]

First, high-speed processors are ultimately limited by memory. It turns out that high-level architectures require less memory bandwidth. Because of the high semantic content of each instruction, fewer instructions are required in order to execute the same task. Moreover, the instruction flow is more regular; the numerous conditional branches encountered during unification can take place at the microcode level and therefore do not perturb the instruction pipeline. The memory system can also be tailored to the data-referencing behavior of the language. The important issues, as far as Prolog is concerned, are (1) the support of its complex memory model, consisting of a *register set*, several *stacks* and a *heap* (by "heap" we mean here the runtime heap; we shall call *global stack* the area called "heap" in the WAM, in order to better correspond to the way it is accessed) and (2) shallow backtracking (that is, backtracking *within* a predicate invocation), which has been shown to be the primary data-memory reference bottleneck of the WAM.[15]

Second, high-level architectures facilitate software development, for example, via simpler and therefore faster compilers. In spite of his confidence in the technology, D. Patterson[16] expresses the concern that RISCs may not provide the same advantages in the cost/performance factor for exploratory environments.

An additional argument was that designing a high level architecture would make it easier to specialize the data paths and capture much of the microparallelism available in each instruction. Also, the technology was well understood and easy to bring into play.[17]

Hardware memory architecture. Reducing memory penalty basically relies on a proper memory hierarchy and an appropriate caching strategy. It turns out that the most classical hierarchy—a register set, local to the execution unit; cache(s), local to the central processing unit; and external memory—fits the memory model of the WAM well.

The idea of a register set, used to perform argument-passing and store the state of the computation, is at the heart of the WAM. A data cache has the good property of being able to catch all types of reference and therefore can cover caching of all the different memory areas of the WAM, including the heap.

Using hardware registers to perform argument-passing straightforwardly suggests separate paths to code and data memory, an organization often referred to as a *Harvard architecture*. Indeed, each source goal, that is, a great part of the source program, is compiled into an argument-passing sequence, basically a sequence of simple load-and-store instructions, with the result that code and data are accessed simultaneously at a high rate. On top of providing twice the memory bandwidth, split code and data caches avoid bad interferences between instruction and data referencing, as demonstrated by Evan Tick.[15]

14.2.2 Modifications to the WAM

The above considerations led us to introduce the following variations to the basic WAM model:

The split-stack model. The KCM assumes a split-stack model. This organization, first suggested by E. Tick and D.H.D. Warren,[15,18] consists of splitting the stack storing the environment and choice-point frames into two separate stacks, an environment and a choice-point stack. This model has the advantage of increasing the locality of environment and choice-point reference. It also fits well with delayed choice-point creation (see below); whereas the standard model imposes a strict order on choice-point and environment creation, the split-stack model makes it possible to start filling an environment before pushing the choice-point onto memory.

Caching choice-point frames. Most of the memory bandwidth loss due to shallow backtracking can be avoided by creating choice-points, virtually, in the register file and pushing them onto memory only when the execution cannot fail any longer. If failure occurs, restoring the computation state is very cheap. A first solution relies on the use of a second, shadow, register set, as in Pegasus.[19] The solution adopted for the KCM, inspired by M. Meier,[20] is slightly less efficient but requires much less hardware. Two new registers are introduced, a backtrack trail pointer and a backtrack program pointer, and the compiler ensures that argument registers are not modified when unification may result in shallow backtracking. Virtual choice-points are then created by simply copying three registers (*top-of-trail*, *environment*, and *global-stack* pointers) into the corresponding backtrack pointers, and setting the backtrack program pointer to the address of the code to be executed in case of failure. In case of failure, a flag *shallow*, set when creating the virtual choice-point, and reset when the virtual choice-point is turned into a real choice-point, indicates whether the state should be restored from a virtual or a real choice-point. In case of success, the flag *choice-point*, set when deep backtracking takes place and reset when a virtual choice-point is created, indicates whether a real choice-point should be created.

Caching environment frames.   In the WAM, permanent variables are allocated a slot in the environment frame. Accessing a permanent variable is always done via an offset in the environment frame. On the KCM, permanent variables may also be allocated a register, as temporary variables. Also, environment frames are not pushed onto memory before the possibility of failure has been discarded.

Environment trimming.   Trimming, a generalization of tail-recursion optimization, or more precisely last-call optimization, makes it possible to reuse permanent variable slots in the environment as soon as these slots are no longer needed. The overall gain over pure last-call optimization is, however, far from being clear. First, the management of the environment stack is more costly. Second, avoiding dangling references may introduce a significant overhead, including numerous memory references because of dereferencing, and may even result in an increase of the global stack (see the handling of *unsafe* variables, in Aït-Kaci's tutorial).[14]

As a result, the KCM does not trim environments eagerly, but rather performs *virtual* trimming at garbage-collection time; a proper layout of the environment frames, with the current size of the environment recorded in all the nonterminal call instructions, as for trimming, allows the garbage collector to distinguish between dead and alive permanent variables.

14.2.3 Implementing Built-in Predicates

Microprogramming the WAM provides all the instructions necessary to execute Prolog programs free of built-in predicates, plus a few predicates, for example, $=/2$, $var/1$, $;/2$, which can be coded in terms of WAM instructions. Implementing a full Prolog system is, however, not possible; even basic facilities like integer arithmetic are missing.

The PLM.   In order to deal with this problem, the instruction set of the PLM, an early WAM-based co-processor developed within the Aquarius project at Berkeley,[21,22] includes a single *escape* instruction that makes it possible to implement built-in predicates in microcode. Most of the time (integer divide and multiply, floating-point arithmetic, I/O, and so forth), the role of *escape* is limited to dumping the necessary arguments and the built-in predicate identifier into a communication area, and subcontracting the work to the host processor.

In such a co-processor approach, sharing the data between the host and the co-processor requires identical data formats on both processors. This means a nonoptimal architectural compromise for at least one of the processors (in the case of the PLM, a Prolog word is restricted to 32 bits). It also means frequent context switches between the co-processor and the host, as well as sharing the memory bandwidth. These points were not acceptable as far as the performance requirements of the KCM were concerned.

PSI-II.   In PSI-II, ICOT's stand-alone Personal Sequential Inference machine,[23] each basic built-in predicate is implemented as a different machine instruction and fully executed by the microprogram of the machine.

This is the best solution, as far as performance is concerned, but a very costly one. On the one hand, the stand-alone approach requires the development of much peripheral hardware and software, and does not make it easy to use existing application software. On the other hand, microprogramming part of the runtime significantly increases the complexity of the system, however good the microprogramming environment may be.

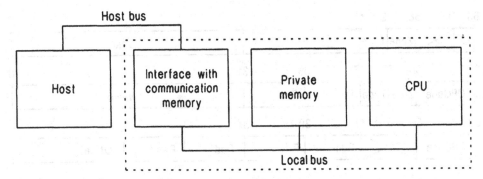

Figure 1. The KCM system.

The KCM. Taking the previous remarks into account, the KCM was designed as a back-end processor, to be connected to a UNIX host, as shown in Figure 1. Thus the KCM acts as a diskless, terminal-less machine with I/O operations supported through remote servers on the host. The whole Prolog runtime can, however, be implemented on the back-end processor. The cost to be paid for such a loose coupling is some limitation on the granularity of host-KCM interactions.

Also, the instruction set of the KCM includes both *Prolog* instructions and *general-purpose* instructions.[24] High-level Prolog instructions, close to the WAM instructions, implement the basic Prolog mechanisms (unification, backtracking, indexing, and cut). Low-level general-purpose instructions constitute a general-purpose instruction set to be used to implement the functionality that the standard WAM does not provide.

The general-purpose instructions, although supporting tagged data, did not need to be tied to Prolog, and therefore make it possible to implement other languages, for example, Lisp or even C, on the KCM. To facilitate such implementations, the KCM kernel and the low-level code-generation tools are language-independent. As a result, although the KCM is dedicated to Prolog, it is not restricted to Prolog, and can be seen as a sketch of a tagged general-purpose machine with support for Logic Programming.

14.2.4 Word Format

A 64-bit tagged architecture. The WAM assumes tagged data words; that is, a basic entity consists of a value plus an additional tag field giving information on the type of the entity.

Most commercial Prolog systems running on general-purpose computers pack tag and value into a 32-bit word, thus reducing the range of virtual addresses and integers. Many tagged architectures store a 32-bit value with a 4-bit to 8-bit tag. The problem is then to switch between this nonstandard word length and the usual 32-bit word format on the host. A solution is to use 40 bits internally but 64 bits externally, that is, in memory and on disk.[25] There are also software systems that use 64 bits to store a Prolog entity; SEPIA is one of them. This solution was adopted for the KCM, which is built as a 64-bit tagged machine: 32 bits for the value part, and 32 bits for the tag part, as shown in Figure 2.

Code words are also 64 bits long. This length has two main benefits. First, it simplifies addressing; there is a single notion of KCM word. Second, the instruction formats can be made regular and simple. Also, apart from the Prolog indexing instructions, all the instruc-

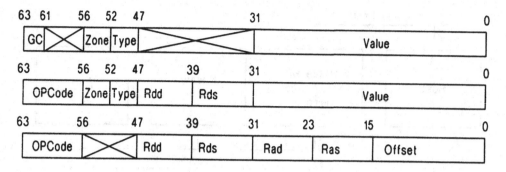

Figure 2.   KCM word format.

tions can be one word long. These are common RISC features. A simple encoding of the in-struction fields removes instruction-decoding time from a critical execution path and saves decoding hardware, at the cost of a slight degrading of memory behavior.

The representation of unbound variables.   The WAM has a self-referencing represen-tation of variables; that is, the value of an unbound variable is its own address. Also, un-bound variables and references do not require different tags. This feature is very convenient; for example, a variable can be loaded in a register without any tag manipulation.

Supporting *debugging* and *metaterms*, used for the implementation of coroutining (see Section 4.2), requires dropping this representation, so that an unbound variable can be as-sociated information like its print name, for debugging purposes, or, more generally, a pointer to a term on the global stack, as is the case with metaterms. Different tags are then necessary to recognize unbound variables, metaterms, and references.

This requirement also means that the trail, a stack used to remember the bindings to be undone on backtracking, becomes a *value* trail; that is, it stores both the address of the bind-ing and its previous value, instead of the address alone.

14.2.5 Practical Hardware and Software Issues

Size.   All the boards composing the KCM were designed to fit into the cabinet of the diskless desktop workstation selected as the host of the prototype systems, that is, a Bull DPX-1000, built around a Motorola 68020. [The pilot systems were also hosted by Siemens MX-300 (NS 32532-based) and ICL PWS-80 (Intel 386) machines.] The CPU was imple-mented on one large printed-circuit board (510 × 310 cm). The interface and the main memory are separate boards of double-Eurocard format.

Technology.   The KCM was implemented using standard TTL (transistor-transistor logic) and CMOS (complementary metal-oxide semiconductor) off-the-shelf components. Top-of-the-range ASIC (application-specific integrated-circuit) technology was not considered worthwhile, in spite of its performance advantage, for an exploratory project. Nevertheless, two small 1.5um CMOS ASIC chips were used in order to fulfill the size requirements.

A Single-task system.   The objective was essentially to simplify the design of the mem-ory system. The absence of context-switch made it possible to implement virtual caches, avoiding a systematic address-translation phase, and to store the whole page table on the processor, getting rid of the usual translation lookaside buffer mechanisms.

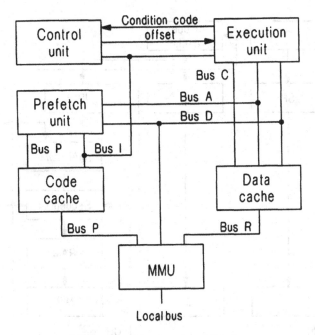

Figure 3. Top level architecture.

14.3 HARDWARE ARCHITECTURE

The data paths of the KCM, shown in Figure 3, follow directly from the above-mentioned considerations. It is a Harvard architecture: a prefetch unit connected to a code cache, and an execution unit connected to a data cache. In between the caches and memory, the memory-management unit deals with address translation and protection. A centralized microcoded control unit drives the processor. The following sections examine these different units in more detail. Further details can be found in reports cited in reference.[26-28]

14.3.1 Control and Pipelining

Figure 4 shows the basic micropipelining and macropipelining.

Micropipeline. Micro-instructions are issued at the rate of one micro-instruction per cycle; while the current micro-instruction, held in the micro-instruction register (MIR), is executed, the address of the next instruction is computed and the instruction read from the microcode RAM (8K × 152 bits). Apart from sequential execution, the control flow can be altered in sophisticated ways, including subroutine calls, conditional execution, and 16-way branch-address calculation.

Macropipeline. The macropipeline is a conventional fetch-decode-execute pipeline. The register TP holds the address of the currently executing instruction, stored in the instruction register (IR), and SP the address of the next instruction, stored in the instruction buffer (IB). The program pointer (P) points to the instruction being fetched from the code cache.

In order to cope with the latency of the cache, instruction fetching is split into two stages: a cache-addressing stage, and a cache-access stage. Decoding involves computing

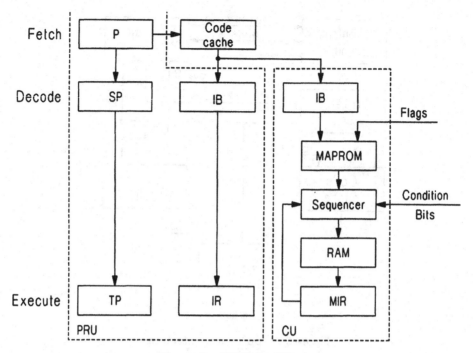

Figure 4.   KCM pipelining.

the address of the microcode routine corresponding to the instruction held in IB. The usual scheme consists of using the instruction opcode as an address into a mapping memory (here a programmable ROM).

In the KCM, five additional bits are taken into account, a macro-interrupt bit, a single-step bit, and Prolog status flags (unification-mode, shallow, and choice-point flags). Specialized entry points can then be associated with each possible configuration of these bits, which therefore do not need to be tested at execution time.

Whereas the first three stages of the macropipeline are always one cycle long, the execute stage has a variable length. The minimum length is one cycle, corresponding to many general-purpose instructions (for example, register transfer, logical and simple integer arithmetic instructions, data write operations). There is no maximum length; many Prolog instructions involve dereferencing, which is an unbound operation.

The basic three-cycle latency of prefetching can be reduced in two cases. First, in the case of control-flow instructions using immediate addressing, specific hardware decoding of the instruction opcode makes it possible to anticipate the pipeline break during the decode stage, and reduce the latency to two cycles. Secondly, the microcoding of conditional control-flow instructions favors the branch-not-taken path; the pipeline does not stall and the instruction costs one cycle. The branch-taken path is then slightly more costly (four cycles) than a standard pipeline break.

As for accessing the code cache, a data-cache access takes two cycles. Only the first cycle is visible in case of a write operation; the actual write is performed transparently by the cache hardware. When microprogramming, read operations can be pipelined (the next address can be sent while getting the previous data). This pipelining cannot be done, however, at the macrocode level; data-load instructions take two cycles.

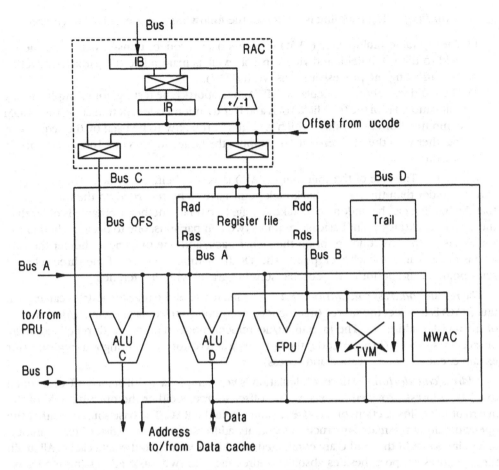

Figure 5. The execution unit.

14.3.2 The Execution Unit

Basic data processing. A basic data processing operation consists of the following operations:

(1) Two words A and B are read from the 64 × 64-bit register file (A can also come from the prefetch unit in case of immediate addressing).

(2) Binary data manipulation is performed on A and B, or unary data manipulation is performed on B, with A used as input to address calculation (which includes plain transfers of A and B to C and D, respectively).

(3) The results, C and D, are written back into the register file.

A conventional arithmetic logic unit (ALU) and floating-point unit (FPU) are used to deal with IEEE standard arithmetic and logical operations. These operations only concern the value part of a word. The tag of the result is simply obtained by passing through the tag of B. The ALU and FPU status flags are stored in a special 32-bit register, the processor status word, together with all the other status flags of the machine (for example, the Prolog flags).

Tag handling. Tag handling is limited to the following few specialized operations:

1) The tag-value multiplexer (TVM) can pass data through, transfer data from the tag field to the value field, and vice versa, as well as manipulate the garbage-collection bits, affecting the processor status word (PSW).
2) The multi-way address calculator (MWAC) supports type testing, for example, during unification. From the type fields of A and B and a microcode function code, this PROM computes a three-bit value, which is stored in the PSW to be used by the sequencer, together with the ALU zero bit, to compute the target address of a 16-way microcode branch.

The trail. The role of the trail unit (TRAIL) is very specific to Prolog. The binding of variables older than the current backtrack point have to be recorded on the trail stack so that the binding can be undone on backtracking. Deciding whether a variable is older than the current backtrack point basically requires two comparisons, one to decide whether the variable is on the environment or on the global stack, and one to decide whether the variable is older than the backtrack point. The TRAIL maintains a copy of the three relevant stack pointers and performs the comparisons in parallel with dereferencing.

The register address calculation unit. The main role of the register address calculation unit (RAC) is to select the source (microcode, macrocode or internal increment/decrement) of the register addresses. The increment/decrement mode, together with pipelined memory access, supports (in microcode) the fast saving and restoring of contiguous registers (for example, choice-point creation and access).

Address calculation. Address calculation is very simple: a 16-bit signed offset is added to a base address provided on bus A. The offset source is either the operand field of the macro or micro-instruction, or an offset coming from the RAC. The base source is either the operand field of the macro-instruction (absolute addressing) or the register file. An important point is that both A and C are connected, as address inputs, to the data cache. All in all, these features support, besides absolute addressing, the two basic addressing modes required by Prolog:

- a pre- and post- increment/decrement addressing mode to access stacks growing in either direction,
- an indexed addressing mode to access control frames (for example, choice-point and environment) and symbol table frames (for example, functor and procedure descriptors).

14.3.3 The Prefetch Unit

The prefetch unit, shown in Figure 6, supports the pipeline described in Section 3.1. P can be incremented every cycle with the registers SP, TP, IB and IR all clocked.

P can alternatively take its value from the value field of the macro-instruction (instruction buffer IB) or from the execution unit via D (that is, either from a register or from memory). Also, SP, the address of the next instruction, can be sent to the execution unit via D (that is, either to a register or to memory). These basic data paths make it possible to implement efficiently both Prolog control-flow mechanisms (that is, continuation and backtracking) as well as a standard call/return mechanism.

Additional multiplexer inputs are used, together with the prefetch unit-execution unit connection, for code access, instruction emulation, interrupt handling, injecting constants from the macro-instruction to the execution unit (EXU), and supporting the Prolog indexing instructions.

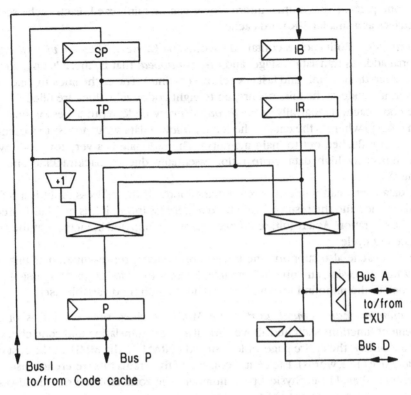

Figure 6. The prefetch unit.

14.3.4 The Memory System

Semantics of an address. The KCM uses word addressing; a KCM address is, as any KCM word (Figure 2), 64 bits long. The 28 least significant bits of the value part of the address cover two virtual spaces of 2 Gbytes each, one for code, one for data. Each virtual space is accessible via a specific set of load/store operations; incremental compilation can then store new instructions directly in the code cache without any cache flush or memory management operation.

In the case of a data address, the zone field of the tag indicates to which *zone* the address is supposed to belong. More precisely, a zone is a contiguous segment of the virtual space with an associated start-address and end-address as well as valid types for read access and write access.

For instance, in KCM-SEPIA, an integer is never valid. Also, since compound terms are stored on the global stack, an address with type list or structure can only address the global stack. There are 16 possible zones, with zone 0 illegal and zone 1 reserved by the kernel for kernel data. Each main data area of the system (heap, environment stack, control stack, and so forth) is mapped onto a different zone.

Zones provide an additional protection mechanism at the virtual level. On each access to the data cache, the consistency of the type, zone, and value of the access is checked. This mechanism is used to detect stack overflow and trigger garbage collection.

Zones are also used to implement a kind of cheap set-associativity. The data cache is divided into eight sections, indexed by the most significant three bits of the zone field; that is, there are two zones in each section. The different zones can then be allocated into different zone pairs so that mutual interferences can be minimized. Each cache section actually behaves as a smaller 1-Kword cache.

The caches.   Both caches contain 8 Kwords (64 Kbytes). They are *virtual*, avoiding an additional address translation stage, and *direct-mapped*; that is, there is no associativity in order to keep them simple and fast (1-cycle access time). The cache lines are one word long. However, if a code-cache miss occurs, up to eight code-cache lines are filled.

The code cache is logically *write-through* (every code write access is flushed out to main memory) whereas the data cache is *copy-back* (a data write access to a cached virtual address is not flushed out to main memory). The rationale is a very low code write ratio and an unusually high data write ratio, essentially due to backtracking and structure copying.[15]

The data cache can work in dereferencing mode. If the address input is a reference, a read takes place and the result is again used as address input; if it is not, hardwired control aborts the operation. As a result, reference chains are followed in memory at the rate of one reference per cycle.

The data cache also supports the non-self-referencing representation of unbound variables. When accessing an unbound variable, it can return, for argument-passing purposes, a reference to the unbound variable rather than the unbound variable itself.

The memory-management unit.   The MMU provides the two levels of memory-management functions sketched above: virtual address translation and zone check. For the sake of simplicity, the entire page table is stored in RAM, in the MMU, at the cost of a quite large page size (16 Kwords). Each entry consists of five status bits (reference history and access rights) and an 11-bit physical page number. The zone table entries are also stored in RAM. Zones have a granularity of 4 Kwords.

Main memory.   The main memory is implemented, using SMD technology, with components mounted on both sides. The design allows for one or two boards with size 16, 32, 64, or 128 Mbytes. Pilot systems were configured with a single 32-Mbyte board using 1-Mbit chips.

The main memory is 32 bits wide. Page mode is used to access two 32-bit words at a time and form a KCM word. A physical memory access via a cache is in the order of 1 microsecond.

14.3.5 The Interface Board

The interface board is the sole mechanism by which the KCM can communicate with the outside world. It provides 4 Mbytes of dual-ported memory, which can be accessed from both the host and the KCM side as well as a programmable timer accessible from KCM. The interface supports interrupting the KCM by the host, and vice versa. It also supports initializing and controlling the KCM via specific configuration and service mechanisms.

14.4 SOFTWARE ARCHITECTURE

Figure 7 gives an overall picture of the KCM software system. This system consists of:

(1) OS software, split between the KCM kernel, on the KCM, and software, on the host, which provides the KCM with standard UNIX services such as secondary storage, file, and terminal access.

(2) KCM-SEPIA, a Prolog system that runs entirely on the KCM, on top of the kernel.

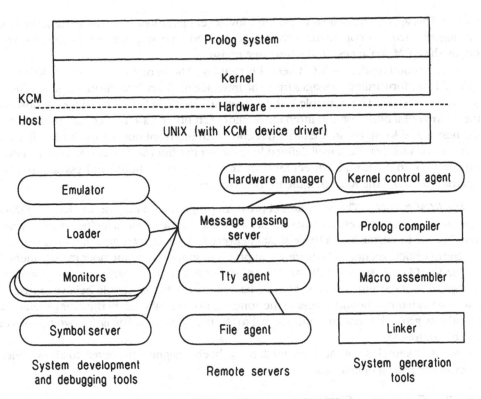

Figure 7. KCM software architecture.

(3) System-debugging and system-development tools, used for low-level system development and debugging, as well as bootstrapping.

14.4.1 Operating System Software

Host software. The UNIX host kernel contains a small driver to support delivery of interrupts between the KCM and a user process on the host, and mapping of the dual-ported interface memory, including interface registers, into the address space of a user-level process on the host. Aside from this driver, all host code for dealing with the KCM operates at user level in order to facilitate the connection of the KCM to different host machines.

A message-passing system on the host is provided to allow a number of processes to communicate with each other and the KCM. Agents can be dynamically added and removed from the system. Blocking and nonblocking communication is supported. The system is broadcast-based with message filtering to reduce overheads. Broadcasting facilitates monitoring; the agent monitoring message traffic, for debugging or development purposes, can be connected at any time.

The file and tty agents handle remote file and terminal input/output operations on behalf of the KCM.

Communication between the KCM and the host. There are two modes for communication between the KCM and the host software. The first mode is used for initial booting of the KCM kernel and for testing and debugging of the KCM at the microcode and hardware levels. Requests from agents wishing to communicate with the KCM (such as a monitor or a loader for stand-alone binary files) are handled by a hardware-access-manager agent

(HAM). This agent knows how to perform low-level operations, such as starting the clock, loading microcode, stepping through macrocode, and accessing internal registers and memory on the KCM, via access to the interface registers.

In the second mode, the KCM kernel is running. The kernel control agent (KCA) is responsible for forwarding messages from the interface memory into the message-passing system and vice versa. The principle is the following. The KCM kernel provides the host with the address of a buffer on the interface memory (empty in case of a communication from the host to the KCM, full in the other direction). An interrupt notifies the host of the availability of this address, in a well-defined location on the interface board. KCA transfers the data, from or to the host, by direct memory access, resets the buffer address, and sends an interrupt to notify the KCM that the transfer has been done.

The KCM kernel. The KCM kernel provides programs running on the KCM UNIX-like operating-system services, via a system call interface. These services include an abstract-file interface for input/output, reliable signal delivery to user-defined handlers with provision for cheap critical sections, debugging and profiling support, and memory management.[29]

The KCM kernel supports the memory model of the KCM. In particular, it is possible to specify, at runtime and on a zone-by-zone basis, how the kernel should behave in case of a trap due to an out-of-bound access to the zone: register a fatal error in the user program, automatically grow the zone, or send a signal to the user program. The latter two options can also be combined.

The KCM kernel is not multithreaded. It has been designed, however, to allow concurrency in the paging operations.

14.4.2 The Prolog System

KCM-SEPIA. KCM-SEPIA is an incremental Edinburgh-like Prolog system that provides the user with a large subset of SEPIA (about 300 built-in predicates), including the following advanced features:

(1) *Coroutining.* Delay declarations define the condition under which a call should be delayed, with resuming taking place when unification results in negating the condition. This modification of the strict left-to-right computation rule of Prolog makes it possible, for example, to get the efficiency of standard backtracking on plain generate-and-test programs or to avoid infinite loops, thus preserving completeness.[30]

(2) *Event handling.* A general and flexible event-handling mechanism connects synchronous events (raised by the program itself, for example, on an incorrect argument to a built-in predicate) and asynchronous events (external to the program, for example, interrupts) to user-defined event handlers.[31]

(3) *A predicate-based module system.* This system facilitates the structuring of large applications, while solving the contradictory requirements of free access for meta-programming purposes and information-access restrictions.[32]

KCM-SEPIA runs on top of the KCM kernel. It is divided into two layers, the runtime layer and the Prolog layer.[33]

The runtime layer is loaded at boot time by the kernel. It is the core of the system. It maintains the Prolog runtime structures: the functor and procedure tables, a low-level runtime database based on property lists, I/O stream descriptors, and an asynchronous event-handler table. It includes basic event-handling and memory-management facilities as well as a Prolog loader. The Prolog loader is in particular used to load incrementally the binary object files composing the upper Prolog layer.

The Prolog layer implements the built-in predicates of KCM-SEPIA. Whereas the runtime layer is static, the Prolog layer can be modified incrementally, greatly facilitating the development of the Prolog system. The Prolog layer includes, quite classically, an incremental compiler, a reader/writer, a debugger, a predicate and internal indexed database (based on the runtime database), and a garbage collector. Coroutining is also implemented at this level. Note that there is no interpreter; the debugger debugs compiled code.[34] The following paragraphs focus on details specific to the KCM.

Stack management and garbage collection. The zone mechanism makes it possible to closely match the virtual space allocated to a stack with the actual size of the stack. M.L. Ross and K. Ramamohanarao have shown that this mechanism drastically reduces page traffic.[35]

The Prolog stacks are initially spread over the whole virtual space, so that a collision is practically excluded, and allocated a limited number of virtual pages. The behaviors of the corresponding zones are set so that the zones are automatically extended, with a notification sent to KCM-SEPIA. This notification is used to keep memory-usage statistics and trigger garbage collection.

Garbage collection, however, is not triggered at each stack expansion but rather after a user-defined amount of global stack has been used up or if physical memory is about to be exhausted. Once garbage has been collected, unused pages, beyond stack tops, are deallocated.

Note that the actual garbage collection cannot occur right on zone growth (which may happen at any time during the execution), but must be delayed until specific points in the execution, namely procedure calls and exits, where the state of the computation (for example, the sources of alive data) is well defined. This delay is achieved by using a PSW bit, set by the signal handler dealing with zone growth, and tested at all the procedure calls and exits. This test, thanks to careful microprogramming, can be done at no cost. When the bit is set, the few registers necessary to resume the execution (basically a program pointer and, on a procedure call, the arguments of the call) are saved, and garbage collection can take place.

This scheme has to be contrasted with the usual software implementations, which rely on explicit overflow checks impeding execution speed.[36]

Another interesting feature of the garbage collector, common to SEPIA and KCM-SEPIA, is its use of 64-bit data words. The possibility of storing a full address plus two garbage-collection bits in any pointer tag makes it possible to build relocation chains during the mark-and-link phase, and thus perform collection in a single pass.[37]

The Prolog compiler. The incremental Prolog compiler bears much resemblance to the compiler of M. Carlsson,[36] for example, construction of an abstract tree, compilation of control structures (including cut) by source transformation, flattening of terms, and support of shallow backtracking. There are, however, significant differences.

For example, register allocation takes place during code generation rather than in subsequent pass, implementing a variant of the algorithm of G. Janssens et al.[38] Also, indexing is done prior to clause compilation. Knowing the indexed argument, selected by the compiler, makes it possible to get rid of redundant unification instructions during clause compilation. Compound terms in the body are compiled in a breadth-first manner, as described by M. Meier.[39]

Finally, arithmetic expressions can be compiled in different modes. In debugging mode, arithmetic expressions are interpreted. By default, they are translated into a series of primitive predicates (for example, Z *is* $X + Y$ is compiled as '+'$(X, Y, Z1)$, $Z = Z1$). When running in coroutining mode, these primitive predicates delay if not sufficiently instantiated;

they raise an error otherwise. For experimental purposes, arithmetic can also be fully compiled in-line, in which case it cannot coroutine, and simply prints a message and fails when an error occurs. A further optimization consists of getting rid of generic arithmetic. Note that, in all cases, arithmetic expressions are type-checked at runtime.

Coroutining. The implementation of coroutining is based on the following sketchy ideas. Delay declarations for a given predicate are translated into normal Prolog clauses, which are prepended to the clauses making up the predicate. This translation is made possible by the introduction of a variant of freeze/2,[40] *freeze(Goal, Vars, NVVars)*, whose semantics are: delay *Goal* until any variable of *Vars* is unified or any variable of *NVVars* is instantiated to a nonvariable term. The link between variables and frozen goals is kept via attributed variables,[41] called metaterms in (KCM-)SEPIA. The unification of metaterms is recorded on a special stack, whose lifetime is limited to a procedure call; in particular it is reset on backtracking, and sets the same PSW bit as the garbage collector. At the next procedure call or exit, a metaterm handler will then retrieve the frozen goals attached to the bound variables and wake them up if necessary.

The point is that very little hardware and firmware support is necessary. As already mentioned, the self-referencing representation of variables has to be dropped and a new tag introduced. Unification instructions include a new case for metaterms, similar to the ordinary case, except that some information has to be pushed onto a special stack. Also, this stack has to be reset on backtracking. Finally the same mechanism can be used to indicate the necessity for a garbage collection or the necessity of coroutining. This mechanism can actually be seen as a general way to resynchronize asynchronous events with the Prolog execution. Handling these events is then slightly delayed but cheaper.

Also, hardware and firmware support, (for example, support for dereferencing in the cache and microcoded multiway branch), makes it possible to completely avoid slowing down part of the execution, using standard Prolog, when another part resorts to coroutining.

14.4.3 System Debugging and Development Tools

A prerequisite to the development of KCM assembly code was the availability of the associated software tools on the host: assembler, linker, and loader. The assembler provides recursive macrocapabilities, conditional assembly, typed expressions, and support for a language-definable symbol-attribute system.[42] A separate preprocessor further supports basic loop and conditional constructs. The loader connects to the message-passing system. It is used to download stand-alone programs, for example, the KCM kernel, to the KCM. For bootstrapping purposes, the Prolog compiler can also run on the host, on top of SEPIA.

Several monitor agents helped debug the system at different levels: micro-code, macrocode, or Prolog. The latter, called the runtime debugger, relies on the kernel-debugging support, via the runtime layer of KCM-SEPIA and the message-passing system, to safely access the registers and memory of the KCM, perform single-stepping, and set breakpoints. It is written in Prolog and runs (on the host) on top of SEPIA. It is therefore able to print KCM Prolog data in its Prolog form. Its extensibility made it easy to add a number of modules specific to the main runtime data structures. The runtime debugger was especially valuable when tracking down problems in the runtime layer, or problems due to incorrect compiled code that could not be pinned down by the Prolog debugger on the KCM. A symbol-server agent supports symbolic debugging within the macromonitor and the runtime debugger.

Table 1. Software size.

Language	KCM	Host	
Prolog	20,000	2,000	15%
C		50,000	33%
KCM ass.	44,000		29%
ucode	34,000		23%
Total	98,000	52,000	

An emulator reproduces the behavior of the KCM, with perfect caches, at the instruction-set level. The emulator allowed validation of the instruction set and testing of major parts of the system long before the hardware and the kernel were available. It was later used to gather execution-profile statistics for evaluation.

14.4.4 Implementation Languages

Four main languages were used to implement the system: C and Prolog on the host; Prolog, assembly code, and microcode on the KCM. Table 1 gives the approximate size of the software (firmware included) and shows the respective shares of the four implementation languages. The sizes are given in number of lines (blank lines and comments excluded).

Quite a lot of code was developed for the host; the macro-assembler is the biggest C program, with 12,000 lines. Also, the weight of firmware and assembly code is very important. The kernel and the KCM-SEPIA runtime layer have been totally implemented in assembly code. They are respectively 13,000 and 10,000 lines long. The Prolog layer of KCM-SEPIA also includes 10,000 lines of assembly code, most of it due to the debugger and the garbage collector. The rest of it is essentially microcode test programs. Finally, more than half of the firmware is also devoted to test programs.

14.5 EVALUATION

14.5.1 Benefit Analysis of Architectural Features

The hardware evaluation[8,43] gives some insight into the performance benefit associated with each of the main architectural features of the KCM. The instrumentation facilities of the emulator made it easy to use a *what-if* approach: the performance degradation was quantified on the basis that a specific part of the hardware is removed or changed.

Table 2 summarizes the results on a set of 22 standard benchmark programs.[43] These programs do not contain built-in predicates other than simple type-testing and arithmetic predicates. The arithmetic predicates were compiled in-line with generic arithmetic.

Removing the facility of the CPU to simultaneously handle tag and value and reducing the data paths of the execution unit and data cache to 32 bits accounts for a performance loss of 60 percent. Without a Harvard architecture and the separate access paths to code and data, the speed of the KCM would decrease by 56 percent, not taking hit ratio degradation into account. Omitting stack support (address calculation and four-port register file) leads to a degradation of 53 percent. The write policy of the data cache has an important influence (50 percent) on the performance as well.

Table 2.   Hardware evaluation of the KCM.

Hardware Feature		Loss
Tagged Architecture		60%
Harvard Architecture		56%
Stack Oriented CPU		53%
Copy-Back Data Cache		50%
Unification and Switch (multi-way branch on tag)	23%	
Prolog Flags (flag dependent execution)	11%	
Dereferencing (following reference chain)	10%	
Trail Operation (pointer comparisons)	7%	
Load Term (argument passing)	6%	
Choice-point (creation/restoring)	2%	
Prolog Support Total		59%

The specific Prolog hardware support sums up to a total of 59 percent. The complexity, in terms of number of gates, of this hardware is small, compared to other architectural features, and has therefore the best performance/cost ratio, but is not sufficient to make a fast machine.[42]

The hardware evaluation also focused on memory behavior and the design of appropriate cache systems, which, because processor speed increases faster than main memory speed, is bound to very much affect performance. The study suggests that some degree of associativity in the code cache may be worthwhile, providing that the cycle time is not impacted too much. Splitting the data cache into sections is shown to perform well for small caches of up to 16 Kwords. A simple direct-mapped cache is then more efficient because of the under-utilization of some sections. Although associative caches are not well adapted to a stack-reference model,[44] some degree of associativity may alleviate, in the case of bigger caches, the weight of interferences. Finally, the time spent on cache misses is shown to be mainly due to write misses, hence the idea of introducing a write buffer after the cache.

14.5.2 The KCM versus ECLiPSe on a SUN SPARCStation II

ECLiPSe.   ECLiPSe (ECRC Common Logic Programming System)[11] integrates within a single system the facilities of SEPIA (compiler, coroutining, polished user interface), Mega-Log (persistence),[45] and Opium (extensible debugging environment).[46] The basic reason why ECLiPSe provides a better basis for comparison than SEPIA 3.0, the reference version of SEPIA as far as KCM-SEPIA is concerned, is that the emulator has been enhanced to use threaded code and make better use of the registers of the SPARC, therefore getting closer to the mode of operation of the KCM, while not altering any language features or important implementation decisions (like 64-bit words). Note that the compiler has also been further enhanced (peephole optimization and indexing) so that it generates code of better quality than the compiler of KCM-SEPIA.

Benchmark figures.   Our comparisons will be based on what will be referred to as the Aquarius benchmark suite. This is a set of benchmark programs put together from a number of different sources as part of the Aquarius project (University of California at Berkeley). This suite is well known in the Prolog community; it has, among others, been used to assess the performance of the BAM processor,[12] the Aquarius Prolog Compiler,[47] and PARMA, a Prolog compiler for the MIPS RISC architecture.[48,49] It is also interesting in that it includes programs of different sizes and programming styles, and does not discard the use of important built-in predicates such as arg/3, functor/3, or write/1, which often represent, as shall be seen, an important share of the execution time. Note that versions of the programs *flatten* and *sdda* without calls to write/1 have been added to the initial benchmarks to get a better feel for the weight of this predicate.

Table 3 compares the speed (CPU time in milliseconds) and static code size (in bytes) of the KCM and ECLiPSe running on a SUN SPARCStation II, a fast SPARCStation built around a 40-MHz SPARC processor with a 64-Kbyte instruction-and-data, direct-mapped, cache.

The execution times have been obtained by incrementally compiling and running each program one after another in a repeat/fail loop such that each program runs about 20 seconds. This procedure guarantees that the timing intervals are well above the clock accuracy. Moreover, it averages some cache behavior due to the initial state of the cache(s). (A further step would be to repeat the process in order to also average the influence of differ-

Table 3.   The KCM versus ECLiPSe/SPARCStation2.

Benchmark	KCM-SEPIA 5.1		ECLiPSe 3.2.1				
	speed (ms)	size (bytes)	speed (ms)	absolute	scaled	size (bytes)	
boyer	3927.00	16792	5970.00	(1.52)	(4.86)	34004	(2.03)
browse	2518.00	5144	7980.00	(3.17)	(10.14)	5180	(1.01)
chat_parser	376.00	51632	1250.00	(3.32)	(10.64)	77220	(1.50)
crypt	28.50	3472	30.40	(1.07)	(3.41)	3432	(0.99)
deriv	0.35	6808	1.08	(3.09)	(9.87)	10048	(1.48)
fast_mu	5.20	2784	13.10	(2.52)	(8.06)	3112	(1.12)
flatten	11.50	8072	8.38	(0.73)	(2.33)	9768	(1.21)
flatten_nowrite	6.12	7928	6.88	(1.12)	(3.60)	9616	(1.21)
meta_qsort	25.70	3464	38.20	(1.49)	(4.76)	5100	(1.47)
mu	2.22	1696	7.78	(3.50)	(11.21)	2336	(1.38)
nand	107.00	33600	216.00	(2.02)	(6.46)	43092	(1.28)
nreverse	0.83	904	2.70	(3.25)	(10.41)	556	(0.62)
poly_10	242.00	4440	565.00	(2.33)	(7.47)	6580	(1.48)
prover	2.94	4600	8.23	(2.80)	(8.96)	7560	(1.64)
qsort	3.00	1520	5.70	(1.90)	(6.08)	896	(0.59)
queens_8	29.40	1264	31.70	(1.08)	(3.45)	1328	(1.05)
query	26.80	2616	30.20	(1.13)	(3.61)	3372	(1.29)
reducer	306.00	15736	357.00	(1.17)	(3.73)	20852	(1.33)
reducer_nowrite	184.00	15640	336.00	(1.83)	(5.84)	20692	(1.32)
sdda	22.70	12416	16.40	(0.72)	(2.31)	14988	(1.21)
sdda_nowrite	2.64	10296	3.56	(1.35)	(4.32)	12824	(1.25)
sendmore	869.00	2328	781.00	(0.90)	(2.88)	2508	(1.08)
serialise	1.78	1968	3.84	(2.16)	(6.90)	2288	(1.16)
simple_analyser	154.00	21392	194.00	(1.26)	(4.03)	24724	(1.16)
tak	1960.00	528	1520.00	(0.78)	(2.48)	572	(1.08)
unify	15.40	12376	24.90	(1.62)	(5.17)	15512	(1.25)
zebra	228.00	2632	385.00	(1.69)	(5.40)	2696	(1.02)
average				(1.83)	(5.87)		(1.23)
standard deviation				(0.88)	(2.81)		(0.29)

ent relative locations, in the direct-mapped caches, of the procedures making up the programs.). On the KCM, the programs have been compiled with default arithmetic compilation.

Ratios are relative to the KCM, that is, a factor greater than 1 indicates that the KCM is faster (speed) or that its code is more compact (size). Two speed ratios are given: an absolute one and a scaled one, the latter compensating for the difference of cycle time between the KCM and the SPARC. The idea is to abstract, as far as can be achieved, from the implementation technology. Let us note, however, that scaled ratios are bound to be favorable to the KCM for two reasons. First, the scaling factor does not apply to main-memory access. Secondly, a much faster clock may require some simplifications of the architecture detrimental to the performance.

Results.   As can be seen from the table, the KCM outperforms ECLiPSe running on a SPARCStation II by an average factor close to 2. This is quite a good result, considering the technology of the KCM and the relative merits of the compilers, all the more as most of the discrepancy between the different programs can be explained by the weight of built-in predicates, as illustrated by Figure 8, which relates absolute speed ratios to the percent of time spent executing built-in predicates. These measures are based on run-time profiling.

In terms of scaled ratio, the KCM is an order of magnitude faster on programs free of built-in predicates, with the performance degrading regularly with increasing weights of the built-in predicates. This behavior is not surprising. Prolog has been used to implement many

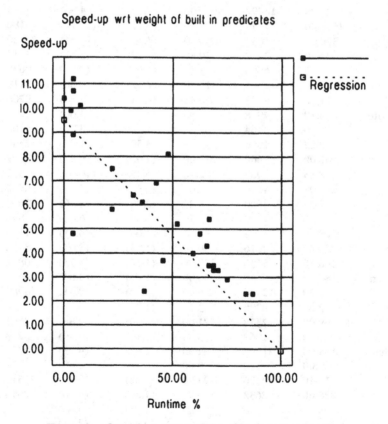

Figure 8.   Speed-up wrt weight of built-in predicates.

bits of KCM-SEPIA where C is used in SEPIA. The compilation technology used on the KCM does not make it possible to match the performance of the C implementation when considering machines of equal raw power. Moreover, the low-level parts of the system, written in assembler, do not benefit from the hardware support for Prolog. It is again the raw power of the machine that matters, and the KCM is therefore outperformed.

The abstract ECLiPSe code is slightly larger than the native KCM code in spite of a more compact encoding, possibly due to larger code for indexing (on more than one argument) and the compilation of compound-term unification into two different unification sequences, a read and a write sequence.[39]

These results have to be moderated by the fact that ECLiPSe resorts to a threaded-code emulator, rather than to native code execution. Running the same benchmarks on SISCtus 2.1 #5, the latest version of the Prolog system developed at the Swedish Institute of Computer Science,[50] shows a speedup of two, on average, between the execution of byte code and native code, in spite of a twofold increase of the code size. Note also that compilation into native code is typically only twice slower than compilation into byte code, which is quite acceptable.

14.5.3 The KCM versus the BAM

The BAM. Following their work on the PLM, members of the Aquarius project took the approach of designing simultaneously a general-purpose microprocessor extended to provide extra support for Prolog, the BAM,[12] and an optimizing Prolog compiler.[47,51]

The overall architecture of the BAM has quite a number of points in common with the KCM: a tagged Harvard architecture, support for stack operations (including a four-port register file), and a direct-mapped cache with a copy-back policy. It is, however, radically different from the KCM in that it is essentially a RISC architecture; in particular:

- There is no microcoded control, although *internal opcodes* can be viewed as a simple form of microcode.
- The execution unit uses a five-stage pipeline. All branch and jump instructions are delayed with the following instruction executed if not annulled.
- The instruction set is about twice smaller than the one of the KCM.
- The Prolog-specific instructions, while being of higher level than typical RISC instructions, are of lower level than the Prolog instructions of the KCM.

Benchmark figures. Table 4 compares the speed (CPU time in ms) and static code size (in bytes) of the KCM and the BAM. Scaled ratios are relative to the KCM. On the KCM, the figures rely on the same methodology as described before. The benchmarks are compiled with in-line arithmetic, to take into account the fact that the absence of coroutining arithmetic and simpler error-handling allows the BAM to compile arithmetic in-line.

Moreover, integer arithmetic is used. In order to get fast arithmetic, the BAM uses the most significant four bits of a 32-bit word for tagging, associating tags (0000) and (1111) to non-negative and negative integers, and compiling arithmetic in-line by using a special version of arithmetic instructions, which trap on 28-bit overflow. The equivalent level of optimization, on the KCM, could have been obtained by microcoding special versions of the most frequent arithmetic instructions, using multiway branching. The timing of these instructions would have been very close, possibly slightly better than the series of simpler instructions generated for in-line integer arithmetic.

The execution times for the BAM are extracted from Van Roy's dissertation.[51] They are simulated in warm start (that is, each benchmark is run twice and the first result is ignored),

Table 4.   The KCM versus the BAM.

Benchmark	KCM 5.1 ms	KCM 5.1 bytes	VLSI-BAM [59] no analysis ms	scaled	bytes	scaled	analysis ms	scaled	bytes	scaled
boyer	3480.00	16784	1410.00	(0.97)	99448	5.93	1360.00	(0.94)	36544	2.18
browse	2500.00	4960	820.00	(0.79)	7452	1.50	741.00	(0.71)	4600	0.93
chat_parser	376.00	51648	151.00	(0.96)	134228	2.60	131.00	(0.84)	82064	1.59
deriv	0.33	6680	0.15	(1.06)	23564	3.53	0.09	(0.66)	4492	0.67
mu	2.13	1640	0.99	(1.12)	4676	2.85	0.78	(0.88)	2924	1.78
nreverse	0.82	904	0.31	(0.90)	1148	1.27	0.14	(0.40)	556	0.62
prover	2.84	4600	1.07	(0.90)	17580	3.82	0.82	(0.69)	5272	1.15
qsort	1.41	1480	0.38	(0.64)	1940	1.31	0.17	(0.29)	860	0.58
queens_8	6.55	1136	1.70	(0.62)	1888	1.66	1.09	(0.40)	584	0.51
query	13.10	2648	5.18	(0.95)	5700	2.15	3.57	(0.65)	1612	0.61
serialise	1.39	2000	0.51	(0.88)	3440	1.72	0.45	(0.77)	2080	1.04
zebra	229.00	2632	84.60	(0.89)	5084	1.93	84.10	(0.88)	3256	1.24
average				(0.89)		2.52		(0.68)		1.07
std deviation				(0.15)		1.36		(0.21)		0.52
crypt	14.50	3232	4.09	(0.68)	4956	1.53	4.00	(0.66)	4108	1.27
fast_mu	2.70	2400	1.12	(1.00)	4660	1.94	0.93	(0.83)	2872	1.20
flatten	10.00	8008	1.46	(0.35)	17068	2.13	1.42	(0.34)	9340	1.17
meta_qsort	24.90	3504	5.33	(0.51)	9936	2.84	4.45	(0.43)	5696	1.63
nand	89.10	33496	18.70	(0.50)	93624	2.80	13.40	(0.36)	82064	2.45
poly_10	207.00	4400	60.40	(0.70)	12092	2.75	35.60	(0.41)	3572	0.81
reducer	273.00	16056	48.80	(0.43)	46904	2.92	44.90	(0.39)	30728	1.91
sdda	22.00	12328	3.18	(0.35)	26104	2.12	2.94	(0.32)	20124	1.63
simple_analyser	113.00	20856	35.40	(0.75)	36228	1.74	31.90	(0.68)	23344	1.12
tak	1070.00	456	71.70	(0.16)	320	0.70	25.40	(0.06)	136	0.30
unify	8.25	12240	1.60	(0.47)	25304	2.07	1.40	(0.41)	16840	1.38
average				(0.54)		2.14		(0.44)		1.35
std deviation				(0.23)		0.72		(0.21)		0.57

assuming a 30-MHz clock, and 128-Kbyte direct-mapped write-back caches. The Aquarius compiler[47] includes a global analysis module that infers implementation-type information and makes it possible to reduce dereferencing and trailing. Results with and without analysis are given.

The benchmarks are separated into two series of programs, with the second series including all the programs written by members of the Aquarius project. In general, the two series of programs use very different programming styles, relying on assumptions on the capabilities of the compiler. In particular, the first series uses cut to express determinacy and assumes that indexing is limited to the functor of the first argument, whereas the second series uses mutually exclusive tests to express determinacy, and assumes better indexing.

Other points to be kept in mind are that the figures given for the KCM correspond to an incremental system (nonrecursive calls within a procedure are indirect calls via the procedure table). Also, garbage collection and coroutining are taken into account, which requires additional work on procedure calls (event test) and during unification (dereferencing, value trailing), and does not allow uninitialized cells to cross procedure-call boundaries. To our knowledge, these issues are not taken into account in the figures of Van Roy.[51]

Results without global analysis. Not taking global analysis into account, the BAM does not, on average, bring any clear performance advantage over the KCM on the first series of benchmarks. The lower ratios of *browse* and *qsort* point to possible compiler improvements in the area of indexing and factoring. The lower ratio of *queens* seems, however, more architecture-related. This program spends most of its time in in-line arithmetic where the KCM is slower than the BAM because of slower dereferencing (the *dref* instruction of the BAM costs 1.6 cycles on average, whereas the corresponding instruction of the KCM is at least three cycles long) and arithmetic operations (catching overflows requires an additional conditional jump).

On the second series of benchmarks, the KCM is, on average, outperformed by a factor of 2. Part of it is due to compilation and programming-style issues. An extreme example is given by *tak*. This program computes a particular value of the Takeuchi function and amounts to recursive invocations of a predicate tak/3 and simple integer arithmetic. An efficient execution of the program relies on the compiler recognizing that $X = <Y$ and $X > Y$ are complementary, deterministic tests, and avoiding the creation of a choice-point. The program results, in standard implementations (for example, KCM, ECLiPSe, or SICStus), in the creation of a choice-point at each invocation of tak/3 and the duplication of many inequality tests. These implementations expect tak/3 to be written with a single test and a cut. (This was the initial formulation of Evan Tick).[52] Such a version of *tak* runs in 231 ms on the KCM, which gives a scaled ratio of 0.74 instead of 0.16.

Another source of inefficiency comes from the weight of the built-in predicate write/1 in *flatten* and *sdda*. Comparing Aquarius and Quintus Prolog, P. Van Roy[51] mentions that these programs perform well on the BAM because write/1 is much faster in Aquarius.

The code size of the BAM remains more than twice the one of KCM, in spite of a much tighter encoding of instructions and data on 32 bits.

The benefits of static analysis. Incremental compilation has been assumed so far; that is, each predicate is compiled in isolation without taking into account any context of execution. Static analysis makes it possible to improve significantly the quality of the code generated by specializing it to its execution context. Much effort has been devoted to the static analysis of logic programs since the early work of C. Mellish,[53] which has led, together with the parallel maturing of basic compilation techniques, to the emergence of optimizing compilers such as the Aquarius compiler and PARMA.

The static analyzers of these systems are based on abstract interpretation.[54] They essentially associate type information with each predicate argument. This association includes knowledge of the instantiation state of an argument (for example, whether it is bound or not) as well as information on its machine representation state (for example, whether it is dereferenced or not). This knowledge makes it possible to greatly simplify unification, possibly replacing it by standard assignment, and improve indexing.

The technique has, however, a number of shortcomings. It is slow and therefore not well suited to quick prototyping. For instance, PARMA analyzes the parser of CHAT-80 in 37 seconds on a MIPS, and it takes the Aquarius compiler 36 minutes, two minutes of which are devoted to global analysis, to compile it on a SPARCStation 1+. This program is compiled in 9s on the KCM or on a SPARCStation II running SICStus (byte code). Also, meta-programming and extra-logical features confound analysis. This topic is extensively covered in Taylor's work,[49] and some partial remedies are considered. Finally, some programs escape static analysis because of their inherently dynamic character (for example, *zebra* and constraint-satisfaction problems in general).

In the case of the BAM, Table 4 shows that global analysis is especially successful in reducing the code size, which gets close to the size of the code of the KCM. The speedup due to global analysis remains low, around 25 percent on average.

It is also interesting to compare the respective performance of the Aquarius compiler on the BAM with PARMA. It turns out that the gain through global analysis obtained by PARMA is close to twice the speedup obtained by the Aquarius compiler on the BAM. The result is that, although PARMA is slower than Aquarius/BAM without static analysis, it is able to catch up when static analysis is used.[49] This is not surprising since one can expect smaller gains from static analysis when starting from a machine with Prolog support. Other important factors are discrepancies in the abstract machines and the respective quality of the analyzers (for example, the types of PARMA are more precise than the ones of Aquarius). Another point to be kept in mind when comparing PARMA with the Aquarius compiler is that PARMA is specific to a given processor. Portability issues may make it necessary to give up some optimizations.

Static analysis and the KCM.   Static analysis techniques can also be applied to the KCM, but not as successfully. Static analysis decreases the weight of high-level Prolog instructions in favor of general-purpose instructions. Delays due to pipeline breaks on load operations and conditional branches become a bottleneck.[9]

14.6 CONCLUSION AND PERSPECTIVES

The ambition of the KCM project was to better understand the benefits and limitations of CPU hardware support for Prolog. An experimental approach was taken: a machine was built and the accompanying software developed, including a full-blown incremental Prolog system. This procedure leaves few doubts as to the feasibility of the approach as well as its difficulties.

Assuming incremental compilation, a first result is that hardware support can indeed significantly speed up Prolog. In spite of a now obsolete technology, the KCM is still twice as fast as its companion system, ECLiPSe, running on a SUN SPARCStation II. This result corresponds to a tenfold scaled speedup ratio on programs free of built-in predicates, and to an average ratio of about 6 on the Aquarius benchmark suite. Experiments with SICStus show that native code compilation may divide these ratios by about 2, which leaves us with still comfortable speedup ratios of 3 (average) to 5 (maximum). A second result is that, according to the results of the comparison of the KCM and the BAM, specialized RISC and CISC architectures exhibit very similar performance.

Static analysis, however, by breaking apart and simplifying basic Prolog operations such as unification, reduces the benefits of dedicated hardware and favors architectures implementing efficiently simple load/store and conditional-branch instructions; CISC architectures are outperformed, and specialized and general-purpose RISC architectures get very close. This is all the more important as, in spite of its shortcomings, static analysis is a very promising technique (see, for example, the comparisons between C and Prolog in the work of Mariën et al[55] and Van Roy).[51] A practical full-blown system mixing incrementally compiled and optimized code remains, however, to be implemented.

Another major aspect of the discussion is that specialized hardware calls for specialized software. On the KCM, firmware and assembly code accounts for 45 percent of the code, and dedicated C code for another 35 percent. This figure is probably close to an upper bound. RISC architectures have the good property of getting rid of firmware. More code can be written in Prolog, especially if a Prolog-optimizing compiler is available. Note, however, that it looks difficult to achieve the portability of symbolic "assembly languages" such as Lisp, by writing, for example, the garbage collector in Prolog. An option would have been to develop an extension of a lower-level language, like C, able to handle tagged words efficiently .

A last point is that Prolog, and Logic Programming, is moving ahead. Prolog implementation techniques that significantly depart from the WAM are put forward. BinProlog,[56] MALI,[57] and the VAM[58] are some examples. At the level of the computational model, the integration of constraints,[59] parallelism,[60] and work on deductive databases[61] break the rigid control strategy of Prolog. The integration of objects[62,63] and functions[64] are also very active research areas.

This view advocates concentrating on software improvements that are at least of comparable potential benefit, but cheaper to unveil, and easier to share. The introduction of user-defined memory management in recent micro-kernel-based operating systems follows the same philosophy, and can actually be used to implement some of the memory-management ideas described above (triggering of garbage collection, improvement of paging).

This approach does not preclude hardware support, but suggests that it be restricted to facilities that may be useful to the implementation of a wide variety of languages. Tagged data, fast conditional branching on user flags, and intelligent memory-model support look like good candidates. Also, performance/silicon area should not be the only criterion; for example, a tagged architecture avoids resorting to tricks when implementing dynamic typing, and may therefore save development and maintenance efforts.

ACKNOWLEDGMENTS

The KCM results from a group effort. At ECRC, the following people directly contributed to the project: Jean-Michel Beacco, Hans Benker, Sylvie Bescos, André Bolle, Michel Dorochevsky, Lindsay Errington, Ludwig Fingerhut, Philippe Holleville, Thomas Jeffré, Liang-Liang Li, Stefano Novello, Anita Pöhlmann, Jonathan Price, Bruno Poterie, Alan Sexton, Heinz Seidl, Olivier Thibault, and Günter Watzlawik. Jean-Claude Syre deserves a special mention for having started the project and led it with enthusiasm until he left ECRC in Summer 1989. Special thanks are also due to the SEPIA team, and especially to M. Meier and J. Schimpf, for their time and expertise. There was joint development work with Bull/GIPSI, Siemens, and ICL for the KCM interface boards and host software. Siemens took part in the design of the memory boards, and manufactured the memory and processor boards. They also assembled the pilot machines. The KCM project would not have been possible without the strong backing of Bill O'Riordan, Owen Evans, and Malcolm Rigg at ICL, Peter Müller-Stoy, Walter Woborschil, and Peter Stock at Siemens.

Mireille Ducassé, Michel Dorochevsky, Micha Meier, Mike Reeve, Joachim Schimpf, and an anonymous reviewer provided valuable comments on drafts of this chapter.

REFERENCES

1. D.H.D. Warren, *Applied Logic—Its Use and Implementation as Programming Tool,* doctoral disssertation, Dept. of Artificial Intelligence, Univ. of Edinburgh, Edinburgh, Scotland, 1977.
2. D.H.D. Warren, "An Abstract Prolog Instruction Set," Tech. Note 309, SRI, Stanford Research Institute, Menlo Park, Calif., Oct. 1983.
3. J. Noyé and J.C. Syre, "ICM3: Design and Evaluation of an Inference Crunching Machine," *Proc. 5th Int'l Workshop Database Machines and Knowledge Base Machines,* Kluwer Academic, Norwell, Mass., 1987, pp. 3–16.
4. H. Benker, et al., "ICM3: Final Specification Report on a High-Speed Inference Co-Processor," Tech. Report CA-23, European Computer-Industry Research Centre, Munich, Germany, Feb. 1987.
5. G. Watzlawik, H. Benker, and J. Noyé, "ICM4," Tech. Report CA-25, European Computer-Industry Research Centre, Munich, Germany, Feb. 1987.
6. H. Benker, et al., "KCM: A Knowledge Crunching Machine," *Proc. 16th Int'l Symp. Computer Architecture,* IEEE CS Press, Los Alamitos, Calif., 1989, pp. 186–194.
7. H. Benker, et al., "A Knowledge Crunching System," *Proc. 11th ITG/GI Conf. Architecture of Computing Systems,* VDE Verlag, 1990, pp. 9–21.
8. O. Thibault, "Hardware Evaluation of KCM," *Proc. Tools For Artificial Intelligence 1990,* IEEE CS Press, Los Alamitos, Calif., 1990, pp. 209–217.
9. M. Dorochevsky, J. Noyé, and O. Thibault, "Has Dedicated Hardware for Prolog a Future?" *Proc. Int'l Workshop Processing Declarative Knowledge,* Springer-Verlag, Berlin, Germany, 1991, pp. 17–31.
10. ECRC, *SEPIA 3.0 User Manual,* European Computer-Industry Research Centre, Munich, Germany, 1990.
11. ECRC, *ECLiPSe 3.2 User Manual,* European Computer-Industry Research Centre, Munich, Germany, 1992.
12. B.K. Holmer, et al., "Fast Prolog with an Extended General Purpose Architecture," *Proc. 17th Int'l Symp. Computer Architecture,* IEEE CS Press, Los Alamitos, Calif., 1990, pp. 282–291.
13. L. Sterling and E. Shapiro, *The Art of Prolog,* MIT Press, Cambridge, Mass., 1986.
14. H. Aït-Kaci, *Warren's Abstract Machine: A Tutorial Reconstruction,* MIT Press, Cambridge, Mass., 1991.
15. E. Tick, *Memory Performance of Prolog Architectures: Frontiers in Logic Programming Architecture and Machine Design,* Kluwer Academic, Norwell, Mass., 1988.
16. D.A. Patterson, "Reduced Instruction Set Computers," *Comm. ACM,* Vol. 28, No. 1, Jan. 1985, pp. 8–21.
17. Advanced Micro Devices, *32-Bit Microprogrammable Products, Am29C300 / 29300 Data Book,* Advanced Micro Devices, 1988.
18. E. Tick and D.H.D. Warren, "Towards a Pipelined Prolog Processor," *Proc. Int'l Symp. Logic Programming,* IEEE CS Press, Los Alamitos, Calif., 1984, pp. 29–40.
19. K. Seo and T. Yokota, "Pegasus—An ASIC Implementation of High-Performance Prolog Processor,"*Proc. Euro ASIC 90,* IEEE CS Press, Los Alamitos, Calif., 1990, pp. 156–159.
20. M. Meier, "Shallow Backtracking in Prolog Programs," tech. report, European Computer-Industry Research Centre, Munich, Germany, Apr. 1989.

21. T.P. Dobry, A.M. Despain, and Y.N. Patt, "Performance Studies of a Prolog Machine Architecture," *Proc. 12th Int'l Symp. Computer Architecture*, IEEE CS Press, Los Alamitos, Calif., 1985, pp. 180–190.

22. T.P. Dobry, *A High Performance Architecture for Prolog,* Kluwer Academic, Norwell, Mass., 1990.

23. H. Nakashima and K. Nakajima, "Hardware Architecture of the Sequential Inference Machine: PSI-II," *Proc. Symp. Logic Programming*, IEEE CS Press, Los alamitos, Calif., 1987, pp. 104–113.

24. J. Noyé, "KCM Instructions," Tech. Reports CA-36 and CA-37, European Computer-Industry Research Centre, Munich, Germany, Jan. 1988; rev. Oct. 1991.

25. M. Hill, et al., "Design Decisions in SPUR," *Computer*, Vol. 19, No. 11, Nov. 1986, pp. 8–22.

26. H. Benker, et al., "KCM—Functional Description," Tech. Report CA-43, European Computer-Industry Research Centre, Munich, Germany, Mar. 1989.

27. H. Benker, et al., "KCM—Hardware Implementation," Tech. Report CA-32, European Computer-Industry Research Centre, Munich, Germany, Mar. 1989.

28. G. Watzlawik, "KCM—Microcoding Manual," Tech. Report CA-41, European Computer-Industry Research Centre, Munich, Germany, Mar. 1989.

29. A.P. Sexton, "KCM—Operating System Interface Manual," Tech. Report DPS-95, European Computer-Industry Research Centre, Munich, Germany, Dec. 1990.

30. L. Naish, *Negation and Control in Prolog,* Lecture Notes in Computer Science, No. LNCS 238, Springer-Verlag, Berlin, Germany, 1986.

31. M. Meier, "Event Handling in Prolog," *Proc. North American Conf. Logic Programming*, MIT Press, Cambridge, Mass., 1989, pp. pp. 871–887.

32. M. Dorochevsky, "Key Features of a Prolog Module System," Tech. Report DPS-103, European Computer-Industry Research Centre, Munich, Germany, Mar. 1991.

33. M. Dorochevsky, "KCM - Sepia Implementation," Tech. Report DPS-98, European Computer-Industry Research Centre, Munich, Germany, Dec. 1990.

34. E. van Rossum, *Implémentation d'un Debugger Prolog*, master's thesis, Facultés Universitaires N.D. de la Paix, Namur, Belgium, 1989. In French.

35. M.L. Ross and K. Rammaohanarao, "Paging Strategy for Prolog Based on Dynamic Virtual Memory," Tech. Report TR 86/8, Univ. of Melbourne, Melbourne, Australia, Aug. 1986.

36. M. Carlsson, *Design and Implementation of an OR-Parallel Prolog Engine,* doctoral dissertation, Dept. of Telecommunication and Computer Systems, The Royal Institute of Technology, Stockholm, Sweden, Mar. 1990.

37. J. Schimpf, "Garbage Collection for Prolog Based on Twin Cells," *Proc. 2nd NACLP Workshop Logic Programming Architectures and Implementations*, MIT Press, Cambridge, Mass., 1990.

38. G. Janssens, B. Demoen, and A. Mariën, "Improving the Register Allocation of WAM by Reordering Unification," *Proc. 5th Int'l Conf. and Symp. Logic Programming*, MIT Press, Cambridge, Mass., 1988, pp. 1388–1402.

39. M. Meier, "Compilation of Compound Terms in Prolog," *Proc. North American Conf. Logic Programming*, MIT Press, Cambridge, Mass., 1990, pp. 63–79.

40. M. Van Caneghem. *L'anatomie de PrologII,* InterEditions, Paris, France, 1986. In French.

41. S. Le Huitouze, "A New Data Structure for Implementing Extensions to Prolog," in *Programming Language Implementation and Logic Programming*, P. Deransart and J. Maluszynski, eds., Springer-Verlag, Berlin, Germany, 1990, pp. 136–150.

42. A. Sexton, "KCM Macro Assembler Reference Manual," Tech. Report CA-48, European Computer-Industry Research Centre, Munich, Germany, July 1989.

43. O. Thibault, "Design and Evaluation of a Symbolic Processor," doctoral dissertation, Université Paul Sabatier, Toulouse III, Toulouse, France, May 1991.

44. V.S. Madan, C.-J. Peng, and G.S. Sohi, "On the Adequacy of Direct Mapped Caches for Lisp and Prolog Data Reference Patterns," *Proc. North American Conf. Logic Programming*, MIT Press, Cambridge, Mass., Oct. 1989, pp. 888–906.

45. J. Bocca, "MegaLog—A Platform for Developing Knowledge Base Management Systems," *Proc. 2nd Int'l Symp. Database Systems for Advanced Applications*, 1991.

46. M. Ducassé and A.-M. Emde, "Opium: A Debugging Environment for Prolog Development and Debugging Research," *ACM Software Eng. Notes*, Vol. 16, No. 1, Jan. 1991, pp. 54-59.

47. P. Van Roy and A. Despain, "High-Performance Logic Programming with the Aquarius Prolog Compiler," *Computer*, Vol. 25, No. 1, Jan. 1992, pp. 54-68.

48. A. Taylor, "LIPS on a MIPS: Results from a Prolog Compiler for a RISC," *Proc. 7th Int'l Conf. Logic Programming*, MIT Press, Cambridge, Mass., 1990, pp. 174-185.

49. A. Taylor, *High Performance Prolog Implementation*, doctoral dissertation, Basser Dept. of Computer Science, Univ. of Sydney, Sydney, Australia, 1991.

50. M. Carlsson, et al., *SICStus Prolog User's Manual*, SICS, Swedish Institute of Computer Science, Kista, Sweden, 1991.

51. P. Van Roy, *Can Logic Programming Execute as Fast as Imperative Programming*, doctoral dissertation, Computer Science Division, Univ. of California, Berkeley, December 1990.

52. E. Tick, "Lisp and Prolog Memory Performance," Tech Report TR 86-291, Stanford Univ., Palo Alto, Calif., Jan. 1986.

53. C. Mellish, "The Automatic Generation of Mode Declarations for Prolog Programs," Research Report 163, Univ. of Edinburgh, Edinburgh, Scotland, 1981.

54. M. Bruynooghe, "A Practical Framework for the Abstract Interpretation of Logic Programs," *J. Logic Programming*, Vol. 10, No. 2, 1991, pp. 91-124.

55. A. Mariën, et al., "The Impact of Abstract Interpretation: An Experiment in Code Generation," *Proc. 6th Int'l Conf. Logic Programming*, MIT Press, Cambridge, Mass., 1989, pp. 34-46.

56. P. Tarau, "A Compiler and a Simplified Abstract Machine for the Execution of Binary Metaprograms," *Proc. Logic Programming Conf.*, ICOT, Tokyo, Japan, 1991, pp. 119-128.

57. O. Ridoux, "Mali v06: Tutorial and Reference Manual," Internal Report 611, IRISA, Institut National de Recherche en Informatique et Automatique, Le Chesnay, France, Oct. 1991.

58. A. Krall and T. Berger, "Fast Prolog with a VAM1p Based Prolog Compiler," *Proc. 4th Int'l Symp. Programming Language Implementation and Logic Programming*, Springer-Verlag, Berlin, Germany, 1992, pp. 245-259.

59. T. Früwirth, et al., "Constraint Logic Programming - An Informal Introduction," in *Logic Programming in Action*, 2nd Int'l Logic Programming Summer School, Springer-Verlag, Berlin, Germany, 1992.

60. J. Chassin de Kergommeaux and P. Codognet, "Parallel Logic Programming Systems," Tech. Report RR 891-I, Laboratoire de Génie Informatique, Grenoble, France, May 1992.

61. C. Delobel, M. Kifer, and Y. Masugana, eds., *Deductive and Object-Oriented Databases*, 2nd Int'l Conf. DOOD, Springer-Verlag, Berlin, Germany, December 1991.

62. J.-M. Andreoli and R. Pareschi, "Linear Objects: Logical Processes with Built-In Inheritance," *New Generation Computing*, Vol. 9, 1991, pp. 445-473.

63. A. Davison, "Design Issues for Logic Based Object Oriented Programming Languages," Research Report, Imperial College, London, England, 1990.

64. S. Hölldobler, *On the Foundations of Equational Logic Programming*. Springer-Verlag Lecture Notes in Computer Science, Vol. 315, Springer-Verlag, Berlin, Germany, 1990.